CAMBRIDGE STUDIES IN
MEDIEVAL LIFE AND THOUGHT

Edited by M. D. KNOWLES, Litt.D., F.B.A.
*Fellow of Peterhouse and Professor of Medieval History in the
University of Cambridge*

NEW SERIES VOL. I

THE ABBEY AND
BISHOPRIC OF ELY

THE
ABBEY & BISHOPRIC
OF
ELY

*The Social History of an Ecclesiastical Estate
from the tenth century to the
early fourteenth century*

BY

EDWARD MILLER

*Fellow of St John's College
Cambridge*

CAMBRIDGE
AT THE UNIVERSITY PRESS
1951
REPRINTED
1969

Published by the Syndics of the Cambridge University Press
Bentley House, 200 Euston Road, London, N.W. 1
American Branch: 32 East 57th Street, New York, N.Y. 10022

PUBLISHER'S NOTE

Cambridge University Press Library Editions are re-issues of out-
of-print standard works from the Cambridge catalogue. The texts
are unrevised and, apart from minor corrections, reproduce the
latest published edition.

Standard Book Number: 521 07778 8

First published 1951
Reprinted 1969

First printed in Great Britain at the University Press, Cambridge
Reprinted in Great Britain by John Dickens & Co. Ltd, Northampton

CONTENTS

MAPS

EDITOR'S PREFACE

SOME thirty years ago, when the threads of academic life were being gathered together after the first world war, the late Dr G. G. Coulton inaugurated a series of *Cambridge Studies in Medieval Life and Thought*. A number of notable books appeared, including the editor's own four volumes, which became one of the best known of books on medieval religious history under the title *Five Centuries of Religion*. Some fifteen years, however, have now passed since any volume appeared save for Coulton's final one, and the series may be considered to have lapsed.

It is now proposed to revive it, principally in order to present in a single collection some of the work submitted for higher degrees or Fellowships by young Cambridge medievalists, though the work of scholars not of Cambridge provenance will not necessarily be excluded. The series should thus serve both to assist publication and to assemble in a single run of books, with a certain stamp of family likeness upon them, work which might otherwise fail to appear in its original shape, or be scattered over a number of publishing houses.

M. D. KNOWLES

PETERHOUSE

April 1951

AUTHOR'S PREFACE

THE character and limitations of the studies which follow have been set out in the first chapter; and nothing more need be said here by way of preface to them. It is, however, pleasant to record the many obligations I have incurred while preparing them. Heaviest of all is my debt to my own College. I was enabled to begin work upon the archives of the Church of Ely by the award of a research studentship more than a dozen years ago; subsequently the award of a fellowship has permitted me to finish this essay. Other obligations have been accumulated by the way. The Bishop and Dean and Chapter of Ely, the Master and Fellows of Trinity College and of Gonville and Caius College, Cambridge, have given me every facility for examining manuscripts in their possession; and I have received the assistance and courtesy always accorded to students by the staffs of the Public Record Office, the British Museum, the Bodleian Library, and the Anderson Room of the Cambridge University Library. In this connection, I would like to acknowledge in particular Mr P. Grierson's kindness in depositing Caius College MS. 485/489 for use in my own College library; and to express my thanks to the Ven. Seiriol Evans for making so many journeys from the Northern Marshland to put at my disposal his unrivalled knowledge of the Cathedral muniments at Ely. I am grateful, too, to Mr L. R. Thurston of the Department of Geography for making two sketch-maps of mine fit for presentation; and to Mr H. P. R. Finberg for reading through my proofs and making a number of suggestions from which I have greatly profited. Finally, three Cambridge scholars have given me far more of their time than I had any right to expect. I owe to Professor M. M. Postan most of the knowledge I have of economic history; and discussion with him over the years has left a mark on almost every part of this book. Professor M. D. Knowles has not only been kind enough to accept my work for the series which he edits; he also read the whole of it in typescript and pruned away some of its worst infelicities. Above all, Professor H. M. Cam has kept a kindly and critical eye on my labours from the beginning. She directed my earliest researches, and ever since has been willing to spend time reviewing their progress. With such guidance the results ought to have been better, but at least I know how much worse they would have been without it. For the defects which remain I must take the sole responsibility.

E. M.

St John's College
Cambridge

27 *February* 1951

LIST OF ABBREVIATIONS

AR	Assize Roll(s).
AS Chron.	*Anglo-Saxon Chronicle.*
BCS	*Cartularium Saxonicum*, ed. Birch.
Bentham	J. Bentham, *History and Antiquities of the...Church of Ely.*
BIHR	Bulletin of the Institute of Historical Research.
BM	British Museum.
Bodl.	Bodleian Library.
Cal.	*Calendar.*
Cart. Rames.	*Cartularium Monasterii de Rameseia.*
Charter R.	*Charter Rolls.*
Chron. Rames.	*Chronicon Abbatiae Rameseiensis.*
Close R	*Close Rolls.*
CRR	*Curia Regis Rolls.*
CUL	Cambridge University Library.
D & C	Dean and Chapter's Muniments, Ely.
Dd	*Domesday Book.*
EcHR	*Economic History Review.*
EDR	Ely Diocesan Registry.
EHR	*English Historical Review.*
FA	*Feudal Aids.*
FFC	Farrer, *Feudal Cambridgeshire.*
GEC	*Complete Peerage*, by G.E.C.
HE	*Historia Eliensis.*
ICC	*Inquisitio Comitatus Cantabrigiensis.*
IE	*Inquisitio Eliensis.*
Inq. pm.	Inquisitions post mortem.
KCD	*Codex Diplomaticus Aevi Saxonici*, ed. Kemble.
KR	King's Remembrancer.
LTR	Lord Treasurer's Remembrancer.
Mem. R.	Memoranda Roll(s).
Mon. Angl.	*Monasticon Anglicanum* (ed. 1846).
Pat. R	*Patent Rolls.*
PCAS	*Proceedings of the Cambridgeshire Antiquarian Society.*
Pipe R	Pipe Roll(s).
P & M	Pollock and Maitland, *History of English Law.*
PN Cambs.	P. H. Reaney, *Place-Names of Cambridgeshire and the Isle of Ely.*
PQW	*Placita de Quo Warranto.*

RBE	*Red Book of the Exchequer.*
Rec. Comm.	Record Commission.
RH	*Rotuli Hundredorum.*
Robertson, *ASC*	*Anglo-Saxon Charters*, ed. A. J. Robertson.
RP	*Rotuli Parliamentorum.*
RS	Rolls Series.
TRE	Tempore Regis Edwardi.
TRHS	*Transactions of the Royal Historical Society.*
Trin.	Trinity College, Cambridge.
VCH	*Victoria County History.*
Whitelock, *ASW*	*Anglo-Saxon Wills*, ed. D. Whitelock.

LIST OF ABBOTS AND BISHOPS OF ELY, 970–1337

ABBOTS

Brihtnoth	970–981?
Aelsi	981–1022?
Leofric	1022–9?
Leofsige	c. 1029–c. 1052
Wulfric	c. 1052–65
Thurstan	1065–72
Theodwin	1073–5
Symeon	1081–93
Richard	1100–7

BISHOPS

Hervey	1109–31
Nigel	1133–69
Geoffrey Ridel	1174–89
William Longchamp	1189–97
Eustace	1198–1215
John of Fountains	1220–5
Geoffrey de Burgh	1225–8
Hugh of Northwold	1229–54
William of Kilkenny	1255–6
Hugh of Balsham	1257–86
John of Kirkby	1286–90
William of Louth	1290–8
Ralf of Walpole	1299–1302
Robert of Orford	1302–10
John de Ketene	1310–16
John of Hotham	1316–37

I

INTRODUCTION

No attempt has been made, in the pages which follow, to rewrite the history of the medieval abbey and bishopric of Ely. It may well be that such an enterprise is long overdue. James Bentham's history, even in its second edition, is now almost a century and a half old; and no later writer has attempted anything on a similar scale. True, the virtue has not gone out of Bentham's work; but since his time, both the methods and the subject-matter of historical investigation have changed out of all recognition. If only for that reason there is room for students who, accepting what Bentham has done, will carry his work forward.

On the other hand, the time may hardly be ripe for a new history of the church of Ely. In the first place, too few of the materials for such a history are yet in print in anything like a satisfactory form. Secondly, although the materials are extremely plentiful, there are also extensive and serious gaps which can only be papered over with comparable data from elsewhere, data not always easily available. The loss of the bishop's central financial records has resulted in what may be the most serious of these gaps; but almost equally serious is the fact that comparatively few manorial account rolls and court rolls seem to have survived from the medieval period. If only for these reasons, the studies which follow have a modest and limited purpose. If they achieve any sort of unity, it will be in the attempt to describe some of the types of social relationship which existed within the confines of a great estate in the high Middle Ages, and therefore above all in the thirteenth century. At the same time, any attempt to describe these relationships involves some concern with the problem of how they came into existence. The society of the thirteenth century had behind it a long history, and above all the long history of lordship. In particular, therefore, these studies are concerned with the workings of the principle of lordship in a fragment of medieval society.

1

This approach to the problems of social history is, of course, one-sided. The predominant influence of territorial lordship upon medieval social arrangements needs no laboured demonstration. The medieval great estate was always something more than 'a unit of ownership. It was equipped, or it became equipped, with coercive powers for distributing and enforcing burdens and responsibilities. Nor were the responsibilities allotted by the great landowner prescribed only by the economic objectives of estate management. The great estate as such, and particularly when it was also a barony or a franchise or both, was itself a subject of political responsibilities; and the landowner had to make administrative and even economic arrangements to discharge them. The great estate, in short, had functions and powers which were derived, not from private right, but from the exigencies of public administration.

Despite these facts, however, there are dangers in viewing medieval social relationships through the records of a single estate—and above all a danger that the efficiency of territorial lordship as a positive social force may be given excessive weight. The structure of medieval society was a result of the interplay of many forces. Previous stages of history everywhere (and not least in East Anglia)[1] left behind them a sediment of customary practice and customary right which lordship might modify but could not always destroy. At every step in the social pyramid rights conceded by lords to their dependants at one point in time tended to acquire a kind of autonomy and were difficult to resume or change in other and different times. Above all, the growing power of the state as the Middle Ages progressed increasingly prescribed the direction of social development. The administrative records of a single estate are hardly likely to give due weight to all of these factors; and we still know too little about the stages of social development in general and of regional social development in particular to have an easy corrective at hand. The conclusions presented here, therefore, can be no more than a contribution to a regional study of eastern England

---

[1] In this respect the student who is concerned with the Ely estate starts with something of an advantage. In part he is covering ground already traversed by Prof. D. C. Douglas in his *Social Structure of Medieval East Anglia*. My debt to this and other works by Prof. Douglas is hardly adequately acknowledged by the large number of references to them which will be found in the following pages.

in medieval times, subject to amplification and correction by other studies within the same region.

The nature of the problems with which these studies are concerned have prescribed, in turn, their chronological limits. In the high Middle Ages the bishops of Ely were lords, not only of a great estate, but also of a great barony and a great liberty. A study of the seignorial resources in the bishops' hands, therefore, demanded first some attempt to deal with origins—with the origin of the barony on this side of the Norman Conquest and of the estate and liberty of Ely in the century before Duke William came. From the time of the Conquest, the story of the combination and the consequences of these different elements which made up the bishop's lordship has been carried down to the early decades of the fourteenth century, when 'feudalism as it had been introduced by the victorious Norman duke had ceased to exist in any real sense'.[1]

To stop at this point may be illogical from many points of view. The estate and liberty of Ely lived on: they survived in some measure, not only the restoration of a centralized state by Henry VII and his son's Reformation, but even the depredations of Elizabeth. On the other hand the context of social relationships in the later Middle Ages was radically changed. The feudal estate not only ceased to exist as a military unit; it also lost much of its cohesion as a social unit. More and more, therefore, a study of the country gentry must view them as a social class rather than as members of feudal communities. In the same way, as great landowners became rentiers, the primary economic problem ceases to be the progress of the economy of the great estate; interest shifts to the progress of the peasant economy. Neither gentry nor peasantry in the later Middle Ages can be studied so profitably within the confines of a single estate as they can in earlier times. With the obsolescence of the vertical stratification of feudal society, the later history of these classes demands a much broader treatment.

On one other matter nothing will be said in the pages which follow. The estate and the liberty of Ely came into existence long before Henry I made the Breton Hervey the first bishop of Ely; and they extended far outside the diocesan boundaries. For that reason, there is no discussion here of diocesan organi-

[1] S. Painter, *English Feudal Barony*, p. 14.

zation. The bishop is looked upon only as a baron and a land-owner, and not in his ecclesiastical capacity; to have done so would have introduced problems quite foreign to the range of questions here considered.

One other preliminary matter calls for a brief discussion at this point. Something has already been said about the qualities and defects of the materials available for a study of the history of the medieval Church of Ely. A brief description of the surviving records will put those remarks into proper perspective; and suggest the large task of editing and publication which remains to be done before a detailed study of the medieval bishopric of Ely can be lightly undertaken.

(i) *Annals*. Chronicles, annals or histories of the abbey, the bishopric and the cathedral priory exist in a number of forms, all apparently interdependent to one degree or another. The earliest surviving form of these chronicles is an account of the refoundation of Ely abbey by Bishop Ethelwold and of the properties which he conferred upon it;[1] a version which took its present shape, at Bishop Hervey's instigation, early in the twelfth century, though resting perhaps upon some sort of earlier Anglo-Saxon collection.[2] This work in turn was, later in the twelfth century, embodied in a chronicle which sets out to tell the story of the church of Ely from the times of St Etheldreda down to the reign of Henry II.[3] There are also concurrent sets of annals of a briefer character, the relationship of which to the

---

[1] This has survived in at least two copies: (i) *Libellus quorundam insignium operum beati Aedelwoldi Episcopi* in Cott. Vesp. A xix; and (ii) *Libellus operum beati Aedeluuoldi Episcopi* in Trin. MS. O. 2. 41. For this latter text, see M. R. James, *The Western Manuscripts in the Library of Trinity College, Cambridge*, iii, pp. 145–6. Both are probably late twelfth-century copies. I am grateful to Miss D. Whitelock for calling my attention to the *Libellus*.

[2] What may be a reference to the compilation of the *Libellus* is contained in the 'Miracula S. Etheldrede' in *Acta Sanctorum Iunii*, iv, p. 541. In the course of an account of the loss and recovery of certain lands at Little Downham after the death of Edgar, the writer remarks: 'Hec de libro terrarum, quem librum S. Aedelwoldi nominant, accipimus.... Aliud sequitur miraculum.... Fratres autem nostri interfuerunt et rem certissime cognoverunt, et in libro iamdicto S. Aedelwoldi Anglice composuerunt, sed nunc temporis in Latinum transmutatum.'

[3] This, of course, is the well-known *Liber Eliensis* or *Historia Eliensis*; it will be referred to throughout this book under the latter title. For a discussion of most of the manuscript copies extant, see W. Holtzmann, *Papsturkunden in England*, ii, pp. 75–93.

larger work has still to be worked out.[1] Finally, in addition to these various sources for the earlier history of abbey and bishopric, there are also annals covering the lives of most of the medieval bishops; generally they are uninformative in character and well represented in those printed by Wharton.[2] A satisfactory text of all this material is still a primary requirement for a definitive study of the history of the church of Ely.[3]

(ii) *Surveys and terriers*. Three surveys have survived, all of them very well known, although only one of them is so far in print. These are: (*a*) The *Inquisitio Eliensis*, based upon the survey of the Ely lands in 1086 by the Domesday commissioners[4] and splendidly edited by Hamilton;[5] (*b*) a survey of the bishop's demesne manors in 1222;[6] and (*c*) a survey of the bishop's demesne manors carried out in 1251.[7]

[1] A good deal of all this, of course, is in print; though unfortunately not always in satisfactory form. The most recent edition of books I and II of the *HE* is the *Liber Eliensis ad fidem codicum variorum*, ed. D. J. Stewart, 1848; but it is sometimes little more than a conflation of a very limited number of the texts. A version of book I was printed by Mabillon, *Acta Sanctorum Ordinis S. Benedicti*, II, pp. 738 ff.; while the Bollandists, in *Acta Sanctorum Iunii*, IV, pp. 493 ff., printed another version of book I, part of book II, and a continuation in the form of annals down to the early twelfth century. These annals are very similar to those which cover the whole history of the abbey down to 1107 contained in Wharton's *Anglia Sacra*, I, pp. 593 ff., where they are followed by book III of the *HE*, though from a text inferior to that contained in Trin. MS. O. 2. 1. The papal letters in book III have been splendidly edited by Holtzmann, *op. cit.* For some further (though hardly exhaustive) notes on the editions and sources of the *HE*, see T. Duffus Hardy, *Descriptive Catalogue* (RS), I, p. 278.

[2] *Op. cit.* pp. 631 ff.

[3] The new edition of books I and II of the *HE*, which Miss D. Whitelock is preparing for the Camden Society, had not yet appeared when these pages were written. References throughout, therefore, are to Stewart's edition, generally by number of book and chapter. Grateful as we shall be for Miss Whitelock's text of the earlier part of the history, a good edition of book III, an important source for the reign of Stephen, is almost as urgently required.

[4] For the sources of the *IE*, see Galbraith, 'The Making of Domesday Book', *EHR*, LVII (1942), pp. 167-9; and for its purpose, my remarks *ibid.* LXII (1947), pp. 452-4.

[5] In *Inquisitio Comitatus Cantabrigiensis*, which supersedes the text printed by the Record Commissioners in the fourth volume of *Domesday Book*.

[6] Cott. Tiberius B II.

[7] This survey has survived in three copies: (i) Cott. Claudius C XI; (ii) the Old Coucher Book or Liber R in the Ely Diocesan Registry; and (iii) MS. 485/489 in the library of Caius College, Cambridge. It should clearly be understood that these are merely different copies of the same survey; and that the dates 1256 and 1277, which Prof. Douglas (*East Anglia*, p. 7) assigned to the Coucher Book and Cott. Claudius C XI respectively, are both

(iii) *Charters, etc.* There seems to be no large collection of charters deriving specifically from the bishop's administrative offices, though a certain number are included in the volumes containing the surveys of the estate referred to above.[1] Many of the earliest charters of the church are embodied in the *Historia Eliensis*; and there are sometimes subsidiary collections in some of the manuscripts of the history.[2] Far more fruitful, however, is the collection of well over one thousand original charters preserved amongst the muniments of the Dean and Chapter of Ely (although most of these refer to the conventual estate), and the series of Priory registers of which five at least have provided materials of some importance.[3]

(iv) *Account Rolls.* The only records of this type which give anything like a comprehensive account of the financial structure of the estate are vacancy accounts, which have survived either as summaries in the Pipe Rolls or in the form of the accounts rendered by the keepers of the see to the Exchequer. Most valuable of these are the engrossed manorial accounts which cover the whole accounting year 1298/9.[4] The only good series of manorial accounts surviving at Ely is that for the manor of Wisbech Barton; and elsewhere the rolls of Great Shelford and, to a lesser extent, Somersham in the Public Record Office. Even then, however, the earliest of these rolls dates from the eighth year of Edward II.

incorrect. Indeed the dating of this survey has always been a source of confusion since Cole inserted the date 1277 in the margin of the Cottonian text, although a correct date was given long ago by Jessop in his discussion of the Coucher Book in *Hist. MSS. Comm., 12th Rep.*, Appx. IX, p. 387. The matter is easily settled. All versions state that the survey was made in the twenty-first year of Bishop Hugh by his steward, Roger of Abington. The reference must be to Bishop Hugh of Northwold (1229–54); for Roger of Abington was his steward and ultimately his executor: Bodl. Laudian Misc. 647, ff. 140, 141; Bullock, *Norfolk Portion of the Chartulary of Lewes*, no. 217; LTR Mem. R, no. 30, m. 9. For reasons of convenience, the Caius College manuscript has generally been used in the preparation of this work.

[1] For example, those to be found in the Coucher Book, ff. 209–42.

[2] One may instance the collection of charters dealing with the liberty of Ely in Trin. MS. O. 2. 41.

[3] By far the most important of these registers is Liber M, a magnificent fourteenth-century cartulary preserved in the Diocesan Registry. Other conventual registers of similar date are Bodl. Laudian Misc. 647 and BM Add. 41612; while two fifteenth-century registers have also been consulted: Liber B in the Diocesan Registry, and Liber A, now BM Add. 9822. For a discussion of these registers see S. J. A. Evans, *Camden Miscellany*, XVII, pp. xvii–xx.   [4] PRO Min. Accts, 1132/10.

(v) *Court Rolls*. With the exception of the Littleport rolls edited by Maitland[1] and those of Walsoken edited by Ault,[2] only one good run of court rolls has survived for the period under discussion. These rolls, preserved in the Diocesan Registry, provide a record of the hundred courts, leets and manor courts of Wisbech and its hamlets. At the same time, a comparison between the Littleport rolls and those deriving from the Prior's manors suggests that business and procedure followed a similar course on both estates. This may justify the use for comparative purposes of the splendid series of court rolls from the Prior's manor of Sutton in the Isle, which go back to 1292 and which are now preserved amongst the muniments of the Dean and Chapter.

Naturally, the sources listed above have merely provided the basic materials upon which this study is founded. Where possible they have been checked against the public records, and the latter in turn have provided a wealth of information of every sort—eloquent testimony to the part played by the liberty and barony of Ely in the work and burden of medieval government.

At the same time, a student's debt is not exhausted by medieval times and medieval records. There are also the packed notebooks of James Bentham in the Cambridge University Library. They do not contain much which cannot be found elsewhere, but they are none the less an excellent guide to a great mass of manuscript materials. More valuable in their way, however, are more than two hundred pages of extracts 'ex archivis Eliensibus' which Matthew Wren copied into a notebook still in the Diocesan Registry at Ely.[3] These extracts include passages from documents which have long since disappeared, passages therefore precious despite their brevity. It is the more pleasant to be able to record this debt to a scholar long dead because his own labours amongst the archives of Ely were brought to a sudden and premature conclusion by the troubles of civil war.

[1] *The Court Baron* (Selden Soc. IV).
[2] *Court Rolls of the Abbey of Ramsey and the Honour of Clare*, 171 ff.
[3] For an account of this book see *Hist. MSS. Comm. 12th Rep.*, Appx. IX, pp. 387–8.

II

ORIGINS

I T is impossible to obtain any comprehensive view of the lands
of Ely abbey, or of the inhabitants of those lands, until we
come down to *Domesday Book*. At the same time a proper
understanding of the information given there calls for some
attempt to get behind *Domesday*, in fact (if this is possible) to go
back to the beginnings of the abbey's history. The difficulty
here lies less in the intention than in knowing where to look for
beginnings. The evolution of the estate which belonged to Ely
abbey in 1086 can be traced with some assurance from the time
of Bishop Ethelwold's refoundation of the abbey in 970. Yet as
early as the twelfth century a tradition had already grown up
which placed Ethelwold's refoundation somewhere this side of
the middle of the abbey's history. It was believed that regular
monastic life had flourished at Ely, with substantial continuity,
since the seventh century; and that these early days had contributed something, had perhaps contributed a very great deal,
to the privileges which the church enjoyed in later times. If we
seek, therefore, to go back to the beginnings of the lands and
liberties of Ely abbey, some attention must be given to its
antiquities—and above all to the dower of St Etheldreda. This
was the traditional beginning; we can do much worse than to
start there before turning to the last and better documented
century of Old English history.

I

The main points of the tradition about the beginnings of monasticism at Ely, as it took shape in the course of the twelfth
century in the chronicles of the cathedral priory, can be briefly
summarized and checked against the eighth-century testimony
of Bede.[1] The foundress of monastic institutions on the island
in the fens was St Etheldreda, daughter of Anna king of the
East Angles. She was married about the middle of the seventh

[1] *Hist. Eccl.* IV, c. 19.

century to Tonbert, chieftain of a people called the Southern
Gyrwe; and it was from her husband, according to the Ely
chronicle,[1] that she received possession of the 'Isle of Ely' as
her 'dower'.[2] Bede, on the other hand, knows nothing about
St Etheldreda's dower. According to his account, Ely was part
of the East Anglian territory: it was a district (regio) of six
hundred families in the province of the East Angles where
St Etheldreda wished to found a monastery because she was
descended from the royal house of that province. There is a
discrepancy in the evidence here to which we shall have
to return.

Tonbert, it seems, died shortly after his marriage to St Etheldreda; but she was unable to carry out immediately her plans
to found a monastery at Ely. Only after a second marriage
to Ecgfrith of Northumbria was she able to return to Ely and
build an abbey there over which she ruled as abbess till her
death. She was succeeded in this office in turn by her sister
Sexburgh, the latter's daughter Ermenhild and granddaughter
Werburgh. After Werburgh's death (which may have taken
place about the year 700) nothing more was known about the
history of Ely abbey in the twelfth century until St Ethelwold's
refoundation, save for a tradition that it had been sacked by the
Danes in the year 870. It is quite clear, in short, that the
chronicler knew very little about the antiquities of Ely abbey.

There can be no question, of course, that a monastery was
founded at Ely by St Etheldreda in the course of the seventh
century; that fact rests upon the incontestable authority of
Bede. But the twelfth-century chronicler was concerned to do
a great deal more than record this simple fact. He desired to
establish a venerable antiquity for the privileges enjoyed by his
church in his own day; and to vindicate for those privileges
some sort of continuity from St Etheldreda's time.[3] In this

---

[1] HE, I, c. 4.

[2] The word 'dower' should no doubt be construed as 'morning gift', i.e.
the provision for a wife's widowhood which a husband made on the morning
after his wedding day. Over property so conferred a woman obtained full
proprietary rights (as HE, I, c. 15 implies in this case) provided she did not
remarry within a year of her husband's death: see Whitelock, ASW, pp. xlvii,
111, 142.

[3] His vindication of a substantial continuity of monastic life at Ely is
important in this connection. He assumes that St Etheldreda's foundation
survived down to the time when it was sacked by the Danes in 870 (HE,

respect he has been more successful than he himself may have anticipated. He has persuaded more than one historian that the medieval Isle of Ely, with its special and extensive franchise, and the modern administrative district of the Isle which is still distinguished from Cambridgeshire proper, are derived ultimately from the dower of St Etheldreda.[1]

Once the initial likelihood of this assumption is admitted a good deal of evidence can be marshalled to support it. The very name of Ely contains the archaic element *gē*—a district; and this suggests that it may have been at some early time the centre of an ancient province. This suggestion, in turn, is strengthened by Bede's reference to the *regio* of Ely, for the term *regio* is rapidly acquiring a technical significance which points to one of the administrative units of the earliest Anglo-Saxon period.[2] Bede's *regio*, moreover, with its six hundred families will bear comparison, even identification, with the province of the Southern Gyrwe which was rated at six hundred hides in the Tribal Hidage.[3] So predisposed, it is not hard to find at Ely some of the characteristics which, we are taught,[4] afford evidence for the fact that a place had once been an ancient provincial centre. At the beginning of the twelfth century forensic agricultural services were still being performed on the Barton farm at Ely;[5] later still the court at the Barton gate in Ely was one which called upon the suit of outland tenures, and Ely was the centre of a group of villages and hamlets intercommoning in the fen.[6] A picture easily takes shape from these details; we can derive the later two hundreds of the Isle

---

I, c. 38), though without facts to back his assertion after the beginning of the eighth century. After 870, he continues, religious life was soon re-established, though by a body of clerks, not monks (c. 41).

[1] See, for example, my own remarks in *Trans. Herts. Arch. Soc.* 1938, p. 295; also Cam, *Liberties and Communities*, p. 185 and Hurnard, *EHR*, LXIV, p. 317.

[2] Stenton, *Anglo-Saxon England*, p. 290; *PN Cambs.* p. 214.

[3] This is one of a number of suggestions made by Chadwick, *Origin of the English Nation*, p. 8; for the Tribal Hidage, see Stenton, *op. cit.* pp. 292–4.

[4] Jolliffe, *Oxford Essays in Medieval History presented to H. E. Salter*, p. 12.

[5] See Bishop Nigel's charter which confirms a grant of Bishop Hervey's to the men of the 'island' abolishing the ploughing services 'totius insule de Ely quam faciebant Bertune de Ely': D & C Charters, no. 56 (see below, Appx. X, p. 286).

[6] See below, pp. 220ff. and the map in Darby, *Medieval Fenland*, p. 71.

of Ely from St Etheldreda's dower, and the latter in turn from the *regio* of the Southern Gyrwe. The Isle, in short, was the district over which St Etheldreda's husband was ealdorman.

Yet there are difficulties involved in this identification which are not entirely easy to gloss over. It demands that we jettison the eighth-century account given by Bede in favour of the tradition written down at Ely in the twelfth century. Bede knew nothing about the dower which Tonbert conferred upon his wife; on the contrary, as we have seen, he implied that Ely was part of the territory of the royal house of East Anglia.[1] True, this might be brought into harmony with the Ely account, at least in part, by a series of assumptions. The Isle of Ely may have been the territory of the Southern Gyrwe; it may have been recently conquered by the East Anglians, perhaps during the time that Redwald had the supremacy over all England south of the Humber;[2] Tonbert may have ruled it as ealdorman during his life and St Etheldreda may have acquired it from her father after her husband's death. We would have to give up only the legend of St Etheldreda's dower—a minor sacrifice in view of the fact that Bede knows nothing of it.

Even these assumptions, however, merely raise new difficulties, particularly in connection with the identification of the Isle of Ely with the territory of the Southern Gyrwe. In the first place, that identification is incapable of proof. All we know of the Gyrwe is that they were a people divided into northern and southern groups. We may believe that, as their name implies, they lived along the fen margins and on the islands in the fen; but no one has yet been able to define the extent of their territory or the boundary line which separated the northern and southern divisions of this people.[3] They may have extended northwards into Lincolnshire; probably they did extend west

[1] For this difficulty see Chadwick, *op. cit.* p. 8 and Darby in *Antiquity*, VIII, pp. 200–1. The fact, moreover, that the early abbesses of Ely followed in some sort of hereditary line may suggest a proprietary right which originated in the East Anglian royal house rather than in St Etheldreda personally (for this sort of succession elsewhere see Levison, *England and the Continent in the Eighth Century*, pp. 27–9).

[2] Darby in *Antiquity*, VIII, p. 194; Fox, *Archaeology of the Cambridge Region*, p. 239.

[3] The evidence, such as it is, has been assembled by Darby in the article referred to above.

along the Nene into Northamptonshire;[1] possibly at some time
their territory included land south of the present boundary of
the Isle of Ely.[2] But any definite conclusion is impossible; the
Gyrwe are shrouded in that obscurity which covers all the
peoples of the Middle Angles.

There is, however, a second and stronger reason for questioning that theory of the origin of the Isle of Ely which has sometimes been deduced from the Ely chroniclers. It is important
to note that they themselves do not imply that St Etheldreda's
dower can be identified with the territory of the Southern
Gyrwe. 'Girvii sunt omnes australes Angli in magna palude
habitantes *in qua est insula de Ely*.'[3] In short, the 'island of Ely'
was part of the territory of the Gyrwe; it was not coterminous
with that territory. More than this, it is also clear that the
chronicle uses the term 'insula de Ely' to describe two different
things. On the one hand it can be used to describe the two
hundreds of the Isle, the modern and medieval administrative
district called the Isle of Ely. On the other, it has a more
restricted connotation; it refers to an island 'seven miles long
from *Cotingelade* to Littleport or to the Abbotsdelf...and four
miles broad from *Cherchewere* to Stretham mere'. This island,
moreover, is distinguished from those other outlying islands
within the Isle upon which lay Doddington, Whittlesey, Thorney
and Chatteris.[4] Although a number of the places in the chronicler's account escape certain identification,[5] this 'island' in the

---

[1] *VCH Northants*, I, pp. 250–1 and see also *Chronicle of Hugh Candidus*,
p. 2 for the belief held at Peterborough in the twelfth century that *Medeham-
stede* had lain in the region of the Gyrwe, men who 'dwelt in the fen or hard
by the fen'.

[2] See Lethbridge's suggestion in *PCAS*, xxxv, pp. 90–5, though he offers
little evidence in support of it.

[3] *HE* (ed. Stewart), pp. 4–5.

[4] *HE* (ed. Stewart), pp. 4, 169 collated with Trin. MS. O. 2. 1, ff. 2d, 50d;
compare also Bentham, p. 79 and Dugdale, *History of Imbanking*, p. 183
together with a similar account of the 'island of Ely' in *Chronicle of Hugh
Candidus*, p. 2 where its dimensions are given as seven miles by seven miles.
The 'islands' of the Isle are shown in map no. II.

[5] Those which present difficulties are the following:

(i) *Cotingelade* has been variously identified with part of the Bean Ditch
which once separated Stretham and Cottenham fens and with the stretch of
the West Water as far as the Car Dyke: see Wells, *Laws of the Bedford Level
Corporation*, II, pp. 175, 177; Fowler, *PCAS*, xxxIII, p. 124 and *PN Cambs*.
pp. lviii, 11.

(ii) The Abbotsdelf has usually been identified with the modern Crooked

narrow sense must be, not the Isle, but the ridge of higher
ground which extends from Aldreth north-eastwards to Littleport.[1] After all, this tract is in a real sense an island; it must
have been literally an island when the fens about it were
a 'wild wilderness', 'immense marshes, now a black pool of
water, now foul running streams'.[2]

This island of Ely, moreover, well down into the Middle
Ages, retained a good deal of coherence as a social unit—partly
due, perhaps, to the complex of intercommoning rights shared by
its inhabitants.[3] It was probably the 'island', too, rather than the
Isle which, up to the beginning of the twelfth century, rendered
ploughing service at the Barton farm at Ely; for in the thirteenth
century miscellaneous services in the bishop's vineyard and
elsewhere were owed only by villages within the island.[4] There
is no inherent improbability in the supposition that the 'island'
may have been the endowment which St Etheldreda conferred
upon her abbey in the seventh century; for as a social unit it has
characteristics which may indicate considerable antiquity. On
the other hand, it is impossible to prove that it was coterminous
with the province of the Gyrwe; and it was merely one of the
elements which went into the making of the medieval Isle of Ely.

Drain (*PN Cambs*. p. 209); but Fowler has suggested that in fact it continued
the Crooked Drain in a north-easterly direction towards Shippea Hill station,
PCAS, XXXIV, pp. 17, 27.

(iii) *Cherchewere* is even more elusive. It appears in this form in most of
the texts, e.g. Cott. Domitian A xv, f. 8 d and Bodl. Laudian Misc. 647, f. 3 d;
but also in the form *Cherechwere* in Trin. MS. O. 2. 1, f. 2 d. Could the *were*
in this name have been transmuted into *mere*? If so, it might underlie the
modern place-name of Crouch Moor in the north of Littleport parish, which
appears as *Krechemere* or *Crechemere* in the thirteenth century and as
Crouchemeere in the seventeenth: Caius 485/489, ff. 19 d, 20 d, 30; Wells,
op. cit. II, p. 164 and *PN Cambs*. p. 227.

[1] See map no. II and also the maps in *VCH Cambs*. II, p. 382 and Darby,
Medieval Fenland, p. 107 (the latter shows the three causeways or bridges
into the island which are mentioned by Hugh Candidus in the passage
referred to on p. 12, n. 4).

[2] Felix, *Life of Guthlac*, cited by Darby, *op. cit.* p. 8.

[3] Darby, *op. cit.* p. 71.

[4] See above, p. 10, n. 5. In the thirteenth century services were owed at
the bishop's vineyard, bakery, brewery and garden by the villeins of Downham, Linden in Haddenham, Stretham, Wilburton and Littleport; but not
from Doddington or further afield: Caius 485/489, ff. 30 d–2, 37, 43 d, 48 d,
55. Likewise on the conventual estate the villeins of Sutton owed services
(commuted only in 1314) at haytime in the prior's meadows at Northney and
Shippea in Ely parish: Sutton Halimote, 4 Edw. II (St Etheldreda); 7 Edw.
II (St Margaret); 8 Edw. II (St Augustine).

The Isle, in fact, seems to have been an administrative area of much later creation, and to have retained some degree of artificiality arising out of the diverse characteristics of its component parts. Scattered references seem to imply that sometimes, at least, in the seventh and eighth centuries the boundary between East Anglia and Mercia may have cut right across the Isle—leaving the 'island' of Ely on the one side and Thorney and Whittlesey (possibly even Doddington and Chatteris) on the other.[1] Further, the social organization of the Wisbech area is quite distinct from that of the rest of the Isle in later centuries. It strongly suggests an early connection with the Norfolk Marshland; and in fact this area was probably a late addition to the Isle, rather awkwardly tacked on to the rest.[2] We cannot say when these various pieces were put together into a composite whole, but it seems likely to have been a good deal later than the times of St Etheldreda. Perhaps it was the work of that Danish 'army which belonged to Cambridge'[3] in the later ninth century; or more likely still of the West-Saxon kings after they had reconquered the Cambridge region from the Danes in the tenth century, in the course of the extensive administrative reorganization which followed upon the reconquest.[4]

If either of these possibilities should be the correct one, it is also important to note that the formation of the Isle would then have taken place at a time when there was also a break in the continuity of religious life at Ely. The twelfth-century chroniclers knew nothing of the history of Ely abbey in the eighth century or the ninth; other abbesses followed St Werburgh, they say, 'quarum nomina solius dei novit scientia, nobis autem prorsus incognita'.[5] Tradition alone established the continuance of the abbey during these centuries, and was evidence for its destruction by the Danes in 870. The tradition may well be a true one; but even so there is good evidence to show that after the reconquest of the Danelaw even the site of St Etheldreda's monastery was in the possession of the West-

[1] This seems to be Prof. Darby's suggestion in *Antiquity*, VIII, pp. 194–7.
[2] See below, pp. 31 ff.
[3] *VCH Cambs.* II, p. 379.
[4] For the 'deliberate remodelling of administrative geography' in the Midlands and East Anglia during the tenth century, see Stenton, *Anglo-Saxon England*, p. 295 and Cam, *Liberties and Communities*, p. 90.
[5] *Acta Sanctorum Iunii*, IV, p. 524.

Saxon kings. Between 955 and 959 King Edwy was in a position to grant 40 'manses' *aet Helig* to Archbishop Oda of Canterbury.[1] This gift seems to have proved of a temporary character, and Ely had returned to the royal estate before 970. On this point all the best sources—the *Libellus*,[2] Aelfric's life of St Ethelwold,[3] the charters of King Edgar[4]—are in agreement. It was from the king that Bishop Ethelwold obtained the site of the monastery he wished to refound, and before the refoundation the service of God had completely ceased there.

In short, the origin of the medieval lands and liberties of the church of Ely is to be sought in King Edgar's charter of refoundation.[5] There is no direct link (possibly no link at all) between the region of the Southern Gyrwe and the medieval liberty of the Isle of Ely, or even between St Etheldreda's dower and the endowment which King Edgar conferred upon the monastery of Ely. Between St Etheldreda's abbey and the abbey which St Ethelwold refounded there had been a break at least of a century. That century may have been, moreover, a most important century; it may have been the century which witnessed the creation of the Isle of Ely as the men of the Middle Ages knew it and as we know it to-day. Some property in this Isle, and rights of some sort over the whole of it were one of the first endowments which King Edgar conferred upon the new foundation. These rights were to be very important in the future; it seems also probable that they were not derived directly from the past endowment of monasticism on the 'island of Ely'.

[1] *KCD*, no. 465; *Crawford Charters*, no. 5. The editors of this latter collection doubted whether the charter in question could refer to Ely, doubts which seem to have been dispelled by Robinson, *Times of St Dunstan*, p. 118.

[2] Trin. MS. O. 2. 41, f. 3. After describing the sack of the monastery by the Danes, the writer continues: 'Sicque per destitutionem regie sorti sive fisco idem locus additus est.'

[3] *Chron. Abingdon*, II, pp. 261–2: 'sed erat tunc destitutus et regali fisco deditus.'

[4] In the Anglo-Saxon version, the king says that the place had been sadly neglected in his time and with less service than was pleasing to him; in the Latin, 'locus denique predictus deficiente servicio dei nostra etate regali fisco subditus est': Robertson, *ASC*, pp. 98–102; *KCD*, no. 563.

[5] Even the *HE* mentions only one property which passed to the refounded church from the old abbey—the manor of Stapleford (Cambridgeshire): II, c. 28. The fact that there is no sign of this in the *Libellus* gives one little confidence in the authenticity of this tradition.

II

At this point we may begin to treat separately the lands and liberties of the church of Ely, and look first at the accumulation of territorial possessions which made Ely abbey a very great landowner. The first foundation is to be sought in King Edgar's charter; *Domesday Book* provides us with an outline summary of what that first endowment had grown to be on the day when King Edward was alive and dead. That summary, however, is testimony to the impressive achievement of the century after the refoundation of Ely abbey. A rough calculation seems to show that, towards the end of the Old English period,[1] the abbey had demesne lands in some 116 villages scattered over six counties and valued at about £900 a year.[2] Further, it had acquired a wide and varied circle of dependants in more than 200 villages, comprising more than 1200 landholders of every sort from holders of a mere acre or less to king's thegns with estates in many counties.[3] All this was no small achievement to set to the credit of a mere century of estate-building. No other period in the history of abbey or bishopric can show anything even remotely comparable. In fact, the later history of the lands of the church of Ely is almost exclusively the history of the assets garnered, with astonishing rapidity, in the two or three generations after 970.

So far as its history can be reconstructed from the twelfth-century accounts,[4] this accumulation of property seems to fall into two well-marked phases. The first is a very short one, ending with the death of Abbot Brihtnoth in 981 and of Bishop Ethelwold in 984. Its main characteristics are well enough summarized by the Old English chronicler who closes his account of the re-

[1] The figures which follow (presented with all the reservations appropriate to Domesday statistics) describe the estate at its greatest extent—i.e. before the alienation of certain properties to Stigand and others in the Confessor's reign (for these, see below, pp. 24–5).

[2] The figures for different counties are as follows: Cambridgeshire and the Isle (£414); Suffolk (£144); Norfolk (£135); Essex (£122); Herts (£55) and Hunts (£34).

[3] The majority (about 800 in all) are found in Suffolk; Norfolk accounts for about 270 and Cambridgeshire for 180.

[4] As pointed out on p. 4, n. 2 above, of course, these accounts were based upon some sort of earlier compilation; and the chroniclers clearly had at their disposal documents which have since disappeared (e.g. *HE*, II, cc. 67, 68). On this point see also Stenton in *VCH Hunts.* I, p. 328.

foundation of Ely abbey with these words: 'then [Bishop Ethelwold] bought many villages from the king and made it very rich'.[1] There are clear signs that Ethelwold was carrying out a deliberate policy of providing an adequate territorial endowment for the refounded monastery, a policy which seems to be evident also in other places during this period of monastic reform.[2] In order to implement this policy, he seems to have set out to purchase land on a very large scale. No transaction was too small to be beneath his notice. Side by side with the acquisition of great manors like Northwold or Stoke, we also read how he bought seven acres from a bishop's son and five acres from a poor widow.[3] Having bought these lands, moreover, he was always ready to defend them—particularly during the troubled time after King Edgar's death—against all who might call in question the abbey's title to them. The rich legacy of ancient land-pleas preserved in the *Historia Eliensis* (the circumstantial character of which calls for some credence) is the monument to his tireless pertinacity.

The major result of this decade or so of purchase was to consolidate, more or less, the abbey's ownership over the 'island of Ely'—and it is interesting to note that, whatever coherence the island may once have had, it seems to have been acquired piecemeal during this period. Edgar's foundation charter conceded to the monks 'the minster lands which lie into Ely'[4] (a phrase which, in the light of the evidence we have for the acquisition of other properties, can have meant little more than the vill of Ely itself with its dependent hamlets). But most of the remaining property on the 'island' does seem to have passed into the possession of the monastery during this phase,[5] though our record of the transactions whereby it was acquired

1 *AS Chron. s.a.* 970.
2 Stenton, *Anglo-Saxon England*, p. 446.
3 *HE*, ii, cc. 3, 20, 39, 42; Trin. MS. O. 2. 41, ff. 5, 36, 60–1.
4 The quotation is from Edgar's Anglo-Saxon charter. Three versions of his donation to Ely have survived: (i) an Anglo-Saxon charter which can be consulted most conveniently in Robertson, *ASC*, pp. 98–102; (ii) a Latin charter similar to (i), but not identical with it: *KCD*, no. 563 and *BCS*, no. 1266; (iii) another Latin charter conceding some, but not all, of the properties conceded in the main charters: *KCD*, no. 564 and *BCS*, no. 1265. For the difficulty of determining the relationship between these documents, see Robertson, *ASC*, p. 347.
5 At any rate Stretham, Wilburton, Linden End, Hale, Witchford, Witcham and Sutton: Trin. MS. O. 2. 41, ff. 9–13, 29–32.

is hardly exempt from difficulties.[1] Elsewhere in the Isle, only a small property in Doddington seems to have been obtained at this time; but in Cambridgeshire land was obtained in seven or eight different villages, in Suffolk in five villages, in Norfolk in two villages, and in one village each in Hertfordshire and Huntingdonshire—generally through the instrumentality of Bishop Ethelwold.

This represented a solid, even a remarkable, beginning for the lands of the church of Ely. But here as elsewhere in eastern England the territorial growth of the new monasticism was interrupted, momentarily but powerfully none the less, by the disturbances which followed the death of King Edgar. During this time of troubles the new monasteries were attacked from many sides. True, there is nothing in the *Historia Eliensis* to suggest that any political motive or any genuinely anti-monastic issues were involved. On the contrary, the real problems seem to have been at root problems of land-title. The attacks were directed, not against monastic reform, but against the validity of some of the transactions which were turning the restored monasteries very quickly into great landowners.[2]

In some instances, men seem to have sought to recover properties to which they asserted a claim on the strength of what may have been little more than a legal quibble. They alleged sometimes that the transaction which had brought land to the monks had been the result of a forced bargain;[3] or that the church had taken advantage of the financial embarrassment of the vendor to obtain property for less than it was really worth.[4]

---

[1] Wilburton provides a typical case. There is one record of the purchase of 12 hides in Linden End, in which Wilburton is included as one of the appurtenances of that manor; but there is also an account of the purchase in Wilburton itself of four hides and 220 acres and of some other lands to make up a total of five hides. The record may have been doctored to bring it into line with the assessment of five hides attributed to Wilburton in *Domesday*: *HE*, II, cc. 8, 11, 17; *Dd*, I, 192.

[2] See Stenton, *Anglo-Saxon England*, p. 367.

[3] E.g. *HE*, II, cc. 10, 12.

[4] *HE*, II, c. 19: King Edgar fined a certain Oslac a hundred pounds, and the latter sold certain of his lands to Bishop Ethelwold in order to pay the fine, lands which Ethelwold gave to Ely. After Edgar's death Oslac seized them again and, in the course of a plea held at Cambridge, asked for a valuation of them (implying clearly that he had received less than they were worth). The court decided, however, that in fact he had received more and ordered him to repay the balance to the abbot. See also c. 11 for lands bought from one Aelfric when he was oppressed by heavy 'tribute'.

There are, however, other and more important cases which suggest that more fundamental issues were involved. If a man sold his lands to the church he was, in effect, disinheriting his family; and some of the controversies that arose after Edgar's death do seem to suggest that the right of a man to do so was not fully conceded in the custom of the time.[1] Indeed, there is even one case in which Abbot Brihtnoth himself came dangerously near admitting a right vested in the heir which required redemption. The monk Goding bequeathed a hide of land to the abbey, but after his death it was claimed by his son; and in the end the abbot agreed to pay the latter twenty shillings before the citizens of Cambridge before he was able to obtain possession of the land.[2]

All that these instances seem to suggest is that the rapid changes in landownership occasioned by the monastic revival provoked a reaction, understandably enough perhaps, amongst the 'disinherited'. At the same time, troubles of this sort may have arisen the more easily because conveyancing procedure was in a transitional state. Land might pass from one person to another in at least two ways. On the one side the act of conveying the land might still be mainly oral and depend for its validity upon a series of traditional ceremonies carried out before witnesses.[3] On the other side, there were also occasions when older procedure was supplemented at some stage or another by the transfer of a written instrument, a charter or a land-book. This latter procedure might apply, not only when land was 'booked' to the abbey by the king, but also when the monks acquired land the grantor's rights over which were buttressed by a land-book. In this last instance, the grantor's

---

[1] This may be the basis of the claim made by Uvi in *HE*, II, c. 18 and see also cc. 27 and 34. The Ramsey chronicle also seems to stress the same point when it talks about the way in which perjured sons forswore the devotion of their fathers: *Chron. Rames.* 46–7. For the 'old restrictive common law' of Anglo-Saxon times, 'the law which keeps land in families', see Vinogradoff, as quoted by Holdsworth, *History of English Law*, II, p. 68.

[2] *HE*, II, c. 26.

[3] For an example of this procedure see *HE*, II, c. 11, the record of an exchange whereby one Aelfric gave the abbey his lands in Downham in return for a sum of money and other lands in Chippenham. The agreement was made and the money paid over, apparently, in the county court of Cambridgeshire; afterwards Aelfric conceded actual possession of Downham to the abbot first before the twenty-four lawmen of Cambridge, and then before witnesses.

land-book generally passed to the abbey along with the land.[1] Possession of a charter referring to a particular property, therefore, in itself became presumptive evidence of title—as it was, for instance, when the monks produced their land-book for Bluntisham to corroborate the evidence already given in their favour by the old and the wise of Huntingdonshire.[2]

It is probably true, of course, that these two methods of conveyancing were appropriate to different sorts of land.[3] Once land had become 'book-land', land demised and endowed with privileges by means of a written instrument, its conveyance would demand a written deed of transfer or at least the surrender of the original deed to the grantee. On the other hand where 'folk-land', land held by ancient custom, was the subject of the conveyance a written instrument was no necessity for a valid transaction. True, land which had passed in the traditional way might later acquire the buttress of a charter; but the object in this was probably not so much to support title as to gain the additional privileges and exemptions which a land-book commonly conferred.[4] But theoretical distinctions of this sort may not always have been so clear in actual practice. When two equally valid methods of transferring land co-existed, it must have been possible for some transactions to fall between the two procedural stools. Book-land, for example, might pass with much formality from grantor to grantee, but without the transfer to the latter of the book. In such a case the grantor's heir might claim the land on the strength of his charter, and a real doubt might arise as to who had the better title to the land.[5]

In such ways, then, did the rapid accumulation of land contribute to the 'anti-monastic reaction' of 975 so far as it affected Ely abbey. It resulted in the loss of some property, and of at

[1] When Bishop Ethelwold gave Sudbourne to the monks he handed over to them the charter wherein King Edgar had conceded the manor to him: *HE*, II, c. 37.

[2] *HE*, II, c. 25: 'quia proprior erat ille ut terram haberet qui cyrographum habebat quam qui non habebat.'

[3] On the questions raised in this paragraph see Jolliffe, *EHR*, L, pp. 1–21 and Plucknett, *EcHR*, VI, pp. 64–72.

[4] See Plucknett, *op. cit.* pp. 71–2. There seems to be an instance in *HE*, II, c. 9, where it is recorded that Bishop Ethelwold gave the monks land in Linden End, and only some time later did the abbot obtain a charter from the king in respect of it.

[5] As in the dispute over the abbey's title to lands in Newton and Hauxton: *HE*, II, c. 27.

least one reputation—for the chronicle of Ely displays ealdorman Aethelwine of East Anglia in a light far less favourable than does the chronicle of Ramsey.[1] He seized Hatfield from the monks of Ely, and drove a hard bargain with them before he would restore it; and on other occasions (the chronicler suggests) he was less zealous in the abbey's interest than was proper.[2] But Brihtnoth, ealdorman of Essex, was to Ely what Aethelwine was to Ramsey, the 'advocate' of their struggling community.[3] Perhaps the latter's patronage of Ramsey arose, not so much out of a devotion to the monastic ideal, as out of the proprietary solicitude of a great landowner towards a church of his own founding upon his own land. That was an attitude rooted deep in the past of the Germanic peoples.[4]

At the same time the set-back of 975 imposed no lasting check upon the building of the estate of Ely abbey. But, in the years after the death of Bishop Ethelwold, a new phase begins. It seems to have become clear that the new monasticism was firmly established and had come to stay. In the next few generations the monks of Ely bought very little land.[5] On the other hand, their abbey became the object of gifts of land on a very considerable scale which filled out the map of the estate to something like its Domesday proportions. The details are of minor importance, though we may note the completion of the process which gave the abbey a virtual monopoly of ownership within the confines of the Isle of Ely. March was acquired between 995 and 1006, Wisbech before 1016, and the Ely manor in Whittlesey from that 'praiseworthy man' Leofwin, a thegn of King Ethelred.[6] By this time there seem to have been

---

[1] *Chron. Rames.* 71–2.

[2] *HE*, II, cc. 7, 27, 49, 55. To recover Hatfield (the timber of which they needed to build their abbey) the monks gave the ealdorman four manors in Huntingdonshire.

[3] 'Advocatus noster' is the description of Aethelwine in *Chron. Rames.* 26.

[4] For *Eigenklöster* in England, see H. Boehmer in *Texte u. Forschungen zur englischen Kulturgeschichte*, especially p. 350, and Levison, *England and the Continent in the Eighth Century*, pp. 27–33.

[5] A few cases noted are the purchase of Hadstock, Linton and Streetley from King Ethelred; the exchange of Cheveley for Wood Ditton with King Cnut; and the purchases in Barham and Teversham from Earl Aelfgar: *HE*, II, cc. 77, 82, 97; *KCD*, no. 725; *Dd*, I, 201 d.

[6] *HE*, II, cc. 60, 67, 75; on Leofwin see Robertson, *ASC*, p. 377. He gave Ely one third of the vill of Whittlesey, which exactly corresponds to the extent of its property there in 1086: *Dd*, I, 191 d, 192 d.

only two manors in the Isle which were not part of the estate of Ely abbey—the manor of Thorney abbey in Whittlesey and the manor of Ramsey abbey in Chatteris.

One other feature of interest about this second period arises out of a study of the men and women who gave lands to Ely abbey. From such a study one fact emerges with some force. The whole picture of benevolence is dominated to a remarkable degree by ealdorman Brihtnoth of the East Saxons, his relatives by marriage (the daughters of ealdorman Aelfgar), and his descendants.[1] Brihtnoth's own gifts to Ely were munificent,[2] and some of them were confirmed and augmented by his widow.[3] This patronage, moreover, continued down to the third generation of his descendants—for amongst the abbey's benefactors are numbered his daughter[4] and Aelfwine bishop of Elmham, said to be his son;[5] his daughter's daughters and the husband of one of them,[6] and finally, perhaps, the latter's son.[7] There are difficulties in the interpretation of some of these gifts;[8] for many of them seem to have been cumbered with life interests and slow to come to fruition. Nevertheless, of the manors which Ely abbey had on the day when King Edward was alive and dead, a score or more can be traced back to gifts by this single family.

Of course, there were many other benefactors: other instances of family generosity,[9] a few other great names amongst them.[10] Many gifts accompanied the sons of important land-holders when they devoted themselves (or were devoted) to the monastic life—gifts amongst which we may notice the half dozen manors brought with him by the future Abbot Leofsige.[11]

---

[1] On Brihtnoth and his connections see Robertson, *ASC*, pp. 315,337,430; Chadwick, *Anglo-Saxon Institutions*, pp. 177, 180; Whitelock, *ASW*, pp. 104–7.   [2] See *HE*, ii, c. 62.

[3] *Ibid.* c. 63, supported by her will in Whitelock, *ASW*, pp. 39–43.

[4] Leofflaed, who gave the monks Balsham: *HE*, ii, c. 88; *KCD*, no. 932. See the remarks on her parentage in Whitelock, *ASW*, pp. 141–2.

[5] Blomefield, *Collectanea Cantabrigiensia*, p. 244; he gave Wisbech to Ely.

[6] *HE*, ii, c. 88.   [7] *Ibid.* cc. 88–9; Whitelock, *ASW*, pp. 80–4, 193.

[8] Some of them are discussed by Whitelock, *ASW*, pp. 189–93.

[9] For example, the gift of lands in eight villages by three brothers when the sons of two of them entered the monastery: *HE*, ii, cc. 66–8.

[10] Another bishop of Elmham, for instance (c. 65), and Godgifu, the widow of Leofric earl of Mercia (cc. 81, 83; for the identification of the Lady Godiva of the text see Whitelock, *ASW*, p. 212 and Robertson, *ASC*, p. 465).

[11] *HE*, ii, c. 74.

Men of thegnly status, however, are also to be found side by side with greater men in the giving of land. Indeed, one of the largest single accessions of territory resulted from the gift of eight manors by King Ethelred's thegn, Leofwin; but then he had the crime of matricide to expiate.[1] More typical of the gifts from this class of men was Aelfelm's grant to the monks of the vill of West Wratting saving the two hides which Aethelric held;[2] or the similar gift of land at Bergh Apton in Norfolk by Aelfric Modercope, a lesser king's thegn allowed by the Confessor to commend himself to the abbots of Ely and Bury St Edmunds.[3]

It would seem, therefore, that it is possible to draw from the record of these benefactions the following conclusions about the accumulation of the Domesday demesnes of Ely abbey. The foundations were laid by Bishop Ethelwold, in the execution of a deliberate policy to provide the new monasticism with firm roots in the soil and by means of lavish expenditure. Then, after a temporary check following King Edgar's death, estate-building continued under somewhat different circumstances. At first, much of the prosperity of Ely abbey may have been due to the patronage of ealdorman Brihtnoth and his family; but it was soon able to draw upon far wider public support extending to all circles of the late Saxon aristocracy. Under these conditions the policy of purchasing land could be relinquished during an age of pious gift. But an even more precise chronology of estate-building is possible. Not more than about half a dozen of the abbey's manors for which information has survived seem to have been acquired much later than the year 1020. In other words, the very considerable redistribution of property in eastern England, which was necessary to create the demesne lands of Ely abbey as they are known to us in *Domesday Book*, was carried out in the brief half-century after 970.[4] This was an

---

[1] *HE*, II, c. 60 and above, p. 21, n. 6.

[2] *Ibid.* c. 73; Whitelock, *ASW*, pp. 31–5, 133–7. He was King Ethelred's 'faithful minister', had roughly the status of a king's thegn and had possessions in some twenty villages in half a dozen counties.

[3] Whitelock, *ASW*, pp. 74–5, 186 and, for the Confessor's writ, *KCD*, no. 877. There is some discussion of Aelfric in Douglas, *Feudal Documents*, pp. cx–cxii.

[4] This seems to accord well enough with the modern learning about the new monasticism. It passes through a period of very rapid expansion in the later tenth century, but this seems to have been over soon after the year 1000: see Knowles, *The Monastic Order in England*, especially pp. 59, 66.

achievement which, in virtue both of its magnitude and its rapidity, must have had major social consequences; it is a chapter of the very greatest significance in the long history of landlordship.

The geography of the estate, furthermore, bears marks which were given to it by both of these periods in its building. During the first phase, the main achievement was the consolidation of the abbey's lordship over the 'island of Ely' and the building up of a not inconsiderable estate in the adjacent districts of Cambridgeshire and north-west Suffolk. During the second period, on the other hand, when most of the new acquisitions consisted of gifts of land, there was less design in their distribution. The scattered estate which resulted was that which, whatever the inroads made upon it by the companions of the Conqueror, was surveyed in 1086 by the Domesday commissioners. In so far as the Norman abbots after 1072 were able to make good in detail their claims to this Saxon heritage, the resources which Bishop Ethelwold and the first few abbots had garnered became the endowment of the medieval bishopric and cathedral priory of Ely. The work which was done in a brief half-century endured for near six hundred years.

Finally, it may be remarked that the work of these early abbots stands in even clearer relief because the last decades of the Old English period saw a slackening, even a reversal, of earlier expansive tendencies. It is true that in Abbot Wulfric's time (?1052–65) there were still a few new acquisitions of property, but once again they were the result of purchase rather than of gift.[1] Yet these can hardly have balanced what were, in effect, losses of land. We read how Esgar Staller seized High Easter from the monks, and extorted from them eventually the right to hold the manor for his life. Before he was dead Duke William came, and it never returned to the abbey; for it passed with the rest of Esgar's property to Geoffrey de Mandeville and became the site of his castle of Pleshy.[2] Archbishop Stigand, too, in 1066 was in possession of four of the abbey's richest manors, manors which passed into King William's

---

[1] Land was purchased in Teversham and *Bercam*, presumably the demesne manor of Barham in Suffolk: *HE*, ii, c. 97; *Dd*, i, 201 d; ii, 383 d.

[2] *HE*, ii, c. 96; *Dd*, ii, 60 d; Round, *VCH Essex*, i, pp. 341, 509.

hands;[1] and Abbot Wulfric's brother, Guthmund, was given a competence from the abbey estate in order to facilitate his matrimonial designs upon the daughter of a noble house.[2] These misfortunes may not be matters of great moment; they do not necessarily point to any real weakening of monasticism, any great corruption in the religious life of the last days of Saxon England. But they do suggest, none the less, that these times must have been different times from those during which Bishop Ethelwold and ealdorman Brihtnoth had endowed the abbey of Ely so richly. The lands of the church of Ely, of which they had laid the foundations, were never to be quite so wide again as they had been in the first decades of the eleventh century.

III

The medieval liberty of the church of Ely, like its medieval estates, had its first beginning in King Edgar's charters of re-foundation. In the Anglo-Saxon version, the king expressed his desire to endow the abbey with its own freedom and special honour. In part he fulfilled this desire by granting to the monks the soke over the fenland in the two hundreds; the soke at Wicklaw in Suffolk over the five hundreds; and the soke over all lands then given to the church or that would be given to it in the future. In addition the abbey was to receive the fourth penny out of the forfeitures incurred in the public courts of Cambridgeshire. The Latin charter differs from this in no important particular; while the subsidiary charter

---

[1] Wood Ditton and Snailwell (Cambs.) with Methwold and Croxton (Norfolk): *Dd*, I, 189 d, 199 d; II, 136, 136 d. According to *HE*, II, c. 98 he retained possession of these properties after he had the custody of the abbey following Wulfric's death; but *Domesday* speaks of his having leased them and the *ICC*, p. 3, names Abbot Leofsige as the lessor. This might point to a transaction round about 1052 (when Abbot Leofsige was last certainly alive) and perhaps near enough to the time of the obscure revolution which put Stigand in the place of the Confessor's Norman archbishop (for which see Stenton, *Anglo-Saxon England*, pp. 458–9).

[2] *HE*, II, c. 97. The full story can be reconstructed from *Dd*, II, 54, 212 d, 238–8 d, 406, 410 d: in Norfolk Guthmund was given the lordship over groups of sokemen in Marham and Garboldisham; in Suffolk, the demesne manors of Livermere, Occold and Nacton; in Essex, Sandon. These lands, with the rest of Guthmund's property, were given by the Conqueror to Hugh de Montfort.

supports the right of the abbey to forfeitures from Ely and its appurtenances.[1]

Thus, from the year 970 onward Ely abbey enjoyed 'soke' over certain hundreds and in all its lands. It is another matter, however, to define the precise nature of the rights implied by this 'soke' as King Edgar would have understood it. We can no longer assume so easily as was once possible that what was conferred in grants of this kind consisted of court-keeping rights, rights of private jurisdiction.[2] The evidence, moreover, which bears upon the early history of the liberty of Ely is particularly scanty. In the main, it is no more than a phrase, found first in a writ of the Confessor's but afterwards repeated on many occasions. It was used to describe the liberty of Ely (though with a few additional terms) in the Conqueror's writ confirming the findings of the Kentford inquest,[3] and in every subsequent confirmation of that liberty down to the end of the twelfth century.[4] The history of the phrase is long enough to warrant some examination of its terms.

The original formula is to be found in the writ in which Edward the Confessor notified to the notabilities of eastern England, somewhere about 1052, the appointment of Wulfric as abbot of Ely. He has given the abbey to Wulfric, he says, 'in all things within borough and without, toll and team and infangentheof, fihtwite and fyrdwite, hamsoke and grithbrice, let his man live where he lives and work where he works'.[5] The Norman version of this formula included an addition which may

[1] *KCD*, no. 564: 'Elig cum omnibus sibi subjectis tam in delictorum emendatione quam in ceteris rebus.'

[2] See Goebel, *Felony and Misdemeanour*, I, pp. 377 ff. He argues that jurisdictional privileges granted by charter had nothing much to do with court holding; they were concerned for the most part with the allocation of the profits accruing from the public courts. It is true that his views have not been in any way fully accepted on this point (see Hurnard, *EHR*, LXIV, p. 292 and the references given there); but at the very least he has made it imperative to scrutinize as closely as we can the precise terms of each particular instance of what once might have been accepted as a grant of court-holding rights without question.

[3] *EHR*, LXII, p. 455.

[4] By Henry I (*Mon. Angl.* I, 482; Bentham, Appx. IX and XVII; *Cartae Antiquae Rolls* 1–10, nos. 50, 52); Stephen (Trin. MS. O. 2. 1, f. 128; Liber M, f. 81); Henry II (Delisle-Berger, *Recueil des Actes de Henri II*, no. 60); John earl of Mortain (*EHR*, LXII, pp. 455–6); and by Richard I in his first charter to Ely (D & C Charter no. 13).

[5] *KCD*, no. 885; *HE*, II, c. 95.

be significant. In the Conqueror's writ it ran as follows: 'sake and soke, toll and team and infangentheof, hamsoke and grith-brice, fihtwite and fyrdwite within borough and without *et omnes alias forisfacturas que emendabiles sunt in terra sua super suos homines*'. The novelty here consists in the addition of the term 'sake and soke' and in the final phrase which might perhaps be rendered as 'all other penalties for which a money amendment can be made'. It should be noted in passing that these liberties were to be enjoyed generally throughout the abbey's lands. No distinction was made between the liberty within and without the hundreds of the church of Ely; no peculiarity was asserted at that time for what afterwards became the special liberty of the Isle of Ely which was 'in divers statutes called a county palatine'.

Some of the terms of this formula seem to be concerned not with a judicial but with a fiscal privilege—with penalties, amendments, *wites*. *Fyrdwite* and *fihtwite* are quite explicitly *wites*; the Conqueror (if his last phrase has the meaning suggested above) seems to be conceding forfeitures for emendable crimes. It is also possible that, at an early date, a grant of *grithbrice* and *hamsoke* may have conferred no more than the right to receive the hundred shillings *wite* which was the amendment due to the king from such causes.[1] On the other hand, the terms *team* and *infangentheof* in the Confessor's writ suggest that throughout his estate the abbot of Ely possessed (or was to be allowed from that time forward) courts where defendants in cases of theft could vouch to warranty and where hand-having thieves could be summarily dealt with.[2] Further, if the Conqueror's writ after the Kentford inquest merely confirmed existing rights, and if it be true that after the Conquest 'sake and soke' normally implied jurisdiction[3]—then the Conqueror's writ is evidence for the fact that the abbots of Ely before 1066 had held courts for all their men in all their lands.

---

[1] Goebel, *Felony and Misdemeanour*, I, pp. 366, 408. It may be of significance that in *Pipe R*, 31 Hen. I, 45, 46 the sheriff of Cambridgeshire received allowance in respect of amercements 'pro pace fracta' paid over to the bishop of Ely. In the light of Miss Hurnard's argument (*EHR*, LXIV, pp. 304–5) the reference may be to pleas of *grithbrice*, in which case it would seem that the bishop was not trying such pleas in all his manors even in 1130.

[2] Hurnard, *op. cit.* p. 292 n.

[3] *Ibid.* pp. 292 ff.

If that were so, then one would also expect those same courts to have exercised jurisdiction in those other matters which receive merely a fiscal expression in the formula under consideration, in those pleas which gave rise to *fihtwite* and so on. There is, of course, no need to assume that this would imply a very far-reaching jurisdiction; in fact it probably amounted to very much the same sort of jurisdiction as the bishop exercised in later centuries in his courts leet. In effect the abbots of Ely in the Confessor's time may well have been doing in their own courts the business which normally would have been done in the hundred courts: and we should remember that the hundred courts had probably already lost to the courts of the shires all the embryonic 'pleas of the crown'—important cases in which the king alone could mitigate the sentence.[1] On the other hand, the fact that it was the hundredal jurisdiction which had passed into the hands of the abbots will explain why no distinction was made in our documents between the liberty they had within and without their hundreds.

Yet if the liberty of Ely was a court-keeping liberty in the Conqueror's reign, and if there is a reasonable presumption that it may have been so in the Confessor's, this constitutes no proof that these were the rights involved in the 'soke' which King Edgar conferred upon the monks. In the only one of Edgar's charters to Ely where there is any gloss upon this 'soke', we hear nothing about courts; there is mention only of 'emendatio delictorum', payments made in emendation of crimes.[2] There is, moreover, other evidence which suggests that the abbey, in the earliest phase, may have enjoyed only a fiscal privilege. In the first place we may recall that King Edgar granted to the abbey the 'soke' over all its lands and over the lands which it would acquire in the future. Had this involved an immediate grant of court-keeping rights, we might expect it to have resulted in the withdrawal of all the abbot's men from the public courts of shire and hundred. Yet in fact that did not happen. In the thirteenth century and outside the Isle of Ely

[1] In fact this had probably taken place by the time of Cnut: Hurnard, *op. cit.* pp. 292–5.

[2] *KCD*, no. 564 quoted above, p. 26, n. 1. We have also been taught that the word 'soke' used by itself (as it is in these charters of King Edgar) 'frequently stands for the profits of justice' rather than for a right to hold courts: Hurnard, *op. cit.* p. 299 n.

even the demesne manors of the bishops of Ely still owed suits to the public courts.[1] It is true that by that time the circle of suitors had probably been narrowed down to certain men for whom suit was a 'real burden', an incident of tenure.[2] It is also true that, in the manors of the bishops of Ely, these suits had been drained of real meaning; for the bishop in his *curie et lete* could exercise all the jurisdiction which the sheriff could exercise. By the thirteenth century the liberty of Ely had, to that extent, become an immunity; but the fact that these suits persisted suggests that this had not always been so, that at some time or another it had been no more than an area of fiscal privilege.

There is more direct evidence still, however, deriving from a place where we would most expect to find the church at an early date exercising the rights of an immunist. The peculiar liberty of the church of Ely in the Isle is thought to be very ancient;[3] and it is probably true that the 'situation most favourable to private court-keeping was the possession of a hundred'.[4] It does indeed seem quite certain that the abbots were holding their own hundred courts in the Isle and elsewhere in the Conqueror's reign[5] and, despite the purely fiscal terminology of *Domesday Book*,[6] we may be justified in suspecting that they had done so before 1066. But it is another matter to assume that in the Isle this was an automatic outcome of the 'emendatio delictorum' King Edgar had given the monks in the fenland; for there is nothing to prove that 'the transition from a right to "wites" to such "jurisdiction" as the feudal lord enjoys' was a 'very easy' transition to make.[7] On the contrary, the special powers which the church of Ely had in the Isle 'are not stressed until after the Conquest'[8] and, more important still, incidental allusions in early land-pleas suggest that the early abbots had no

[1] See below, pp. 214–16.
[2] P & M, I, pp. 541–2.
[3] Hurnard, *op. cit.* p. 317.
[4] Goebel, *Felony and Misdemeanour*, I, p. 377.
[5] See Henry I's writ in Bentham, Appx. XXIII. It is discussed below, pp. 240–1.
[6] Eg. Mitford hundred: 'tota soca istius hundredi jacebat ad sanctam Adeldredam TRE et valet 60 solidos': *Dd*, II, 214; and compare the entry for the Suffolk hundreds: *ibid.* 385 d.
[7] Maitland, *Domesday Book and Beyond*, p. 278.
[8] Hurnard, *op. cit.* p. 317.

immunity at all even in the Isle, and may not even have had a court-keeping franchise. We find ealdorman Aethelwine presiding over a plea about land in Witchford, a plea which was heard at Ely 'within the cemetery at the north gate of the abbey, with all the hundred present'. We find Wulfstan of Dalham, sheriff apparently both of Cambridgeshire and West Kent,[1] coming to Ely with many thegns (barones) and, the two hundreds being present, presiding over a plea about lands in Stonea. In a later plea about land in the same place, ealdorman Aethelwine once more presided successively over courts held at Ely and at Cambridge.[2] In short, although the abbots of Ely may have been exercising the hundredal jurisdiction generally throughout their lands before the end of the old English period, it is very doubtful whether they were exercising it even in the Isle of Ely in the earliest days after the refoundation. Furthermore, there is nothing at all to show, even after they had begun to exercise such a jurisdiction, that the two hundreds of the Isle were in any way distinguished from the rest of the abbey's hundreds or the rest of the abbey's lands. The quasi-palatine liberty which the bishops enjoyed later in the Isle receives no mention in the Confessor's writ or the Conqueror's; in fact it receives no mention in a public record until the time of Richard I.[3]

Whenever the church of Ely began to hold courts in its hundreds (hundreds it was to hold for the rest of the Middle Ages), some rights in all of them were acquired in Anglo-Saxon times. The five and a half hundreds of Wicklaw in Suffolk[4] and the two hundreds of the Isle of Ely were both given to the abbey by King Edgar as part of its first endowment. The monks also claimed at a later time that Edgar had also given them the hundred and a half of Mitford in Norfolk: but this was in a passage inserted into the chronicle in the latter part of the twelfth century.[5] However, the matter is of little importance.

[1] Chadwick, Anglo-Saxon Institutions, p. 231.
[2] HE, ii, cc. 12, 18 and 24.
[3] In Richard's first charter to Ely: D & C Charter no. 13, and see Hurnard, op. cit. p. 317.
[4] I.e. the hundreds of Plumesgate, Loes, Wilford, Carlford and Colneis and the half hundred of Parham. This district, like the eight hundreds of St Edmund's in the same county, may preserve the outlines of a far older administrative area: see Cam, Liberties and Communities, pp. 88–9 and Douglas, Feudal Documents, pp. cli–clii.
[5] HE, ii, c. 40; it does not appear in the Libellus: Trin. MS. O. 2. 41, f. 60.

Ely abbey certainly had the soke of this hundred in 1066 as an appurtenance of its manor of East Dereham;[1] it had come into their possession through the grant of one or other of the Old English kings.

Out of all these pre-conquestual hundreds, only the two hundreds of the Isle seem to have left traces which allow us to say just a little about their internal structure and organization. The first point would seem to be that, administratively speaking, these two hundreds were originally in fact one hundred. Traces of this original unity were slow to disappear. Even in the thirteenth century and the fourteenth there was still a court at Ely which called upon suitors, quite irrespective of their tenure, from the whole of the Isle with the exception of Wisbech and its appurtenant hamlets.[2] At this late date that court had no more than a nominal existence; but its ancestor would appear to be the court which, in the twelfth century, might meet at Ely or Witchford or *Modich*.[3] Traces of a court, calling upon suitors from both the two hundreds of the Isle and meeting at the north gate of the monastery, have survived from Saxon times;[4] and even *Domesday* can be read in a similar light. True, it divides the villages of the Isle between two hundreds, but a glance is enough to show that those hundreds were not geographical entities. The division, in fact, was a purely fiscal one designed to produce two hundreds of roughly forty hides each. Administrative reality, on the other hand, was represented by the rubric which spoke of the two hundreds of Ely which met at Witchford.[5] The process which produced first two and then three

[1] Cam, *op. cit.* p. 185; *ICC*, 195; East Dereham was probably in the abbey's possession by 1029–35: *HE*, II, c. 84 (for the dating of this chapter see below, pp. 37–8).

[2] See below, pp. 219 ff.

[3] 'Et omnes homines duorum centuriatuum insule de quindecim in quindecim diebus debent convenire ad Ely vel ad Wicheforda, que caput centuriatuum insule dicitur, vel ad Modich, que quarta pars est centuriatuum': *HE*, II, c. 54. There was nothing to prevent a hundred court meeting at more than one place within the hundred. In the fourteenth century Witchford hundred met regularly both at Witchford and Witcham, and sometimes also at Sutton and Haddenham: EDR Court Rolls, C 7; Wren's Note Book, f. 276.

[4] E.g. *HE*, II, c. 18 and see above, p. 30.

[5] *Dd*, I, 191 d: 'De duobus hundretis de Ely qui conveniunt apud Wiceforde'. The plural 'hundreds' in a charter of Bishop Hervey's in 1128 to Thorney abbey may have a similar significance: 'Omnes illas consuetudines et causas seculares quas habebat Elyensis ecclesia in hundredis suis de Wichefort'—Thorney Red Book, I, f. 166.

distinct hundreds in the Isle was a long one. Even in the thirteenth century divers inquests were required to establish the boundary which marked off Witchford hundred from Wisbech hundred to the north.[1]

In connection with this latter hundred, we must turn for a moment to *Modich* where, as we have seen, a court was held in the twelfth century to serve a quarter part of the hundreds of the Isle. *Modich* has been identified with a place called *Mudeke* mentioned amongst the fisheries of Littleport in the thirteenth century,[2] although its exact location does not seem to be known. It would appear, however, that the commons and fisheries of Littleport in early times stretched deep into the marshy no-man's-land between the island of Ely and the northern group of villages about Wisbech.[3] If *Modich* indeed lay somewhere in that direction, this would strongly reinforce other evidence which seems to suggest that the court held at *Modich* was a court for the Wisbech district. In the chronicler's description of the gift of Wisbech to the abbey, he describes it there as 'a quarter part of the hundred of the Isle'.[4] In *Domesday*, again, Wisbech was assessed at ten hides—one quarter of a forty-hide hundred. The distinct character of this part of the Isle is not without interest. It looks as though a separate court may have been held for Wisbech and its hamlets from an early date—probably of necessity, because they were a long way from the compact group of villages on the island about Ely and Witchford. That would be the first step in a development which created eventually a separate Wisbech hundred.

Yet this hardly exhausts the interest of this 'quarter part of the hundreds of the Isle'. That phrase immediately calls to mind the *ferdings* which crop up from time to time in East Anglia.[5] They were districts which, Abbot Samson's kalendar

[1] Cott. Claudius C xi, f. 357d.

[2] *PN Cambs.* p. 213; Cott. Tiberius B ii, f. 96; Caius 485/489, ff. 35d–6.

[3] It may be noted that the name *Horninges* appears both in the boundaries of Littleport and of Upwell in the thirteenth century: *ibid.* ff. 35d–6, 97d.

[4] *HE*, ii, c. 75.

[5] Round, *Feudal England*, p. 101. Normally, *ferdings* are associated with Suffolk, where they are twice mentioned in *Little Domesday* (Lees, *VCH Suffolk*, i, p. 358); but they have also been found in the Happing hundred of Norfolk: see West, *Register of St Benet of Holme*, i, pp. 169–70 and Stenton, *EHR*, xxxvii, p. 227.

tells us, were also and in other places called leets;[1] and they were capable of acting as units of government and police.[2] In short, the *ferding* of Wisbech would seem to preserve traces of an organization which preceded the time when it was embodied into the two hundreds of the Isle; and there would seem to be some characteristics which connect it with the adjoining villages round West Walton over the border in Norfolk—villages in which the leet organization has left particularly clear traces.[3] In the same connection it may not be without significance that, in the thirteenth-century organization of the bishop's estate, Wisbech was associated precisely with this group of Norfolk manors in the Marshland Bailiwick, and not with the manors of the rest of the Isle.[4] That association may have a very venerable origin.

In short, we may say that the hundredal organization in the Isle of Ely in the eleventh century was an artificial thing and probably a relatively recent thing. More than that, however, it fitted the facts of social structure loosely, but for reasons which may have been different from those which lent artificiality to the five and a half hundreds which the abbey had in Suffolk. There, the hundredal organization may have been superimposed upon a pre-existing administrative district; in the Isle, on the other hand, it seems to have given unity to a number of different components.[5] We shall probably never know how the patchwork was sewn together; but the original diversity of the elements fused in the two hundreds retained some vitality and some importance. To some measure, of course, diversity was subdued by the conjunction of landowning rights and jurisdictional privilege which the church of Ely enjoyed over most of the area of the Isle from the tenth century onwards. But it was never entirely subdued; and many of the peculiarities of the later hundred courts of the Isle may derive in the last resort from the differing origins of its different parts.

All this discussion of the pre-conquestual liberty has been

---

[1] CUL Add. 6006, f. 102d: 'Hec sunt ferdinges in Babeberge quas in aliis hundredis vocamus letas'; and see also Douglas, *Feudal Documents*, p. clxvi.

[2] *Pipe R*, 5 Henry II, 10: 'Idem vicecomes reddit compotum de ferdingo de Sudburna pro murdro,' etc.

[3] See especially Douglas, *East Anglia*, pp. 195–200.

[4] *Ibid.* p. 196n. and PRO Min. Accts, 1132/10.

[5] There is further discussion on this point above, p. 14.

2

based upon evidence which is fragmentary in the extreme; and it is a dangerous thing to draw conclusions from it. Yet there may be signs of progress and change in the brief century which separates Bishop Ethelwold from William the Conqueror. King Edgar granted the abbey merely the soke of certain hundreds and of the lands the abbey had—a soke which even in the abbey's hundreds may have been no more than a fiscal privilege. But the liberty of Ely was not always as limited as that. At least as early as the Conqueror's reign the abbots had begun to hold courts in their hundreds, as they may not have been doing in the time of the ealdorman Aethelwine. By the Confessor's time, they had also acquired the right to receive a whole variety of *wites* and forfeitures, whatever the tribunals may have been which imposed them. Furthermore, it should be noted that this was a right which extended, not over the land of the abbey, but over all its men—let them live wherever they lived and work wherever they worked.[1] This also seems to be the main characteristic of the soke about which *Domesday* has so much to say. In the vast majority of instances, the abbot had the soke of all his men (whether or not their land was the abbot's land);[2] and this soke involved at least a fiscal privilege which was vested in the abbot. That will explain why we read about certain men of Feltwell in 1071–5: 'wheresoever they do wrong, the abbot will have their forfeiture'.[3] We need only remember once again that the abbey had many dependants in 1066; this was one of the ways in which the abbot's men were profitable to him.

At the same time, these notices of soke over men are significant from a wider point of view. They indicate for us that the lordship exercised by the Anglo-Saxon abbey of Ely did not cease to extend its influence even after rapid territorial expansion had come to an end early in the eleventh century. King Edgar's charter was concerned with soke over the abbey's hundreds and

[1] *KCD*, no. 885 and above, p. 26.
[2] This emerges very clearly from the Domesday account of the Suffolk hundred of Claydon. Normally the soke there belonged to the king and earl; but wherever the abbey had dependants it also had the soke over them: *Dd*, II, 294d–5, 298d, 305d–6, 360d, 376–6d, 446–6d. We shall have much more to say on this matter below, pp. 53ff.
[3] 'Ubicunque forisfecerint abbas forisfacturam habebit et de illis similiter qui in eorum terris forisfecerint'; and compare the similar entry regarding men at Sudbourne: 'ubicunque deliquerint emendacionem habebit et de omnibus illis qui in terris eorum deliquerint': *ICC*, 193, 194.

the abbey's demesne land; the Confessor's writ was concerned
with soke over the abbey's men, because in the interval the
abbey's lordship had been pushed far outside its own territories.
On the whole this extension of personal lordship was a transitory
phase in the development of the seignorial rights vested in the
church of Ely. The Norman land settlement drastically narrowed
the circle of the abbey's dependants; and those who remained
were turned quite soon into tenants. From that time onwards
it was territorial rather than personal dependence which involved dependence also in judicial matters. None the less, the
extension of the abbey's lordship over men's persons before
1066 was more than merely testimony to its pre-conquestual
influence. It provided some of the materials out of which territorial dependants were created after 1066; and those dependants,
according to their station, became suitors to the domanial and
feudal courts, the development of which the Conquest unquestionably stimulated. Some of the powers, moreover, which
the medieval bishops and priors of Ely exercised in such courts
were influenced and justified by the privileges already enjoyed
by the abbots in the Confessor's day—even if the precise
meaning which was later attached to such privileges was something which the Confessor would barely have recognized.

III

THE OLD ENGLISH ESTATE AND THE NORMAN CONQUEST

CERTAIN features of the liberty of Ely abbey in the eleventh century have shown quite clearly that the accumulation of demesne lands represented only one of the ways in which the lordship of the Old English abbots had been extended. The care the Confessor took to define the rights which Abbot Wulfric enjoyed over all his men, wherever they might live and wherever they might work, is testimony to the ever-widening circle of dependants established around the periphery of the demesne lands of the abbey. A study of the lordship exercised by the abbey at the end of the Old English period, therefore, must take account both of the methods employed in the management of its demesnes and of the character of the dependent ties which extended often far outside those demesnes. Such a study raises very many problems; but it is an essential preliminary to an attempt to estimate the changes involved in the Norman settlement so far as it affected the abbey of Ely.

I

It is clear enough, of course, that the methods of organization which prevailed on the estate of Ely abbey before and after 1066 were determined largely by the character and needs of a monastic community. Such a community was immobile: it could not move about the estate eating up the produce of the manors as a layman or even a bishop could. Its numbers (including servants) were considerable, though they might be smaller in 1066 than they were to be at a later date.[1] Both of these charac-

[1] In the early twelfth century Ely had fifty monks; and later in that century seventy (still its statutory complement at the beginning of the fourteenth century): *Anglia Sacra*, I, 617; 'Ely Chapter Ordinances', *Camden Miscellany*, XVII, p. 14. For monastic numbers in general, and the fact that they were lower before 1066 than in the reign of Henry I, see Knowles, *The Monastic Order in England*, pp. 425–6; for servants, see *ibid.* pp. 439–41, where it is shown that the system of lay servants was firmly established before 1066. At Ely in the twelfth century the number of servants about equalled the number of monks.

teristics demanded methods of estate organization which may have been more regular and inelastic than those which prevailed on other sorts of estate at this time. At the same time, the devices adopted for the management of the lands of the church of Ely correspond well enough with what is known of contemporary monastic estates.[1]

The methods of estate management can be approached most conveniently through the terminology of *Domesday* and its satellites. The same manor can be described as lying 'always in the church in demesne' or 'always in the church in demesne *farm*'.[2] Again, a manor which lay in the church also lay in the demesne of the church;[3] whilst a demesne vill of the abbot, a vill which had lain always in demesne, was one that had lain in demesne farm.[4] A demesne manor, once more, was one which might in King Edward's time have provided food for the monks.[5] Amidst all this revelling 'in the use of synonym and paraphrase',[6] there seem to be certain underlying assumptions. A demesne manor is almost of necessity a manor which renders a farm, a *firma*,[7] though it is another matter to say what a farm might be. Certainly on the Ely manors of Croxton and Methwold it may have meant a fixed amount of food for the monks; but sometimes in 1066 renders of food may have been one element only in a farm and in other cases deliveries in kind may already have been commuted into money payments.[8] On this subject, the evidence of *Domesday* is too enigmatic to stand alone.

The Ely tradition about the origins of the farming system in

---

[1] See for instance Smith, *Canterbury Cathedral Priory*, pp. 113–14 and Neilson, *VCH Kent*, III, pp. 185–6.

[2] *Dd*, I, 191d; *IE*, 115 (Whittlesey).

[3] *Dd*, I, 190d; *IE*, 104; *ICC*, 18 (Stetchworth).

[4] *Dd*, I, 190d; *IE*, 104; *ICC*, 19 (Westley Waterless).

[5] *IE*, 138 (Croxton and Methwold): 'iacebat TRE ad victum monachorum'.

[6] Round, *Feudal England*, p. 26.

[7] Where a manor had not been at farm TRE it might even be difficult for the Domesday jurors to say how much it had been worth before the conquest; see Vinogradoff, *English Society*, p. 378 quoting *Dd*, I, 179d (Lugwardine, Hereford).

[8] For commutation on the royal demesne, see *ibid.* pp. 374–6; Poole, *The Exchequer in the Twelfth Century*, pp. 26–35; Round, *Feudal England*, pp. 111–15 and *Commune of London*, pp. 68–74. For similar evidence from a monastic estate soon after the conquest see Douglas, *EHR*, XLIII, pp. 376ff. and *Feudal Documents*, p. cxxxiii. On the whole subject of farms see also Knowles, *The Monastic Order in England*, pp. 441–4.

its demesne manors is relatively straightforward.[1] It was in-
stituted, we are told, by Abbot Leofsige with the permission of
King Cnut and must date, therefore, from the years 1029–35.
Previous to this time the management of the abbey's lands had
been entrusted to a monk with full discretion over the whole of
its property; his responsibility was clearly that assigned to the
cellarer in St Benedict's rule.[2] Once the monastic community
had achieved some sort of stability, however, and once the
period of rapid territorial expansion was over, the cellarer's
discretion was confined within stricter limits. Abbot Leofsige
'assigned farms which would suffice for the provision of the
church throughout the year, and more especially he chose for
this purpose from its lands and villages those which were known
by their more abundant fertility and fruitful fields to produce the
better crops'. In other words, the central feature of the exploitation of the abbey's demesnes from that time forward was
the institution of a system of food farms in the proper sense of
that term. The units of this system were one week's supply of
food for the abbey, and altogether thirty-three manors contributed fifty-six of these units. At the same time, as the chronicler
indicates, the burden was a selective burden. The manors of the
Isle of Ely were specifically held in reserve in case deliveries
should not be made from manors burdened with a farm—a large
reservation for such a contingency which suggests that farms
must have been fixed somewhere near the maximum these other
manors could produce. Apart from the manors of the Isle,
however, a considerable number of manors elsewhere (perhaps
not far short of thirty in all) were not called upon to contribute
food farms. It is not easy to say how such manors were exploited. They may well have been farmed like the rest, but
farmed for a cash payment, or payments both in cash and kind,
since it is at least probable that food farms by no means exhausted the liveries in kind which the monks obtained from the
manors. We hear of rents paid in the form of honey,[3] and of
astronomical numbers of eels delivered by the fenland manors.[4]

---

[1] *HE*, II, c. 84.

[2] *HE*, II, c. 54 and see Knowles, *The Monastic Order in England*, pp. 431ff.

[3] At Histon and Larling, for instance: *Dd*, I, 190d; *IE*, 140.

[4] These manors produced some 95,000 eels in 1086, and long before King
Edgar had given the abbey a yearly rent of 10,000 eels from Outwell: *Dd*, I,
191d; Robertson, *ASC*, pp. 98–102.

We know also that Hatfield was valued as a source of timber;[1] and that the abbot's saltpans in the manors of the Norfolk Marshland must have been as necessary as they were useful in the domestic economy of the abbey.[2]

At the same time the fact that a manor was included in the list of those which rendered food farms in the early eleventh century did not mean that this arrangement was irrevocable. Some manors may have been granted away,[3] while others may have taken their places in the scheme. There may even have been a more important revision of the scheme in some places. Barking and Drinkstone were two of the manors on which food farms had been imposed in 1029–36. In 1086, on the other hand and if the words of *Domesday Book* mean what they say, they were paying money farms and the complaint was that the farm was greater than the manor could bear.[4] We cannot be absolutely sure, because we cannot be absolutely sure that the words of *Domesday* do mean what they say;[5] but there may be a suggestion here that some food farms were being turned into money farms. Complaint may have arisen because it was a recent change, a recent break in traditional arrangements. At the same time, such a change may have been the easier to make because some manors, even in the earlier eleventh century, had always fallen outside the system of food farms and may well have paid money farms from the beginning.

If such a change from food to money farms was taking place around the time of the Norman Conquest it was not, however, a universal change. So much is suggested by an arrangement which dates from the very end of the eleventh century.[6] It professes to be an account of the division of the abbey's revenues between the abbot and the monks and provides particulars, unfortunately, only of that part of those revenues which was

---

[1] *IIE*, ii, c. 8.   [2] *Dd*, ii, 213, 276.
[3] If the Ditton included in the manors rendering food farms in 1029–35 is Wood Ditton, it had passed into Stigand's hands; while Sandon was in the hands of Guthmund: see above, pp. 24–5.
[4] *Dd*, ii, 381 d, 382 d–3.   [5] See below, p. 42, n. 5.
[6] *HE*, ii, c. 136 collated with the version in Trin. MS. O. 2. 1, f. 112 where the rubric runs: 'Institutio Willelmi regis Anglorum *primi* et abbatis Symeonis et Rannulfi capellani.' This might date, however, from the reign of William II when the abbey was in the king's hand after Abbot Symeon's death, a circumstance which would demand special provision for the monks (see Knowles, *The Monastic Order in England*, pp. 435–6, 612–13).

assigned to the monks. But at least a part of the abbey's income was still drawn in the form of food farms. The monks were to receive two hundred pigs a year and those which fed in the grounds of the abbey; all the butter and cheese of the estate except that which was included in the farms delivered by the reeves; and over 700 quarters of wheat and 1000 quarters of malt which, we may guess, formed part of those farms. These liveries were supplemented by cash payments of £70 a year for clothing and £60 a year for the abbey kitchen. In this record, there is strong testimony to the persistence of the food farm system after the Conquest, whatever may have been happening at Barking and Drinkstone; and the farms would seem to have included butter and cheese as well, presumably, as grain. Indeed, some food farms (especially on the conventual estate) had still a long history before them. An early twelfth-century charter about Fen Ditton,[1] which owed a farm at that time both to the bishop and the cathedral priory, suggests that, while the bishop's farm was a money farm, the farm paid to the monks was still a farm in kind. At Shelford later in the century, the Scalers family was burdened with a farm of 126 quarters of grain a year to the monks;[2] and the same family submitted to a similar impost for lands they held of the monks in Melbourn down at least to the reign of Edward I,[3] perhaps even to the reign of Edward III.[4]

It is clear, of course, that these renders in kind were part only of the abbey's revenue in the eleventh century, and very possibly a declining part. Some manors from the beginning may have been farmed for a cash income, and this method of exploitation may have been extended by the later abbots. Over and above these money farms, there may have been other sources of cash income. Some of the Domesday free tenants may have paid money rents about which the great survey offers no particulars. Some old food rents were perhaps being com-

[1] Liber M, f. 145 (printed below, Appx. VII, p. 284).

[2] This farm, Stephen de Scalers asserted, was so heavy that it was ruining him; he therefore refused to pay it in King Stephen's reign, a refusal which caused that king some considerable concern: Trin. MS. O. 2. 1, ff. 145, 163–4; Bodl. Laudian Misc. 647, f. 98; Cott. Titus A 1, f. 34. The convent eventually gave up its demand in return for a grant of land in Newton: Liber M, f. 605.

[3] Chancery Inq. pm, Edw. I, File 38 (4).

[4] Liber M, f. 615.

muted into cash payments.[1] There were profits of jurisdiction which were carefully registered by the Domesday commissioners.[2] Stock-farming, finally, must sometimes have been a source of cash returns (whether as part of a money farm or as a separate item of account). Doddington in the Isle had a stock of over one hundred cattle and twenty-four mares in 1086; it must have been a breeding and dairying centre of more than manorial importance.[3] Then there were nearly 2000 pigs on the demesne manors of *Domesday Book*; and even if the monks consumed 200 a year or more[4] pigs multiply quickly and mature rapidly,[5] and some were probably sold. The sheep flocks, lastly, were almost certainly a commercial asset. In 1086 there were some 9000 of them on the demesne manors;[6] and although they may have been valued largely for their manure (as the mention of fold-soke suggests)[7] the income from the abbey's wool-clip cannot have been inconsiderable.

There is much in all this to indicate that the economy of the Ely estate must already have been involved, to a degree there is no means of calculating, in market exchanges. The fact that Abbot Leofsige imposed the food farm system upon only a proportion of the abbey's manors suggests that this had been true from the beginning. If there was some tendency, in the years the Confessor and the Conqueror spanned between them, to substitute money for food farms this margin of cash revenue

---

[1] Some of the fish rents in the fenland manors were at least expressed in terms of money payments: Dd, I, 191 d.

[2] The Suffolk hundreds were worth £11 and Mitford Hundred £3 in 1086: IE, 134; Dd, II, 385 d.

[3] IE, 116. A great many of these cattle may have been cows, for Doddington at a later time had important vaccaries and the 'animalia otiosa' of Domesday often did include cows: Round, VCH Essex, I, p. 367.

[4] Their allowance in the arrangement is discussed above, p. 40. Some two centuries later the monks received 161 pigs in the course of a year from the conventual manors: D & C Treasurer's Roll, 18–19 Edw. II.

[5] At Wisbech and Soham in the early fourteenth century 50–60% of the pig stock in any given year represented that year's increase: EDR Bailiff Rolls, D 8; Duchy of Lancaster Min. Accts, 288/4716, 4717.

[6] The figure of 13,400 in Power, *Wool Trade*, p. 33 includes the flocks of the abbey's dependants.

[7] E.g. Dd, II, 214 (Hoe). These notices are confined to Norfolk, but suit to the lord's fold was probably far more widely spread in the light of later evidence, especially amongst the villeins. On the large part played by the demand for manure in the history of the human race, see also Maitland, *Domesday Book and Beyond*, p. 76.

(and the participation in a market economy it implies) may well have been growing in importance. Yet we should not make too much of this; it involved no necessary or far-reaching change in economic attitudes. Whether manors were responsible for producing food or money, they may well have been handed over in much the same way to bailiffs or reeves or farmers burdened with fixed and certain payments to the abbey.[1] Whether these payments were in cash or kind, the underlying assumptions were the same. The needs of the monks were known and capable of precise calculation; it was merely a matter of subdividing this burden amongst manors, the productive capacities of which in crops or cash were also known. The objective was consumption rather than profit; indeed, the Old English abbots seem to have had scarcely any of the economic virtues.

It is not even clear that the farming system as such was in any way an outcome of purely economic forces, still less that it was a temporary economic expedient to offset the effects of falling prices and economic depression in the last century of Saxon England.[2] The system may only have been recently adopted by monasteries like Ely abbey, because these monasteries themselves were new; it was none the less an old and well-tried device which, at least on the royal estates, stretches back into the mists of time.[3] Further, the very prominence of food farms amongst the farms rendered to the monks is something which, by later analogy,[4] would have been a strange solution for a fall in agrarian profits. The fact, moreover, that food farms persisted after the Conquest (concealed or partially concealed though this may be in *Domesday*[5]) and often long after the Conquest; the

---

[1] See Knowles, *The Monastic Order in England*, pp. 441–3; in 1086 Henny, close to Ely itself, was held by a bailiff 'in presto', here presumably 'at farm': *IE*, 119.

[2] This would seem to be Professor Postan's suggestion, *EcHR*, XIV, pp. 131–4.

[3] For some of the evidence see Maitland, *Domesday Book and Beyond*, pp. 318–19; Stenton, *Anglo-Saxon England*, pp. 275–6, 284–6; Seebohm, *Tribal Custom in Anglo-Saxon Law*, pp. 431–2; Vinogradoff, *Growth of the Manor*, pp. 223–4.

[4] A reversion to rents in kind was one of the methods adopted by Cambridge colleges in the sixteenth century to offset a rise in agricultural prices; see Stat. 18 Eliz. c. 6 which legalized expedients which had been anticipated in the practice of my own college: Howard, *Finances of St John's College*, pp. 33–4.

[5] In view of the fact that there were still food farms on the Ely estate when its revenues were divided between abbot and monks, some of the money

fact that the farming system in general (involving renders both in cash and kind) persisted on all the church's lands down to the later years of the twelfth century[1]—these things suggest that the farming system may have been anchored more firmly in tradition than in economic calculation. It seems to have managed to continue through more than one cycle of economic expansion and decline.

In the long run, indeed, it may be better to banish from our minds those economic motives which modern learning has imposed upon the practical arrangements of the remote past; or, at least, to substitute for them calculations which are simpler and more primitive. The farming system was a device well suited to the peculiar character, to the stable and regular requirements of a monastic community. It could ensure, as the chronicler said, sufficiency throughout the year. Even if, in the earliest Norman period, some food farms were being turned into money farms, these new burdens had still much of the fixed and customary character of the old burdens. The idea of sufficiency was still there, it still conditioned the allotment of responsibilities to manors; and this attitude to a considerable extent insulated the eleventh-century great estate from economic fluctuations. Its face was turned inwards towards the church on the island in the fens, and the monks who lived there show little sign of having regarded their lands as assets which should be rationally exploited in order to produce an ever greater yield. 'Statuit etiam...firmas...que per annum ecclesie in cibum sufficerent', such was the motive the chronicler saw at work, a motive which was still powerful long after the last of the Saxon abbots. The transformation of this motive worked by rising prices and the demands of the state before Hugh of Northwold became bishop is one of the major revolutions in the history of the lands of the church of Ely.

valets of _Domesday_ must be instances of the use of money merely as a 'unit of account' (a practice for which Professor Postan argues that 'no historical proof has so far been adduced': _loc. cit._ p. 126). On this see Poole, _Exchequer in the Twelfth Century_, p. 27.

[1] See below, pp. 98–9 for the fact that almost every one of the bishop's manors was being farmed during the vacancy after the death of Bishop Nigel.

II

In 1066, however, this change was still in the future; and for the time being we must turn back to the burdens imposed by the Old English abbots upon the peasantry. This demands that attention be given to the rights which the abbots claimed to exercise over some 1200 freemen and sokemen, 1100 villeins, 950 bordars and cottars and nearly 300 *servi*. The lines which marked off these classes one from the other were probably not easy to draw. Degrees of dependence varied, while they had been distorted and perhaps not always understood in the confusion of conquest. Even the broad categories of dependence implied no essential uniformity of obligations, and still less did they stand for marked differences in economic standing. Sometimes the villein may have stood higher in the social scale than the freeman, despite the superior status of the latter in the eyes of the law.[1]

For these reasons it may be best to begin with the classes standing closest to the demesne—villeins, bordars, cottars and *servi*. So far as the last of these classes is concerned, there is little to be said. There are *servi* on 80% of the abbey's manors in 1066. They are found on every manor in Essex and Hertfordshire; after that they are most ubiquitous in Norfolk and Suffolk; they are absent only in Huntingdonshire. If this means anything more than a mere difference in the classification of the peasant population, one can only guess that their importance varied inversely with the degree of manorialization and the more adequate supply of villein labour which manorialization implied.

At the same time, it is very hard to draw fine distinctions about the degree to which, by 1066, manorial organization had been imposed upon the different parts of the estate. Only six out of eighty-six demesne manors were without villeins at that date; only two without bordars or cottars; and there was not a single manor without representatives of at least one of these classes, whether that manor lay in 'manorial' Huntingdonshire or in 'free' Suffolk. This may no more than indicate the effects upon social organization of the uniform and heavy demands which the

---

[1] Economically, at any rate, freemen and sokemen were often no better than their villein neighbours: Stenton, *The Lincolnshire Domesday*, pp. xx–xxi and *Anglo-Saxon England*, p. 509; Lennard, *Economic Journal*, LVII, p. 186.

monastery made of its estate; but at least it is clear that, despite the extreme variety of social traditions which was the raw material at its disposal in such diverse counties, the estate of St Etheldreda was a great leveller.

It is another matter to decide what were the burdens these villeins sustained. To say the least, it is likely that they performed labour services, for such services were demanded of freemen and sokemen even in Norfolk and Suffolk. One fact may give some indication of the burden. In the Isle, Cambridgeshire and Hertfordshire demesne and villeinage were assessed at roughly the same total number of hides; on the other hand, the demesne contained only about one-third of the total number of ploughs.[1] To put the matter in another way, if the division of the fiscal burden between demesne and villeinage bears any relation to the actual allotment of land between them, ploughs were relatively thicker on the ground in the villeinage than in the demesne. This might be due in part to a greater economy in the use of ploughs on a larger area of exploitation; but some part of the surplus, so to speak, of villein ploughs was probably called into being by the services which the abbey demanded of its villeins. If that is true, the comparison between ploughs actually in the manors in 1086 and the ploughs that could or ought to have been there also assumes a new significance. The deficiency of 'actual' (as compared with 'potential') ploughs on the demesne amounted to 25% in Cambridgeshire and the Isle and to 40% in Hertfordshire; the corresponding figures for the villeinage were a mere 6% and 15% respectively. The villeinage as a source of ploughs for the demesne husbandry seems to be growing more important under our very eyes.

Domesday appears to tell us little more than this about the burdens of the villein; and it is equally taciturn about his economic standing. From time to time it reveals the fiscal assessment of his holding in acres or in virgates; but such data, we know, provide no standard of comparison between holdings in different manors and no means of calculating the real acreage of tenements in a given manor. Materials taken from the survey of the estate of Ely abbey suggest also that information about villein plough-beasts, recently used as an index of peasant

[1] The demesne's share of ploughs falls as low as one-fifth in Huntingdonshire, and one-quarter in Essex.

economic standing,[1] may also be inadequate for the purpose. Perhaps the point ought to delay us a moment, for it means that we are denying ourselves the use of a means of social measurement which is attractive because it is simple.

If the number of a villein's plough-beasts is taken to be an index of the size of his holding as compared with other villeins or other peasants, use presumably should be made, not of the plough-beasts he actually had in 1086, but those which *Domesday* tells us he ought to have had. The former figure may be in a high degree artificial and transitory, reflecting such accidental circumstances as the devastation of a district in the course of the conquest. That means, in turn, the assumption that there is a more or less constant (and therefore comparable) ratio between a man's beasts and his holding, between the amount of land in a manor and the number of teams there ought to be there; in short, that 'the land for one plough', the 'team-land', is indeed a measure of area.[2] These assumptions are a somewhat abrupt solution to an ancient controversy,[3] and that despite many weighty reasons for scepticism about their acceptability. Even in a single village, the ratio between hides and team-lands varies considerably from manor to manor, or, to put it another way, the team-land does not always carry the same assessment to the geld within the village.[4] If this can be explained in terms of beneficial hidation or differences of farming practice, it is also notable that the value of the team-land varies markedly in quite a restricted area. The classic instance of the Cambridgeshire hundred of Staine is a case in point. If the hide varies in value from 30% above to 25% below a mean of 30s., the value of the team-land also varies by about 30% on either side of a mean of 20s. If the variation in the value of the hide helped to destroy the notion that it might be a measure of area,[5] then for the same

---

[1] See Lennard, *Economic Journal*, LVI, pp. 244–64.

[2] *Domesday*, of course, does not always provide information about team-lands—i.e. we do not always find the formula that here 'there is land for X ploughs'. But the same information is provided by the formula that here 'there are X ploughs and Y more could be made'; in other words, there are X plus Y team-lands, land for X plus Y ploughs.

[3] The main poles are to be found in Vinogradoff, *English Society*, pp. 158 ff. and Maitland, *Domesday Book and Beyond*, pp. 421–4.

[4] See, for instance, the six manors of Grantchester described in *ICC*, 70 (summarized by Maitland, *op. cit.* p. 418).

[5] Round, *Feudal England*, p. 45.

reason the notion of the team-land as a measure of area is also difficult to sustain, and with it the notion that plough-beasts can provide a comparative index for the economic standing of the villein.

None the less, the plough-team data from the lands of Ely abbey in *Domesday Book* may tell us something more about the total burden imposed by the lord upon the villeinage and about the factors which influenced the distribution of ploughs within the manor. Attention has already been drawn to the fact that the ratio between plough-teams and hides differed between the demesne and the villeinage within the abbey's manors.[1] In Cambridgeshire proper, there was a plough for every hide on the demesne; in the villeinage, a plough for every half hide. In the Isle of Ely, there was a plough for every 0·6 hide in the demesne and 0·3 hide in the villeinage.[2]

Of course, there may be more than one explanation for this disparity. It may be that the demesne was bearing a geld burden twice as heavy as that borne by the villeinage. But it is rather more probable that the land per team in the villeinage was in fact a different thing from the land per team in the demesne;[3] and the reason would appear to be the very simple one that the villeins on the average, over and above the tillage of their own tenements, provided about a third of the ploughing which the lord required upon his demesne. This may be a rough and ready result; but it is important in putting labour services in their place. Even in the time of *Domesday Book*, even on a monastic estate with a fairly extensive villeinage, labour services were but one of the ways by which the demesne farm

---

[1] See above, p. 45. For the reasons given in the text, the figures which follow are calculated from 'potential' in preference to 'actual' ploughs.

[2] These figures are, of course, averages. The precise ratios differ from manor to manor; but the teams per hide are everywhere almost exactly doubled in the villeinage as compared with the demesne. Incidentally, these figures suggest that the Isle was more lightly assessed than the shire proper, perhaps because much reclamation had taken place there from the fen without a corresponding increase in fiscal burdens.

[3] The same suggestion seems to be made by Mr O. C. Pell in *PCAS*, VI, pp. 22–3. So much agreement, however, does not imply a real understanding of the higher flights of Mr Pell's mathematical fancy or acceptance of his main contention that the hide is a measure of area. At most the argument advanced above assumes that within a single manor the allotment of geld between demesne and villeinage roughly corresponds to the actual distribution of land.

obtained labour. There will be the less to surprise us when we find that, in the midst of the 'manorial reaction' of the thirteenth century, wage labour and villein labour were working side by side in the fields of the bishop of Ely.

Finally, we may conclude from this that the distribution of plough-beasts within a manor, and in particular on the holdings of the villeins, was probably influenced by a number of factors. The capacity of the villein's holding to support his beasts was but one of these factors; and some part must have been played by the lord's need for labour from his villein. This in turn might vary with the size of the demesne and with the relative areas of the demesne and the villeinage; and with the success with which the lord could impose his demands against, for example, the formidable tradition of peasant freedom in much of eastern England. Although St Etheldreda's abbey was a great leveller, and the villeins on the abbey's estate bore a fairly constant share of the demesne ploughing throughout Cambridgeshire and the Isle, even there some variants are found, and the general average bears no necessary relationship to that found on other estates in the same county.[1] The distribution of plough-beasts within a manor was the result of a series of equations peculiar to that manor of that estate.

If little that is precise can be said about the villeins of Ely abbey in the eleventh century, the cottars and bordars are even more obscure. At best we know something of the fiscal assessment of their holdings. The average tenement of a bordar in Cambridgeshire, the Isle and Hertfordshire was assessed at five acres, of a cottar at one acre. But averages as usual do violence to individual instances. The bordars of Horningsea had only their messuages, those of Balsham ten fiscal acres apiece; while there were cottars at Impington each with holdings assessed at five acres.[2] What those figures mean in terms of field acres there is no means of knowing, so a precise definition of the economic position of these classes eludes us. Only a very general conclusion emerges: that already in 1066 there existed

[1] On six of the manors of Ramsey abbey in Cambridgeshire, for example, there is somewhat less than one team per hide in the demesne and something over two teams per hide in the villeinage; yet at Elsworth there are three ploughs to the villein hide: *Dd*, 1, 192 d.

[2] *ICC*, 24, 28; *IE*, 113. At Impington there were also three other cottars with messuages and gardens only, like the bordars of Horningsea.

something of that later distribution of the villein population between holders of whole or half standard tenements on the one side[1] and holders of mere cottages with scraps of land on the other. We can only guess that, arising out of this unequal division of land, there was also something like the graded obligation for labour service which was also characteristic of a later age.

III

When we turn from the villeins to the 'free' dependants of Ely abbey in 1066—the men called *homines* or *liberi homines* or *sochemanni*—the principles of classification appropriate to the former cease to have validity. The villeins can be discussed, properly enough, in connection with plough-teams and team-lands;[2] their status, their tenements, their obligations are all governed by the requirements of the demesne husbandry. They fall into sub-groups defined by the contribution they make to the lord's economy; and lines of economic division between them had probably already acquired something of that regular character associated with the 'classical' notion of the manor. But the abbey's free dependants have a very different appearance; and amongst them the regularity characteristic of the villeinage is replaced by extreme variety. They include every sort of men and women from king's thegns with possessions in many counties down to holders of a mere acre or two. The social ties between abbot and man are expressed in more than one formula; and it is at least probable that words like soke and commendation used in describing these ties do not always possess the same significance. Likewise, the *consuetudo* or the *servitium* which the dependant owes is expressed in words which are 'the widest of words', and which must have assumed different meanings for the different sorts of the abbot's men. Perhaps, too, the abbot's stake in the lands of his dependants varied from group to group, if not from man to man.

Historians may have been too anxious to over-simplify the

---

[1] A number of manors in the Isle show that not all the villeins had the same amount of land; there were, so to speak, greater and lesser villeins as at Littleport, Wilburton or Witcham: *IE*, 116, 117, 120.

[2] One of the numerous calculations made by the compiler of the *IE* (pp. 168ff.) was a digest from the Domesday materials of data about villeins, serfs and ploughs; see my remarks in *EHR*, LXII, pp. 453-4.

main tendencies in late Old English society—and, because the facts were anything but simple, to generate much controversy about commendation, about soke, about sokemen and about freemen.[1] The layman, in consequence, is faced by a jungle of current controversy, as well as by the difficulty of knowing where to begin in studying a society where confusion was so much the essence of things as it was in eastern England in the eleventh century. The choice made here to begin with the land—with the lord's rights and the man's rights in the man's land—may be governed more than it ought to be by the change the Normans made in this society by turning all social relationships into tenures. A trend towards tenurial dependence was present in the Old English great estate; although it may have been merely one trend amongst many and one that is overstressed in *Domesday Book* by Norman preconceptions about what Old English facts should have been.[2] But, used with due caution, a study of territorial relationships as they existed in 1066 can provide an introduction to the study of social relationships as those relationships are presented to us in *Domesday*.

So let us begin with the main categories of land in the estates of Ely abbey as they appeared to William the Conqueror.[3] First, there was demesne land: comprising, no doubt, not only demesne in the narrow sense, but also the villeinage appurtenant to it.[4] Secondly, there were two sorts of land held by the abbey's dependants: 'thegnlands' and 'sokelands'. It is this second category that is relevant to the present range of problems; and the broad significance of the terms used in describing it is well enough known. The holder of thegnland cannot alienate

---

[1] A starting point for any investigation of these problems is still to be found in Round, *Feudal England*, pp. 28–35; but they have again been subjected to much discussion whilst these pages were being written. Professor Stephenson initiated this new controversy in *EHR*, LIX, pp. 289–310; and he has provoked an interesting rejoinder from Miss B. Dodwell, *EHR*, LXIII, pp. 289 ff. Very full references to the available literature will be found in these articles, which have been much in my mind in constructing the argument which follows.

[2] This may be one of the difficulties about Domesday evidence for Old English conditions for which sufficient allowance has not always been made; almost inevitably it emphasizes (even where it does not invent) a territorial basis for social relationships.

[3] See his writs in *ICC*, pp. xviii–xix (nos. III and IV).

[4] Cf. Vinogradoff, *English Society*, p. 353 and *Villainage in England*, pp. 55–8.

the land; the holder of sokeland can do so. It may be a broad distinction, but it does seem to have been regarded as fundamental.[1]

Taking the thegnlands first, it may seem logical to make some attempt to find out how they came into existence. It is clear, in the first place, that some of them originated in grants from above, in a demise to a tenant of the abbey's demesne. In 1086, for instance, Picot the sheriff held 12 hides at Milton; in 1066 more than half of this land had been held by Ailbert, the abbot's steward, 'so that he could not sell or separate it from the church, and after his death it should return to the church'. This holding, no doubt, was part of the 21½ hides of the abbey's thegnlands which Picot held in Cambridgeshire.[2] A similar arrangement may underlie the tenure of a carucate of land in Suffolk which Saxo held 'pro suis solidatis'.[3] If in these cases the Old English abbots were creating something very like administrative tenures,[4] other grants from the demesne partook rather of the character of leases[5] or even of the sale of the land in question for a limited period of time.[6] In each of these cases, the Old English abbots were creating something not very different from the tenures of later times; and even their limitation to a single life, which was the commonest term on this estate, might not long have withstood pressure from the tenants to make them into hereditary tenures. It seems to have been in this way that the *feudum* became an hereditary holding on the continent before it was introduced into England after 1066.[7]

[1] In addition to Round, see also Salzman, *VCH Cambs.* i, pp. 349–50.
[2] *IE*, 114, 176; *Dd*, i, 201 d.   [3] *Dd*, ii, 418 ('Tusemera').
[4] Such tenures may have appeared very early, for the first of the abbots of Ely gave land in Haddenham to Grim the son of Wine, ever busy about the affairs of the monastery, 'so that he should have it as his payment so long as he served them well': *HE*, ii, c. 15.
[5] See the abbey's claim to Methwold in *IE*, 138: 'jacebat *TRE* ad victum monachorum et abbas eam prestavit Stigando archiepiscopo ut post mortem ejus redderetur abbacie'.
[6] *Dd*, ii, 373: 'hanc emit Beornus...ab abbate eo conventione quod post mortem suam rediret ad ecclesiam'. The abbey's agreements with Esgar Staller and Guthmund (see above, p. 24) were probably couched in similar terms: see, for instance, Guthmund's tenure in Nacton—*Dd*, ii, 406; *IE*, 143–4. For 'loans' of land for a specified period in return for a lump sum down see Holdsworth, *History of English Law*, ii, p. 70 and Maitland, *Domesday Book and Beyond*, p. 303; and for some of the considerations behind such 'loans', Vinogradoff, *English Society*, pp. 229 ff.
[7] Where land was granted only for one or more lives, there was nothing to preclude regrant to the heir of the last holder; in this way the hereditary

But thegnlands had arisen, not only out of action from above, but also out of action from below. There was, for example, a freeman of St Etheldreda at Starston in Norfolk who (according to what is probably the best account of his position) had commended himself to the abbey *so that* he could not sell his lands away from the church.[1] He had 'bowed' to the abbot and he had brought his land with him; he had become a tenant of the land, now firmly under the abbot's control. Nor did he stand alone; there is another freeman who had similarly commended himself at Rattlesden in Suffolk.[2] Another Suffolk entry, though far from clear, may mean that a man might first commend himself and then later bring his land into the bargain. Edmund the priest in King Edward's time was a freeman of St Etheldreda, he was commended to St Etheldreda; it was land that he obtained with his wife that he granted to the abbey so that he could not sell or give it away from the church.[3] Whatever the correct interpretation of this particular case, however, it seems clear at least that commendation could involve a man in becoming a tenant. The development of tenurial relationships in the Old English estate arose both from the small man's search for protection and the church's requirement for service. Tenant lands, thegnlands, were created both out of the property of the former and from the demesne of the abbey.

One final point about the Ely thegnlands. Presumably all or most of their tenants owed some sort of service; but except in the case of a few groups of sokemen in Norfolk who rendered agricultural services[4] there is seldom any information about their obligations. Yet one thing does seem clear. The holders

---

principle may have invaded the tenure of the Worcester thegnlands before 1066: Hollings, *EHR*, LXIII, pp. 479–81. For the slow development of the hereditary character of feudal holdings, see Bloch, *La Société féodale: formation des liens de dépendance*, pp. 293 ff.

[1] *IE*, 141: 'In Sterestuna unus liber homo S. Aedeldrede commendationis ita quod non poterat vendere terram suam extra ecclesiam, sed sacam et socam habebat Stigandus in Hersham'. *Dd*, II, 186 seems to conflate and confuse the two relationships mentioned here; and it seems dangerous to argue from this case alone (as Maitland seems to do) that restraints on alienation may be 'the outcome of soke': *Domesday Book and Beyond*, p. 103.

[2] *Dd*, II, 303; *IE*, 141; perhaps a similar bargain lies behind the entry for Alburgh in *Dd*, II, 246.

[3] *Dd*, II, 431 d. Miss Dodwell's comment on this passage is not very easy to follow: *EHR*, LXIII, p. 295 n.

[4] See Round, *Feudal England*, pp. 30–3.

of thegnlands were men of every sort: not only the abbey's servants, but also at one end of the scale a great king's thegn like Tochi who held Trumpington and Weston Colville of the abbot;[1] and, at the other, the two sokemen with a virgate in Babraham or the two men in Charsfield with only seven acres.[2] The kind of service rendered by such a variety of men from such a variety of holdings can hardly have been any specialized sort of service. The terms in which the obligations of thegnland were conceived must have been wide enough to comprehend whatever honourable service a king's thegn or the abbot's steward would perform and also that of a tiny sokeman, whose burdens are likely at least to have been peasant burdens and may well have been near to servile.[3]

Despite the unspecialized character of thegnland, there is, in the light of later developments of landed society, something familiar and recognizable about it. The sokelands of Ely abbey are another matter; and their unfamiliarity is perhaps good cause for much of the controversy which has arisen about them. But let us look first at a description of them, written after the Norman Conquest, before facing the difficulties in it. 'Those who held this land *de soca* in King Edward's time were able to sell [it], but sake and soke and commendation and service always remained to the church of Ely.'[4] This description is very similar to another and well-known one, of certain men at North-wold and Feltwell in Norfolk to whom *Domesday* sometimes hesitates to apply the name sokemen because they can sell their land.[5] Taking the Feltwell entry as typical of both, we read that

[1] In addition to extensive properties in four other Cambridgeshire and at least fifteen Norfolk villages: *Dd*, I, 196–6d; II, 157d–70.

[2] *Dd*, I, 191, 199; II, 373d.

[3] These facts may be of some value in considering thegnland generally, and in particular the argument that the service demanded from it was 'primarily military service': Vinogradoff, *English Society*, pp. 370–2. It is an easy way to solve the problem to suggest (as Professor Stephenson does) that the terminology of the *IE* reflects only 'the vagaries of a local scribe': *EHR*, LIX, p. 306; it seems to be assumed that it has a wider comprehensibility in the Conqueror's writs. Moreover, even the selection of entries from *Domesday* quoted by Vinogradoff includes one where the tenant is a priest (et poterat cum ea ire quo volebat'!); and for another case of a priest holding thegnland and owing service, though he could not depart, see *Dd*, IV, 135–6 ('Stratona', Somerset). In short, there may still be room for further investigation here.

[4] *IE*, 121–2, 123, 124.

[5] *Dd*, II, 162, 213d; *IE*, 132, 139. These entries are discussed by Round, *Feudal England*, pp. 30–3; but he is in error in describing all of them as men

there are forty-one sokemen pertaining to that manor; or alternatively thirty-four sokemen and seven others who are *liberi
homines* or free with their land. It seems clear from the record
of the plea of 1071–5 that all of these men owed agricultural
service, so the distinction did not lie there; but rather in this
matter of being free with their lands. The seven men who can
only with doubtful propriety be called sokemen, who are free
with their lands—these men 'can sell their lands but sake and
commendation remains to St Etheldreda'.[1] In Cambridgeshire
they would have been put under the rubric of holders *de soca*,
just as their thirty-four companions in labouring for the abbey
would have been described as holders of thegnlands.

So far there is little difficulty. The holders of sokeland can
sell their land. But what is meant by the proviso that 'soke etc.
remains to the abbey'? Does it mean soke over the person of the
man who sells, the commendation of his person, service which
was a personal obligation? Or does it mean that commendation,
soke and service were already 'inhering in the land'; and would
be taken up by the purchaser of the land as the modern house-
purchaser takes up the obligation to pay the local rates? To put
the matter another way, was the land in question land in which
the holder had a full proprietary right; or was it land over which
the abbey had a superior dominion and the holder enjoyed only
something like a possessory right? These are the points of recent
controversy.

On the Ely estate, particulars about the soke[2] which was
reserved when sokelands were alienated are the most revealing.
Take the land which Fridebert had held in Harston: he could
depart, he could sell it, he could depart with the land, 'sed
semper remansit socha *eius* in ecclesia S. Aedeldrede'.[3] If this

who could not depart. *Domesday* can be compared with the detail of the
services owed by these men in the plea of 1071–5: *ICC*, 194 and see Maitland's
comment in *Domesday Book and Beyond*, p. 77.

[1] *IE*, 132.

[2] This word has been retained throughout this section in view of the
doubts (discussed above, pp. 26 ff.) about its precise significance; fortunately
it is not altogether material here whether it implied a right of jurisdiction or
merely a right to appropriate judicial profits.

[3] *IE*, 106 and see the parallel entries in *ICC*, 46 and *Dd*, 1, 200. The
former reads: 'potuit recedere quo voluit sed soca remanebat Harlestone';
suggesting, not only that the abbot retained the soke, but that these rights
remained attached to the manor of Harston.

entry means what it says, even if Fridebert sold his land the abbot still had the soke over him, over his person. Nor does this instance stand alone: it is the same with twelve sokemen in Whaddon,[1] ten sokemen in Meldreth,[2] eight sokemen in Melbourn,[3] six sokemen in Snailwell,[4] and two others in Kingston and Hardwick.[5] In most of these instances some of the parallel texts merely say that 'soca remansit ecclesie' or something of the sort; so that where this latter formula stands alone, it may mean that the abbot retains the soke over the man who sells the land rather than over the land he has sold. If this is true of the soke, moreover, presumably it is also true of the commendation and the service which are bracketed with the soke: it was the man's commendation, the man's service which remained to the abbey even if the man sold his land and departed. In instances of this sort, we do seem to be concerned with men whose lands were their own; whose dependence was a purely personal dependence. Soke and commendation in these cases were not yet relationships which had become attached to the land.

At the same time, late old English society was not a static society, and it was impatient of the permanence of a half-dependence. Even in instances where men had the right to dispose of their land, soke had sometimes become attached to the land itself; it would therefore become an obligation that would be assumed by the purchaser.[6] In addition, the proprietary rights of men in sokeland, their freedom to sell or withdraw, were also being curtailed in some instances. This was so at Shelford, where six or seven sokemen held a hide and a half and six acres; it was land 'de socha abbatis', but in 1066 only three virgates could be sold without the abbot's licence.[7] Similarly in Meldreth

[1] IE, 108; ICC, 63—'socha eorum remansit in ecclesia.'
[2] ICC, 65; Dd, 1, 199d—'soca omnium remanebat ecclesie.'
[3] IE, 109 ('soca eorum remansit'); Dd, 1, 200 ('soca de viij⁰. sochemannis remansit abbati').
[4] ICC, 3—'socham eorum habuit archiepiscopus'.
[5] IE, 110; ICC, 87.
[6] This seems to have been demonstrated in a number of instances by Miss Dodwell; see particularly her discussion of the records concerning Feltwell and Sudbourne in the plea of 1071–5: EHR, LXIII, pp. 298–9; ICC, 193–4.
[7] IE, 107; the parallel passages in Dd, 1, 191, 198 and ICC, 48 have compressed this passage (or even omitted part of it) so that they hardly make sense as they stand.

out of ten sokemen holding there 'de soca S. Etheldride', one or two could no longer give or sell their land in 1066.[1]

Perhaps we may say that, in such cases, sokeland was being turned into thegnland; or, at least, that the abbot was acquiring a right in the land not dissimilar to that which a lord would have in his socage at a later time. In 1066 every one of the sokemen in the Isle of Ely was unable to sell or depart without the abbot's licence; but that did not necessarily mean that they were tied to the soil as the villeins were or that the abbot would set his face against all alienation. The position may have been not unlike that which is described in the charters of a later date: in Bishop Nigel's charter, for instance, confirming to the monks of Ely lands in Stretham which Wigar the priest had given them 'sicut liberam terram suam quam dare et vendere potuit'; or in Bishop Eustace's charter confirming a similar grant from his socage land in Witcham which a certain Osbert had held 'et quam de assensu nostro dare potuit eisdem monachis'. In both cases the monks were to hold freely, saving that they were to take over and perform that service which Wigar and Osbert had owed to the bishop's hundreds.[2] Here, the service due to the bishop's hundreds 'inheres in the land'. In the same way, when sokeland lost that quality of free disposition which had been its predominant characteristic before 1066, obligations which had been personal obligations probably tended to become territorial obligations. The service due to the hundred in the twelfth century may have some similarity to the soke of *Domesday*; and commendation may easily have shaded off into homage for land once the abbots had asserted a superior dominion over the land. Once attached to land, these rights must have gained in stability by comparison with those personal rights which the abbots had enjoyed over most of the holders of sokelands in the estates of the Old English abbey.

The thegnlands of Ely abbey, the tendency to convert the obligations of the holders of sokelands into territorial obligations—both suggest that tenurial relations were making progress at the end of the Old English period. At the same time, such relationships were hardly typical as yet. In Cambridgeshire less than three-fifths of the abbey's dependants were involved;

[1] *Dd*, I, 200; *ICC*, 65; *IE*, 108.
[2] Liber M, ff. 158, 163 (2), and see below, Appx. IX, p. 285 and XII, p. 287.

in Norfolk and Suffolk, though it is impossible to arrive at an accurate figure, the proportion was a good deal less.[1] Thegnland, in the sense it had on the Ely estate, looks rather like a new category of landholding introduced into a society which previously had known only the dichotomy between *dominium* and *soca*, between the lord's land and the land of the man. Landlordship and tenant land, so far as freemen were concerned, were growing (but still sporadic) features of this society. Lordship, on the other hand, was everywhere; and it is time to turn once more to the soke and the commendation which were the symptoms of that lordship.

To deal first with soke, it must be clear that there was more than one sort of soke and that it may not always have meant the same thing. In some cases the man may have been the justiciable of a court held by the abbot; in others it is probable at least that the abbot's right was a fiscal rather than a judicial right—a right to *wites* and forfeitures. Sometimes men may have been subject to the abbot's soke (though they were men of other lords) because they lived in a hundred of the abbey's or even in one of its manors.[2] At other times, the abbot had the soke over a man simply because that man was the abbot's man: it was an outcome of personal dependence. This was commonly true, as we have seen, in the sokelands of Cambridgeshire. It may also have been true of one Anant, who held at Fincham in the Norfolk hundred of Clackclose. He was commended to Ely abbey and the abbot had the soke over him; but the soke over his men belonged to Ramsey abbey[3]—doubtless in virtue of the Confessor's grant that Ramsey should have the soke of all moot-worthy men in Clackclose hundred.[4] Ely's soke here can have extended little beyond Anant's person.

Domesday Book itself, however, can distinguish between these different sorts of soke and introduce us to yet another. In the account of Earsham half hundred in Norfolk we read that Archbishop Stigand had the soke of the half hundred: but St Edmund's had the soke in Thorpe Abbots and Ely in

---

[1] A rough calculation for Norfolk suggests a figure of between one-quarter and one-third.

[2] E.g. *Dd*, I, 195, 202, 202d; II, 266.

[3] *IE*, 139.

[4] *Cart. Rames.* I, pp. 218ff. and compare Ault, *Private Jurisdiction*, p. 97 and *Dd*, II, 215d.

Pulham; Earl Ralf had the soke of Redenhall and of his own commended men; and Reimund Girald the soke of his own land.[1] Here Stigand has the hundredal soke of the sort Ely abbey had in the Isle and elsewhere; and there is also mention of the personal soke that Earl Ralf had over his commended men and Ely abbey in its sokelands. But there is, in addition, reference to a territorial soke—the sort of soke which Ely had in its demesne manor of Pulham and Reimund Girald in his land. We may assume that such territorial soke was co-extensive with the demesnes of Ely abbey. It must also have covered most of the thegnlands of the abbey, since those thegnlands had either once been part of the abbey demesne or were lands which had been transferred to the abbey. At least in some cases it had been extended to sokelands, even where their holders were still free to sell and depart.

These, moreover, are precisely the conclusions that the privileges of Ely abbey would suggest that we should reach. King Edgar had granted the monks soke over their hundreds and over all their lands and all the lands they might acquire in the future; Edward the Confessor had confirmed to them the forfeitures of all their men wherever those men might be. So in the demesne and in the thegnlands and in sokelands becoming thegnlands soke was already rooted in the soil in 1066; and the tendency for soke to become a territorial burden, even where a properly tenurial relationship hardly yet existed, may well have been one of the forces which were giving to the abbey a stake in the land of its dependants. But this territorial soke was supplemented by a far-reaching soke over persons, defined apparently by the commendation relationship.[2] This force of the commendation tie comes out very clearly in entries like the description of Eudo *dapifer's* lands in Brettenham. Seven freemen held there, and the soke of six of them lay in the king's manor of Old Buckenham; but the seventh was commended to

---

[1] *Dd*, ii, 139d.

[2] At the very least we can say that commendation and soke very commonly go together; and that it is a gross understatement to suggest that a commended man 'might occasionally' be drawn into jurisdictional dependence (Vinogradoff, *English Society*, p. 127), at least where a man's lord had the right to enjoy the soke of his dependants. In Suffolk we can be sure where the soke lay in respect of over 330 commended men of the abbot of Ely: the abbot had the soke of all but twenty-four of them.

Ely abbey and the abbey had his soke.[1] So closely, indeed, did soke follow commendation that sometimes (though not always) where commendation was divided, so also was the soke and in the same proportion.[2] When a landowner was as privileged as the abbey of Ely was, the act of commending oneself to the abbey had extensive implications. It is perhaps time to consider this commendation tie a little more closely.

It is, of course, the commendation relationship which has aroused the most intense controversy in recent times. Not a little of this controversy may have been due, in the last resort, to an inclination to invest the relationship with too precise a character: to make it something to which all else might be added but which was, in itself, a slight and insubstantial bond between lord and man.[3] If this view merely implies that commendation *could*, under certain circumstances, establish ties which were both slight and fragile, there is nothing to quarrel about. Looked at from the point of view of western Europe generally, the act of commendation was an act of personal subordination.[4] It had no essential connection with the establishment of tenurial relationships, and still less of servile tenurial relationships which commonly had other and different roots.[5] Sometimes it might limit a man's freedom, even his personal freedom, to the slightest extent; and leave him free to revoke the contract he had made with one lord and seek another in his place.[6] But it is another matter to say that this slightness and this fragility were of the nature of the commendation relationship. What counted in practice in determining the character of any given contract was likely to be the 'might' on one side and the 'unmight' on the other. It was this which would fix the price which a lord would be in a position to demand for his protection and which a man would be willing to

---

[1] *Dd*, ii, 239d.

[2] E.g. Lustwine at Barham, over whom Wisgar and Ely had each half the soke and commendation; or Turchill at Pettaugh: *Dd*, ii, 352, 384.

[3] This would appear to be Maitland's presupposition: *Domesday Book and Beyond*, pp. 67ff.; and see also Douglas, *East Anglia*, pp. 124–6 and Dodwell, *EHR*, LXIII, p. 305.

[4] Stephenson, *EHR*, LIX, p. 290.

[5] Bloch, *La société féodale: formation des liens de dépendance*, pp. 233ff.; Ganshof, *Qu'est-ce que la féodalité?*, pp. 7ff.

[6] Dopsch, *Economic and Social Foundations of European Civilisation*, pp. 218, 287.

pay to obtain it. In consequence, each commendation contract would tend to be subject only to its own conditions; but the fact that the parties were generally unequal parties made commendation a powerful force in widening the effective range of lordship and in extending it from the persons of men to bind also their land.[1]

In the light of these general considerations, we would naturally expect the working of the commendation tie to produce a wide variety of dependence. But before trying to analyse this variety, let us look first at one side issue which has helped to confuse the problem. Maitland made much of certain entries in *Domesday* which refer to 'mere commendation', the commendation 'which seems put before us as the slightest bond that there can be between lord and man'.[2] 'Unus liber homo commendatione tantum' or something like it is the phrase in question; though it might also appear in other guises. We find sometimes that 'over these men such a lord has nothing except commendation ('in his non habuit nisi commendationem')'.[3] The phrase 'mere commendation' used to translate these entries is an evocative phrase; it carries with it an implication of the slightness of the commendation tie. But is that the implication which *Domesday Book* is trying to convey?

Let us take a random sample from the Ely estate in Suffolk in a search for bearings. If the villages in that county in which Ely abbey had lands or men are arranged alphabetically, the first two dozen or so provide details about some 160 dependants of the abbey. Of these, the abbot had the soke and commendation of 133; about 24 of the rest we hear only that he had their commendation. But in one or two of these instances, *Domesday* is more communicative. A freeman is only commended to the abbot, but the king and earl have the soke;[4] or Wihtgar, a freeman of the abbot's by commendation only, has two carucates of land in the soke of the king and earl.[5] Outside this arbitrary group of villages, there are similar entries elsewhere;[6] and

---

[1] Bloch, *Cambridge Economic History*, i, pp. 252–60.
[2] *Domesday Book and Beyond*, pp. 68–9.
[3] See Dodwell, *EHR*, LXIII, p. 300.
[4] *Dd*, ii, 383d ('Hassa'): 'unus liber homo commendatione tantum dimidiam acram.... Rex et comes socam.'
[5] *Dd*, ii, 411 (Creeting).
[6] *Dd*, ii, 382 (Livermere), 383 ('Uledana').

generally in Norfolk and Suffolk, where we hear only of the abbot's commendation without further qualification, the soke is often specifically stated to lie somewhere else.[1] On this estate at least, then, such expressions as 'commendatione tantum' are exclusive rather than descriptive; they imply only that the abbot did not have the soke of such a man, as he commonly did over his commended men.[2] But they tell us nothing about commendation, about its slightness or its character.

In fact it would seem that, if commendation might mean very little, it could also mean almost everything. There were, no doubt, men about in 1066 who could both sell their land and 'withdraw to another lord',[3] though clear instances on the Ely estate are hard to find. On the other hand, a man who commended himself to the abbot of Ely (even without committing his land) very commonly came under the abbot's soke. Moreover, the fact that very often 'his soke remained' even if he sold his land and departed suggests that the commendation relationship might be indestructible,[4] even if it was not exclusive.[5] And the man might go further. He might commend himself *so that* he could not sell his land, as we have already seen.[6] Here, presumably, if son were to succeed father, the former would likewise

---

[1] In Suffolk in 1066 St Edmund's abbey had the soke over Ely's commended men in Drinkstone (*Dd*, II, 291); the king and earl at Blakenham (351 d) and Coddenham (375) and Ash Bocking (383); the bishop had the soke in Hoxne at Wingfield (385); the king at Buxhall (398) and St Edmund's at Elvedon (398). For similar instances in Norfolk, see Starston (186 d) where Stigand had the soke in Earsham; or Banham (213 d): '3 liberi homines...de quibus non habuit nisi commendationem. Soca in Keninchala regis'. For similar formulae where Ely abbey had the soke and the commendation lay elsewhere, see the 'invasions' of Hermer de Ferrières in the Ely hundred of Mitford (274 d–5).

[2] Similarly, we can find cases of 'mere soke' which are explicable in the same sort of way, as in the case of a freeman in Bridgeham 'unde abbas habet sacam et socam tantum' (*IE*, 140). Probably this man lived in the abbot's demesne manor of Bridgeham, over which the abbot had soke; but he was attached by commendation to the manor of John nephew of Waleran in Brettenham (see *Dd*, II, 266).

[3] Dodwell, *EHR*, LXIII, pp. 304–5.

[4] As Stephenson argues, *EHR*, LIX, p. 290.

[5] Commendation to more than one lord was particularly common in Suffolk; for men half under Ely and half under Edric of Laxfield or Wisgar or Haldein or Gyrth, see *Dd*, II, 296 d–7, 318, 352, 386 d–8, 403, 412, 415. The Confessor himself had approved of Aelfric Modercope commending himself both to the abbot of Ely and the abbot of Bury: *KCD*, no. 877.

[6] See above, p. 52.

have to become the abbot's man; and so the little man had gone far towards giving away the freedom of his posterity. Finally, as at Feltwell in Norfolk, men who could sell their land and men who could not do so performed the same services—and those agricultural services—to the abbey of Ely. Commendation, it would seem, could bring a man near enough to servility even without making him a tenant.

This may be enough to indicate, not only the variety of the dependence which commendation could involve, but also something of its force in consolidating the lordship of St Etheldreda's abbey. Commendation was the all but universal bond between the abbey and its free dependants.[1] It was hardly 'a second and lesser degree of dependence' than soke;[2] on the contrary, it was one of the things that determined where a man's soke would lie. It was a means, not only of recruiting dependants subject to service, but also of recruiting tenants. Commendation contracts with small men and greater men were a fruitful method of extending and consolidating the abbot's lordship even after the age of purchase and pious gift, which had created the demesnes of Ely abbey, was over and done with.

And even after 1066, the force of the commendation tie was not quite spent; it had still some part to play in defining the boundaries of the feudal estate of Ely abbey. Such was the case at Banham, in Norfolk. There had been three freemen there of whom the abbot had had only the commendation (their soke lay in the king's manor of Kenninghall); they had been appropriated, first by Ratfrid and later by William de Scohies, but afterwards the abbot seized them 'propter commendationem suam'.[3] In other and similar cases the abbot recovered seisin of his commended men by means less suggestive of self-help—in the course of one or the other of the great Ely land pleas of the Conqueror's reign, no doubt, and backed often by the king's express command.[4] The abbot was unwilling to give up his

[1] Even where not expressly mentioned in *Domesday*, the existence of a commendation contract is sometimes revealed in the parallel texts. Compare, for instance, *Dd*, II, 346, 385 and *IE*, 149, 159 (Culpho, Grundisburgh, Kembrook and Tuddenham) where the two texts seem to supplement each other to some degree; and *IE*, 121-4 shows that the holders of the Cambridgeshire sokelands were the commended men of the abbot despite the silence of *Domesday*.

[2] Vinogradoff, *English Society*, p. 423.

[3] *Dd*, II, 213 d; *IE*, 133.   [4] E.g. *Dd*, II, 383, 383 d, 385, 385 d.

claim even to half a freeman;[1] and in one instance where the abbot had been only one of two lords to whom a man had been commended, the problem was solved by making the man into a tenant of the abbot for half the holding and of the Norman successor of his other lord for the other half.[2] If commendation had been making men into tenants before 1066, that process was abruptly completed by Norman land settlement. The Normans obliterated the old distinction between thegnland and sokeland; they made all men into tenants and followed very commonly the criterion of their pre-conquestual commendation in discovering who their post-conquest landlord should be.

A final point remains. Is it possible to discover, in the light of what has been said, any consistent distinction between those men described as sokemen and those called freemen in the estate of Ely abbey? It is almost certainly not possible to do so, if we are seeking a definition applicable to all the counties in which the abbey had land. In Norfolk, for example, a sokeman does not seem to be distinguished by the fact that he owed 'consuetudines' in the form of agricultural services; freemen had similar burdens.[3] On the other hand, it does seem to be commonly assumed that a sokeman should perform such services; and, more important, that he should not be able to alienate his land—that if he could do so, he was no sokeman but a freeman.[4] In Suffolk, likewise, the sokemen were closely attached to the demesne manors, no doubt because of the services they performed there;[5] and again they were commonly stated to be

---

[1] E.g. Dd, II, 424 (Hemley).

[2] Dd, II, 443: 'In Horapola tenet Odo unum liberum hominem commendationis S. Aedeldrede et dimidium Edrici 16. acras et valet 3 solidos.' IE, 146: 'In Horapola unus liber homo Wenelincg dimidia commendatione abbatis de 8. acris.'

[3] See above, pp. 53–4.

[4] See especially Dd, II, 159d, 162, 178d (Marham, Feltwell, Mundford, Northwold and Banham). The agricultural services owed by the sokemen no doubt explain their grouping about demesne manors: see Dd, II, 215 for the groups about Pulham and Bergh Apton.

[5] As in Norfolk, sokemen have no monopoly of the liability to perform agricultural services. In 1071–5 there were some 264 men burdened with consuetudines to the abbey in the county, as compared with thirty-five sokemen recorded in Domesday. No doubt some sokemen have been displaced and lost; but most of these men must have been of the sort described at Bromeswell (Dd, II, 387d): 'In eadem villa tenet Herveus 70 liberos homines unde abbas habuit commendationem, socam et sacam, et omnes consuetudines.' This may mean much the same thing as those entries for the

unable to sell their land. In the Isle of Ely, finally, the sokemen were surveyed, so to speak, 'within the manor', and they could not sell or depart. In all of these districts, with very few exceptions, the sokemen were peasants—men with smallish holdings, no bigger (and often less) than the holdings of the villeins.

In each of these areas, then, the sokemen look like small free peasants who have been turned into tenants tied to the soil and who have been absorbed into the abbey's manor to which they owe their service, commonly agricultural service. In Cambridgeshire, on the other hand, there is not even this much approximation to uniformity. A number of the sokemen had holdings there which can only be described as manors;[1] while others were clearly peasants with holdings no bigger than those of their peers in the Isle and elsewhere. While two-fifths of them could not alienate their lands, the other three-fifths could do so. There are references to service, but what this service was is nowhere described; and it is hard to imagine that it could have meant the same thing for holders of manors and for holders of mere peasant tenements. So, the Cambridgeshire sokeman remains a mystery; and it has to be admitted that even elsewhere no dividing line is absolute. Even freedom to sell or depart was not quite necessary for a freeman[2]—perhaps because, when a man has bartered away this right in the commendation contract, he did not lose his old status (or not at once) in the common estimation. At best then, so far as the East Anglian manors of Ely abbey are concerned, we can only conclude that, while a sokeman could very often not sell or depart, a free man was very often able to do so.

It would, perhaps, be too much to expect any more definite conclusion than that about this or any other of those problems which have been discussed here. If the major impression which remains is that the Old English abbey was extending and consolidating its lordship, it is also clear that this objective was being pursued along no single path. It was acquiring an ever-

St Edmund's estate like the following: 'Berardus tenet de abbate 7. liberos homines....Hi potuerunt dare et vendere terram, sed saca et soca et commendatio et servitium semper remanebat sancto' (*Dd*, II, 358).

[1] E.g. Aelfric at Quy, Fridebert at Harston, and other sokemen at Arrington, Lolworth and Impington: *Dd*, I, 191, 193 d, 200, 201.

[2] E.g. *Dd*, II, 303: 'In Ratesdana tenuit unus liber homo sancte Aldrede commendatione et soca...quod non poterat vendere 60. acras terre'.

widening circle of commended men, whose personal subordination might also involve service and jurisdictional dependence. It was acquiring a widening circle of tenants, either through the man surrendering his land at the time when he entered into a commendation contract or by the demise of the abbey's demesne to procure service. Even those rights of soke which Old English kings had conferred upon the abbey—over its men and its lands and its hundreds—might be a factor in estate-building once they became definitely rooted in the soil. Such were, so to speak, the modes of operation of the new and pushing lordship of Ely abbey, still only a century old when *Domesday Book* was made. They were working upon stubborn material, upon even older regional custom and traditions of personal standing which were not easily transformed. The interaction of these many forces over an eventful century can have done nothing to simplify the structure of society.

IV

Ultimately, some measure of simplification was achieved not by evolution but by revolution, by the land settlement of the Norman Conquest. No doubt much that was archaic, much that was anomalous, remained; but systematic and all-embracing change was equally notable. Like other monastic houses Ely abbey was quickly absorbed into the Norman pattern of strong aristocratic leadership in society; Norman ecclesiastics were the instrument. Abbot Thurstan had no English successor. He was followed by Theodwin of Jumièges, first of a line of Norman abbots who applied the discipline necessary to fuse the Old English monastery into the fabric of the feudal state. Some of them were well fitted to do so by birth as well as nationality. Abbot Symeon was brother of the notable Bishop Walchelin of Winchester and in some degree related to the Conqueror himself;[1] Richard, last of the abbots before Ely became a bishopric, was son of Richard fitzGilbert (ancestor of the house of Clare) and of a daughter of Walter Giffard.[2] Such men were well fitted for the task which William I and Lanfranc entrusted to them.

[1] Wharton, *Anglia Sacra*, I, p. 255.
[2] Round, *Feudal England*, pp. 469, 472.

3

In one respect, however, the history of Ely abbey in the immediate post-conquest days is not quite typical. The implication of the monks in Hereward's revolt; the long vacancies of 1075–81 and 1093–1100; even the pre-conquest misrule of abbot Wulfric—all combined to make Ely the 'special prey of the Norman spoiler'.[1] The monotonous reiteration of the losses suffered by the abbey in *Domesday* is some measure of the catastrophe which befell it after 1066, and this in turn helped to speed up and intensify the transformation wrought by the conquest. If only for that reason the 'invasions' suffered by the Ely estate call for some comment.

These 'invasions' sometimes led to a permanent diminution of the lands and men that had been under the abbey's lordship. Some of these losses were probably due to confiscation during the course of Hereward's revolt.[2] In other cases, land held of the abbey by Saxon notables was apt to pass after the conquest to their Norman successors, and was never very easy to recover.[3] But above all the confusion of pre-conquest dependent relationships tended to give rise after 1066 to a multiplicity of claims to the land of a great many of the abbots' men; and the abbots did not always manage to assert their rights 'propter commendationem'. What, in the long run, decided the fate of many such holdings was the pertinacity of the abbots in asserting their claims, the efficiency of eleventh-century legal process in adjudicating upon them, and the power of Norman kings to enforce upon some of their greatest subjects the verdicts of English juries and the detail of general precepts. Many questions were still undecided in Henry I's time,[4] perhaps in Henry II's;[5]

[1] Round, *VCH Essex*, I, pp. 340–1.   [2] *HE*, II, c. 107.
[3] So Stigand's manors in Snailwell and Wood Ditton passed to the king and later to the baronies of Percy and Camois (*FFC*, pp. 42–5, 150–2); Esgar Staller's misgotten property in High Easter became the *caput* of the Mandeville honour (Round, *VCH Essex*, I, p. 341); Tochi's manors in Trumpington and Weston Colville passed, the one to the honour of Skipton by gift of Henry I (*FFC*, pp. 219–20), and the other to the honour of Warenne (*Cal. Inq. pm.* II, 136, 420; *FA*, I, pp. 141–2).
[4] See his charter commanding restoration of lands 'quas carta mea Wintonie...testatur fuisse iuratas tempore patris mei ad feodum ecclesie de Ely': D & C Charter no. 6 (Bentham, Appx. XIX).
[5] It was not until the last decade of his reign that settlement was finally reached about the military service owed by the earl of Norfolk to the bishop, some of which was assessed on lands usurped soon after the Conquest: Liber M, f. 89 (see below, Appx. III, p. 281).

and in 1086 the abbey's losses were still far more striking than property regained. It retained only about a quarter of the dependants who had been subject to its lordship on the day that King Edward was alive and dead.

Moreover, even where lands and lordship were recovered, this commonly did not mean a restoration of the pre-conquestual state of things. So far at least as sokelands and thegnlands were concerned, it seems to have been both the Conqueror's will[1] and the compromise eventually reached that restoration should take the form of an enfeoffment of the intruding occupier in the land he had usurped.[2] Such a solution had much to recommend it. Particularly where the pre-conquest tenant or man had been a landholder of substance, it permitted both a recognition of the abbey's lordship and the grant of complete Saxon estates to a single Norman successor.[3] It involved as little change as possible in claims already established in the first days of the conquest. And, by joining with recognition of the abbey's lordship obligations for military service, it enabled the abbots to shoulder a new burden—the burden of their *servitium debitum*. The 'invasions' which followed the Conquest did much to establish the boundaries of the medieval barony of Ely.

The chronology of these arrangements is well enough known.[4] The abbey's obligation to provide forty knights for the king's army is first heard of in connection with the Scottish campaign

[1] See his writs in *ICC*, pp. xviiff. (nos. III, IV and X). This policy was still being pursued by Henry I, as when he commanded holders of lands sworn to Ely abbey in *Domesday* to recognize the bishop's lordship 'et teneant de predicta ecclesia et episcopo de Ely...faciendo inde ecclesie servicium milicie secundum tenuras et secundum hoc quod servicia statuta sunt in eisdem terris': D & C Charter no 6; *Cartae Antiquae Rolls 1–10*, no. 51; Bentham, Appx. XIX and compare Appx. XVI (from Liber M. f. 76).

[2] See *IE*, 124 ('De hac servit Hardwinus abbati iussu regis....Et inde Wido servit abbati iussu regis'); 113 ('Modo Picotus tenet eam sub abbate de Ely'); 135 ('Hos tenuit R. Bigod de rege sed abbas diratiocinavit eos coram episcopo Constantiensi. Modo tenet eos predictus R. Bigod de abbate'); *Dd*, I, 200 ('De hac hida et dimidia servit Picot abbati et tenet eam iussu regis'). These entries should be read in the light of the Conqueror's writs referred to in note 1 above. It is not a question of the king ordering the enfeoffment of mesne tenants (as suggested by Douglas, *EcHR*, IX, p. 131). Picot and Guy were ordered to serve, not the abbot to enfeoff them.

[3] It was a matter of 'administrative convenience' to give to one man 'all the scattered lands of one English thegn': Stenton, *English Feudalism*, pp. 63–5.

[4] See Chew, *Ecclesiastical Tenants in Chief*, pp. 2–3, 114–15 and Round, *Feudal England*, pp. 299–302.

of 1072. At first these knights were quartered in and about the monastery; but so troublesome did this arrangement prove that many of the great men who had intruded upon the abbey's property were allowed to hold their usurped estates *in feudum* in return for military service.[1] The circle of military tenants was, no doubt, slowly increased by recovery effected as a result of the land-pleas of the Conqueror's reign and of the Domesday inquest.[2] As a consequence, some of the later fees of the barony of Ely, as recorded in returns of the early thirteenth century,[3] can be traced back through Bishop Nigel's *carta*[4] to *Domesday Book* itself and the agreements which preceded or succeeded that great inquest.

A few examples will illustrate the fruits of this policy. Already in 1086 Picot the sheriff of Cambridgeshire held of the abbot lands which later made up four or five of the knight's fees held of the barony of Ely by the Pecche family, barons of Bourn, to whom much of Picot's property came.[5] In other places, too, Picot served the abbot at the king's command—for the manor of Quy, for instance, which was to remain in his family and answer for the service of one knight.[6] Other fees were probably also created as early or nearly as early as these—one in Impington and three in Milton which Picot held; three held by Hardwin and three by Guy de Rembercurt;[7] and one in Landbeach which two carpenters had. It may not have been long after 1072 that Cambridgeshire, from these holdings alone, was providing seventeen knights towards a quota of forty assessed on the barony as a whole. In the same way, in Norfolk and Suffolk, the 'invasions' of Ralf de Savigny, Godric *dapifer*, Ralf de Belfou, Frodo and Hervey de Bourges, in later times at least,

---

[1] *HE*, ii, c. 134: 'Ex hoc enim abbas compulsus non ex industria aut favore divitum vel propinquorum affectu quasdam terras sancte Edeldrede invasoribus in feudum permisit tenere', etc.; and see also Douglas, *Feudal Documents*, p. lxiv.

[2] On these land pleas see my notes in *EHR*, lxii.

[3] The returns of *c.* 1210–12 in *RBE*, ii, pp. 524–7 collated with Coucher Book, ff. 228d–9d; Cott. Tiberius B ii, ff. 247d, 251; Cott. Claudius C xi, ff. 19d–20d; and Caius 485/489, ff. 15d–16d.

[4] *RBE*, i, pp. 363–6.

[5] *Dd*, i, 191, 200; *IE*, 112–13 (Rampton, Lolworth, Madingley and Harston).

[6] *Dd*, i, 190d, 200.

[7] For the recognition of the abbey's lordship by Hardwin de Scalers and Guy de Rembercurt, see *IE*, 124.

would provide another ten or so; those of Eudo *dapifer*, Rainald *balistarius*, and Hugh de Berners in Essex half a dozen. The assertion of the abbot's right to this service took time, no doubt; sometimes a considerable time if the mandates of Henry I are any guide in the matter.[1] Once asserted, however, the abbot was not far from securing the quota of service demanded from his barony. The end result, moreover, was not very different from that achieved by normal processes of subinfeudation elsewhere. The medieval bishops of Ely were very normal ecclesiastical tenants-in-chief.

There is no need in these days to stress the significance of this new element introduced into the framework of Old English society.[2] It was not only that strict tenurial superiority replaced earlier and more varied forms of lordship, and that the obligations of the knightly tenant were more narrowly and more rigidly defined than ever those of the Anglo-Saxon thegn had been.[3] It was equally important that the point of departure for these changes was not the convenience of estate administration or the mere progress of private lordship, but a wholesale revision of political responsibility imposed by the Crown. So it was in 1086 that Picot and Hardwin, Guy de Rembercurt and Roger Bigot stood between the abbey and the lands which twenty years before had been demesne lands, lands held by thegns, lands held by the abbey's servants, lands held by peasants. In turn, it was Picot and Hardwin and the rest who, in the first instance and from these very heterogeneous elements, created knight's fees; though of course, in later years, abbots and bishops carried this process a good deal further.

The creation of fees by these mesne tenants had already made considerable progress by 1086. Picot, for example, had already enfeoffed Roger in Lolworth, Long Stanton, Cottenham and Rampton; his son-in-law, Ralf de St Germains, in Milton; and Walter in Impington.[4] Hardwin, too, had enfeoffed Ralf in

---

[1] See above, p. 67, n. 1.

[2] See especially Douglas, *Feudal Documents*, pp. lxxxii ff. and Stenton, *English Feudalism*, ch. IV.

[3] Cf. Mitteis, *Lehnrecht und Staatsgewalt*, pp. 356 ff. and Darlington, *History*, XXII, pp. 1–13.

[4] *Dd*, I, 200–1 d; and for extensive subinfeudation on Picot's estate in general *c*. 1092 see (if it be genuine) his foundation charter to Barnwell Priory: *Ecclesie de Bernewelle Liber Memorandorum*, 40.

Over,[1] and Eudo *dapifer* Turgis in the Rodings and Richard in Rettendon.[2] This meant, of course, that in the barony of Ely there were commonly three rungs in the feudal ladder from the very beginning; but for the moment there are other consequences of subinfeudation of more immediate importance.

These consequences are obvious enough in general terms. In the first place, compared with the years before 1066, the area of demesne directly exploited was reduced; and this may have stimulated rationalization and increased economic pressure upon the manors which remained. Secondly, the general imposition of a military burden upon the aristocracy contributed to a revision of social relationships at all levels, to a regrouping of land and men into units with a prime responsibility for maintaining the members of the feudal army. Though they are interrelated, these two developments demand separate discussion.

There are no readily available data to document an account of reorganization and rationalization in the demesne economy. Moreover, the Domesday survey of the abbey's manors clearly reflects a number of temporary factors: the income from some of them had fallen, perhaps because of devastation occasioned by military operations,[3] perhaps sometimes in consequence of a policy of *Raubwirtschaft* pursued by their new Norman tenants.[4] Still, despite distortion by such imponderable influences, one general trend does seem to be implicit in Domesday statistics. The value of the demesne manors in Cambridgeshire and Hertfordshire in 1086, for example, was 12% lower than in King Edward's day; but it had risen 18% above the low levels prevailing in the years immediately after 1066.[5] Elsewhere, values seem to have risen (often very considerably) above preconquest figures.[6] Thus, despite the devastation of some of its

---

[1] *Dd*, I, 199. [2] *Dd*, II, 49, 51.

[3] For the effects of military operations in south-west Cambridgeshire see Fowler, *Archaeologia*, LXII, pp. 41–50 and Darby, *PCAS*, XXXVI, p. 44. The value of nineteen of the abbey's manors fell by 20% or more between TRE and 1086; of these fourteen were in Cambridgeshire and the Isle, and ten of them about the south-west border of the Isle where, no doubt, a large part of the operations against Hereward took place.

[4] See Lennard's conclusions drawn from a study of Domesday woodland in the eastern counties: *EcHR*, XV, pp. 36 ff.

[5] I.e. above the valuation 'quando recepit'.

[6] The average rise in values between 1066 and 1086 amounted to 8% in Essex, 18% in Huntingdonshire and 30% in Suffolk.

property, the income the abbey was receiving from those manors still in demesne in 1086 was no lower in aggregate than the income from those same manors twenty years before. Moreover, in 1086, the curve of income was a rising curve almost everywhere and there is no reason to suppose that reconstruction was over by the time of *Domesday*. Therefore, in so far as the farms paid by the manors were expressed in the values assigned to those manors in *Domesday Book*, farms were rising. To that extent there is evidence that rationalization was on foot.

How this appreciation of the abbey's income was achieved is another matter. It has no very obvious connection with more intensive cultivation. It was quite possible for the value of a manor to rise[1] (or at least to be maintained[2]) even though there were fewer ploughs than there ought to have been or even if the number of ploughs had definitely fallen.[3] In the same way, a fall in the manorial population did not necessarily cause a fall in the value of a manor;[4] on the contrary, its value might increase.[5] The only hypothesis which readily suggests itself is that there had been a steady increase in economic pressure upon the manorial population, a scaling up of farms. If so, this must have contributed to a general worsening of the social and economic status of the peasantry, or at least of those peasants already deeply committed to the manorial organization.

However, this was not the only way in which the peasantry were 'depressed'. The intrusion of mesne tenants between the peasant and the abbey, the carving out of new baronies and new knight's fees from a mass of heterogeneous elements,[6] often

---

[1] *Dd*, I, 190d (Balsham). [2] *Dd*, I, 135 (Kelshall).

[3] Land values rose despite a fall in the number of demesne ploughs at Aythorpe (?) Roding (Essex) and on eight of the abbey's manors in Suffolk: *Dd*, II, 19, 381d–5. There was one (though not a demesne) manor where manorial profits seem to have been increased by laying the land down to grass. At Roding (? Morel) both ploughs and population decreased, but the value of the manor rose. This can hardly be dissociated from the increase in the number of cattle from 10 to 25, of pigs from 6 to 89, of sheep from 50 to 225, and of goats from none to 55: *Dd*, II, 49.

[4] As at Bluntisham, Feltwell, Kingston, Melton and Wetheringsett: *IE*, 167; *Dd*, I, 204; II, 213, 384d, 386, 387.

[5] This was true of Drinkstone where, despite a fall in population, the value of the manor rose from £2 to £3 and it had been let at farm for £5, though it would not stand so much: *Dd*, II, 381d; *IE*, 154.

[6] The Cambridgeshire baronies of Picot and Hardwin de Scalers are well-known examples. There was no question here of the Norman taking

resulted in something we may call the 'making of manors', at least if we invest that term manor with the minimum of technical content.[1] It is true enough that many of the usages of an older England continued to exist under the regime established by the Norman aristocracy and their feudal custom; true, too, that in eastern England (the classic terrain of peasant depression) a free peasantry survived and sometimes even flourished. For all that, however, there is no arguing away the magnitude of some of the catastrophes which occurred. Two striking instances from Cambridgeshire may illustrate, if they provide no means of measuring, the sort of change which took place in many another village.

Let us take first the village of Whaddon where, in 1086, Hardwin de Scalers had a manor assessed at four hides. Before the Conquest one hide had been held by Turbert of Ely abbey so that he could not depart. The rest had been divided amongst fifteen sokemen—twelve of them men of Ely abbey, one a man of Archbishop Stigand's, one of Earl Aelfgar's, and one of Esgar's. All of them could sell their land. In 1086, on the other hand, two hides of this land were in Hardwin's demesne; and the only other inhabitants of the manor mentioned were nine villeins and twenty cottars.[2] In the thirteenth century, the customary tenants of this manor would be performing regular week-work.[3] If this labour cannot be argued back with any certainty to the time when Hardwin came to Cambridgeshire, neither can the catastrophe be disguised which then befell the sokemen of Whaddon. Hardwin was a far harder master than the Old English abbey of Ely.

Picot's manor in Long Stanton is equally a case in point. Fifteen sokemen held those three hides in King Edward's time;

over from a specific Saxon *antecessor*. Hardwin's barony, for example, was composed of the holdings of some 300 Saxon landholders (mostly sokemen) who had been commended to sixteen different lords. See also the making of knight's fees in High Easter from the holdings of two substantial sokemen and the glebe of the manorial church: *Dd*, ii, 60 d.

[1] See the evidence collected by Maitland, *Domesday Book and Beyond*, pp. 60–7, 138, 149 and Vinogradoff, *The Growth of the Manor*, pp. 299 ff.; although these passages should be read in connection with certain modifications introduced by Douglas, *Feudal Documents*, pp. cxviiff. and *EcHR*, ix, pp. 138–9.

[2] *Dd*, i, 198 d.

[3] In 1284 the customers of Geoffrey de Scalers in Whaddon owed, for the most part, two days' work a week: Chancery Inq. pm, Edw. I, File 38 (4).

all save one could give and sell their land; and they were men, some of King Edward, some of Ely abbey, and one of Sexi. In 1086 Guy held of Picot land for two ploughs in demesne, and the rest of the population consisted of six bordars and five cottars.[1] Once again, in the thirteenth century, there is something approaching a regular manorial organization here. The estate passed to the Foliot family and the honour of Wardon;[2] and in 1279 it was held by Henry Cheney of William Latimer, with 120 acres in demesne. Certainly there were thirteen free tenants, but these were hardly the wretched survivors of the Domesday sokemen, for they had but thirty acres of land amongst them. The bulk of the land was held by sixteen villeins with a half virgate tenement apiece who, apart from a money rent of 4s., owed considerable labour services, though no regular week-work by that time.[3]

Of course, to generalize from these instances would be neither wise nor legitimate. In East Anglia generally, 'the manor was clearly a very artificial institution' in the eleventh century.[4] In a large measure and despite the slow depression of the peasantry between the conquest and the extents of the thirteenth century, it often remained so.[5] Even in Cambridgeshire, though more 'orthodox' than Norfolk, the manor of classical theory was not the predominant form of social organization in the thirteenth century,[6] and it had been even less so in the eleventh.[7]

All the same, for all these vestiges of an older society which survived, the evidence on the other side does not simply fall out of the picture. Even in the demesne manors of Ely abbey, there are signs that the church was pressing more heavily upon its peasants and asking more of its manors in food or money or labour. Already, this had had the consequence of restoring the

---

[1] *Dd*, I, 201.   [2] *FFC*, pp. 201–4.

[3] *RH*, II, 463.   [4] Douglas, *East Anglia*, p. 217.

[5] Three random examples illustrate how true this could be on lay estates. Robert Tony's great manor of Saham Tony was worth nearly £90 a year in 1309; out of this the works of his customary tenants were valued only at 70s. Similar were William Mortimer's manor at Barnham in 1297, where works were valued only at 4s. 2d. out of about £22; and the Argentem manor at Ketteringham where the only labour services in Edward II's time were harvest boons: Chancery Inq. pm, Edw. I, File 80 (1); Edw. II, Files 2 (14), 15 (3) and 62 (8).

[6] Kosminsky, *EcHR*, v, pp. 32–3.

[7] Dodwell, *EcHR*, xiv, pp. 163–4.

value of those manors to somewhere near their value in the last days of Saxon England, or raising the abbey's income from them even beyond that value. Doubtless, on an ecclesiastical estate of this sort, we must account for this by changes which were evolutionary rather than revolutionary in their character. The villeins and sokemen who had worked and carried for Ely abbey in the days of Abbot Wulfric, who had paid their dues to the abbot, were no doubt working in the same way at the same tasks, were carrying the same goods along the same roads, were paying similar dues in Abbot Symeon's time. But already they were probably working just a little harder, perhaps they were paying just a little more.

Furthermore, although on the abbot's land the social framework may have changed slowly and almost imperceptibly, there are also signs that, as subinfeudation progressed, more radical changes were more brutally effected in many places. This transformation was hardly uniform; still, some free men were being displaced, some demesnes were being created, some 'manors' imposed upon the conquered. Apart from that, in all cases, lines of dependence were sharpened and rooted in the soil, and obligations were more rigorously defined. At bottom, such changes have little to do with the economic virtues of the Normans. They stem rather from their conception of the political (and above all the military) responsibilities of the aristocracy; and they were distributed the more universally and exacted the more rigorously because of the very slender hold the invaders had upon England in the first desperate days. And because they were rooted in the soil, in the land settlement of the Conquest, the political aspects of that settlement became the solvents of anterior social relationships. No absolute uniformity replaced the luxuriant confusion of Old English society. Much that was archaic remained in the demesne manors of Ely abbey, even in the lands of Picot or Hardwin; and this was passed on by them to the bishops and barons and knights who succeeded them. But even the abbots of Ely were moving with the changing times; and the very existence of Picot and Hardwin, with all that they stood for, was something new.

IV

THE MEDIEVAL ESTATES OF
THE BISHOPS OF ELY

AFTER the lands of the church of Ely were surveyed by the
Domesday commissioners in 1086, the abbey as such had
only a brief history. At a council held at Nottingham in the
autumn of 1109, because the diocese of Lincoln was 'very
full of people', Henry I established a bishopric at Ely with
Cambridgeshire as its diocese. The matter had been under
discussion for some time. Abbot Richard seems to have
broached the idea to the king in the last months of his life,
and to have found favour there; after his death the project
was not allowed to sleep by Bishop Hervey of Bangor, whom
Henry had put in charge of the abbey during the vacancy. In
1108, it was discussed at a council held in London, and Hervey
was sent to Rome bearing royal and archiepiscopal letters asking
papal consent for the new bishopric. In due course he brought
back a favourable answer, and papal recommendations for his
own advancement. So the council of Nottingham formally
ratified the creation of the see of Ely, and Hervey became its
first bishop.[1]

The creation of the bishopric of Ely did not, of course, involve the disappearance of monastic life from Ely. The monks
remained as the inhabitants of the cathedral priory, which
gradually achieved a considerable degree of institutional independence of the bishop. One aspect of this independence which
is relevant to the problems which will be discussed in this
present chapter is the fact that very soon the monks acquired
territorial endowments specifically set aside for their own use.
It is probably true that the final division of the lands of Ely
abbey between the bishop and the monks took time—far
longer, at least, than the monks may have claimed during some
later period. The commonly accepted record of the division of

---

[1] The proceedings attendant upon the creation of the bishopric are fully
discussed by Bentham, pp. 119 ff.; and he has printed most of the relevant
materials in his Appx. VI–VIII.

the abbey lands seems in fact to be a forgery,[1] and the vicissi-tudes suffered by the conventual estate in the middle years of the twelfth century take up many of the pages of the conventual chronicle. A stable territorial settlement between bishop and monks may not in fact have been reached much before the early years of Henry II's reign; and there is certainly no sign that it was achieved during the time that Hervey was bishop or in the early years of Nigel when, as a charter of Prior Alexander tells us, 'he had our lands and possessions in his seisin'.[2]

Once a settlement had been made, however, the conventual estate developed along its own lines. Confined in the main to Cambridgeshire and Suffolk, it was geographically more com-pact than the bishop's estate; and the methods of organization found upon it in the thirteenth and early fourteenth centuries were characteristic enough of the Benedictine economy in the age of high farming.[3] Externally, the conventual manors were divided between a home group mainly concerned with provi-sioning the monastery and a revenue group in Suffolk managed for the purpose of producing a cash revenue.[4] Internally, there was the usual strict centralization of finance in the hands of the treasurers.[5] This system, no doubt, was peculiarly suited to fulfil the more or less stable requirements of a monastic cor-poration, a stability which cannot be postulated for the con-temporary establishment of the medieval bishops of Ely. The episcopal estate was subject to different stimuli and developed its own pattern of organization. If only for that reason, it can

---

[1] This is Hervey's charter printed, from chartulary sources, by Bentham, Appx. XXVI. Its very phrasing is suspicious; but its authenticity is more seriously impugned by the fact that Hervey's charter (which differs quite markedly) has survived in original: D & C Charter no. 51 (printed below, Appx. IV, p. 282).

[2] Cott. Claudius C xi, f. 338 d (printed below, Appx. XIII, p. 287).

[3] Still best described in the work of that fine young scholar, R. A. L. Smith, especially in his Canterbury Cathedral Priory and his Collected Papers, pp. 54–73; and see also Knowles, The Religious Orders in England, pp. 32–63.

[4] These remarks are based upon D & C Treasurers' Accts, 10–11, 12–13 and 18–19 Edw. II; Granatar's Accts, 1–2 and 7–8 Edw. II; Cellarer's Acct, 9–10 Edw. III; and Hostiller's Acct, 2–3 Edw. III. In 18–19 Edw. II only 4% of the grain grown in the home group of manors was sold.

[5] The administrative system of the conventual estate can be studied in 'Ely Chapter Ordinances', Camden Miscellany, xvii; see especially p. xii, where it is shown that the Treasurers controlled resources greater than all the rest of the Obedientiaries put together.

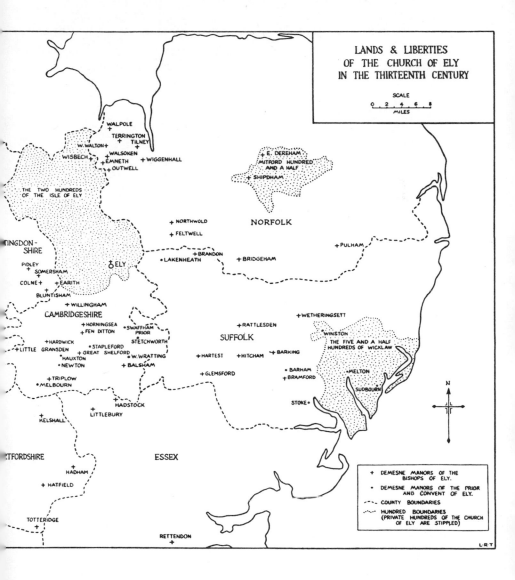

LANDS & LIBERTIES
OF THE CHURCH OF ELY
IN THE THIRTEENTH CENTURY

SCALE

0 2 4 6 8
MILES

WALPOLE
TERRINGTON
TILNEY
W. WALTON
WALSOKEN
WISBECH
EMNETH
WIGGENHALL
OUTWELL

E. DEREHAM
MITFORD HUNDRED
AND A HALF
SHIPDHAM

THE TWO HUNDREDS
OF THE ISLE OF ELY

NORFOLK

NORTHWOLD
FELTWELL

HUNTINGDON-
SHIRE

PULHAM

PIDLEY
SOMERSHAM
COLNE
EARITH
BLUNTISHAM

BRANDON
LAKENHEATH
BRIDGEHAM

ELY

WILLINGHAM

CAMBRIDGESHIRE

HORNINGSEA
FEN DITTON
SWAFFHAM
PRIOR
STETCHWORTH

RATTLESDEN

WETHERINGSETT

WINSTON
THE FIVE AND A HALF
HUNDREDS OF WICKLAW

SUFFOLK

HARDWICK
LITTLE GRANSDEN
STAPLEFORD
GREAT SHELFORD
HAUXTON
W. WRATTING
NEWTON
TRIPLOW
MELBOURN
BALSHAM

HARTEST
HITCHAM
BARKING

GLEMSFORD

BARHAM
BRAMFORD

MELTON

SUDBOURN

STOKE

N

HADSTOCK
KELSHALL
LITTLEBURY

HERTFORDSHIRE

ESSEX

HADHAM
HATFIELD

DEMESNE MANORS OF THE
BISHOPS OF ELY.
DEMESNE MANORS OF THE PRIOR
AND CONVENT OF ELY.
COUNTY BOUNDARIES
HUNDRED BOUNDARIES
(PRIVATE HUNDREDS OF THE CHURCH
OF ELY ARE STIPPLED)

TOTTERIDGE

RETTENDON

L·R·T

be studied in isolation and in the light of factors which were to some degree peculiar to itself.

I

The differences between the episcopal and the conventual estates arise, no doubt, from many causes. The bishop's possessions, to begin with, were far more scattered; for they were disposed in fifty manors lying in six different counties. But it is perhaps more important that a bishop was a different sort of landlord from a community of monks. There was a stability and regularity about the requirements of an immortal corporation, and about the administrative devices appropriate to fulfilling those requirements, which cannot be expected in the lordship of a peripatetic medieval bishop,[1] ever drawn into the affairs of state and subject to the common fate of mortal man. There was nothing unusual in the fact that Nigel, presented to the monks of Ely as their bishop by Henry I, should have departed immediately after a hurried consecration to resume his public duties.[2] The itineraries of men like Longchamp, Eustace, William of Kilkenny or John of Hotham would illustrate equally clearly the way in which episcopal lordship might be conditioned by public service.

These men, however, were to some extent civil servants first and bishops afterwards; yet their preoccupation with public affairs differs in degree rather than in kind from that of Hugh of Northwold. Though better known as builder and high farmer, as Grosseteste's friend[3] and Matthew Paris's ideal of the good monk-bishop,[4] there was no way for him to escape the obligations of his high office in church and state. He is to be found in Wales with the king; he acted as papal delegate against those who disturbed the peace of the realm, an office which took him to Worcester; he inspected on behalf of Gregory IX the bull declaring Henry III to be of age; he was Henry III's ambassador

---

[1] Even his episcopal duties compelled a bishop to be ever on the move; one visitation compelled Bishop Swinefield to sleep in thirty-eight different places in fifty-one days: Moorman, *Church Life in England*, p. 176.

[2] Wharton, *Anglia Sacra*, I, p. 619.   [3] Grosseteste, *Epistolae*, 297.

[4] M. Paris, *Chron. Maj.* V, 454 and compare the man 'of meekness, simplicity and dignity' of the *Memorials of St Edmundsbury*, II, p. 41 cited by Gibbs and Lang, *Bishops and Reform*, pp. 9–10.

to the Emperor and brought the king's bride across to Dover in 1236; even in his old age he was an 'executor' of the crusading tithe granted to the king in 1252.[1] Hugh left little obvious mark upon the general history of his time; but these were no more than duties natural to his station.

So it would be with any bishop. He would be much away from his diocese and his estate, and such absences would vary greatly in frequency and duration. Equally variable would be his responsibility for entertainment, for the provision of military service, and for expenditure which in a broad sense may be called political. Even at home, the bishop's habits would depend to some extent upon temperament, and Somersham chace would naturally be a favourite residence for a mighty hunter. But even for men of more sedentary disposition, a wandering life seems to have been assumed to be normal. Hugh of Northwold built halls in many of his manors, and signs of the bishop's presence at Downham in the Isle, at Wisbech castle, at Hatfield and many another place are not far to seek. Indeed, in 1251, in almost every manor, the obligations of the villeins in food and forage and the bearing of burdens upon the bishop's coming or going were minutely described.[2] Hugh of Northwold, we suspect, would have found nothing strange in the twenty-sixth of the rules which his friend Grosseteste drew up for the Countess of Lincoln.[3]

These, no doubt, are some of the reasons why the organization of the episcopal estate is so much more flexible than the system which is found on the priory lands. A settled framework of

---

[1] *Close R*, 1231–4, 84, 321; 1234–7, 222; 1251–3, 214; *Pat. R*, 1225–32, 477; *Cal. Pat. R*, 1232–47, 4; *Royal Letters*, I, 430–1, 556; M. Paris, *Chron. Maj.* III, 335, 393.

[2] At Doddington even the hundredors found a man to transport the bishop by boat to Somersham, Ely, Willingham or Downham; and the men of March provided the same service if the bishop wished to go north to Wisbech, etc. At Willingham, too, each villein carried the lord's baggage when necessary, threshed fifteen sheaves of oats 'ad prebendum domini', made malt for the bishop's coming, and found hay and forage for his horses. At Hitcham in Suffolk the bishop's forester fed in the *curia* during the bishop's stay; at Glemsford the villeins had each to house a member of the bishop's *familia* and his horse, and on the first night find hay and forage for the latter: Caius 485/489, ff. 63, 64, 73, 118, 303 d, 323.

[3] *Walter of Henley's Husbandry*, p. 145: 'Every year at Michaelmas… arrange your sojourn for the whole of that year, and how many weeks in each place', etc.

supply and revenue manors would be neither so necessary nor
so convenient for a lord normally peripatetic; and the bishop
may commonly have demanded from most of his manors an
income in cash rather than in kind from a very early date.[1] Of
course, the bishops still consumed some of the natural produce
of their estate even in the fourteenth century; and even when
John of Hotham was as far away as York carrying out his duties
as chancellor.[2] But a decision to take manorial revenue in kind
from any given manor at any given time must very early have
become merely one amongst a number of ways of using its
productive capacities. Indeed, by the thirteenth century, so
flexible had the estate administration to be that a large bureaucracy was required to exercise over the whole economy a minute
and detailed supervision. Through the medium of this bureaucracy the bishop's lordship attained the summit of its economic
influence.[3]

It is, of course, also true that 'the will of the bishop' and the
activities of his servants were only one force amongst many
which prescribed the pattern of agrarian relationships which are
to be found on the Ely estate. Even bishops of Ely had to take
account of things which were natural or traditional, and had to
use them where they could not change them. There were, as we
shall see, many vestiges of an earlier peasant freedom which
demanded accommodation. Different sorts of land demanded
different sorts of cultivation; so that pigs were prominent in Hatfield woods, cows in the water meadows at Doddington,[4] and oats
the predominant crop upon the marginal lands of the Marshland.[5]

---

[1] It may be significant that even in Bishop Hervey's time, while the
conventual farm from Fen Ditton was a food farm, the bishop's farm was
a money farm: Liber M, f. 145 and above, p. 40.

[2] Wisbech Barton Accts, 13–14 Edw. II (a payment to two mariners
taking wheat and oats by sea to York 'ad victualia domini') and compare *Cal.
Pat. R*, 1317–21, 209 for a safe conduct to one of the bishop's men taking
corn and victuals to the north for the sustenance of the bishop and the clerks
of chancery.

[3] For some discussion of this point, see ch. VIII below.

[4] The vaccaries here were able to support 100 cows and five bulls in 1251:
Caius 485/489, f. 61.

[5] At Wisbech Barton oats accounted for 40% of the corn sown between
1315 and 1322; while on the neighbouring manor of Coldham in Elm in 1308
oats were sown on 630 out of 860 acres—and this on land later to be described
as 'terra morosa et marisci' of which only one acre in ten could be sown yearly:
PRO Min. Accts, 766/10; Chancery Inq. pm. Edw. III, File 27 (13).

Field arrangements, too, partook of many of the peculiarities of a district which lay outside the three field-region;[1] and great expanses of fen and forest appear not only to have favoured peasant freedom by providing easy outlets into reclaimed land, but also to have contributed to a wide distribution of supra-manorial units, generally called 'sokes', based upon extensive commons in which a number of villages had joint rights.[2] Such units are to be found, not only in Norfolk,[3] but also in Huntingdonshire,[4] in the Isle of Ely,[5] and even up the valley of the Cam to the south of the Isle.[6] This was the sort of material with which the 'will of the bishop' had to work. It is perhaps time to see the kind of results which were achieved.

II

It is an unfortunate thing that the medieval bishops of Ely have not, like their contemporaries at Winchester, left behind them any pipe rolls or, for that matter, any central financial records

[1] The terriers describe a three field lay-out only at Downham, Linden, Littleport and Wilburton in the southern part of the Isle; at Willingham just outside it; and at Triplow on the Cambridgeshire-Essex border: Caius 485/489, ff. 29d, 34d, 46d, 51, 116. There were also three fields in the Prior's manor of Sutton, near Wilburton: D & C Charter no. 216. The wide distribution of arrangements akin to those found in East Anglia may not be without interest—as suggested by the 'wongs', furlongs, crofts, 'hays' and 'hegs' amongst field names at Somersham (Hunts); by the crofts and 'dales' at Wisbech; by the 'doles' and 'hays' in the West Cambridgeshire manors of Hardwick and Little Gransden; and by the 'bredes' or broad strips at Fen Ditton: Caius 485/489, ff. 99d, 120d, 121, 145, 149; Cott Claudius C xi, f. 72d; for the field names quoted here see Douglas, East Anglia, pp. 21-9.

[2] On these, see Douglas, op. cit. pp. 196-8 and Darby, The Medieval Fenland, pp. 67-78.

[3] Not only the groups of villages commoning in Westfen and the marsh of 'Well' in the Marshland (Beloe, Norfolk Archaeology, xii; Pipe R, 6 Joh., 117); but also a similar group round the North and South Fens near Feltwell and Northwold, and yet another about the commons of East Dereham: Caius 485/489, ff. 236, 252, 275, 283d.

[4] The bishop's soke of Somersham was merely part of a group of inter-commoning villages which included the St Ives and Ramsey manors in St Ives, Holywell and Needingworth and which comprised most of Hursting-stone hundred: ibid. f. 101.

[5] See Darby, op. cit. pp. 67-78.

[6] Fen Ditton may have been the centre of a group including Horningsea, Eye and Clayhithe and given cohesion by intercommoning rights (see Bracton's Note-Book, iii, plac. 1582). In this case, however, the group had reached an advanced stage of disintegration by the thirteenth century: see RH, ii, 441-3.

at all. For any comprehensive view of the working of the episcopal estate as a whole, therefore, we must fall back upon the accounts rendered to the exchequer by the king's keepers during vacancies. These accounts, for the purposes we have in view, have many defects. They exclude the bishop and his household from the picture; they must be expected to display an exploitation of the estate designed to make the most of a windfall and to produce a quick cash return for the king. At best, therefore, they indicate no more than the possible order of magnitude of the main heads of the bishop's income. For lack of better evidence, we can hardly afford to dismiss such indications.

The most detailed and useful of the vacancy accounts is that which covers the full year from Michaelmas 1298 to Michaelmas 1299.[1] The manorial accounts are enrolled in it bailiwick by bailiwick; so it is possible to analyse income into its various components. Furthermore, it gives details of the manorial surpluses of corn available for the king's use (they were mainly sent to Gascony) which, valued at current prices and added to the cash income set down in the rolls, should give some sort of indication of what the bishop's income might be.

The results of this calculation suggest that the bishop of Ely at the end of the thirteenth century may have enjoyed a gross income of about £3500 a year and a net income of about £2500. These figures may be too high; indeed, they are too high if they are compared with the figure of £2000 a year at which the prior farmed the vacant see after 1337[2] and the identical figure at which the bishop's temporalities were valued for the taxation of Pope Nicholas in 1291.[3] On the other hand, the sum with which the prior was charged was fixed more than a generation after 1298 and at a time when landowners' incomes may already have begun to contract; and the taxation of Pope Nicholas, despite the lamentations of a Cambridgeshire chronicler,[4] was not always based upon a *verus valor* of ecclesiastical property and may sometimes have underrated it.[5] Equally, of course, some

---

[1] PRO Min. Accts, 1132/10.   [2] Chapman, *Sacrist Rolls of Ely*, I, p. 54.
[3] Black Book of Ely, f. 68d; Lunt, *Valuation of Norwich*, p. 597.
[4] *Ecclesie de Bernewelle Liber Memorandorum*, 191; 'Usque ad ossa excoriat' is his phrase.
[5] Graham, *English Ecclesiastical Studies*, p. 294, where it is also pointed out that the principles of the assessment are completely baffling. In that

allowance must be set against the figure for net income of £2500 calculated from the vacancy account; the fact that there were no liveries of foodstuffs to the bishop's household must have left a larger surplus than normally there would be for sale. Perhaps the truth lies somewhere between the two figures; but wherever it lies, it is clear that the bishop enjoyed an income which placed him amongst the wealthier members, not only of the episcopate, but also of the aristocracy as a whole.[1]

Much more revealing, however, than this tentative figure for the bishop's net income is a breakdown of the figure for gross income in 1298–9 into its component parts. In very round figures appropriate to a calculation which can make no claim to minute accuracy, just under half of the total is accounted for by rents and quasi-rents (including the sale of labour services); just over one-tenth by seignorial profits from courts, markets, feudal dues, etc.; and 40% only by the profits of agriculture.[2] It will be well to remember this last figure when we speak of the bishop of Ely and high farming in the thirteenth century. In terms of income and by the end of that century agricultural production was no longer the most important segment of the bishop's economy. At the same time, since demesne agriculture represented the most direct and the most striking impact of the medieval landlord upon social relationships, the sources of agricultural income have still the first call upon our attention.

Travelling back from 1299 towards the extents of 1251, the importance of demesne agriculture appears to increase. A calculation based upon the vacancy account for 1255–6[3] suggests that income from this source accounted, not for 40%, but for 50% of gross revenue. In 1251, too, it absorbed the major part of the bishop's manors; for out of 70,000 acres or thereabouts, 20,000 were demesne acres and 20,000 more disposed in tenements of which the primary purpose was the provision of labour for the demesne.[4] Much of the balance of rented land consisted of

connection it might be pointed out that the bishop's property in the Isle and Cambridgeshire were valued at £1042 and property outside the diocese at £948. In fact the latter property produced about 60% of the bishop's income.
[1] For ecclesiastical incomes, see Moorman, *Church Life in England*, p. 169; and for laymen, Painter, *English Feudal Barony*, p. 174 and Denholm-Young, *Seignorial Administration in England*, pp. 22–3.
[2] See Table II below, p. 94.   [3] See Table II below, p. 94.
[4] See Table I below, p. 87.

tenements of recent creation, formed often from new land altogether, from assarted land. The further back we go, in short, the greater the comparative importance of the demesne.

Of the purely agricultural aspects of demesne farming little need be said here. As in most parts of England, cereals were the crop *par excellence*; and their culture did most to determine the sort of work which would be required of a villein. But there was mixed farming too. The cows in the Doddington meadows have already been mentioned; and so have the pigs in the woods at Hatfield (and, we might add, at Somersham).[1] Sheep were ubiquitous as they had been in Domesday times; and if they were valued first for their manure and wool, there is no reason to suppose that their mutton was an unconsidered trifle.[2] The bishop also had many fisheries in his fenland manors producing astronomical numbers of eels,[3] which there often replaced the herring as the villein's food on boon days[4] and were considered not unworthy of the royal table.[5] Finally, from the marshland manors and above all from Terrington[6] came the salt essential to preserve fish and flesh outside their season.

Well into the fourteenth century some proportion (though no doubt a very variable proportion from year to year) of all this produce was still finding its way to the bishop's table at Ely or in the course of his peregrinations about his estate and diocese. This was true of the wheat, oats and pigs of Wisbech[7] in the second decade of the century; it was true also of the malt and pigs of Great Shelford in the third and fourth decades;[8] and

---

[1] These woods, indeed, provided pannage for the pigs of a great number of the bishop's manors—including Balsham, Great Shelford and Fen Ditton in Cambridgeshire: Caius 485/489, ff. 123, 130, 138.

[2] The prior, at least, did not think so; in 1324-5 the steward of his hospice received no less than 90 sheep from Stetchworth and Witchford: D & C Treasurer's Acct, 18–19 Edw. II.

[3] 8000 'sticks' at Littleport, for instance: Caius 485/489, f. 40.

[4] Deliveries of eel rents by lessees of fisheries were often timed to coincide with boon days, as at Littleport again: Cott. Tiberius B 11, f. 97.

[5] See Pipe Roll no. 102, m. 7 for the sheriff of Cambridgeshire purchasing eels for the king.

[6] This manor provided some 16 'ways' or 672 bushels: Caius 485/489, f. 200; Cott. Tiberius B 11, f. 238; Hall and Nicholas, 'English Weights and Measures', *Camden Miscellany*, xv, p. 28.

[7] The proportion sent to Ely might be as high as one-third of the produce of the manor in some years, e.g. Wisbech Barton Acct, 13–14 Edw. II.

[8] In 19–20 Edw. II wheat and pigs were sent to Ely; flour to Somersham at Christmas; malt and fish to Willingham, Glemsford and Littlebury. Pigs

even in the reign of Richard II much livestock might still be sent up from Somersham for the bishop.[1] The carrying services which were so carefully recorded in 1251 seem often to have been designed to facilitate this flow of goods for consumption from the manors. The men of Hardwick were to carry 'ad opus episcopi' and this might mean taking food to Ely.[2] Alternatively, like their contemporaries at Triplow,[3] they might take it no further than another neighbouring manor, either because the bishop was staying there or as a stage on a longer journey in which the villeins of a number of manors were called upon to co-operate.[4]

Even in 1251, however, these villein carrying services were already serving other purposes. In the first place they may have been already, as they certainly were in later times, a link between the bishop's manors which helped his servants to treat the whole clumsy edifice of the estate as something like an economic unit. They might serve to make good the deficiencies of one manor from the surpluses of another, to distribute good breeding stock from the pastoral manors, to replace worn out seed; and in this way turn to profit the specialization imposed by natural conditions and local variations in fertility.[5] In such manner the old routes which villeins and sokemen had trodden in the days of the abbots, carrying food and forage to the abbey gates, became the arteries of a high-farming estate economy.

were likewise sent to Ely in 1–2, 2–3 and 6–7 Edw. III; in 2–3 Edw. III malt was sent to the lord's hospice at Littlebury and flour to Balsham; in 6–7 Edw. III nearly half the wheat grown in the manor and all the malt made there went to the lord at Willingham, Balsham and Kelshall. In 1 Edw. III malt from this manor was even taken to the lord's household in London: PRO Min. Accts, 1132/14–15.

[1] For the delivery of 2 oxen, 3 young cattle, 57 muttons, 47 pigs, 6 capons, 318 hens and 720 eggs in 4–5 Ric. II see PRO Min. Accts, 1307/3.

[2] Caius 485/489, f. 146.   [3] *Ibid.* f. 143.

[4] In 1326–7 the customers of Great Shelford took malt and other food, together with the bishop's baggage, as far as Littlebury in Essex on the way to the bishop's town house in Holborn: PRO Min. Accts, 1132/14.

[5] This use of carrying services is frequently illustrated by the Great Shelford rolls. Timber for fencing and to build a new mill when the old one fell down came from Balsham, Littlebury and Hadstock; grain, and especially seed grain, was obtained from Fen Ditton, Littlebury, Hadham, Balsham and Triplow; and livestock from Balsham and Little Gransden. In turn, the reeve of Shelford sent grain to Balsham and Fen Ditton and young cattle and lambs to Hatfield and Balsham; and he bought pear and apple seedlings in the village to replant Somersham orchard: PRO Min. Accts, 1132/14–15, 1133/1.

Secondly, carrying services provided the link between the bishop's manors and their markets: in county towns like Cambridge, Norwich, Bury St Edmunds, Huntingdon, Ipswich, Hertford; and even in London in the case of some of the Essex and Hertfordshire manors.[1] But most important of all of these markets, in terms of the frequency with which it was mentioned, was the regional centre of Lynn; it was offering to all the valleys of the Cam and of the Great and Little Ouse a way to the sea, and to the coastal and continental traffic based on its harbour. In this way the carrying services made possible a complex system of buying and selling: the purchase of necessaries for the manorial economy;[2] the purchase of common foodstuffs and medieval luxuries—figs and raisins, almonds, pepper and ginger, nuts and sugar, honey and wine, salmon and porpoises;[3] but above all the sale of the surplus produce of the bishop's manors. Notices of carrying services 'ad bladum domini vendendum' are so numerous that citation would be tedious.

Of course, even intermanorial carrying services might serve the same end; for the bishop had fairs and markets in a number of places.[4] It was laid down in 1251 that corn grown at Downham might be taken to Ely market for sale;[5] and the bishop's corn was not something which could be spoken of lightly, as Alice Balle discovered at Littleport in 1320, for she was amerced there for defaming the lord's corn so that buyers avoided it.[6]

---

[1] Caius 485/489, ff. 153, 161, 183; Cott. Claudius C xi, f. 165 d.

[2] Cart-horses were bought at Bishop's Stortford and mill fittings in London for Great Shelford: PRO Min. Accts, 1132/14, 1133/1; in 1251 the customers of Hardwick were to go to Royston or Hatfield to buy cartwheels; those of Fen Ditton to Bury St Edmunds to purchase livestock: Caius 485/489, ff. 116 d, 146 d; in the fourteenth century the purchases of the reeves of Wisbech at Lynn included building timber, oil, and pitch for the shepherd: Wisbech Barton Accts, 20 Edw. II, 1 Edw. III, 3–4 Edw. III.

[3] This list comes from D & C Prior's Hospice Acct. 4–5 Hen. IV. Of course the villeins might carry less exciting viands; the customers of Kelshall are simply to carry from the market anything the bishop wants: Caius 485/489, f. 153.

[4] These included Ely, Balsham, Shipdham, Needham Market, East Dereham, Pulham, Wisbech, Hatfield, Hadstock and Barking: PRO Min. Accts, 1132/10; Liber M, ff. 84, 112, 117; Cal. Charter R, i, 287; iii, 403; Rot. Litt. Claus. ii, 109, 112, 183.

[5] Cott. Claudius C xi, f. 35 d.

[6] Maitland, Court Baron, p. 130. Of course, markets and fairs were probably more valued as a source of tolls than for their convenience in manorial marketing. It was because he was losing his consuetudines that the

The wool clip of the Barton farm at Wisbech seems also to have been normally sold at Ely in the fourteenth century.[1] Even apart from markets, there seems also to be a tendency in this century to concentrate manorial surpluses in local collecting centres, no doubt because this arrangement facilitated sales in bulk.[2] This, in brief, is the background of the agricultural income of the bishops of Ely. Their manors were involved in the whole gamut of commercial transactions of their time: transactions which ranged from sale in penny packets in a local market (the sort of sale, no doubt, which might be marred by the disparagement of an Alice Balle) up to bulk transactions with merchants of substance, who bought up the produce of a whole group of manors and perhaps sold it in markets far distant from this fertile corner of eastern England.[3]

The foregoing account of what we might call the motives of the demesne economy—of production for the market and production for consumption in the episcopal establishment—has

abbot of Bury objected to the prior of Ely's market in Lakenheath in 1202 and paid for an inquest to see if it was to his damage: *Pipe R*, 4 Joh., 114; *CRR*, II, 136.

[1] There are only five notices of sales of wool at Wisbech itself in a fairly complete series of rolls covering the years 1313–64; and the amount concerned was only considerable in 1326/7. On most other occasions it seems to have been sent to Ely.

[2] Fen Ditton seems to have been such a centre in Cambridgeshire to judge from the Great Shelford rolls (PRO Min. Accts, 1132/14–15). Almost every year corn was taken from Shelford to Ditton for sale to merchants there; and on one occasion the villeins of Shelford also carried corn and wool from Balsham to the same destination. Ditton had obvious conveniences from this point of view; it was on the river which linked Cambridge with Lynn.

[3] Many of the lots of corn sold at Wisbech Barton were quite large. In 8–9 Edw. II they included 80, 60 and 40 qrs. of wheat, 80 qrs. of mixtill and 99 qrs. of oats; in 13–14 Edw. II 34 oxen were sold *in grosso*; and in 14–15 Edw. II lots included 90, 60 and 50 qrs. of oats and 130 and 100 qrs. of mixtill. Wisbech, too, of course was on the way to Lynn; and probably enjoyed a considerable share of the trade we see moving down the fenland waterways to this latter town. Certainly in 1319 no fewer than fourteen of the bishop's men received safe conduct for going with their ships to Lynn, Boston, etc. to sell their ale and other goods; and John Chamberleyn was given leave to export 200 barrels of ale so long as he did not sell them to the Scots. It is this trade which provides a background to the complaint of the good men of Ely in the parliament of 1335, in which they declared that they and their ancestors from time out of mind had sold ale and all other manner of victuals, goods and merchandise in the town of Lynn, as well wholesale as retail, and as well to merchants and foreign traders as to the men of Lynn themselves: *Cal. Pat. R*, 1317–21, 311; *Cal. Close R*, 1318–23, 160, 165, 175; *RP*, II, 93.

had to be purely descriptive. There is little evidence for estimating quantitatively the disposition of manorial produce between sale and the bishop's table, still less for striking a balance
between these two uses. It may be best, therefore, to leave for
the time being the problem of the development of the bishop's
agricultural income; and turn to the way in which labour was
provided for the bishop's farming in general.

III

A study of labour organization can be based most firmly upon
the data provided by the extents of 1251; and some statistics
drawn from this source have been summarized in Table I. The

TABLE I. *Land, ploughs and villein work on the estate
of the bishop of Ely, 1251*

Bailiwick	Utilization of land (in '000 acres)				Demesne acres per demesne plough	Week-works per villein acre per year
	Total	Demesne	Vil-leinage	Rent-paying land		
Cambs. and Hunts.	11·9	4·3	5·2	2·4	200	9
Isle of Ely	8·3 (?10·0)[1]	4·1	2·5 (?4·2)[1]	1·7	130	9
Marshland	16·6	1·8	1·5	13·3	130	9
Essex and Herts.	10·5	3·6	3·2	3·7	200	5
Suffolk	9·5	2·7	2·5	4·3	165	8
Norfolk	14·8	3·5	5·3	6·0	200	7
Total	71·6 (?73·3)	20·0	20·2 (?21·9)	31·4	—	—

figures there which concern the disposition of land between
different sorts of income-producing uses show that, in all
counties, the amount of land held in demesne and the amount
of land in the villeinage was roughly equal. Local and regional
differences were reflected rather in the relative area of rent-

[1] The difficulty here is that villein holdings are usually expressed in 'ware
acres' and the demesne, apparently, in field acres; and that 'ware acres'
commonly each represented two field acres (Maitland, *Court Baron*, p. 108 n.)
though at Ely itself, it would seem, only one and a half field acres. The
figure in brackets, therefore, represents some approximation towards a true
and comparative assessment of the area of the villeinage.

paying land about the nucleus formed by demesne and villeinage. From this point of view, in short, the labour organization on the bishop's lands adheres closely to the manorial pattern.[1]

At the same time, the factors which come into play in the organization of labour are clearly very complex factors. On the demand side, clearly what matters is the size of the demesne. On the supply side, one factor again is the relative extent of the villeinage, so that the slight variations from bailiwick to bailiwick shown in the table may be important. For these variations may help to explain another factor on the supply side—the relative severity or lightness of the labour burden imposed upon the villeinage. These burdens are not easy to assess in comparative terms; it does not mean very much, for example, to point out that the villeins of Fen Ditton owed only two days' work a week, while those of Walpole owed six—for the villein tenement at Walpole was twice as large as the villein tenement at Ditton.[2] Perhaps a better index, therefore, is provided by calculating the incidence of week-work per villein acre. The results of that calculation which are given in Table I show once again that (except for Essex and Hertfordshire, for which the explanation is anything but obvious) villein burdens did not vary very widely between the different parts of the estate. On the other hand, the minor variations in the relative extent of demesne and villeinage are probably reflected in these figures. The villeins of Norfolk did not work quite so hard as the villeins of the Isle and the Marshland; and part of the reason for that was probably the fact that the villeinage was relatively very large in Norfolk, and not nearly so large in the Marshland and the Isle.

On the other hand, there may be dangers in accepting the villeinage and its burdens as a source of labour supply which responded easily to variations in demand from the side of the demesne. The information given by the 1251 extents about demesne ploughs, taken in conjunction with data about the size of the demesne, shows that there was at least one other variable in the situation—the amount of demesne cultivation carried out

---

[1] On the other hand, this does not apply to manors acquired at a late date, like Totteridge and Bramford (Caius 485/489, ff. 164, 358). At Bramford there were only nineteen acres of villeinage and no regular villein tenements; at Totteridge there was no villeinage at all, and one wonders in fact whether there ever had been any.

[2] Caius 485/489, ff. 122, 203.

by the lord's own implements and by hired labour. In Cambridgeshire, for example, demesne ploughs were relatively thin upon the ground; only one for every 200 demesne acres. This presumably can be explained by reference to the fact that the villeinage was relatively large and fairly heavily burdened. Demesne ploughs were thin on the ground in Norfolk, too; presumably because, although the villein's burdens were slighter, the villeinage was relatively very extensive. On the other hand, in the Isle and the Marshland, although the villein's burdens were as heavy as in Cambridgeshire, the villeinage was relatively smaller. In consequence, there were more demesne ploughs about: one for every 130 demesne acres.

Overall averages of this sort may, of course, be thrown badly out by any number of disturbing factors. But the same sort of result seems to emerge from a more detailed comparison of manorial staffs on particular manors as they are set out in the vacancy accounts of 1302 and 1316.[1] At Doddington and Kelshall, for instance, the demesne was roughly of the same dimensions (331 and 357 acres respectively); but while the former manor had only three full-time labourers, the latter had five. This was probably due to the fact that Doddington had a large extent of villeinage (448 acres) and Kelshall comparatively a much smaller area (293 acres). Again, although the demesne at Little Gransden (518 acres) was much larger than the demesne at Downham (444 acres), there were only four full-time labourers on the manor as compared with seven at Downham; again probably because, while the villeinage of Gransden extended to 517 acres, there were only 318 acres at Downham. The fact, finally, that the great central manor at Ely had only 1200–1300 acres of villeinage to serve a demesne of over 1500 acres may in part explain the very large full-time staff of eighteen to be found there.

The following conclusions, then, would seem to follow from the foregoing discussion. Throughout the bishop's estate a roughly similar amount of labour service for the demesne husbandry

---

[1] PRO Min. Accts, 1132/11, 1132/13. In the figures which follow only full-time labour is accounted for, although (and this will receive further discussion later) part-time labour is at least as important. Secondly, shepherds, swineherds, etc. have not been included since their importance would vary greatly between manors according to differences in natural conditions.

was provided by a roughly comparable amount of villein land. This would suggest that by the thirteenth century the villeinage had become a somewhat inelastic source for the supply of labour. It continued to play a vital and important part in the provision of labour for the lord's demesne; in that respect the bishop was orthodox enough. But it is less clear that it would react quickly or easily to new demands imposed by an increase in demesne acres or by the quickening tempo of a more highly commercialized economy. In fact, as we shall see,[1] it seems to have been hard to augment the burdens of the villeins; hard to add to the numbers of the villein tenements; and to all seeming almost impossible to create a villeinage at a late date in places where new settlements were arising, as they were in the Marshland. The villeinage, in brief, was a variable factor in labour supply only to a limited extent; far more variable, apparently, was the growing pool of wage labour which could compensate for the relative lightness of villein burdens or the relative paucity of villein acres.

The real importance of hired labour in the bishop's economy is substantially underrated by a mere count of full-time workers in a few manors of the sort attempted above. So much is clear from a glance at one or two of the account rolls of Wisbech Barton.[2] In 1316 (as is shown by a roll which covers only part of a year), five ploughmen were hired for about a penny a day to do 147 days' ploughing; two men for a fortnight after Michaelmas to load manure; other men at piece rates to spread it; and yet another man for a few days to help with the sowing. The services of a blacksmith, likewise, seem always to have been paid for; there were numerous payments to carpenters working on the fold and the buildings; and the whole of the harvest was threshed at piece rates. All this was casual labour, over and above a regular or near-regular manorial staff—four ploughmen, three or four carters, a swineherd with a boy to help him in spring and summer, an oxherd, a shepherd with two assistants at lambing time. This large amount of wage labour is not to be explained by the sale or the commutation of services. Only about 14% of the winter works and 7% of the autumn works were sold; and the tale of services was more or

---

[1] See below, pp. 101 ff.
[2] Wisbech Barton Accts, 8–9 and 13–14 Edw. II.

less the same as in 1222 and 1251.[1] Wage labour, we may say, was hardly a novelty introduced during the break up of the manor.

This proposition, moreover, is not seriously modified by the argument that the marshland economy of Wisbech Barton makes it a somewhat exceptional example. The same combination of wage and villein labour is to be found elsewhere: at Great Shelford, for example, where in 1323–4, although half the autumn week-work was sold, the autumn boons were not and only 10% of the week-work was sold during the rest of the year. Yet there were four ploughmen, a carter, a shepherd and a dairymaid continuously employed, as well as a very great deal of casual labour.[2] At Somersham, too, a manor with a very large area of villein land, there was about the same time a regular staff of five ploughmen, two carters, two shepherds, an oxherd, a swineherd and a gardener.[3]

These examples may be enough to suggest that any very rigid distinction between villein and wage labour, in considering the sort of labour force characteristic of the medieval manor, is a distinction perilously drawn. It is true that we hear very little of these wage-workers in the thirteenth century; but then our information about that century is drawn very largely from the extents and there is no place for labourers, as labourers, in a 'liber de inquisicionibus terrarum'.[4] Their existence, however, is almost presupposed by variations in, and the inelasticity of, the supply of villein labour; and it has very little connection with the 'rise of a money economy'. Indeed, there was at least one of the bishop's manors at the beginning of the fifteenth

[1] 1315 winter and summer works and 520 autumn works were due from the 'werkelondes' of Wisbech in 1321—almost the same figure as the 1815 week-works due in 1251; as in 1222 and 1251, moreover, these were due from ten 'werkelondes', one of which lay in Leverington: Caius 485/489, ff. 80–82 d, 83 d; Cott. Tiberius B II, f. 147.

[2] PRO Min. Accts, 1132/14.

[3] PRO Min. Accts, 1135/8 (1–2 Edw. III).

[4] It might be that criticism from this side would reveal the most serious deficiencies in the general approach of Prof. Kosminsky to this problem: *EcHR*, v, pp. 24–45. He has based his thesis throughout on extents of one sort or another, records which cannot be expected to describe the population except as landholders, or that part of the population not holding land. Nor does the fact that labour obligations existed provide any clue as to the proportion of those services which were actually being exacted or the proportion of the labour required by the demesne which was supplied from this source.

century where there was no charge to enter under the heading of 'stipendia famulorum' because that year the labourers were paid entirely in corn;[1] and a century earlier liveries in kind were at least as important as money wages in the payments made to regular employees of the manor.[2]

At the same time, this system of hiring labourers paid in cash and kind may itself be a fairly recent method of providing a full-time staff for the demesne husbandry. The extents suggest that, in the first half of the thirteenth century, the same purpose was achieved by turning some of the villein holdings into what we might call temporary manorial 'serjeanties'. A villein might, in this way, for one year or more give full-time service on the demesne instead of part-time villein service; in return he would be excused all his rents and services (or most of them) and commonly received some sort of payment or concession from the lord.[3] Almost every sort of labour the demesne might require could be provided in this way: carpenters and blacksmiths, cowherds and dairymen, shepherds and swineherds, and above all ploughmen. But prominent as such arrangements seem to have been in the middle of the thirteenth century, they have all but disappeared by the early fourteenth century.[4] Wage labour, both regular and casual, by that time seems to have been

[1] CUL Doc. 817: Wilburton Acct, 6–7 Hen. IV.

[2] E.g. Wisbech Barton Accts, 13–14 Edw. II where members of the regular staff of the manor were paid a money wage (commonly 5s. a year) and a quarter of corn for every six weeks during harvest and for every eight weeks during the rest of the year. At Great Shelford in 1333–4 part of the rye needed for a livery of a quarter for every ten weeks had to be bought outside the manor: PRO Min. Accts, 1132/15. These liveries, normally, went only to the regular staff; casual labour was paid only a money wage.

[3] *Censuarii*, as well as villeins, might have to serve in this way: see for example the entry regarding William Akerman at Pulham, which also illustrates most of the points made above. He held 7 acres for a rent of 2s. 4d. and various boon services: 'vel ibit ad carucam domini et tunc erit quietus de predictis denariis redditus et consuetudinibus. . . . Et si teneat carucam iste et socius eius habebunt escaeta foragii in boveria per visum prepositi. Et quolibet die Sabbati habebunt carucam domini arantem super terram suam propriam. Et habebunt in estate unam vaccam propriam in pastura cum bobus domini'—Caius 485/489, f. 227.

[4] At Somersham in 1348 there were still two ploughmen who turn out to be villeins excused services for so acting; but at Wisbech in the reign of Edward II, and at Ely and Doddington at the end of Edward I's reign there is no sign of this sort of arrangement; while at Linden, Stretham and Downham the village smith is the only example of it: PRO Min. Accts, 1132/11, 1307/2; Wisbech Barton Accts, 8–9, 14–15, 15–16 Edw II.

found elsewhere, though precisely where is nowhere stated. Presumably it was drawn from cottars, toft-holders, small molmen or even small free tenants—as well as from landless men and small subtenants in the holdings of the bishop's tenants.[1] Quite likely, too, men of these groups had been working for the bishop and for others for many generations; for they are all there in those same extents which describe the manorial 'serjeanties' we have discussed. They must have had the same need in 1251 as later to supplement the produce of their inadequate tenancies with work for food or wages. In fact, as far back as we can see, the labour force on these manors must always have been a mixed labour force; so much so that the *servi* of *Domesday* may some-day appear as the progenitors (in function if not in blood) of the *famuli* of the later account rolls.

IV

It is perhaps time now to leave this long digression on labour organization; and to remind ourselves once again that in 1299 all the work of villeins and wage labourers upon the bishop's demesne lands in the end went to produce only 40% of the bishop's gross income. Yet above and outside this profit he made from demesne agriculture, the bishop had also a non-agricultural income of over £2000 a year made up as follows: 20% was income from courts, markets, feudal dues etc.; 30% from more or less fixed customary rents; 10% from the sale of labour services; and 40% from variable and contractual rents for manors, demesne land, villein holdings, mills, fisheries, herbage rights and indeed from almost everything that was leasable.

One or two observations upon these figures very quickly suggest themselves. In the first place, at the end of the thirteenth century, the bishop of Ely was drawing half his income from

[1] These last two sorts of men are, of course, the 'anilepymen' and 'undersetles' who are 'a distinct feature of the Ely extents': see Douglas, *East Anglia*, p. 31; Maitland, *Court Baron*, p. 112; and especially Homans, *English Villagers of the Thirteenth Century*, pp. 136–7, 210–12. We are only beginning to realize the importance of this 'proletarian' element in the medieval manor. In this connection some figures drawn from the records of thirteenth-century Wotton Underwood may be of considerable significance: there were twenty-two villeins and cottars, but thirty-one *valletti*, landless men: Powicke, *Wirtschaft und Kultur*, pp. 388–9.

rents: that would appear to be a fact which requires a certain amount of explanation in this century of 'high farming'. Secondly, the larger part of this income from rents was derived from short-term contractual rents, and not from customary rents. On the face of it this part of the bishop's rent income would appear to be of recent origin, suggesting even a drift away from cultivation in this century of 'high farming'. Clearly, then, a discussion of the bishop's income from rents, if it is to have very much meaning, must bring us back to the more general economic development of the estate as a whole.

In this connection, an attempt has been made in Table II to summarize a certain amount of statistical data illustrative of the general expansive trends of the twelfth and thirteenth centuries,

TABLE II. *Estimates of the Income of the bishop of Ely, 1086–1299*

Type of income	1086 (£)	1171–2 (£)	1256–7 (£)	1298–9 (£)
Rent income:				
1. Customary rents	—	—	610	630
2. Sale of works	—	—	105	170
3. Contractual rents	—	—	345	900
Total rent income	—	—	1060	1700
Agricultural income	—	—	1160	1400
Income from courts, etc.	—	—	80	400
Total gross income	484	950	2300	3500
Expenses	—	30	370	950
Net income	484	920	1930	2550

although changes in the value of money during the period make it quite impossible to use these figures for measuring the magnitude of expansion achieved.[1] The first column is simply an addition of the Domesday valuations of those manors which remained in the bishop's demesne; and this is followed in sequence by figures drawn from the vacancy accounts of 1171–2,[2]

[1] For the rise in prices beginning in the twelfth and ending in the fourteenth century, which may have been 'one of the most violent price revolutions in English history, comparable in speed to the revolution of the sixteenth century', see Beveridge, *Economic History*, I, p. 164. Such a price movement, of course, makes crude figures of income valueless for comparative purposes.

[2] *Pipe R*, 18 Hen. II, 115–17.

1256–7,[1] and 1298–9.[2] The fact that these last three calculations are all based upon the same sort of record may justify a feeling that they ought to be roughly comparable sets of figures. Stated in the baldest terms, such comparison would suggest that the bishop's income increased threefold between 1170 and 1300; and that agrarian profits may have increased fivefold between the time of *Domesday Book* and the reign of Edward I. Other indications contained in it about changes in the sources of income may be left for the time being until we have looked at some other indices of the expansive movement to which these statistics bear some sort of testimony.

It is clear that some part of the expansion of the bishop's income was the fruit of an increase in the amount of land subject to his control, mostly newly reclaimed land. The most spectacular gains of this sort were made, as we might expect, in the fenland area. In Norfolk during the century after the Domesday inquest the work of those early pioneers, who built the Roman Dyke and founded the villages of the Marshland on land won from the sea, was carried further; and the bishops of Ely did their part in creating a manor in the Wiggenhalls.[3] But the minor place-names of the area suggest that in fact the bishops were winning new land in all their manors;[4] and they carefully safeguarded their gains by minutely apportioning duties for maintaining dykes and ditches upon all their tenants in those villages which commoned in Smeeth and Marshland fens.[5] It

---

[1] Pipe R no. 101, m. 4: this account covers fifteen months and had to be brought into line with the other figures by a pro rata reduction of one-fifth at all points. This will hardly present an accurate picture, but it may serve for the present rough comparison. [2] PRO Min. Accts, 1132/10.

[3] See Beloe, *Norfolk Archaeology*, XII, pp. 311 ff.; Douglas, *East Anglia*, pp. 119–21; Darby, *The Medieval Fenland*, pp. 47–8 and Blomefield, *Norfolk*, IX, p. 176. There was, of course, some sort of settlement at Wiggenhall in 1086 (*Dd*, II, 274 d), but the first mention of the Ely manor seems to be in 1160: *Pipe R*, 6 Hen. II, 5.

[4] E.g. the Frithlond, Senewelond, Rednewelond and North-frithlond at Terrington; the Newefeld and Newecroft at Walpole; and the Newelond and Newcroft at West Walton: Caius 485/489, ff. 187 d, 200; *Norfolk Portion of the Chartulary of Lewes*, nos. 159–62.

[5] At Terrington, for example, almost every tenant 'debet operari portionem suam super fossata versus mare et mariscum': Caius 485/489, ff. 188 d–9, 190. It was the same on the other estates in the neighbourhood: in the St Edmund's holding at Wiggenhall we note 1½ acres burdened 'cum toto onere fossati maris ad dictum terram pertinente': CUL Mm. IV. 19, f. 47; and cf. *Norfolk Portion of the Chartulary of Lewes*, no. 163.

was the same in the Cambridgeshire fenland. At Leverington, for example, we read much about land in the new field, the new purpresture, and the foreign purpresture,[1] in the making of which the whole of the free population of the vill may have taken their part (for we find them entering into a covenant to give to the abbot of Thorney a certain share in the assarts they had made and would make in the future).[2] At Wisbech, too, Longchamp was able to give the convent 800 acres for celebrating the anniversary of Richard I 'de quibus nunquam prius Elyensis ecclesia vel eiusdem ecclesie episcopi aliquod servicium habuerunt';[3] and Geoffrey de Burgh could provide a tenement of new purpresture for his steward.[4] Over all this area, moreover, as in the Norfolk Marshland, there was a minute subdivision of responsibility for the maintenance of dykes and ditches attached to every plot of land.[5]

Some of the examples quoted above show clearly enough that many of these marshland assarts involved very large areas of land; though it is probably true that these numerous acres were often marginal acres unsuited to intensive tillage,[6] and that these gains from the waters were sometimes precarious.[7] At the

---

[1] Thorney Red Book, I, ff. 182–5.

[2] Thorney Red Book, I, f. 186d, printed below, Appx. XV, p. 289.

[3] Liber M, ff. 162–3.

[4] This consisted of 300 acres in Wisbech and 100 acres in Elm, the rent for which was later given to the convent: *ibid.* f. 174.

[5] E.g. D & C Charter no. 852 which records a grant of three acres in the Newfield at Leverington in 1313 and 'inde de fossatis et essewyciis tantum quantum pertinet ad predictas tres acras', and compare the similar obligations of holdings of fourteen and one acres respectively at Wisbech: *ibid.* nos. 699, 718.

[6] So we may infer from the description of Edmund Peverel's demesne at Elm in the early fourteenth century. He had 2400 acres of land; but it was 'terra morosa et marisci' and only 240 acres could be cultivated yearly: Chancery Inq. pm, Edw. III, File 27 (13).

[7] This perhaps is best indicated in the description of the bishop's tiny demesne of 44½ acres at Leverington in 1251 which 'quandoque decrescit et quandoque accrescit per mare': Caius 485/489, f. 84. By the beginning of the fourteenth century, some of this reclaimed land may even have been lost again: on Edmund Peverel's manor referred to above, 960 acres were under water in 1331; in 1299 decayed rents due to recent inundation in the Marshland amounted to £17; and in 1316 at Terrington and West Walton 'magna pars terrarum submersa est in mare': PRO Min. Accts, 1132/10, 13. Even earlier, disasters of this sort might make things difficult for the king's justices; in 1269, when they wished to have John de Marisco before them, they could find nothing whereby he might be distrained because his lands were under water: AR no. 83, m. 9d.

same time, this fenland assarting was no more than part of a far more widespread effort to extend the boundaries of cultivation. Longchamp's gifts to his cathedral priory included, not only land and rent in well over 2000 acres of purpresture in Wisbech and its hamlets,[1] but also 100 acres of land, rent from 240 acres, and tithes from a further and unspecified area—all representing new reclamation in the soke of Somersham.[2] A little later, when John of Fountains gave to the monks the tithe of his demesne land in Hadham, he was constrained to specify that his grant should apply to new assart as well as to land anciently cultivated.[3] Some of these assarts were almost certainly made, not from the fen, but from the forest; a type of reclamation which brought the church of Ely into conflict with the officers of the crown at the end of the twelfth century.[4] These incursions into the forest were the background to that charter in which Richard I gave the bishop pardon for his assarts in Hadstock, Littlebury, and Somersham.[5]

This extension of the cultivated area in the bishop's lands, then, is further indication of a general expansive trend in the economy of the estate during the twelfth and the thirteenth centuries. However, as we shall see, most of this new land went into new tenancies, not into demesne; may we not say, therefore, that the population of the estate was also increasing? The lengthening of the bishop's rent roll would surely point to such a conclusion. But it is another matter to make any sort of measurement of this growth of population. Very little is known yet about the structure of the peasant family in the twelfth century; and many of the new tenants who appear in the thirteenth century extents may simply have escaped from the anonymity which had previously obscured them as members of a peasant family group.[6] Even where new centres of population

---

[1] Liber M, ff. 161–2; D & C Charter no. 62.

[2] Liber M, ff. 161, 162; Bodl. Laudian Misc. 647, ff. 113d–14d.

[3] D & C Charter no. 75: 'omnes decimas de dominico nostro de Hadham bladi et leguminis tam de terra antiquitus culta quam de novo essarto'.

[4] See, for instance, the forest amercements which the elect of Ely had to rebut by the king's writ in *Pipe R*, 1 Ric. I, 24, 27, 193.

[5] This charter and King John's confirmation of it have both been printed in *Cartae Antiquae Rolls* 1–10, nos. 65–6.

[6] This problem of peasant family organization has been the subject of some pioneer work by Homans, *The English Villager of the Thirteenth Century*, pp. 109ff., the implications of which are still to be worked out.

were growing up, the evidence of the records is such that it documents movement rather than growth of population;[1] new settlements offered an outlet to the land-hunger of a prosperous peasantry, who were able to realize opportunities for their younger sons which had never before existed. There is probably no need to doubt that the growth of population should be added to the expansive factors influencing the development of the bishop of Ely's estate in the twelfth and thirteenth centuries. But like most of the other factors, it is one which cannot be described with statistical exactness.

If these are the general tendencies, it still remains necessary to make an attempt to describe their working with a greater preciseness and a more exact attention to chronology. Turning first to the bishop's agricultural activities, we are faced once again by the fact that no central financial records of the estate have survived. A connected account, therefore, of the bishop's agriculture cannot be worked out. We must fall back upon scattered indications of progress: the vacancy accounts, which suggest that the bishop's revenue from agricultural sales was still growing in the second half of the thirteenth century;[2] and the few runs of manorial accounts which imply that 'high farming' may have reached its highest pitch of intensity and profitability in the reign of Edward II.[3] Where these pointers fail us, more indirect testimony has to be sought; and in particular that provided by fluctuations in the area of the demesne, in the area of the villeinage and in the amount of service contributed by villein land.[4]

The significance of such indices, moreover, acquires an added weight in view of one major change in methods of exploiting the Ely estate which took place at some time before the early thirteenth century. The system of farming manors for a fixed

[1] See, for instance, the growing community of craftsmen at Needham Market in Suffolk described in the 1251 extents. The names of the inhabitants are indicative of the kind of skills attracted to such a centre: there was a smith, a baker, a cordwainer, a miller, a merchant and a 'huckstere'. But apart from that we are informed only that these men must have moved from elsewhere—from Bures, Stonham, Barking, etc.; Caius 485/489, ff. 334–4 d.

[2] See Table II above, p. 94.

[3] See below, pp. 105–6. This would be in line with the evidence from the Christchurch estate collected by R. A. L. Smith, *Canterbury Cathedral Priory*, pp. 141–3.

[4] See Postan, *TRHS*, 4th ser. xx, pp. 169–73.

return in money or kind, which may have been universal at the end of the eleventh century and which was still the prevalent practice in 1169–73,[1] was replaced by a system of direct exploitation through the agency of reeves and bailiffs—held to account for the current issues of the manor at the bishop's exchequer, and controlled by itinerant auditors and stewards.[2] In this way, the profitability of demesne agriculture would respond immediately to changes in the factors of production; and for this reason fluctuations in the area of the demesne and in the extent and obligations of the villeinage may be taken as fairly sensitive indices of fluctuations in the bishop's income from agriculture.

So far as the extent of the demesne is concerned, there is no direct evidence for the period before 1222. A few scraps of information suggest that, on this estate as elsewhere, some parcels of demesne may have been leased out in the twelfth century;[3] but notices of this sort are few and hardly outweigh others indicating a rapid expansion of the demesne from the later part of that century onwards, continuing at least down to the end of the first quarter of the thirteenth century. The field names of the demesne in the Norfolk Marshland,[4] the demesne assarts at Hadham,[5] the fenland purprestures at Wisbech and those in the Huntingdonshire woodland at Pidley and Bluntisham[6]—all are indicative of the way in which the bishop was adding to his own acres during this period. In the second quarter of the thirteenth century, similar trends can be more precisely measured. In twenty-nine of the bishop's manors between 1222 and 1251 additional land was added to the demesne in the Isle, Cambridgeshire and Norfolk; but this was almost exactly balanced by contraction in the Marshland and Suffolk. In those districts where expansion did continue,

[1] *Pipe R*, 16 Hen. II, 95–6; 17 Hen. II, 115–17; 18 Hen. II, 115–17; 19 Hen. II, 161–2: only Hartest and Rettendon were not at farm and were managed by *servientes*.

[2] There are very few exceptions to this rule; the manor of Hardwick is the only consistent one, though Little Gransden was also at farm in 1251: Caius 485/489, ff. 149, 151 d; PRO Min. Accts, 1132/10, 13.

[3] There are a few notices like that under Hartest, where the heirs of Thomas de Burgo held twenty acres which were demesne in Longchamp's day: Caius 485/489, f. 308.

[4] See above, p. 95.   [5] See above, p. 97.

[6] Cott. Tiberius B II, ff. 110d–11, 143.

a little of it may have been due to purchase of land;[1] but in the main it was still due to assarting.[2] The very slightness of the net gain, however, seems to show that the growth of the demesne was now coming to an end, and that only a small part of the total amount of reclaimed land was going by this time into demesne.[3]

There is, moreover, a certain amount of evidence to suggest that the second half of the thirteenth century was an age of stabilization. There is no obvious sign that demesnes grew any further; notices of assarting dry up, and there may even have been a tendency for some of the land reclaimed at an earlier date to revert to the fen by the end of the century.[4] By that time, too, earlier expansive tendencies had begun to go into reverse, and leaseholds were carved out of the demesne in a few places.[5] In the first half of the fourteenth century this dispersion of the demesne continued to gain ground.[6] It was a tendency

[1] Like the 30 acres of arable and 6 acres of meadow which Hugh of Northwold bought and added to the demesne at Willingham: Caius 485/489, f. 116.

[2] Particularly in the Isle of Ely, where 165 acres were taken in from the fen at Doddington and 36 acres from Chettisham wood at Ely between 1222 and 1251: Cott. Tiberius B II, ff. 86, 97d; Caius 485/489, ff. 19, 60d.

[3] It is particularly significant that the demesne contracted in the Cambridge and Norfolk Marshland where reclamation was being most actively carried out. Wisbech is not untypical; and there the demesne declined from 752 to 719 acres between 1222 and 1251, although one list of new rents describes assarts totalling over 500 acres during the same period: Cott. Claudius C XI, f. 72d; Cott. Tiberius B II, ff. 143, 241d–2.

[4] See the references to decayed rents above, p. 96, n. 7.

[5] Generally these leaseholds are still small, as at Somersham (51 acres), Hadham (22 acres), Bramford (37 acres), Hitcham (5 acres), Rattlesden (15 acres), and Hartest (17 acres). Only in two cases were large amounts of land involved: at Pulham where a large part of the demesne had been leased sometime after 1290 and at East Dereham where most of the demesne of 380 acres seems to have been leased before 1286: PRO Min. Accts, 1132/9–10.

[6] The surviving records permit the compilation of the following (no doubt) incomplete list of leaseholds:

Downham	264 acres, 1299–1337.
Stretham	135 acres, 1316–45.
Linden End	362 acres, 1316–45.
Somersham	51 acres in 1299, 473 acres in 1348.
Great Shelford	50 acres, 1325–46.
Willingham	150 acres in 1357.
Wisbech Barton	income from demesne leaseholds rose from 53s. 4d. in 1320 to £48. 10s. in 1345.

These figures are taken from: PRO Min. Accts, 1132/10, 13, 14, 15; 1133/1; 1135/8; 1307/2; EDR Bailiff's Accts, D 5 (1), D 5 (2), D 8; KR Extents and Inquisitions, Bdle. 9, File 2.

which may have been checked, in places at least, by the Black Death; but that is something which falls outside the period under review. For the moment it is enough that, in the early fourteenth century, the bishop of Ely was becoming a rentier. To some of the reasons for that fact we may return after looking first at parallel trends in the bishop's villeinage.

These trends, we might expect, would be in the main a direct reflection of those changes we have surveyed in the demesne. Yet how far that proposition would be true of the twelfth century is not altogether certain. There is no very clear evidence for a contraction of any magnitude in the size of the demesne during that century; there is considerable evidence for an expansion of the demesne in the later part of the century. On the other hand, as we shall see in the next chapter, a study of the free tenants, *censuarii*, etc. of the thirteenth century would seem to show that in Cambridgeshire almost exclusively, in Huntingdon and Essex to a large degree, and even to a surprising extent in traditionally free Norfolk and Suffolk, these men were commonly recently recruited from the ranks of the villeins, their lands taken out of the acres of the villein land. This diminution of the villeinage, moreover, did not quite cease even in the thirteenth century, although it was turned less often into free tenancies and more often into tenancies at will.

It is true that this may have been only one amongst a number of contradictory tendencies. At least in the second quarter of the thirteenth century, the bishop was extracting an increasing amount of service from his villeins: the total amount of week-work due increased, in fact, on the average by about 10% over the estate as a whole between 1222 and 1251.[1] In a few cases, this may have been due to an increase in the area of the villeinage,[2] although this increase in some places may well have been balanced by a decrease in others.[3] In still fewer cases, the

---

[1] This average, as usual, conceals marked regional variations. The increase in service was slight in the Marshland (1%) and Essex (4%), and considerable only in Cambridgeshire (21%).

[2] Additional villein tenements were created, for example, at Triplow (1), Fen Ditton (2) and Feltwell (1); but there are not many cases of this sort.

[3] There was certainly a contraction of the villeinage at Littleport, Linden End, Little Gransden and Kelshall.

actual amount of service demanded from the villein tenement may have been augmented.[1] But what may have been more important, although less spectacular in its results in any given place, was further progress in defining and registering villein obligations, and in dividing up villein tenements.[2] This division of tenements may represent a continuous tendency stretching well back into the past;[3] it might also mean a real gain in service, since the obligations of the 'half land' were often proportionately heavier than those of the 'full land'.[4]

There are many things, in all this, which suggest that the history of the villeinage may not be quite so much a mere reflection of the history of the demesne as it is sometimes thought to be. If the demesne, in the late twelfth and the early thirteenth centuries, was a growing thing, one tendency in the villeinage was towards contraction. Even if, despite that tendency, the tale of services owed by the bishop's villeins in the early thirteenth century had increased, it is another matter to say how many of those services were performed. In 1299, although the drift away from demesne cultivation had not made large progress in most places, over one-third of the week-work seems to have been sold; and the income from this source was already considerable in 1256.[5] One wonders how far some of the increase in villein services in the early thirteenth century may have been a concealed way of raising rents; how far villein services were increased in order to be commuted. One wonders,

---

[1] A number of instances were adduced by Maitland, *Collected Papers*, II, p. 369; but not all of them can be sustained. The extra work per week he found at Linden and Stretham is not new; it appears in 1222 as ploughing service done over and above the week-work. At Triplow, on the other hand, the villeins do seem to have been made to do an extra work per week between Michaelmas and the following August: Cott. Tiberius B II, ff. 103d, 108d, 219d.

[2] Between 1222 and 1251 one full land was partitioned in each of the manors of Linden End, Hadstock and Fenton and four full lands in the soke of Doddington.

[3] There is further discussion on this point below, pp. 143–5.

[4] This is illustrated by the manor of Great Shelford. There, when a half-virgater did two works a week, a quarter-virgater did only one; but when the former did three works the latter did two; and both of them did three works a week in harvest time. It was the same with boon works. The quarter-virgater did only half the amount of govel ploughing, but he did the same work at haytime as the half-virgater and provided six men in the harvest field against the latter's seven: Cott. Tiberius B II, ff. 216–17.

[5] See Table II above, p. 94.

also, what difference it would make if more were known about the *famuli*. Can it be that, to some extent at least, demesne and villeinage could develop in different directions—the one growing or being maintained, the other contracting or actually providing less than its established obligation for labour—because the gap could be bridged by the employment of 'free' labour? There seems no possibility of answering this question.[1]

Whatever the answer might be, however, the great terrier of 1251 marked the end of an epoch in the history of the villeinage. Thereafter, the area of the villeinage and the obligations to which it was subjected were more or less stereotyped; so far as we can see, there were no new villein tenements, no more adding to the burdens of the villein. On the other hand, with the quickening of the movement away from demesne cultivation at the end of the thirteenth and the beginning of the fourteenth century, the bishop quite naturally wanted less labour from the villeins. This might lead to two different arrangements, both of which had been tried out as early as 1299.[2] All the services of specified tenements might be commuted for fixed contractual rents, though these rents might be variable at the will of the lord from year to year; this arrangement we find in manors like Pulham and East Dereham where a very considerable part of the demesne was already at farm. More commonly, however, any labour services surplus to requirements in any given year were sold at a standard rate. This latter expedient was essentially temporary, and variable according to the vagaries of the farming year. The former, despite all safeguards, was potentially permanent.

It is not surprising, therefore, that even in the middle of the fourteenth century, by which time demesne leaseholds had made further (though still limited) progress, the sale of a fluctuating number of services each year was still much commoner than the leasing of complete villein tenements. But as more of the demesne was leased, so the amount of service sold rose too. At

---

[1] At the same time, this may be one of the important consequences of the growth of population in the high Middle Ages. There was a large supply of labour available and competition for employment kept wages low, just as competition for land kept the levels of rents high. This fact may have contributed something, perhaps a great deal, to the maximization of agrarian profits in thirteenth-century England.

[2] PRO Min. Accts, 1132/10.

Great Shelford average sales amounting to £2 in 1319–31 had risen to £12 by 1340–2; at Wisbech three times as many works were sold in 1345 as had been sold in 1320; at Somersham income from this source rose by about the same amount between 1327 and 1342.[1] The sale of services, already a considerable item in 1299, was a part of the bishop's rent income which was growing rapidly in the early fourteenth century.

Meanwhile, slower progress was being made in leasing complete villein tenements. This practice was still sporadic in 1299;[2] but from that date onwards it gradually became commoner.[3] No doubt it was possible enough for tenements so demised to revert to services in many cases if the bishop wished it;[4] but difficulties might arise. In 1299, the three tenements at farm at Littlebury had been demised to four tenants; one of them, therefore, must have been divided, and it might not be so easy in the future to reintegrate it as a unit responsible for a specific quota of labour service. The peasant land-market was already, as we shall see, making it hard for the bishop to preserve the integrity of the villein tenements; once he began to lease out these tenements for a money rent, the tendencies making for disintegration were almost inevitably strengthened. It became harder, as a result, for the bishop to reverse the steps he had taken to free the villeinage from its labour services.

[1] PRO Min. Accts, 1132/14–15, 1133/1, 1135/8, 1307/2; EDR Bailiff's Accts, D 8.

[2] PRO Min. Accts, 1132/10: at Hatfield there were 2 virgates at farm; at Hadham a cotland; at Littlebury 3 virgates and at Barking 4; at Glemsford 12 acres and at Brandon 4 tofts.

[3] The following list of villein tenements at farm is anything but complete, but it may provide some illustration of the progress made:

Ely	1 (1302), 2 (1316).
Doddington	1 (1302).
Hadham	1 (1302).
Littleport	2 (1302).
Rettendon	3 (1302).
Linden End	1 (1345).
Downham	2 (1357)
Hardwick	all villein land (1357).
Hatfield	4 virgates, 2 half-virgates, 1 cotland (1316).
Somersham	21½ full lands, 17 cotlands, 41 tofts (1342).

[4] Some of the villein tenements put to rent at Somersham reverted to labour in 1347 for reasons which do not seem to be immediately obvious: PRO Min. Accts, 1307/2.

Still, it would hardly be fair to leave an impression that the bishops of Ely were simply drifting into the position of rentiers. The few sets of manorial accounts which have survived from this period suggest that there was much more of policy in these trends than that. They suggest, in fact, that there was a catastrophic fall in agrarian profits in the second quarter of the fourteenth century; and it is hard to avoid connecting the more pronounced turn away from demesne farming during that period with these indications of economic recession. There is little enough to go upon; but what there is can be found in the rolls of the bishop's manors of Great Shelford and Wisbech Barton.[1] The fact that Great Shelford was a very conventional sort of manor, and a manor in which demesne leasehold and commutation of services made relatively slow progress, makes the evidence of its rolls particularly interesting.

At Shelford, then, there can be no question of the severity of the depression which set in about the year 1325. Agricultural income from the manor, which had been averaging about £80 a year between 1319 and 1323, fell by more than a half in the period 1325–33 and averaged only £10 a year during the period 1333–46. The leasing of about 50 acres out of a demesne of 350–400 acres can only have accounted for a small part of this decline of revenue; and by far the most important cause seems to have been a heavy fall in agricultural prices.[2] Exactly the same trend, moreover, makes its appearance in the great fenland manor of Wisbech Barton about the same time. There, the average agricultural income drawn from the manor in the years 1333–48 had fallen by about two-thirds from what it had been in the years 1319–33.

One immediate consequence of this decline in the profitability of demesne agriculture seems to have been to cramp the whole scale of the bishop's economy. First, the proportion of the produce of the manor going into the market was apparently

---

[1] For what follows, see PRO Min. Accts, 1132/14–15, 1133/1 and EDR Bailiff's Accts, D 8 which provide a fairly continuous series of rolls for these two manors from 1319 to the eve of the Black Death.

[2] Without making any pretence of producing weighted averages, some rough figures from the Shelford rolls are indicative enough of the general direction in which prices were moving. In the early 'twenties wheat was selling at from 10s. 6d. to 14s. a quarter; in the years 1325–33 the average price was around 5s. 6d.; in the late 'thirties and early 'forties it was little over 4s.

restricted, and more of it was diverted instead to direct consumption in the bishop's household.[1] Secondly, and from the long-term point of view more important, there was a sharp reduction of capital investment of all sorts in these manors;[2] and one consequence of this was that the contraction of net revenue from the manors was for the time being less marked than the fall in agrarian profits in general. None the less, clearly the agricultural activity of the bishops of Ely was running down; its contribution to the gross income of the manor had fallen by two-thirds at Shelford and by a half at Wisbech before the Black Death. Its place in manorial revenues was more and more being taken by income from rents.

It is time, therefore, to turn back to the main features in the development of the bishop's rent income; features which, in many ways, simply illuminate from another side many of the developments in demesne husbandry which have been under discussion. The expanding share of rent in the bishop's revenue in the fourteenth century was not something either new or unprecedented; for the bishop had long been adding to his rent roll. If there is something novel, at this or other times, the novelty usually consists in changes in the nature of rent itself.

In any fourteenth-century account roll, income that may properly be called rent income would normally at least be entered under a considerable variety of headings. The heading which covered the oldest component of rent revenue was clearly the heading *redditus assise*; although equally clearly this item comprised a far from homogeneous group of payments. It included many ancient dues, some of them of public origin; payments in commutation of personal service and rents in kind; and payments which arose out of the bishop's franchisal privi-

---

[1] This was particularly true of Shelford. In the 'twenties, most of the corn not used in the manor itself was sold. True, 70 quarters of wheat and malt were sent to the lord's household in 1321–2 and 1326–7; but the only other liveries seem to have been 32 quarters of malt in 1328–9 and 8 quarters of wheat in 1325–6. In the 'thirties, on the other hand, yearly liveries seem to have averaged about 70 quarters.

[2] At Shelford the average annual expenditure on new seed was more or less halved after 1325; and after 1333 there was no further large expenditure on the mill, fold or houses. On the other hand, the average wage bill was 60% higher in 1340–6 than it had been in 1319–33 owing to increased employment of casual labour to compensate for commutation. The result was that manorial costs were rising and net income falling again.

leges.[1] But even in the early thirteenth century, customary dues of this sort were no longer a significant proportion of the assized rents, the great bulk of which consisted in payments from freemen's and molmen's holdings. Since so many of these holdings, in turn, had been created during the twelfth century from the villeinage, clearly the arrentation of villein land during the course of that century was one of the things which made a considerable contribution to that body of payments later comprehended under the head of assized rents. Clearly, too, although it is not possible to define precisely the chronological stages through which it travelled, the curve of assized rents in the twelfth century must have risen fairly steeply.

This trend was also projected into the thirteenth century, though it is probable that the steepness of the ascent gradually flattened out. In forty demesne manors the volume of assized rents rose by 20% between 1222 and 1251, and by a further 10% between 1251 and 1299. The sources of this expansion, moreover, can be analysed a little more closely than is possible with the similar tendency at an earlier date. A little of it (though not very much) may still have come from the arrentation of villein holdings; but generally, as we have seen, the tide had turned for the time being against this practice. Something may have been added, though again very little, through the purchase of rent charges.[2] A good deal of it may have been due to a gradual rise in the levels of rents,[3] even to the prosecution of a definite policy to raise rents by Hugh of Northwold.[4] But

---

[1] Such payments on the Ely estate have been carefully classified by Neilson, *Customary Rents*, especially pp. 18, 50, 54, 63, 131 ff., 184–5.

[2] Hugh of Northwold's purchase of 19s. of rent at Kelshall and 8d. rent at Hartest, for example: Caius 485/489, ff. 10, 308 d.

[3] At Pulham, in 1251, the main body of the *censuarii* paid rents averaging 4d. an acre; but a group of *novi feoffati* paid something more like 6d.: *ibid.* f. 224 d.

[4] There are records from in and about 1230 which show that Hugh managed to double (or very nearly) the rents due from eight holdings in Little Gransden, Doddington, Somersham, and Wisbech: Cott. Claudius C xi, ff. 10 d–14; Cott. Tiberius B ii, ff. 256 d–7. It is not, unfortunately, possible to say how these agreements were reached; for the legal record of them is very uncommunicative (see CRR no. 104, mm. 5 d, 26 d, of which the following entry is typical: 'Rogerus capellanus...dat dimidiam marcam pro licencia concordandi cum episcopo Eliensi de placito terre per plegium', etc.). It is clear, none the less, that the bishop missed no opportunity. A gift of land to Chatteris abbey was a chance to raise the rent as the price of the bishop's confirmation: Cott. Julius A i, f. 79; and when a man abducted and married

the main contribution, both in the late twelfth and in the early thirteenth century, seems to have been made by diverting to the rent paying fringe of the estate the major gains from the assarting movement. That is the reason why the bishop's rent revenue increased so much more markedly in areas of extensive reclamation than it did elsewhere. Compared with the average of 20% for the estate as a whole, in the Marshland bailiwick assized rents rose by 60% between 1222 and 1251. As a result, one of the striking things about the fenland—about Doddington[1] or Elm[2] or Wisbech[3] for example—was the way in which large communities of rent-paying peasants had been settled on reclaimed land before 1250. Equally striking, though the scale is smaller, were the additions made to peasant holdings from forest assarts in the wooded areas of Hertfordshire and Huntingdonshire.[4] In brief, in the late twelfth and early thirteenth centuries assarting, and no longer the conversion of the villeinage into free or semi-free holdings, was the method adopted by the bishops to augment their income from rents.

Some of these facts may not be without their particular significance. First, although the methods of achieving their object had changed, the bishops appear to have tried to increase the amount of income they obtained from rents both in the twelfth and in the thirteenth centuries. Secondly, even in the thirteenth century, 'high farming' was not the only method of

the heiress of a tenement in Tilney, the charter regularizing his title was bought at the cost of a higher rent: Cott. Tiberius B ii, f. 172d; Caius 485/489, f. 214d.

[1] There is an early thirteenth-century note of £7. 0s. 6d. 'de novo incremento per assartum' from the fen; and by 1251 new enfeoffments in the whole soke totalled about 600 acres of land producing an income of over £12 a year: Cott. Tiberius B ii, f. 244d; Caius 485/489, ff. 65d–73.

[2] In various memoranda relating to assarts at Elm in the time of Hugh of Northwold, we read of new tenancies amounting in all to over 1200 acres producing £22 of new rents: Cott. Tiberius B ii, ff. 147d, 153d, 242d–4.

[3] One list from the early thirteenth century gives particulars of 500 acres of assarts and £10 of new rents: ibid. ff. 241d–2.

[4] At Hatfield in 1251 very many of the free tenants held assarted land as the whole or part of their tenements; while at Somersham one free tenant had a plot of 90 acres of assart, and all the 100 acres which Sir Giles de Wachesham held in Pidley (a hamlet of Somersham) was reclaimed land granted to him by Bishop Geoffrey de Burgh. Even many of the villeins here had often plots of assarted land for money rents in addition to their regular holdings: Caius 485/489, ff. 109–9d, 112–12d, 157d.

maximizing a landlord's income; the area paying money rents was also extended and more vigorously exploited. Finally, the choice between these two alternatives may have had very little to do with the state of the market. Where the land was well settled, and there was little opportunity for assarting, the very prevalence of customary standards of rent would be likely to check the previous trend towards a dissipation of the villeinage and turn lords, under the stimulus of rising prices for agricultural produce, to a more intensive exploitation of their demesnes and of both wage and villein labour. On the other hand, where there was much land to be reclaimed, the lord might not venture too willingly upon its cultivation when so much of it might be very marginal land. It was easier to divide it up into rent-paying tenures, since their creation here would involve no diminution of demesne or villeinage; the rent from each new tenement could be counted as pure gain.

Up to the middle of the thirteenth century, then, attention can be concentrated in the main upon the history of the various items which went to make up the assized rents of the later account rolls. In the second half of the century, however, the total volume of income from this source ceases to grow at any significant rate; and the amount of each of the individual payments contributing to it seems to have acquired a customary stability that was to endure for the rest of the Middle Ages. One consequence of this was the attempt to develop new types of rent which were more flexible, more precarious, more easily changed as economic circumstances changed. Between 1251 and 1299 the assized rents increased only by 10 %; in the same period the volume of contractual rents of one sort and another increased threefold. It is true that once again this figure is arrived at by adding together a bewildering variety of different items. The most important subjects of short-term, precarious contracts at an early stage may have been mills, fisheries and grazing rights in the bishop's meadows and pastures.[1] But as early as 1251, the same principle had been applied to contracts involving villein land, for some tenements were already held 'de anno in

---

[1] The value of such things likewise seems to have risen very rapidly. The fisheries of Stretham for example, which in 1251 were leased for £8. 12s. 0d., were bringing in about £24 a year in 1345: Caius 485/489, f. 41 d; EDR Bailiff's Accts, D 5 (2).

annum ad voluntatem domini' for money rents which might be as high as 1s. 5d. an acre.[1] By 1299, finally, the invasion of the demesne by leaseholds had begun.

The gradual increase in the proportion of manorial income accounted for by contractual payments of this sort may be illustrated from the manor of Somersham in Huntingdonshire. In 1299 half of the bishop's rent income from the manor was already made up of contractual rents, leaving only half for customary rents and the sale of labour services at the customary rate. In 1342, the share of contractual rents had risen to 57%; in 1381 to 79%; and in 1445 to 91%. Further, these estimates of the proportionate increase of contractual rents as compared with other forms of rent conceal in part the rate at which the former were increasing absolutely in the first half of the fourteenth century. During the whole of this period the bishop was selling progressively more of the labour services of the villeins from year to year; and the proceeds of these sales have to be added to the yield of customary rents. But if customary rents in this way were pushed up from £33 to £53, the yield of contractual rents rose from £33 to £70.[2]

What may have been more important, however, for the time being was the level rather than the ubiquity of these new types of rent. Penny acres, twopenny acres, even fourpenny acres— still common enough in 1251—were little in evidence in the leaseholds and copyholds made out of the demesne and the villeinage in the fourteenth century. When the bishop in 1336 leased 28 acres of demesne at Great Shelford to John Byrne, the latter paid 1s. an acre for it;[3] at Somersham a dozen years later, where 460 acres of demesne were at farm in 26 plots, the tenants were paying from 8d. to 2s. 4d. an acre.[4] It was the same in the villeinage. At Somersham a virgater was farming his tenement for 20s. a year; a century earlier he might have had it for 6s. 8d.[5] Illustrations of this sort could easily be multiplied, pointing to a threefold rise or more in the levels of rents since

---

[1] E.g. Caius 485/489, ff. 184–5, and below, pp. 135–6.
[2] PRO Min. Accts, 1132/10, 1135/8, 1307/2–4.
[3] BM Add. 41612, f. 78.
[4] PRO Min. Accts, 1307/2; we might compare with these rents of about 2s. an acre at Stretham and of 1s. to 2s. 6d. an acre at Downham in 1316: PRO Min. Accts, 1132/13.
[5] PRO Min. Accts, 1307/2; Caius 485/489, f. 101 d.

the earlier thirteenth century.[1] Customary rents there might still be upon the bishop's rent roll, but it was hardly to be expected that they would develop much when these far more lucrative forms of rent were at the bishop's disposal.

Finally, it may be added that some of the economic gains reflected in the high levels of leasehold rents seem to have been preserved even in the recession of the second quarter of the fourteenth century. Not all contracts were maintained; and at least at Great Shelford and Wisbech there was some fall in income from these sources. That indeed is what might be expected; it was part of the essence of these new rents that they were precarious, and revision might now work in the interest of the tenant. But revision, where it took place before the Black Death, seems to have affected in the main the rents paid for mills, pasturage rights and so on;[2] as yet it had hardly touched the rents paid for land. In so far as the bishop was able to maintain these high rents or even something like them, the temptation to disperse more and more of the demesne and villeinage into rent-paying tenements as prices fell would have all the attractions of economic advantage.

It was, in all probability, calculations of this sort which, in the next century or so, made the bishop of Ely into a rentier. This, no doubt, was no straightforward progression. The Black Death must have undermined the new standards of economic rent; the bishop's interest must have shifted from short-term precarious contracts to long-term fixed contracts; and fluctuations in prices during the later fourteenth century may sometimes have retarded the break up of the demesne husbandry. But, whatever may have been the setbacks, the proportion of rents, and of the new forms of rent, in the income which the bishop drew from his manors went on growing.

[1] Comparative figures for the same tenement in the mid-thirteenth and early fourteenth centuries include the following:

Linden End	2s. and 5s. 6d.
Hardwick	2s. and 8s.
Rettendon	5s. and 20s.
Barking	10s. and 20s.
Littleport	2s. and 15s.

[2] At Great Shelford rents for herbage rights, etc. fell by about one-half after 1330; and the farm of the mill was reduced from £10 to £8 in 1326, then to £6. 13s. 4d. in 1327 and finally to £5. 6s. 8d. in 1338: PRO Min. Accts, 1132/14–15, 1133/1.

Yet this growth in the last days of the Middle Ages was merely carrying forward a trend which, under different guises and in different circumstances, may go back to the first bishops. It may find its first roots in a simple need for an income in cash rather than in kind: a need satisfied in the first instance by transforming old food farms into new money farms. It may even have been farmers, called upon to produce more in cash from the manors, who did something in the twelfth century to turn villein lands into free, rent-paying lands; though bishops themselves may have carried on the dissipation of the villeinage, perhaps making good some of the loss of service by increasing the burdens of the villein or by placing two villeins in a holding which had maintained only one previously. In the thirteenth century, the contraction of the villeinage did not quite cease; but more particularly the bishop maximized his cash income by creating a multitude of new holdings upon assarted land, by pushing up the levels of rent and emphasizing the precarious character of the rent contract, and by playing his part in the contemporary 'high farming' activities. When in the fourteenth century the profitability of commercial agriculture was undermined by economic recession, however, he fell back upon the new high rents which the thirteenth-century inflation had made possible. It was a matter then of getting rid of demesne and villeinage on terms that were as near as possible to thirteenth-century contracts. How successful the bishop was in this attempt is not a matter for this study, though it is hard to believe that he can have been fully successful. At least, it was in the course of this final phase of medieval landownership that the peasantry became the heirs both to feudal bishop and high-farming bishop. But the leaseholders and copy-holders of the fourteenth and fifteenth centuries would already find the land full of folk established there in each preceding stage of the continuous drift of medieval landownership from cultivation.

V

THE PEASANTRY

THE peasantry entered into the heritage of the high-farming bishops; but that word peasantry includes many and different sorts of men, and did so even at the time when Edward III was still a young man. There were villeins who continued to labour, side by side with hired workers, in the farmyards and the fields of the bishop of Ely. There were other villeins who were mainly payers of rent, having commuted their service entirely or bought out a substantial portion of it year by year. These rent-paying villeins were beginning to look more like the various other rent-paying tenants of the time—demesne leaseholders, free tenants, and men we may call semi-free tenants who inhabited a shadowy borderland between freedom and servitude. Underneath all of these, there was a submerged proletariat of cottagers, squatters, and even plain landless men. This was still a society which stood half-way between the predominance of a 'high-farming' demesne economy and the absorption of the demesne by what had been originally merely a periphery of rent-paying tenants. It was also this mixed society, rather than a society still cabined by any 'manorial system', which was overwhelmed in the economic blizzard which swept over agrarian England in the later Middle Ages; and all the elements in it, including the servitude in it, helped to draw the lines of social and economic standing which retained some of their force in the peasant England of the fifteenth century and in the agrarian problem of Tudor times.[1]

Where there is so much confusion, it is perhaps best to start with an over-simple distinction: with that broad difference of tenure between the man who holds freely and the man who holds unfreely. No doubt this distinction, even in the thirteenth century, was in the law of England confused (or rather fused) with another—with the distinction between free blood and

---

[1] See Savine, *Quarterly Journal of Economics*, vol. XIX, for the influence of the dead hand of the past upon the legal standing of customary tenants in the Tudor period.

unfree blood. The men who surveyed the lands of the bishop of Ely in 1222 and 1251, however, were not concerned with legal niceties. They were concerned with the way the bishop's land was held; and where difficulties might have arisen they avoided them by inserting between the free tenant and the villein an intermediate category of *censuarii, consuetudinarii*, molmen— men we may call the semi-free. There might be much of the free tenant about their tenurial position. There might also be much of the villein about their personal status. But like the free tenants, they belong to that broad stream of social evolution leading towards a peasant England; if only for that reason, the free and the semi-free must be considered together.

At the same time, it is well to point out at the very beginning that these tenurial distinctions can be used only for a preliminary classification of the peasantry. They offer less and less guidance to social and economic standing as time goes· on. Two sons of the same father might hold, the one as a villein, the other as a free tenant;[1] the free and the semi-free often bear many of the same marks from the tar-brush of an older servility; villein tenants, like free tenants, might hold their tenements for a money rent; and more and more there was room for enterprise, whether a man was a free man or a villein, so that the yeomanry of a later England were able to trace their descent from no common sort of ancestor. Still, the broad distinction of tenure offers a point of departure; and since the road led eventually to an England of rent-paying peasants, the free and the semi-free who were first on that road demand our first consideration.

I

In the bishop's manor at Somersham in 1251, two groups of tenants fall outside the survey of the villeinage. There were fifteen *libere tenentes*, with holdings ranging from 120 acres down to the half acre for which Elyas Puttehund paid 4*d*. a year.

---

[1] This was so at Hardwick in 1251, where Peter de Stavenesby was a free tenant with 3 acres in the fields and a croft of 2 acres for a rent of 6*s*. 6*d*.; he also had 3 acres in another fee which his father had bought. William his brother, on the other hand, appears among the villeins. He owed no labour service except boons; for he held 6 acres for being the lord's woodman and another acre for 2*s*. rent. But he did owe servile incidents: Caius 485/489, ff. 145 d, 148.

Most of them paid only money rents; but five did harvest boons and two of these five (with a virgate apiece) paid pannage, tallage with the freemen, and suit to the manor court. Then there was another group appearing at the end of the extent and called *minuti censuarii*. They did boon service at hay and harvest and weeding time; they paid servile dues like leyrwite and heriot and merchet; they paid an entry fine on succession and carried the bishop's letters each in their turn. But they did not do week-work; they paid a money rent, though if the lord wished he could put their tenements again to works and forgo the rent. In short they were cottars whose labour services had been com-muted. Although the rent they paid had not the permanence of a freeman's rent, these men had already taken a step away from the villeinage proper. Such commutation is one of the sources for the recruitment of the free and the semi-free.[1]

There is nothing peculiar about the two sorts of rent-paying tenants to be found at Somersham in 1251. Manors without some representatives of both of them at that date were not common; and there were no manors without some representa-tives of one or other of them. Of course, the importance of the free and semi-free element in the manor varied from place to place. They were more numerous in traditionally free Norfolk and Suffolk than in Cambridgeshire and Huntingdonshire; they were very numerous in the areas of rapid reclamation, and in the Cambridge and Norfolk Marshland in particular. These are further indications about the origins of the free peasantry. They might be the descendants of the freemen and sokemen of an older England; they might be beneficiaries from the expansion of cultivation during the twelfth and thirteenth centuries.

In one or two instances, the continuous existence of a free peasantry[2] in the bishop's manors can even be adequately documented. That is so in the case of the foreign sokemen pertaining to the manor of Bramford in Suffolk in 1251, then recently purchased from the church of Evreux;[3] they can be traced back through charters of Richard I and Henry II[4] to the

[1] Caius 485/489, ff. 109, 111–11d.
[2] On this whole question see Douglas, *East Anglia*, especially pp. 27 ff., 87 ff.
[3] 'Istud manerium est de perquisicione domini Hugonis episcopi et in comitatu Suffolchie et in hundredo de Bosemere. Sed quidam de forinsecis sokemannis manent in hundredo de Claydone': Caius 485/489, f. 358d.
[4] Liber M, ff. 88, 90.

original grant of the manor by Henry I,[1] and thence to *Domesday Book*.[2] Even in the thirteenth century one of these sokemen was liable for a payment called 'relief' which still had some of the characteristics of the Anglo-Saxon *heregeatu*.[3] In a very similar fashion, the 'tenmanlot' unit of free landholding in 1251 at the Marshland manor of Walpole[4] can be followed back through an early thirteenth-century charter[5] to a time before the middle of the twelfth century, where it appears in a confirmation of the possessions of Lewes Priory.[6] No doubt it goes further back still to the 'landsharing' arrangements of the Scandinavian settlers.[7]

Documentary proof of this sort, however, is not very common. More generally, the continuous existence of a free peasantry from Saxon times is a matter of inference: from traces of ancient tenemental arrangements, of standard rents which may have originated in the transfer of public burdens to private hands, or of a special connection of the free tenant with the hundred rather than with the manor. With the aid of these criteria, it has been possible to show how very generally in Norfolk and Suffolk the descendants of the Domesday freemen and sokemen appear as free tenants and *censuarii* in the thirteenth century. Since so much of the evidence has been drawn from the Ely surveys, so far as these counties are concerned the point need not be further laboured here. It is enough to conclude that, on the lands of the bishop of Ely as elsewhere in Norfolk and Suffolk, ancient freedom contributed one element to the free tenantry of the high Middle Ages.[8]

The same is true in the Isle of Ely. There, as in Norfolk and Suffolk, sokemen if not freemen had survived the Conquest; and

---

[1] Liber M, f. 80, printed in Douglas, *op. cit.* Appx. 60: 'Sciatis me dedisse ...episcopo Ebroicensi manerium meum de Brantfort et 40 solidatas in sochemannis de Claiendone hundredo et in Bosemere hundredo'.

[2] *Dd*, II, 282d–3.

[3] Caius 485/489, f. 365: 'Et dominus habebit palfridum suum cum toto hernesio post mortem eius pro relevio vel meliorem bestiam si palfridum non habuit et si nullam habuit bestiam tunc habebit dominus 5. solidos et 4 denarios tantum. Et post mortem eius filius et heres eius quietus erit de suo relevio propter predictum herietum'; and see Vinogradoff, *Growth of the Manor*, pp. 347–8.

[4] Caius 485/489, ff. 201d–5 and compare Cott. Tiberius B II, ff. 167d f.

[5] Douglas, *op. cit.* Appx. 55.

[6] *Monasticon Cluniacense Anglicanum*, I, 69ff.

[7] On all this see Douglas, *op. cit.* pp. 29–30.

[8] See Douglas, *op. cit. passim*.

very commonly in those same villages where this was true we find in the thirteenth century groups of men called *hundredarii*,[1] one of whom in 1251 still bore the name of Geoffrey le Sokeman.[2] They were more than mere suitors to the hundred court. They paid no rent; instead, they paid 'sixtypenny' (apparently a charge of sixty pence upon every hide, though not a uniform charge per acre within the hide[3]) and wardpenny, no doubt in commutation of a personal guard duty.[4] These payments, moreover, belonged to the hundred,[5] and were probably paid to the hundred bailiff rather than to the manorial reeves;[6] the *hundredarii* were, in many senses, tenants of the hundred[7] rather than of the manor. That fact would seem to suggest that their origins lie before the time when they had been embodied into the manorial structure, to which they were already deeply committed in Domesday times.[8]

Here, then, may well be a case where public burdens have been transformed into private rents; but which, since the bishop of Ely was lord also of the hundred of Witchford, had never been dissociated from the hundred and transferred to the manor. Quite probably these payments, as well as suit of court, formed part of the service to the hundred which the bishop commonly

---

[1] *Dd*, i, 191 d–2; Cott. Tiberius B ii, ff. 100, 105, 107 d–8; Caius 485/489, ff. 47, 53, 63–4 (Doddington, Wilburton, Linden End). On these men see Douglas, *op. cit.* pp. 145 ff.; Vinogradoff, *Villainage in England*, pp. 188–92, 441 ff.; and Homans, *English Villagers in the Thirteenth Century*, pp. 249, 335.

[2] Caius 485/489, f. 53 d; a man called Henry Sokeman of Haddenham was also juror for Witchford hundred in 1286: AR 90, m. 6.

[3] See Cott. Tiberius B ii, f. 100: 'Baldewinus Blancgernun tenet 24. acras et dat de sixtepen' quantum ad eum pertinet, quia sciendum quod quelibet hida dat de sixtepen' duodecim denarios.' It is very probable that the 12*d.* here ought to be 60*d.*; for the Domesday sokemen here held a hide, and the *hundredarii* of 1222 about 120 acres; while in 1251 the total charge for sixtypenny was 58¾*d.*: Caius 485/489, ff. 63–4.

[4] At Linden, at least, each hundredor paid 1*d.* quite irrespective of the size of his holding: Cott. Tiberius B ii, ff. 107 d–8; Caius 485/489, f. 54.

[5] 'Isti denarii...pertinent ad hundredum': *ibid.* f. 50 d.

[6] *Redditus hundredi* appear only once in the enrolled manorial accounts during vacancies—in that for Linden End in 1286 (PRO Min. Accts, 1132/9). For rent paid to the hundred see also a Chatteris charter in Cott. Julius A i, f. 79: 'reddendo inde nobis annuatim et successoribus nostris et hundredo nostro de Ely decem denarios', etc.

[7] 'Et sciendum quod quilibet tenens de hundredo dabit unum denarium de wardpen'': Cott. Tiberius B ii, f. 108.

[8] This would seem to be the distinctive character of the hundredors, rather than the mere duty of representing the manor in the hundred court and other public courts.

reserved when he consented to the alienation of land in the Isle.[1] It is, at least, characteristic that these holdings were very commonly described as consisting of so many acres 'de wara', acres of fiscal responsibility which diverge somewhat from their field equivalents.[2] Sometimes they were even described more exactly still, as consisting of so many acres 'de wara hundredi'.[3] But the charters do more than stress the traditional connection of these holdings with the hundred: they also document the qualified freedom going back to the Domesday sokemen and beyond. They tell us of the land which Ralf the clerk had held of the bishop's socage in Witcham for which he had owed services to the hundred;[4] they tell us also of land which, subject to the bishop's confirmation, Wigar the priest could grant away in Stretham 'sicut liberam terram suam quam dare et vendere potuit', though even then the bishop saved to himself the service which pertained to his hundred.[5] He could sell, but the soke remained? Perhaps not quite; but this charter of the mid-twelfth century is near enough to the terminology of *Domesday* to be suggestive of the connection between the sokemen of 1086 and the *hundredarii* of 1251.

To that extent it is clear that one of the forces which had subjected these men to the lordship of the church of Ely had been the rights the church enjoyed in Witchford hundred. The old public dues of the hundred had become something like rents, though they were still 'redditus assise hundredi',[6] not manorial rents. But it is also clear that at an early stage, this sort of subjection had been reinforced by another. In 1222 Simon Lisle held 16 'ware acres' amongst the hundredors of Wilburton. He paid sixtypence and wardpence to the hundred, he did suit to the hundred; but he also did suit to the manor court and the court of Ely. More, he did two days' ploughing in winter and two in spring in the manor; he found all his tenants for the great boon in harvest time; he paid heriot at his death, and others of his peers owed merchet and tallage as well.[7]

---

[1] E.g. Liber M, ff. 155 ('salvo servicio meo quod ad hundredum pertinet'), 161, 163 (2); Bodl. Laudian Misc. 647, f. 116d; Caius 485/489, f. 11d.
[2] See above, p. 87 n. [3] Bodl. Laudian Misc. 647, f. 116d.
[4] D & C Charter no. 58 (printed below, Appx. XI, p. 286).
[5] Liber M, f. 158, and see above, pp. 55–6 and below, Appx. IX, p. 285.
[6] See Wren's Note Book, ff. 277–80.
[7] Cott. Tiberius B II, f. 105: Caius 485/489, ff. 47–7d.

Hundredors like Simon, in fact, had become dependent upon
the manor as well as the hundred, and that probably before
Domesday Book was made.[1] In fact, their status probably had
changed very little between the Norman Conquest and the time
of Hugh of Northwold. They were in many ways merely an
anachronistic survival, in an arrested stage of depression, from
an older and freer society. It might be added that, in terms of
the contribution they were making to the rent of the thirteenth-
century bishops of Ely, they were probably an insignificant
survival.

No count of the men who may have been the descendants of
the old free peasantry would be likely to come anywhere near to
accuracy; but it is fairly certain that the great majority of the
free and semi-free tenants on the estate in the thirteenth century
were of much more recent ancestry. Most recent of all was the
substantial element contributed by settlers on newly reclaimed
land in the twelfth and thirteenth centuries: settlers whose
numbers we can watch growing in the extents. In such a way,
the bishop might create a new manor consisting of a contractual
group of peasants, as he did at Wiggenhall;[2] and the similar
settlements about Wisbech in the Cambridgeshire fen were
probably, in the main, also established during this period. Elm
is typical enough of these hamlets of Wisbech.[3] Its lands were
extended at nearly 7000 acres in 1251; and of these more than
600 acres were still described as *nova terra, purprestura*, etc.,
pointing to fairly recent occupation. Four military tenants held
nearly half the land; their fees were created after 1166 and even
in the early thirteenth century had not quite ceased to grow.[4]
A further 1500 acres were held by ten *libere tenentes*, with
holdings ranging from 30 to 300 acres for which they paid only
money rents at rates which vary from 1*d.* to 4*d.* per acre. The
remaining 2400 acres were distributed amongst about a hundred
tenements held by *censuarii*—tenements which range from
a mere cottage to one of 150 acres. Their tenants do a few boon
and carrying services, but these are charged upon their houses

---

[1] See above, pp. 63–4.   [2] See above, p. 95.
[3] Caius 485/489, ff. 91 ff.; cf. Cott. Tiberius B II, ff. 153 d f.
[4] In 1222 the Melkesham fee consisted of a core of 380 acres, together
with an assart of 60 acres and 120 acres which had belonged to Roger Coggere;
in 1251 a further 140 acres in Lodwere had been added for which a money
rent was paid.

and not upon the land: perhaps because, as elsewhere,[1] the work of reclamation had been the work of the villagers themselves. For their land, the *censuarii* paid money rents only, which varied widely between tenement and tenement and even between the different pieces of a particular tenement (for many of them consisted of a number of different plots). Commonly, too, there was no very close correlation between acreage and rent: the latter in fact seems to be fixed at a convenient round figure, suggesting some amicable bargain between lord and tenant as the latter took in some additional plot from the fen.

What happened at Elm was happening too at Leverington, Wisbech and Upwell; and for that matter over the Norfolk border at Walpole, West Walton and Terrington. All over this area, the acres of the demesne were being swamped by the rapidly expanding periphery of lands held by rent-paying tenants. The same sort of thing, of course, was happening elsewhere on a much smaller scale—and particularly in the forest lands. There, assart might well form part of a man's holding[2] or even the whole of it.[3] But it was only in the fenland that the fund of reclaimed land was used on a wholesale scale to endow a rent-paying peasantry in the twelfth and thirteenth centuries; it was only there that new land predominated over the old. Even so, that does not altogether minimize the importance of the assarting movement in the creation of the free and semi-free peasantry of the thirteenth century. For some measure of its importance we need only remember that the Marshland bailiwick, where its most spectacular results were achieved, contributed in 1222 one-third, and in 1299 two-fifths, of all the assized rents paid by the tenants of the bishop of Ely.

In such ways, then, the origin of many of the free and semi-free tenants of the thirteenth century can be explained. These men were descendants of the old Saxon free peasantry; while those were men later established upon assarted land or even the men

[1] For Leverington, see above, p. 96. Something of the same joint-stock action by the villagers may underlie the entry in 1251 which tells us that the men of March and Marchford hold about 700 acres from the bishop by charter: Caius 485/489, f. 69.

[2] A block of 60 acres of assart was part of the 80-acre holding which William the farmer had accumulated at Rettendon in 1251: Caius 485/489, f. 182 d.

[3] Like the 100 acres 'de novo assarto' held by Sir Giles de Argentem at Pidley in Huntingdonshire at the same date: *ibid.* f. 113.

who had carried out the assarting. But ancient freedom did not survive everywhere even in 1066; and assarting on a revolutionary scale was only possible in some places. By contrast, the free and the semi-free, though their numbers might vary from district to district, were ubiquitous in 1251. There remains therefore a third and more universal source from which their ranks had been recruited: they were men holding land which had been villein land or demesne land at some earlier period, and probably most of them were holding land which had been villein land. At least, notices in the records which establish the fact that such a plot had once been demesne are not very common. We hear of worn out demesne distributed amongst the *censuarii* at Balsham;[1] 20 acres of demesne leased at Hartest in the last years of the twelfth century;[2] a hide of land at Hadham held in 1222 for military service and boon ploughing.[3] Doubtless, other free tenements were similarly created; but where there is no explicit reference there are no circumstantial signs which identify them. By contrast, it is far easier to identify holdings which had been originally villein holdings.

Once again, the number of explicit references to early commutation are not very numerous. There is a plot of land at Linden End, a half-virgate at Hadstock; two full lands at Balsham; a virgate at Little Gransden; plots of land at Pulham and Terrington—all of these had been villein lands owing works,[4] though that might have been as long ago as the time of Bishop Nigel.[5] But circumstantial evidence suggests that the enfranchisement of villein land had been a far more widespread thing; and for such evidence we can look in particular to the survival in free holdings of the tenemental framework characteristic of the villeinage and of villein obligations which had persisted despite the fact that a man had become a free tenant or a molman.

Traces of villein tenements amongst the free holdings are evident enough even in areas of traditional freedom, where

---

[1] Caius 485/489, ff. 129–30d.
[2] *Ibid.* f. 308: the heirs of Thomas de Burgh 'tenent 20. acras...de wara a tempore W. episcopi, scilicet de dominico, pro 4. solidis equaliter'.
[3] Cott. Tiberius B II, f. 132, and cf. D & C Charter no. 75.
[4] Cott. Tiberius B II, ff. 127, 161d, 184d; Caius 485/489, ff. 54d, 150, 169d, 189d.
[5] Cott. Tiberius B II, f. 127.

many of the free tenantry were descendants of the Domesday freemen and sokemen. At Shipdham in Norfolk, for instance, a very pointed contrast can be made. Most of the free tenants and many of the *censuarii* in 1251 had holdings which seem to have been made up from 10-acre and 12-acre units; but a seventh of the semi-free holdings, on the other hand, were clearly derived from the 16-acre virgate which was the unit of villein holding.[1] Similar traces of villein holdings amongst the free tenantry can be found elsewhere in Norfolk,[2] as they can in the Marshland,[3] Suffolk[4] and the Isle of Ely[5]—all areas in which a free peasantry had a continuous existence. It is clear that, in these counties in the thirteenth century, the descendants of the Domesday sokemen and of the Domesday villeins were standing side by side in the ranks of the free and the semi-free.

It is hardly surprising that similar evidence should be even more plentiful in counties where the free peasantry in the bishop's manors had been less numerous in 1086. This was true of Essex, where at Hadstock, for example, there were only seven free tenants in 1251; but two held half virgates and two others quarter virgates. It is, moreover, specifically stated that the half virgate which Sylvester, son of Henry Miller, held had been at one time *terra operabilis*; and it is probably significant that the coheiresses of Ralf de Brenninge owed tallage with the customers for their half virgate.[6] Many similar instances could

[1] Caius 485/489, ff. 253 d–63.

[2] At Pulham, for example, the 20-acre virgate and subdivisions of it underlie many of the holdings of free tenants and *censuarii*. One of the latter, William Howard, held 46 acres; but he paid a heriot for 20 acres of this, while for the rest he paid only one year's rent (*ibid.* f. 224 d). The inference would seem to be that the core of the holding was a virgate of land that had once been villein land, which had then been added to by purchase from socage lands. At Northwold, too, there were no less than five 48-acre virgate holdings in the possession of free tenants, as well as holdings of 120, 96, 72, 24, 12 and 6 acres (*ibid.* ff. 284–5).   [3] At Terrington and West Walton.

[4] At Hartest, Rattlesden, Hitcham, and Wetheringsett.

[5] The clearest instance here is the manor of Ely itself. There were no free tenants or sokemen there in 1086; but a number of free holdings had been created by 1222. In 1251 the villein holdings were 18, 12 and 6 acres; the extent and numbers of the free tenements were as follows: 36 acres (2), 18 acres (6), 12 acres (1) and 6 acres (3) together with three holdings of 5 acres each: *ibid.* ff. 21–1 d.

[6] *Ibid.* ff. 169 d–70 d. One might compare with this the even more striking case of Littlebury, where there were nine *censuarii*. Seven of them held half virgates and the other two cotlands; all of them did boon services and paid tallage, marriage fine and heriot as the villeins did: *ibid.* ff. 174–4 d.

be cited from the Huntingdonshire villages which make up the soke of Somersham;[1] and it is probably no exaggeration to say that the majority, even the vast majority, of the free and semi-free tenants of Cambridgeshire without the Isle were holding lands which had once been villein lands. The numbers of such tenants were not large, at least by comparison with Norfolk; but at Willingham there were three virgates and two half virgates amongst the free holdings, and strong traces of servility about the services due from them.[2] Much the same might be said of Balsham, Great Shelford, Fen Ditton and Triplow; and in this last village the enfranchisement of the villeinage had not quite finished in 1222. At that date there were still two complete virgate tenements in the villeinage, as well as twenty-three half virgates. But before 1251 one of these virgates had been granted to Ralf the Red for a money rent by the bishop's charter, and the other had been divided, half being held by a free tenant for a money rent, boons and servile dues, the other half remaining a villein holding.[3] At Hardwick, again, the only free tenant of importance held a full land burdened with services obviously servile;[4] at Little Gransden, there were only two free tenants apart from the parson, and he had only a messuage. One, John de Spineto, had two virgates for a money rent together with 4½ acres for a rent, boon service and court service. The other, Geoffrey of Tilney, had a virgate for a money rent and court

---

[1] At Colne the basic unit in the free holdings was the virgate, and three men holding virgates paid tallage with the customers; at Earith there were virgate and half-virgate tenements; at Bluntisham the free tenants held four virgates, three cotlands and three other holdings which add up to a virgate; at Somersham and Fenton the virgate was equally prominent: Caius 485/489, ff. 101–12.

[2] *Ibid.* ff. 116d–17. Thomas the son of Olive, for his virgate, paid only 6d. rent; but he did a variety of boons; carried the bishop's letters; paid tallage, leyrwite, marriage fine and heriot; and did suit to the lord's court, mill and fold.

[3] *Ibid.* ff. 141d–2d; Cott. Tiberius B II, ff. 219–19d. In addition to the one and a half virgates, a 9-acre villein holding had also been enfranchised between 1222 and 1251 on much the same terms as the half virgate.

[4] Caius 485/489, ff. 145–5d and cf. Cott. Tiberius B II, f. 134d and *RH*, II, 539. With some of the services on the bishop's manors may be compared those owed in 1326 by the molmen on the prior's estate; at Newton, for instance, they did boons, they and their *sequela* owed suit of court, they were liable to be reeve or *messor*, they paid tallage, leyrwite, marriage fine and heriot: D & C Extenta Maneriorum, 18 Edw. II.

service; this was definitely villein land which had been granted to him by Bishop Geoffrey de Burgh.[1]

All this is a clear and natural enough result of that twelfth-century movement towards the dispersion of the villeinage about which we now know a great deal more than once we did;[2] although it may have been noted that some villein tenements were also being enfranchised by such thirteenth-century bishops as John of Fountains and Geoffrey de Burgh. Some of the reasons which may have underlain this policy have already been discussed in connection with the economy of the bishop's demesne. Here, however, it may be pertinent to add one minor influence which may have helped to turn a few villein tenements into free holdings—the bishop's need for land to endow his administrative staff.

The workings of this need at a very early date and in connection with a very humble member of the administrative hierarchy can be illustrated from a charter of Bishop Hervey's to which reference has already been made.[3] In it the bishop gave to his reeve at Ditton the tenements of three *rustici* (probably villeins) to hold for rents in money and kind. This grant, moreover, extended to the reeve's immediate heir and to all his other heirs after him; it would seem to be an early form of an instrument granting land to be held freely in fee and heredity.

The way in which such arrangements had stimulated the creation of free tenements in the villeinage is nowhere better illustrated than in the thirteenth-century survey of the manor of Ely itself—a manor where the tenemental framework derived from the villeinage is particularly clear in the description of the free holdings.[4] Two tenements, for example, were burdened with the duty of going to Cambridge to claim the bishop's liberty on the coming of the justices in eyre; they can hardly be of earlier creation than the reign of Henry II.[5] Three others, again, required their holders to be coroners, a duty that can

[1] Caius 485/489, f. 150: 'Gosfridus de Tylneya tenet unam virgatam terre de dono episcopi Galfridi pro duobus solidis et sex denariis equaliter que prius fuit operabilis. Et debet sectam ad curiam domini episcopi.'
[2] See particularly Postan, *TRHS*, 4th ser. xx.
[3] Liber M, f. 145, printed below, Appx. VII, p. 284.
[4] See above, p. 122, n. 5.
[5] E.g. Walter the son of Elyas held 36 acres for 10s. rent, 'et ibit cum senescallo domini et militibus apud Cantebrigiam in adventu iusticiarii ad postulandum ibidem libertates domini': Cott. Claudius C xi, f. 25 d.

only have been imposed towards the end of the twelfth century.[1] Yet another holding was held by a more intimate service, by the serjeanty of being the bishop's baker:[2] an office which can be traced from its first creation by Bishop Hervey down to the time when it was bought out by Bishop John de Ketene in 1310.[3]

Tenements similarly held for administrative service of one sort or another are common enough throughout the estate. Jurisdictional obligations upon the bishop's land were very commonly acquitted by such means: there were tenements upon which lay the duty of representing the bishop's manors in the courts of shire and hundred;[4] and others which seem to have been enfranchised because they provided a man towards the little group of the reeve and four men representing a village before the king's justices or at a royal inquest.[5] The bishop provided not only his baker but also his boatmen with land;[6] and even tenements burdened with purely agricultural duties might, perhaps by analogy with these more honourable serjeanties, slip over into the categories of free or semi-free holdings. This was fairly often so in the case of tenements held by foresters and parkers;[7] but it could happen even in the case of holdings of swineherds, blacksmiths, ploughmen or shepherds.[8]

[1] Cott. Claudius C xi, ff. 26, 26d; Cott. Tiberius B ii, f. 87; the three men who ought to be coroners probably correspond to the three knights who ought to be elected in each county for this office according to the articles of the eyre of 1194: Stubbs, Select Charters, p. 254.

[2] Cott. Claudius C xi, f. 29: John of Hatfield had 18 acres 'pro ministerio custodiendi officium pistrine episcopi'.

[3] Coucher Book, f. 217 (Hervey's charter is printed below, Appx. V, p. 283).

[4] At Triplow, for instance, Thomas the son of Henry held a virgate 'per servicium sequendi comitatum et hundredum': Caius 485/489, f. 141d; and cf. ff. 117 (Willingham), 308 (Hartest).

[5] Ibid. ff. 253, 324, 342 (Brandon, Hitcham, Wetheringsett).

[6] In 1251 Eustace de Tornes had land in Soham for which he owed a rent of 5s. and the duty of sailing the bishop's baggage from Soham to Ely; and John le Steresman had a messuage in Ely for 'navigating the bishop': ibid. f. 21d. John was probably a descendant of that Engelram, steersman of Bishop Nigel, who was given a fishery for 2s. annual rent and 'pro servicio suo de esnecca', a description of his office similar to that found in connection with the king's boatmen about the same time: Liber M, f. 158; Delisle-Berger, Recueil des Actes de Henri II, i, no. 26; Poole, Exchequer in the Twelfth Century, p. 157.

[7] Caius 485/489, ff. 130, 157d–8d, 223d, 324 (Balsham, Hatfield, Pulham, Hitcham).

[8] Ibid. 129d–30, 170d, 174, 227, 308d (Balsham, Hadstock, Littlebury, Pulham and Hartest). These references are, of course, a selection only; but they do illustrate the fact that this was no mere local tendency.

But these sorts of arrangement were probably the device of an early period which was coming to an end in the thirteenth century. Some of these holdings, like the baker's holding, were ultimately bought out by the bishop,[1] just as the king in this same century was converting royal serjeanties into leaseholds held for little silver pennies.[2] In the meantime, however, the administrative and agricultural serjeanties of the twelfth century had done something to determine the way in which property was distributed in the bishop's estate; they had been one factor (though perhaps not a major one) in the creation of the free peasantry.

It is now time to look a little more closely, in the light of what has been said about their origins, at the status and obligations of *libere tenentes* and *censuarii*. We may hardly expect that the facts will be simple facts, for more than one line of social evolution met and mingled in this rent-paying periphery of the bishop's estate. The obligations of some of these men might be determined, both by the trend towards personal and manorial subjection which had characterized the later Anglo-Saxon period and by the great deal of liberty that many a *liber homo* had still possessed at the time of the conquest. Other men might find the measure both of their freedom and of their remaining servility in the fact that once their land had been villein land and their ancestors villein tenants. Yet again, where a man had been settled in the demesne or on assarted land, it might make some difference to the bargain struck between him and his lord whether he was the son of a villein or the son of a free man. 'Omnes homines aut liberi sunt aut servi', Bracton would say; and that would be true enough in the eyes of the law. But the law, and especially a law so Roman as this, was no very good guide to social relationships. In law, there may be no degrees of personal unfreedom; in society, and in his relationships with his lord, it is clear that the tenant of the bishop of Ely

---

[1] Another serjeanty had been sold at Ely before 1222: 'Willelmus filius Philippi tenuit aliquando sex acras que pertinere debent ad ministerium rosci, sed modo eas vendidit et terra illa debet duos denarios et obolum de witepunt.' Again, the serjeanty of looking after the bishop's hawks at Somersham had been commuted for a money rent between 1222 and 1251: Cott. Tiberius B II, ff. 87, 116 d; Caius 485/489, f. 112.

[2] Powicke, *Henry III and the Lord Edward*, I, p. 104.

could he both variously unfree and variously free. That was no more than the natural consequence of the fact that a variety of men had become the bishop's free tenants and *censuarii* in a variety of ways.

In general, of course, the *censuarii* bear the strongest traces of servility: clearly their ancestors had very commonly been villeins by birth, just as commonly their land may have been villein land. The sort of obligations which this involved may well be illustrated by a single example, typical in general terms (if not in detail) of most of the men who fall under this rubric in any manor on the estate. Robert, son of Maud Hovel, had a 20-acre (a virgate) tenement in Balsham. He paid a substantial money rent, and rents of fowls and eggs. He did a variety of boon works at ploughing, hay and harvest times. Like the villeins he paid marriage fine for his daughter, tallage and heriot; he could not sell his colt or ox without the lord's licence; he did suit to the lord's fold and the lord's mill.[1] He was marked off from the villeins only by the fact that he did no week-work and no carrying service; not by his personal status, but by the conditions of his tenure on that single point. There is little doubt that his fathers had been villeins holding in the villeinage. More important, the relationship which stemmed from such an origin seems to have become a sort of norm, to which other relationships with a different origin tended to conform. Men whose ancestors had been sokemen, men whose ancestors had probably been villeins but who had found a holding in assarted land outside the traditional area of the villeinage—such men might be saddled with similar obligations to those acknowledged by Robert the son of Maud.

If there is this much likeness amongst the *censuarii*, there is unfortunately no clear dividing line between them and the *libere tenentes*. It is true that many of the latter paid only a money rent for their holdings—especially in the assarted lands, but more sporadically elsewhere. Yet very many of them did boon services: once or twice even a military tenant did so,[2] and certainly military tenants owed boons for tenements they held as *libere*

---

[1] Caius 485/489, f. 129.

[2] Thomas Aliquid had a hide at Willingham for service of a quarter of a knight; but he also did suit to the manor court and found all his tenants for the ale-boon in autumn 'et ipsemet equitabit cum eis ad videndum quod bene agant': *ibid.* f. 116d.

5

tenentes over and above their knight's fees.[1] The services due from three free tenements at Willingham however, are warning enough not to expect any too sharp a distinction between free and semi-free in our records. In addition to money rents, their holders owed boon services and suit at the lord's court, mill and fold.[2] They were liable to be tallaged at will—though it might be argued on other occasions that such an impost was incompatible with a free estate;[3] and commonly enough the free tenant was liable only for a general aid authorized by the king's writ.[4] They paid marriage fine for their daughters and leyrwite: yet other free tenants were explicitly excepted from the former payment,[5] and free status was regarded as an adequate plea in an action at law for non-payment of leyrwite.[6] Finally, heriot was due after they died, though sometimes it would seem that a free tenant should pay relief rather than heriot[7] or even in addition to heriot.[8]

[1] Philip Lisle and Nigel de Chewelle both had military holdings of the bishop; but they also held as 'hundredors' in Linden End. For these latter holdings they owed boon services, marriage fine and heriot: Caius 485/489, f. 52d–3d.

[2] *Ibid.* f. 117.

[3] It was on this ground that Isabella Atteholdehalle brought an action against the bishop for illegal distraint when she refused to pay: *Year Books*, 34–5 Edw. I, 133–7, 339, 347.

[4] See the terms of a fine regarding land at Terrington in 1246: 'salvo generali auxilio quando ponitur per episcopatum...super liberos homines... per preceptum domini regis'; or the entry recording the tenure of Alan son of Thomas in Totteridge: 'dabit tallagium quando generaliter ponitur per episcopatum per preceptum domini regis': Caius 485/489, ff. 12, 164d. Hugh of Northwold obtained such writs in 1229 to pay his debts and in 1233 to cover the cost of the confirmation of the charters of Ely: *Pat. R*, 1225–32, 271; *Cal. Pat. R*, 1232–47, 21.

[5] John Crikat, holder of a free tenement at Rettendon, did *not* pay marriage fine: Caius 485/489, f. 181d.

[6] Wisbech Hundred, 2 Edw. II (St Barnabas): 'Preceptum est attachiare Aliciam filiam Ade Symond ad satisfaciendum domino episcopo de leyrwite facta cum Johanne filio Ade Reynold etc. Et modo venit dicta Alicia et dicit quod libera est et quod non debet finem facere pro leyrwite etc.' But this was a difficult case. Alice's ancestors had been free, but they had held villein land and performed villein services; so the case was postponed to the next court 'et interim consulendum est'.

[7] This might be true even of a *censuarius* as in the following entry from Hardwick: 'Et si moriatur tunc dabit relevium pro terra sua, sed non herietum': Caius 485/489, f. 148d. At Wisbech, too, relief seems to be the normal charge against the heir of a free tenant, whether he be the holder of a military tenement of 20 acres or merely a shop: Wisbech Hundred, 31 Edw. I (Conversion of St Paul); Wisbech Halimote, 34 Edw. I (Michaelmas).

[8] Alan son of Thomas of Totteridge again 'dabit herietum, scilicet meliorem bestiam domus in obitu suo; et si non habuit bestiam tunc dabit pro

The *libere tenentes* then were various sorts of men: how various, indeed, is brought out very succinctly in the 1222 and 1251 extents of the little manor of Wiggenhall.[1] There was a messuage holder who paid only a money rent 'et est liber'. One holder of land was so free that he did not give marriage fine for his daughter. But there was another in 1222, a priest, who paid marriage fine for his daughter; in 1251 he had been succeeded by two other men, one of whom paid also tallage and relief, the other tallage and leyrwite. Yet another man at this latter date owed tallage, marriage fine, leyrwite and heriot. Yet they were all *libere tenentes*: hardly freemen, but certainly free holders. In other words, it is quite clear that the surveyors were relatively incurious about personal status so far as' classifying the peasantry was concerned, and found the sort of problems which were perplexing Bracton and his predecessors[2] more or less irrelevant to the economic and tenurial classification they produced. Even so, the facts were so various, the sorts of relationship between lord and tenant so numerous, that any real consistency was probably impossible; men would appear as free tenants in one place who in another would have been called *censuarii*, and vice versa. Of course, every jot and tittle of servile obligation was carefully registered as the source of future profit; but in fact the surveyors saw only one great dividing line between the bishop's tenants which really mattered. On one side lay the men who performed week-work; on the other side lay the men who did not,[3] though some of them might be equally men of villein blood and equally liable to the personal disabilities of the villein. Because those disabilities were profitable to the bishop, they were not easily forgotten; they were registered in the extents and continued as the badge of personal unfreedom. So there was no easy transition from tenurial to personal freedom; free tenants, many of whom had been villeins in recent generations, did not easily become free men. They were free only from week-work.

---

herieto tantum quantum dat de redditu assiso per annum. Sed heres nichilominus dabit relevium suum': Caius 485/489, f. 164 d.

[1] *Ibid.* f. 215 d; Cott. Tiberius B ii, f. 172 d.

[2] In 1203 a case involving the status of a typical semi-free tenant in Suffolk proved so difficult for the king's judges that it was postponed 'et inde consulatur dominus G. filius Petri': *Earliest Northants. Assize Rolls, plac.* 793.

[3] At Fen Ditton and Horningsea there was even a category of *liberi cotarii*, cottars who paid only rent: *RH*, ii, 441–2.

Leaving the free tenants for a time, and looking for a moment at their land, there was no necessary reason why it should have always been freely alienable (apart even from specific restrictions imposed in the contract of enfeoffment).[1] There were certainly some socage tenements which could only be sold if the bishop's licence had been obtained.[2] Much of the land held by free tenants and *censuarii*, however, would in the later thirteenth century have been described, not as socage, but as customary land—land which could normally only be alienated by a formal act in one of the bishop's courts.[3] In fact, however, much buying and selling must have gone on, whatever the mechanism of the transaction. One indication of this fact is provided by the constant integration and disintegration of holdings which we can see going on (in the extents) under our very eyes.

It is clear, moreover, that this market in land was already fully active in the first half of the thirteenth century. At Littlebury in Essex in 1251, for example, John of Littlebury's holding was composed of no less than eight separate elements; and Warin the *messor's* 92 acres of four, two of which at least had formerly belonged to other men.[4] At Hatfield, Richard de Blauncheville's 66 acres comprised five holdings: two of them were assarts, another had formerly belonged to Thomas de la Bare, and half a virgate had once belonged to Robert Bolle, though Richard had purchased it from a third party, Geoffrey de Waytesype.[5] In the soke of Somersham, John son of Henry of Colne had even built up a manor by much patient accumulation,[6] one of the sources of the wealth which allowed members of this family to play no inconsiderable part in local

---

[1] Like those many provisions in charters which anticipate the Statute of Mortmain. A proviso prohibiting alienation to a religious house appears as early as a charter of John of Fountains (1220–5): Liber M, f. 171. The same sort of restriction might be embodied in a peasant charter; as when Walter Dho enfeoffed Geoffrey the clerk in a messuage at Sutton, with power to demise it except to religion or Jewry: D & C Charter no. 203.

[2] Liber M, f. 163 (2).

[3] See below, pp. 138–9, 149.

[4] Caius 485/489, f. 173 d.   [5] *Ibid.* f. 157 d.

[6] *Ibid.* ff. 101–101 d: he was holding a virgate of the Prior of Ely; a virgate, a messuage and a cotland formerly belonging to Azo of Colne; two more cotlands; 2½ virgates—one assart, one which had belonged to Henry George, and half a virgate which had belonged to Sylvester the son of Stanina; another 36 acres of assart; and a messuage which had belonged to Robert of Colne.

administration in the thirteenth century.[1] Examples of this sort, and those which show tenements disintegrating as well as accumulating could be multiplied indefinitely; but they are already very familiar.[2] Free tenants were buying and selling land amongst themselves; they were dealing also with the *censuarii*[3] and, as we shall see, with the villeins; and naturally enough such transactions were not restricted by the boundaries of the bishop's own manors.[4] But clearly, at least, there was a very flourishing land-market amongst the peasantry in the estate in the early thirteenth century; in that market high prices were being paid for land;[5] and it was mainly (though soon not exclusively) the free and the semi-free who were paying those prices.

One result of this activity in the peasant land-market was a rapid erosion of standard tenements in the free holdings. No doubt there were a number of factors which contributed to this end. Because the services performed by free tenants and *censuarii* were not closely tied to the size of their holdings,[6] the

[1] This family had other lands in Caxton, and at the latest by the fourteenth century half a knight's fee in Mepal and other lands in Steeple Morden: *Cal. Inq. pm*, I, no. 46; *RH*, I, 54; II, 542; *FA*, I, 151, 173; AR 86, m. 7; Liber M, ff. 605, 606. John's father, Henry, was sheriff of Cambridgeshire and Huntingdonshire 1236–42; and Baldwin, one of his descendants, a most active figure in local affairs at the beginning of the fourteenth century who represented Cambridgeshire in parliament three times in 1312–13.

[2] See Douglas, *East Anglia*, pp. 61–4.

[3] At Terrington, for instance, one free tenant in 1251 had added to his 12-acre holding no less than 33 acres in divers plots acquired from the 'husbonds' of the bishop (holders of lands which had owed labour service as recently as the time of Bishop Eustace): Caius 485/489, f. 189d.

[4] At Hardwick there is a note that two of the free tenants also hold land they have purchased 'de alieno feodo', for which they have to pay a small rent to the bishop as well as the due service to the feoffor: *ibid.* f. 145d.

[5] So we may judge from prices being paid later in the thirteenth century and at the beginning of the fourteenth century. At Downham, men were paying 21s., 36s., even 44s. an acre for arable land; at Ely 26s. 8d.; at Sutton prices which range from 15s. to 44s. once more. There were transactions in which large sums passed: as when John Pelryn sold 20 acres for £40 to Geoffrey de Fresyngfeld (though the latter may have been acting for the prior); and there were astute dealers in land like Thomas de Wulwenhaye, who bought a messuage and four acres for 10 marks, and sold it again almost immediately for £20: D & C Charters nos. 193, 209, 269, 314, 323, 749, 761, 804, 942, 958–9, 966, 1007.

[6] At Hardwick, for example, there was little difference between the boon services performed by Henry le Eyr for his 20 acres and those of William the son of William for a croft containing 1 acre: Caius 485/489, ff. 145d, 148d.

bishop had not the same interest he had in the villeinage in maintaining the integrity of tenements. A contributory factor in Norfolk,[1] in some parts of the Isle,[2] possibly even in some Cambridgeshire villages[3] may have been the fact that socage tenements were often partible between heirs male. Such a custom might put these tenants 'clean outside the common law';[4] but it was apparently accepted and enforced by the bishop's courts.[5] At the same time, by favouring the creation of uneconomic tenements through continuous subdivision, it must have acted as a stimulus to acquire land to supplement an inadequate holding and have provided a fund of land available for purchase in the shape of holdings that could no longer support a family.

The results are clearly evident in the mid-thirteenth century extents. In Norfolk and the Marshland, particularly, where buying and selling of land was combined with the disintegrating effects of partible inheritance, most of the free tenements were held, not by individuals, but by groups. These groups may sometimes have been merely coheirs; but far more often their members show no signs of relationship one to the other; and very commonly a man may have a stake in a number of such groups. This, in turn, was no more than an illustration of a far

[1] The common occurrence of partible inheritance in Norfolk was noted long ago in P & M, ii, 270 and see also Homans, *English Villagers in the Thirteenth Century*, pp. 109ff.; the many examples in the Ely extents, therefore, need hardly be quoted. Similar customs in Suffolk leave a number of traces in the records: e.g. CRR no. 104, mm. 9d, 19.

[2] At Elm in 1251 amongst the *consuetudinarii* there were no less than twelve pairs of brothers holding land; at Leverington there were six pairs of brothers, five lots of three brothers, and one lot of five brothers; at Wisbech amongst the *novi feoffati* four pairs of brothers, one lot of three brothers, and one or two cases of holdings in the possession of brothers and their nephews (i.e. their brother's sons): Caius 485/489, ff. 75–5d, 85–7, 92d–95d. There is also a twelfth-century charter from Witcham in the south of the Isle where the bishop permits a man to divide his hereditary lands between his two sons: Egerton MS. 3047, f. 62d (printed below, Appx. VIII, p. 285).

[3] On the prior's manor at West Wratting in 1318 Alan and Richard Sewale held 15 acres 'conjunctim' as heirs of their father: D & C Extentat Maneriorum, 12 Edw. II.

[4] *Year Books*, 2–3 Edw. II, 95–7 (Emneth, Norfolk).

[5] Wisbech Hundred, 31 Edw. I (Circumcision): 'Petrus Wedircok capellanus dat domino 12. d. ad habendum equalem porcionem de terris et tenementis quondam Symonis Wedircok patris sui, ita quod dividentur per halymotum de Leveryngton et ballivum et alios legales homines eiusdem ville.'

more widespread tendency. As the free and the semi-free created sub-tenancies in their holdings, and themselves became sub-tenants of other men, a great shuffling of actual occupation took place. There is no reason to suppose that this was reflected very accurately in the bishop's records—indeed, there is good reason to suppose that it was not accurately reflected;[1] so long as the original tenant remained primarily responsible for the service due from the land, that was what concerned the bishop. The mayor of Lynn might be one of the bishop's tenants at Wisbech; and the bishop no doubt held him responsible for the $1s. 4d.$ rent due from the $7\frac{1}{2}$ acres he held. It is less likely that the mayor cultivated this land; but we will probably never know who did.[2] In other words, the tenurial pattern revealed by the extents is no longer a very safe guide to the economic occupation of the free land.

At the same time, in so far as the extents do provide a rough indication about the way land was distributed, they do seem to reveal one consequence of the flourishing market in free land. By contrast with the still more or less ordered succession of villein grades, there was already much variety in the economic standing of free and semi-free tenants in the first half of the thirteenth century. At Totteridge in Hertfordshire in 1251 one man had less than an acre of land; seven had between 1 acre and 10 acres; eleven between 10 and 20 acres; six between 20 and 30 acres; and four more than 30 acres.[3] At Littlebury in Essex at the same date, six men had under an acre, and there were other holders of 1 acre, 2 acres (2), 4 acres (3), 8 acres (2), 15 acres (2), 18 acres, $27\frac{1}{2}$ acres, 45 acres, $92\frac{1}{2}$ acres, 342 acres.[4] At Doddington in the Isle, again, there were eight men with under an acre; twenty-three had between 1 acre and 10 acres; seven between 10 and 20 acres; three between 20 and 50 acres; four between 50 and 100 acres; and one man had over 100 acres.[5]

One trend is quite clear: a few men were building up very substantial holdings indeed. Geoffrey the clerk at East Dereham

---

[1] In many cases, there is simply no information given about the degree of peasant sub-infeudation, as at Triplow where we know that Thomas the son of Henry had 2 virgates and William the archdeacon 6 acres of the bishop; but only that William had also some of Thomas's land (not how much): Caius 485/489, f. 141 d.

[2] *Ibid.* f. 74. [3] *Ibid.* ff. 164 d–5.
[4] *Ibid.* ff. 173 d–4. [5] *Ibid.* ff. 63 f.

in 1251 was showing already genuine yeoman enterprise: he held himself three messuages and 36 acres in no less than eight separate parcels; and over and above this he was a partner with another man in a tenement of 13½ acres, and with yet another in an 18-acre holding.[1] Even in 1222 Ralf the clerk had accumulated four different holdings to make up his 41 acres, though this tenement had disintegrated by 1251,[2] by which date part of it had been acquired by Walter of Buckenham, whose 90 acres had previously been held by seven different men.[3] In the Marshland, some very large holdings had appeared. At Elm in 1222 Oky at the Bridge already had a tenement of 70 acres; in 1251 his son John had added to this 193 acres brought to him by his wife and 32 acres he had bought from Thomas at the Hall—a total in all of 295 acres.[4] True, these were Marshland acres; nevertheless, John Oky and his like were already considerable farmers. They might also be considerable sheep farmers —and yet owe heriot at their death like any of the villeins.[5]

If veritable yeomen were appearing at the top of the scale, there was also at the other end a number, often a considerable number, of very small men. That was true in Norfolk where, at Shipdham, ten out of twenty-seven free tenants had less than 5 acres; it was true also in Cambridgeshire at Fen Ditton, where nine out of thirteen free tenants had similar minute holdings.[6] Of course, such figures cannot be taken at their face value. In villages divided amongst several lords, a small holder in one manor may be an important tenant in another;[7] and in any case, the extents record liability for rent and service rather than the actual distribution of land. Still, having made all such provisos, there may well be a residuum of free tenants who were in fact

---

[1] Caius 485/489, ff. 241 d, 243.

[2] Cott. Tiberius B II, f. 181; Douglas, *East Anglia*, pp. 62–3.

[3] Caius 485/489, f. 269.

[4] Cott. Tiberius B II, f. 154; Caius 485/489, f. 92. We might compare with this a widow's holding of 229 acres at Elm in 1319, which included 10 acres of recent purchase and 80 acres leased from the bishop for term of life: Elm Halimote, 12 Edw. II (Epiphany).

[5] Caius 485/489, f. 35 for a grant of a fold for 100 sheep at Littleport to a man who owed heriot. [6] *Ibid.* ff. 121 d–2, 252–3 d.

[7] The case of John Segyn at Fen Ditton is instructive. He had only an acre in the bishop's manor in 1251; but in 1279 we find that he had an additional 34 acres of his brother Alan in the same vill; and in 1261 he was claiming rights of fold there and was in possession of a considerable holding in Great Shelford: *RH*, II, 441; AR 82, mm. 4, 6.

small men. In some places, bye-employments may have provided some compensation for exiguous holdings of land—in the growing market towns like Needham Market and East Dereham;[1] in the forest land[2] and the fen,[3] each with their peculiar industries. But the general economic trend, once the lord's interest in the integrity of peasant holdings was removed, seems to have been towards a rapid differentiation amongst the peasantry: if there was concentration of property in a few hands at the upper end of the scale, this almost inevitably produced impoverishment at the other end. This, indeed, was to be the general direction in which the peasant economy evolved in the later Middle Ages;[4] but it had already modified very markedly the social structure of the rent-paying peasant fringe by the early thirteenth century. Whatever the law might say or the surveyor, the free and the semi-free at that date were no longer (if they had ever been) anything like an economic class. Amongst them we can find every sort of man from quasi-yeoman to pure proletarian—a man from whose roof the rain fell upon his neighbour's land.[5]

One final point calls for notice. By the middle of the thirteenth century, the expansion of the classes described as free tenants, *censuarii*, etc. seems to have been to all intents complete. Such tenements tended to be tenements in fee and heredity; they were created by contracts which might obtain the protection of the royal courts; and the terms of the contract had a finality about them ill-suited to an age of continued inflation. As a result and as we have seen, the curve of assized rents began to flatten

---

[1] On Needham Market see above, p. 98, n. 1; the *novi feoffati* at Dereham had only 47 acres of land amongst fifty-one tenants; but they included such suggestive names as dyer, potter, baker, vintner, tailor, smith and even Master Ralf the doctor. Some of them, too, had workshops ('fabrica') in the market: Caius 485/489, ff. 247d–8d.

[2] For the potters and charcoal burners of Somersham, see Cott. Tiberius B II, f. 117d.

[3] Richard son of Thomas had a mere messuage at Wimblington and Richard Gase only 12 acres of new assart; but between them they had a fishery in Stanimere for which they paid the substantial rent of 13s. a year: Caius 485/489, ff. 62d, 65, 65d. On the 'amphibious race' of men at medieval Littleport, whose movable wealth consisted mainly of boats, nets and bundles of sedge, see also Maitland, *Court Baron*, p. 107.

[4] Tawney, *The Agrarian Problem in the Sixteenth Century*, pp. 72 ff.; and cf. Hilton, *Economic Development of some Leicestershire Estates*, pp. 94–105.

[5] Stepniak, *The Russian Peasantry*, p. 75.

out in the later thirteenth century, and was overhauled and surpassed by the growing volume of contractual rents. Even in 1251 there were signs of the times. Villein holdings were still being turned into rent-paying tenements; but they were now tenancies at will and they remained within the survey of the villeinage.[1] In this sense, in the thirteenth century, twelfth-century practices were decisively reversed; but this reversal did not change the direction of economic evolution, merely the forms which that evolution assumed. The incidental profits of villein land and villein status were preserved for the peasant England that was to come; the insecurity of villein status and villein tenure made a contribution to the more flexible types of rent-contract devised in the thirteenth century and put into widespread operation in the fourteenth; and ultimately the copyholder and the leaseholder, rather than the freeholder, became the typical peasant farmer of the later Middle Ages.

II

In these respects, the surveys of 1222 and 1251 marked the end of a period. They defined the broad types of land and men; and this classification of land and men which they laid down, with the burdens appropriate to each holding, remained for many generations to come.[2] The drift from villeinage into freedom was checked; from 1251 onwards right down to the end of the Middle Ages 'the manor seems to have kept with wonderful conservatism what we may call its external shape'.[3] In other

---

[1] At Balsham Adam Marshal gave 5s. 10d. de novo for the works due from his virgate; at Willingham nine or ten tofters made a money payment for their works at the lord's will, though they still did their boon services; at Littleport the services of one full land and one 9-acre tenement had been similarly commuted; at Stretham one cottar paid 5s. for relaxation of his works; at Rettendon two tenements 'que soletur esse operabilis' had been turned into tenancies at will by Hugh of Northwold, and nine others had been so converted which had owed works in the time of Bishop Eustace. Some of these were held 'de anno in annum ad voluntatem domini' and in all 138 acres were involved: Caius 485/489, ff. 37d, 45, 119d, 132, 184–5.

[2] The authority of the 'terrier' is still clearly unimpaired at the beginning of the fourteenth century. Reference could be made to it to determine the proper liveries to boon workers at Shelford in 1322/3; it could be vouched as warranty for a man's title to his land in the manor court at Littleport, and for settling the rights and duties of the 'undersetles' there: PRO Min. Accts, 1132/14; Maitland, Court Baron, pp. 133, 146.

[3] Maitland, Collected Papers, II, pp. 369–70.

words, the tenemental framework of the villeinage persisted; villein acres were still unfree acres or at best customary acres. Equally, the descendants of the men who held such acres were unfree men, irrespective of what or where they continued to hold. In law, those were the facts: but economically the picture was very different. Even in the thirteenth century dealings in the peasant land-market had made inroads upon the villein land; by the end of our period those inroads had become deep indentations. The 'external shape' of the villein tenements might remain; but that shape was ceasing to have exclusive reality in economic fact.

Before dealing with these changes, however, we must look a little more closely at the villeins. Broadly speaking, as we have seen, they were distinguished by the surveyors as the men who owed week-work; broadly speaking, indeed, that was still true at the end of the thirteenth century when, though many works were being sold, few had yet been commuted as a normal arrangement. But this fact alone did not make them into an economic class; in fact quite clearly there were at least three main groups of men who would be called villeins. There were men with complete standard tenements; there were men with half standard tenements; and there were cottars, men with a mere acre or so who could not have subsisted entirely on their land. The common ground between them was the sort, though not the quantity, of their obligations to the bishop.

A number of these obligations were incident, not so much upon the villein as upon the villein holding. First and above all, in this context, was regular labour: roughly an equal burden upon equivalent holdings throughout the estate. This basic obligation had, in turn, a number of consequences. The holder of a tenement had to be capable of shouldering it: he could not be too young, too infirm or too old;[1] and he had to be able to keep the tenement in a state of cultivation and repair adequate

---

[1] See for an example Sutton Halimote, 18 Edw. II (St Valentine). John Muchet had died holding a virgate of land, and Agnes his wife surrendered it into the lord's hand for the use of her son Peter because she was old and infirm; but the seneschal was doubtful of Peter's ability to pay the entry fine, nor could the latter find sureties that he would perform the services. In the end Peter was given the holding 'on approval' until Michaelmas to see if he was 'sufficient'.

for a work-producing unit.[1] But with these qualifications, and although villein land was unprotected by the king's courts, normally villein holdings were heritable holdings according to customary rules enforced in the bishop's own courts: that was doubtless the easiest method of guaranteeing that the due service would always be forthcoming generation after generation.[2]

A further corollary to the function of the villein holding as a unit upon which labour service was assessed was that, in theory at least, it was inalienable and impartible. From a very early date it may have been hard to enforce that principle; and in the end the rule seems to have been that, whatever happened to parcels of the tenement—even if they had been demised to someone else—the liability of the bishop's immediate tenant for the service due remained unimpaired.[3] At the same time, this rule may reflect a change which was taking place in the lord's attitude. For a long time, the bishop set his face against the disintegration of villein holdings and backed prohibition with confiscation.[4] But by the reign of Edward II transactions in villein land had become a flood; and the bishop in the end seems to have given up insistence upon prohibition for insistence upon

[1] For a half land and cotland taken into the lord's hand because they were not properly maintained, see Sutton Halimote, 6 Edw. II (Christmas).

[2] Generally villein tenements went to the eldest son, though there were some cases where the village custom of partibility might even apply to the villeinage: Homans, *EcHR*, VIII, pp. 48–56. For the way in which succession was dealt with in the bishop's courts, see for example Wisbech Hundred, 33 Edw. I (Pentecost): 'Agnes Eyr, qui nuper obiit, tenuit de villenagio domini medietatem unius messuagii et terciam partem unius virgate terre que debet heriettari. Et venit Robertus Eyr et petit se admitti ad hereditatem tanquam filius et heres et dat domino pro herietto etc.' Quite commonly from this stage the procedure follows that of an inquest *post mortem* in the higher ranges of society. A jury was empanelled in one of the bishop's courts to declare what holding a dead customary tenant had held and who was the next heir. This verdict given, the heir was admitted in the presence of the court: e.g. Wisbech Halimote, 34 Edw. I (Michaelmas); Wisbech Curia Bondorum, 5 Edw. II (Ascension).

[3] Wisbech Curia Bondorum, 11 Edw. II (Purification): Walter Ketil is allowed to demise 3 acres of villein land to Reginald the son of Stephen for a term of five years 'et predictus Walterus et heredes sui acquietabunt... omnia servicia et consuetudines que ad predictam terram pertinent'; and for what appears to be a similar case see Wisbech Hundred, 35 Edw. I (Lent).

[4] E.g. Wisbech Hundred, 31 Edw. I (Circumcision) and 34 Edw. I (Lent). In the latter year the bishop seems to have set on foot a real campaign against unlicensed alienation of villein land, and special *custodes* were appointed to look after such land taken into the lord's hand: Wisbech Halimote, 34 Edw. I (Michaelmas).

registration in his court, so that at least he could make what profit he could from the entry fine which attended upon the transfer of land.

A few miscellaneous burdens to which holders of villein tenements were subject may be briefly mentioned. Suit to the bishop's mill was almost universal in 1251; suit to the lord's fold was less common and was sometimes restricted to the cottars.[1] More or less universal again was prohibition of the sale of young oxen or colts: either to give the bishop a right of pre-emption, or so that the stock of plough-beasts in the villein holding would be maintained. The payment of heriot, finally, at the death of the holder of a villein tenement was again all but universal. In 1251, in most places, this was commonly the best or second-best beast the villein had; and a money payment was exacted only if the villein had no beasts of any sort.[2] By the beginning of the fourteenth century, however, it was far more commonly a money payment—an entry fine for succession to villein land like the entry fine payable on alienation. True, the heriot was still sometimes exacted over and above the entry fine, sometimes in kind though by this time more commonly as an additional cash payment; indeed, it might continue to be exacted for many generations to come.[3] But on frequent occasions there is at least no mention of it in the court rolls; presumably it had been merged with the entry fine, and, even if exacted, was commonly dwarfed by the latter. For entry fines were an important and profitable charge, not least because they partook of the arbitrary character of many charges against villeins.[4] That was one good reason for seeing that the identity of villein land, even after it had ceased to be burdened with labour service, was not lost to sight.

But villeinage, we know, had its personal as well as its tenurial

---

[1] As at Ely itself: Caius 485/489, ff. 25 d–27.

[2] *Ibid.* ff. 67 d, 147, 271–2.

[3] On the fees which the Lisles and the Pelhams had held of the Bishop in Cottenham, the tenant lands were still said to be heriotable when the village was enclosed in 1843: CUL Add. 630 (87).

[4] The profitability of entry fines is suggested by the fact that, at the prior's manor of Sutton in the decade beginning 1304, they accounted for about 75% of the profits of his halimotes and leets there. Their arbitrary character is equally marked. The entry fine for a cotland might be 1s., 4s. or 10s. The entry fine for a full land might be 30s., 40s., 46s. 8d., 50s. or even 100s. Those for miscellaneous plots of land range from 1s. to 35s. per acre.

aspect;[1] and the bishop had good reason, too, for not losing sight of his villeins. So much we may judge from the case of Adam, son of Bartholomew the Pinder, heard in the hundred court at Wisbech in 1307. He had sought the seneschal's permission to alienate both his villein and his free land to Ralf Hawys; more than that, apparently he wished to become a clerk. So the hundred court ordered the halimote to look into the matter, and a jury empanelled there declared that, if Adam became a clerk, the lord would lose his bodily service; and that, if he were allowed to sell his lands as well 'the lord would lose a man completely and in process of time the whole succession of his blood'.[2] The value of this blood seemed little impaired by the fact that Adam's father had been doubtfully sane; and the jurymen were compelled to admit that Adam himself was somewhat queer. So a 'man', a villein man, was valuable as such; and not merely as a labourer. His value lay in the personal incidents of servility.

These incidents were not numerous. Firstly the villeins could be tallaged at will; and this might produce some considerable revenue (the king's keepers made tallage yield £190 in 1298, £215 in 1290 and £400 in 1286).[3] Secondly, the villein was justiciable in the bishop's courts, and justice was a profitable thing. Thirdly, the villein paid the fine called leyrwite if his daughter became pregnant outside the bonds of legitimate matrimony.[4] Fourthly, the villein generally[5] paid a fine upon the marriage of his daughter and occasionally of his son;[6] sometimes he had to pay when he himself married.[7] Fifthly, the

---

[1] P & M, i, pp. 358–9.

[2] Wisbech Hundred, 35 Edw. I (Lent): 'Dicunt in hoc quod dominus amitteret unum hominem totaliter in principio et in processu temporis totam successionem sanguinis sui.'

[3] PRO Min. Accts, 1132/9, 10; 1307/2; Madox, *Exchequer*, pp. 429–30. In 1256 the villeins of the whole estate and the free tenants of the Isle of Ely were tallaged to the extent of £250: Pipe R, no. 101, m. 4.

[4] Though the girl might have to pay herself if she was no longer in her father's custody; and if her seducer later made an honest woman of her, he might be excused payment of a marriage fine: Caius 485/489, ff. 102–4, 123.

[5] But at Hatfield 'si...filiam suam maritare voluerit alicui consuetudinario domini in ista villa tunc non dabit gersumam pro ea, nisi maritaverit eam alicui homini libero seu alicui de alieno feodo': *ibid*. f. 161 d.

[6] *Ibid*. ff. 68, 70, 245, 347 d.

[7] *Ibid*. f. 67 d. His widow might likewise have to pay a fine if she remarried: *ibid*. ff. 102–4, 153 d; Wisbech Hundred, 2 Edw. II (St Margaret).

villein was tied to the manor; he could not withdraw from the lord's subjection[1] or, if he did so, he had to pay chevage to the bishop in recognition of the latter's lordship.[2]

These disabilities of villein status were an important sanction in maintaining the stability of the villeinage as well as a source of profit. They allowed the bishop periodically to reassert his lordship in a pointed manner. He could exercise some control, in his authority over villein marriage, upon that mingling of free and villein blood (and all the tenurial tangles which might follow) which created so many insoluble problems. He could take action through the coercive machinery of his own courts which, so far as the relation of lord and villein were concerned, were courts of last instance. So a villein was profitable; where status and tenure combined in a villein holder of villein land, he was even a piece of property. If a villein was a man who could be lost, he was also a man who could be granted or sold, he and his heirs for ever, with his land and his services, and possibly without his land.[3]

This question of villein status becomes increasingly important with the passage of time. In the early thirteenth century, the personal obligations of many free tenants and perhaps most molmen were hardly distinguishable from those of men who held by labour service. But as these men escaped from the villeinage, it may well have been more difficult to maintain intact the marks of their villein origin. On the other hand, as the creation of free holdings slackened, the very intrusion of rent-paying tenancies into the villeinage and the disintegration of villein holdings

---

[1] E.g. Wisbech Halimote, 34 Edw. I (Michaelmas): John Mariot and Nicholas his son have withdrawn 'extra subiectionem domini', so their lands are immediately taken into the lord's hand.

[2] In 1251 twelve men from Kelshall (Herts) were paying capons as chevage because they were living on the abbot of Wardon's fee at Horwell and at Therfield, Westmill, Sandon and St Albans: Caius 485/489, f. 155.

[3] See for instance D & C Charter no. 70, a charter of Hugh of Northwold: 'Noveritis nos concessisse et dedisse . . . priori et conventui Elyensi Gummerum filium Radulfi Muscelberd cum tota sequela sua et cum tota mansione simul cum tota terra sua quas de nobis tenuit in villa de Ely etc.'; and for other sales or gifts of villeins, see Liber M, ff. 184, 185, 194. For the sale of serfs 'severed from their tenements', see P & M, I, p. 414 and also Bodl. Laudian Misc. 647. f. 121 for what seems to be an instance of it: 'Sciant presentes et futuri quod ego Johannes filius Willelmi . . . vendidi domino Eustachio Elyensi episcopo Godwinum Mukere cum tota sequela sua nativum meum pro undecim marcis mihi solutis.'

(which we must notice in a moment) laid an increasing emphasis upon villeinage as a status. It mattered that a man was a villein, even though he held no tenement from his lord and was not to hold one in the immediate future,[1] even though in fact he was a servant in the employment of another.[2] This status was still profitable to the lord in the incidents it entailed, even in the last resort because it could only be extinguished by the villein buying from the lord a charter of manumission.[3]

In all this, there is a point of some significance. In the early thirteenth century, we seem to catch glimpses of an ideal villein—an ideal from which even then reality may have been departing but which, as a traditional notion, we may take the more seriously the further back we go. A villein then was a holder of villein land, land which owed regular labour service; he was also personally a villein, subject to servile incidents and seignorial coercion. By the beginning of the fourteenth century, on the other hand, this connection between tenure and status was being ruptured. A man could be a villein and yet hold no land or hold free land; he could live elsewhere and work for another; he could do no labour service; the lord's right over him had such slight intrinsic value that it could simply be bought out for a cash payment.

Many things, no doubt, made their contribution to this result. The gradual drift of landownership from cultivation from the twelfth century onwards whittled away both the area subject to labour and the determination of the bishop to maintain the integrity of labour-producing units. But this solvent from above was reinforced by economic and social movements amongst the

[1] Sutton Halimote, 20 Edw. I (Nativity of St John): '12 d. de Waltero Aylbern quia traxit bona et catalla sua super feodum episcopi: in misericordia. Walterus Aylbern cognovit se esse servum domini prioris et de servili condicione. Et quia nullum tenementum tenet de domino, set se esse sub advocacione domini prioris eadem condicione sicut ceteri villani, quousque aliquod tenementum possit recipere de domino, dabit quolibet anno domino priori 1. gallinum ad Nathalem domini et 6. ovad [sic] ad Pascha.' Walter was soon taught some of the consequences of this recognition; for a few lines further on we read: 'De Waltero Ailbern pro licencia se maritandi 18 d.'

[2] For a fifteenth-century example on the Ely estate, see *Select Cases in Chancery*, p. 154.

[3] Robert Richard, in the case quoted in the previous note, paid £10 for his freedom; in fact the bishop seems to have been doing a flourishing trade in manumissions in the fifteenth century; see Liber B, nos. 246, 253, 257, 291–316, 344–8, 353, 366, 371–2, etc.

peasantry themselves. The scramble for land which appears amongst the free tenantry in the thirteenth century, probably even in the twelfth, did not respect the boundaries of the villeinage and did not fail to produce emulation amongst the villeins.

In turning to the chronology of these developments, we must naturally be concerned very largely with the reverse side of the coin, to the history of the demesne and free tenantry. Furthermore, so far as the twelfth century is concerned, we must work largely from inference. One thing which bulks large, quite clearly, is that many free holdings and many semi-free holdings were created during that century from the villeinage. Some villeins were rising in the legal scale, and entering into a freeholder's opportunities for rising in the social scale. On the other hand there may also be another side to this century of peasant progress. In a sample of a dozen manors or so in Cambridgeshire and the Isle, there were about 190 villein tenements in 1086: most of them virgate tenements in the shire although, in the Isle, they were generally described as containing from $7\frac{1}{2}$ to 15 acres. In the same villages in 1251 there were some 270 full lands, many of them divided into half lands and even into quarter lands. The numbers of the villeins would seem to have been growing despite the drift of some villein land towards freedom.

There is no documentary evidence that will readily explain away this apparent paradox. It is very probable that some new assarted land was put into the villeinage; but if so this had already happened before 1222, after which date the growth of the villeinage was slight.[1] At least one instance, the case of the bishop's manor in Triplow, is suggestive of another explanation. In 1086 there were twelve villeins holding 12 virgates in that manor; in 1251 there were twenty-four villeins still holding 12 virgates in half-virgate tenements. Here, it might seem, the virgates of *Domesday* had simply been divided, and two men now stood in the place where one had stood before.[2] There are other things which suggest that such had been the tendency, perhaps over a long period: the very prominence of half virgates amongst the villein holdings;[3] the many occasions when, even

[1] See above, pp. 101–3.
[2] *Dd*, i, 191; Caius 485/489, ff. 142 d–3 d.
[3] E.g. at Willingham, Balsham, Horningsea, Fen Ditton and Great Shelford (Cambs.), Kelshall (Herts.), and Hadstock (Essex): *ibid.* ff. 117, 122, 123 d, 132 d, 136 d, 153, 170 d.

though the unity of the tenement remained formally unimpaired, it was held by two or more partners not obviously related;[1] and the few instances where such division actually took place in the thirteenth century.[2]

Such a policy might well be advantageous from the bishop's point of view. We have seen that two half lands might be more productive of work than one full land;[3] and applied on a large scale the fission of holdings may therefore have given the bishop a fund of land to play with, the fund wherewith many of the free and semi-free were accommodated. It may well be that we cannot use the prevalence of half-virgate holdings and less in the thirteenth century as an index of the depression of the villeinage in the twelfth century; for we cannot be sure that the Domesday villein exhausts the population of the villein holding at that date. None the less, the signs of fission are there in the thirteenth-century extents; and for that reason we must see the shadows in the history of the villeinage in the time before the extents. Some villein land, even some villeins may have become free; but for others seignorial pressure may have become heavier, their burdens greater and their holdings less. We might even suppose that this was one factor in the slow but steady expansion in the bishop's income which goes right through from *Domesday* to the end of the thirteenth century—and perhaps behind *Domesday* to the increase in the farms of manors of which the Domesday villagers complained.

On the other hand, seignorial pressure may not have been the only factor at work. The division of tenements may equally have been the result of an absolute increase in villein population; not merely the way in which the bishop accommodated more men, but also the way in which the villeins themselves provided for their increasing numbers. Certainly the villein tenements of the

[1] At Little Gransden 9 out of 25 virgates were held by two partners; at Doddington 17 out of 23 full lands (though the second partner in seven of these cases was a woman and in two the mother of the other holder; some divided holdings, therefore, may have been due to customary dower rights); at March 9 out of 11 and at Downham 11 out of 20 full lands were held by two or more partners: Caius 485/489, ff. 30d–2d, 68, 70–70d, 151–1d.

[2] E.g. at Hardwick in 1222 and 1251 there were 14 full and 11 half lands; in 1279 (as in 1357) there were 13 of each. One of the full lands had clearly been divided: Cott. Tiberius B 11, ff. 135–5d; Caius 485/489, ff. 145d–8; *RH*, 11, 538; KR Ext. and Inq. Bdle 9, File 2.

[3] See above, p. 102.

thirteenth century, whether they had been divided or remained undivided, seem full of folk: men and women who appear in the extents as joint holders; and others who retain a splendid anonymity as 'anilepimen' or 'undersetles' and who appear in the record only because they owe some service on the demesne at harvest time.[1] This populousness of the holding might in many cases be due to the persistence of customary kin-rights which had resisted the standardizing efforts of seignorial interest. Even villein tenements might be partible amongst a man's heirs where that was the custom of the place.[2] A widow, too, might have a right in her husband's holding for her life by way of dower,[3] even the power to take the holding to a second husband, the second husband to a second wife, and so on.[4] 'Anilepimen' and 'undersetles', finally, might merely be sons and daughters,[5] or the widowed mother and younger brothers of the holder of the land;[6] but the latter group, the undertenants, had some sort of subtenancy in the holding. Such rights, such practices, might easily be destructive of the unity of the tenement, though how destructive it is hardly possible to say.

But 'undersetles' were not all members of the family; sometimes they were 'strangers coming from without who hire houses from divers persons and hold nothing of the lord'.[7] Such hiring of houses, moreover, is merely indicative of a far more widespread economic movement in the villeinage—of the great deal of buying and selling of land by villeins, of the large amount of dealing that was going on even in villein land. Some

[1] At Littleport, for example: 'scilicet quod quilibet anlepiman et anlepiwiman et quilibet undersetle metet dimidiam acram bladi in autumpno'— Caius 485/489, f. 38 d.

[2] See above, p. 138, n. 2.

[3] These rights of widows were very various: sometimes they kept the whole tenement for life or until remarriage; sometimes they retained only a half or some other portion; once at least they retained the land only if the heir was under age: Caius 485/489, ff. 183 d, 245, 317 d, 347 d. But such practices no doubt explain the not infrequent record of joint tenancies by mother and son.

[4] This seems to have been the somewhat curious custom prevailing at Sutton: Halimote, 24 Edw. I (St Barnabas); Leet, 31 Edw. I (St Luke).

[5] Caius 485/489, f. 266 d (Shipdham): 'Et sciendum quod unusquisque anylepiman vel anilepiwyman qui lucratus fuerit in autumpno duodecim denarios vel amplius dabit domino episcopo unum denarium per annum de chevagio... preter illos qui fuerunt in servicio patrum vel matrum suarum.'

[6] Ibid. ff. 305 d–6.

[7] Maitland, Court Baron, p. 146 (Littleport, 1326).

preliminary consequences were already apparent even in 1251: villein tenements were often clustered about with subsidiary holdings, and some villein tenements were breaking up.

It was perhaps natural that, at that date, these tendencies should have been most evident in Norfolk, where kin-right was most persistent and traditions of ancient freedom had been best maintained. A picture of no little confusion emerges, for instance, from the extent of East Dereham. Henry le Wyneter and Ralf de Humbletoft were both partners, with half a dozen other men, in a ten-acre holding under the heading of *censuarii*; but the former also held half an acre from a villein virgater and an acre from a half-virgater, while the latter had a whole villein virgate in addition. Amongst the villeins, Martin le Neve had two complete virgates together with 22 acres and a purpresture as additional holdings for money rents. Amongst the half virgaters, a number of men had additional holdings of this sort, and one paid 5*s*. 10*d*. rent for 17 acres. Even amongst the holders of a mere 6 acres, there was one with additional holdings totalling 14 acres; another with a half virgate and half an acre besides; and two others who also held land as *censuarii*.[1] At Pulham, there was even greater confusion; subletting of plots from villein holdings was common, and the addition to villein holdings of other parcels of land equally common. In one instance, too, we seem to see a half virgate of ten acres which had completely disintegrated. Thomas the son of Ranulf held 5 acres of land; but there were four other men who held plots of land ranging in size from ¼ acre to 2 acres which had once belonged to Thomas's father. They total exactly those five acres needed to make up Thomas's holding into half a virgate.[2] In brief, in these manors, a reshuffle was taking place in the occupation of land similar to that which, in this period and earlier, had been taking place in the free land. It is hardly surprising that these were manors in which the bishop very early gave up the struggle to maintain the villein tenement, and leased the villein land in both of them before the end of the thirteenth century.

At the same time, similar tendencies were making themselves evident elsewhere. At Hitcham in Suffolk,[3] no doubt for some of the same reasons which prevailed in Norfolk, there were

[1] Caius 485/489, ff. 238 d–47 d.   [2] *Ibid.* ff. 228 d–33 d.
[3] *Ibid.* ff. 325–9 d.

likewise many joint tenancies of villein holdings and much adding of small plots held for money rents to the original tenements. There, again, one Ralf the Tinker held 2 acres each from two separate villein virgates; and Ralf le Neve $2\frac{1}{2}$ acres from a virgater, $\frac{1}{2}$ acre of meadow from a half virgater and $\frac{1}{2}$ acre of land from a quarter virgater. At the other end of the estate at Hatfield,[1] where there was much assarting from the woodland going on, there was again much adding of small plots to villein tenements; and so there was and for similar reasons in the great Marshland manor at Wisbech Barton.[2] Even at Horningsea, near Cambridge, Thomas le Longe paid the enormous rent of 2s. to have $\frac{1}{2}$ acre from Alice Alwyne's villein half virgate.[3] So, despite many symptoms of the depression of the status of the villein tenant in both the twelfth and thirteenth centuries, there was also another trend. The barriers set up against the alienation of villein land were being broken down; and social evolution amongst the villeins began to follow similar lines to those we have noticed amongst the free tenants. Behind it all we must discern, presumably, the growth of a market for peasant produce and the habitual dealing in that market even by the villein.

In these circumstances, everything would tend to emphasize the difference made by natural disparities of capacity amongst villein tenants. Despite the uniformity of the demands made by seignorial administration upon the villeinage, the information given in the extents about villein plough-teams suggests that the bishop could not always feel confidence that men with equal land would be of equal economic standing. At Horningsea, certainly, it was assumed that four villeins would unite to produce one 'caruca integra' for the lord's ploughing.[4] But the survey of Downham was perhaps more realistic. The ploughboons of a holder of a full land were defined in terms of what he should do if he had a full team; if not, the same amount of work was to be done by such a group of partners as was necessary to make up a full plough-team.[5] Perhaps the survey of Somersham was most realistic of all. 'And if by any chance any virgater has

[1] Caius 485/489, ff. 161–3. [2] Ibid. ff. 81–2 d.
[3] Ibid. f. 126.
[4] Cott. Tiberius B II, f. 240; Caius 485/489, f. 122; RH, II, 442.
[5] Caius 485/489, f. 31.

no beast in his plough on account of his poverty, he will be obliged to plough nine acres every year with his pennies (cum denariis suis)'.[1] The ideal of a villein tenement as a unit capable of the same economic effort as any other villein tenement required much modification in fact.

Yet this very existence of men who had become so poor that they had no beasts to their plough offered opportunities to the enterprising. By 1251 many prosperous villeins, busy adding acre to acre, were to be found elsewhere than in Norfolk or Suffolk. At Rettendon in Essex there were twenty-four half-virgaters; amongst them they had a large number of additional holdings which add up to 92 acres in all. They included John Terri with two half virgates (he had bought out the services of both of them and paid a money rent), in addition to which he held 15 acres as a free tenant; and also Alice the widow of Maurice who held a half virgate (15 acres) for which she did service, 5 acres for a rent of 5d., and 15 acres as a tenant at will for 2s. 6d.[2] At Hadstock two villeins with 20 acres apiece also held 10½ and 20 acres respectively amongst the *censuarii*; another with 10 acres held an additional 20 acres as a free tenant.[3] In the Isle, the assarts from Apeshall made at Littleport and Downham were taken up almost entirely by villeins, in plots as large as 41 acres.[4] Such examples could be multiplied many times; and even if we admit that such men were still exceptional, the important thing is that they are to be found in so many parts of the estate and so early as this. Even in 1250 there were already quasi-yeomen in the ranks of the villeins.

In view of the evidence of the terrier, there need be no surprise, therefore, at Maitland's conclusion about peasant society at Littleport two or three generations later. 'A class of thriving yeomen seems to be forming itself, a manorial aristocracy, but still an aristocracy of villeins'.[5] Though there is no longer a terrier to guide us, the thriving villeins of an earlier date had probably grown in stature. They had gone on buying and selling both free land and villein land, so that by the fourteenth century it became very hard to speak of a man's land without specifying

[1] Cott. Tiberius B II, f. 112d. [2] Caius 485/489, ff. 182–4d.
[3] *Ibid.* ff. 169d–71.
[4] By Thomas the reeve of Littleport, who had a full land besides: *ibid.* ff. 37d, 39.
[5] *Court Baron*, p. 113.

that it was both bond and free. The bishop too was offering facilities in his courts for such transactions through the medium of the procedure of surrender and admission, which needs no illustration here. This in turn was transforming the rolls of the bishop's court into registers of peasant titles: a record which could be vouched to warranty in a case at law.[1] Here we are well on the way towards the customary tenure of copyhold.

From the court rolls, then, as well as the village charters there is something to be learnt about that village aristocracy of villeins which seems to be forming. John Albin of Littleport might be accounted a member of it. In 1322 he held a full land and two half lands—perhaps some 50 acres in all—and he made a bargain with the bishop to commute his services for a rent of 30s. a year.[2] Such another engrosser of villein holdings was Reginald de Beringhale of Sutton. He may well have been a younger son, for his father's lands did not come to him; but he acquired a full land and a half land which John the Smith had held when he died; and he had already a half land in addition as well as a number of other plots.[3] Reginald's father had also been a sheep farmer, and had kept the sheep of three other men besides his own in his fold when all of them ought to have been in the lord's fold.[4] One contemporary villein, Roger Aylbern, had a flock of 80 sheep of his own;[5] and many others in and around Wisbech were in continual trouble for overcharging the common with their sheep.[6] To return to Reginald de Beringhale's

[1] E.g. Wisbech Curia Bondorum, 11 Edw. II (Purification): 'Et ad hoc vocat ad warrantum recordum rotuli etc. Et datus est ei dies etc.' and compare *Court Baron*, p. 134. This character of the court rolls may have stimulated the preparation of books or rolls of extracts, like the St Albans court books, or rolls like those that have survived from the Prior of Ely's manor at Swaffham; on the former see Levett, *Studies in Manorial History*, pp. 79–96.

[2] Maitland, *Court Baron*, p. 135; and see also John Tepito of the same place who, in 1324, had an interest in at least seven tenements, one of them presumably the half land he took up in 1316 (pp. 113, 122).

[3] Sutton Courts Leet, 3 Edw. II (St Andrew), 6 Edw. II and 7 Edw. II (St Faith); Halimotes, 6 Edw. II (Christmas) and 7 Edw. II (St Peter in Cathedral).

[4] Sutton Court Leet, 8 Edw. II (St Luke).

[5] Sutton Halimote, 7 Edw. II (St Margaret).

[6] E.g. Elm Court Leet, 35 Edw. I (Pentecost); Wisbech Court Leet, 28 Edw. I (Pentecost). At Linden in 1251 it had been assumed that a villein might have a fold for his sheep, and that even an 'anilepiman' might have sheep to put in the lord's fold: Caius 485/489, ff. 52, 57d.

father, he had at least one labourer working for him; for on two occasions his *famulus* was in trouble in the prior's court.[1] These same villeins were making wills, and neglecting sometimes to obtain the consent of the lord's bailiff in doing so;[2] they were even making charters to record their dealings in land, and sealing those charters with their own seals.[3] Things had changed much since the day when Richard de Lucy had said that 'it was not the fashion of old time that every petty knightling should have a seal'.[4]

But the particular may be more telling than the general, and with a little trouble it is possible to reconstruct some fragments of the biography of a member of this villein aristocracy.[5] His name was Stephen Puttock, and he lived on the prior of Ely's manor of Sutton at the end of the thirteenth and the beginning of the fourteenth century. There can be no doubt about his villeinage: he was described as *nativus* in a charter; he paid a fine for the lord's licence to marry both his wives, as did his sister when she married (and leyrwite as well). There can be no doubt that he owed labour services, for he was amerced from time to time for carrying them out with less than proper care. Yet he was an important man in the village. Almost certainly he held a full land at least; for only two other men paid as much as he did when the prior tallaged the manor in 1294. He was ever in office—reeve in 1310, a chief pledge for quarter of a century, ale-taster more than once, a frequent member of inquest juries. Like others of his kind he was a sheep farmer: receiving 'foreign' beasts into the fen and keeping other men's sheep in his own fold and outside that of the lord.

But above all he was a great buyer of land. In 1300 he bought three-quarters of an acre without licence. A charter of 1303, recording the purchase of an unspecified parcel from another villein, is still extant. In 1304, he took up Northcroft (con-

---

[1] Sutton Courts Leet, 21 Edw. I (Martinmas) and 6 Edw. II (St Luke).

[2] Sutton Court Leet, 7 Edw. II (St Luke); for the conditions upon which a villein might make a will, see Caius 485/489, f. 183 d: 'non potest facere testamentum suum nisi in presencia ballivi domini vel prepositi'.

[3] There is one charter, with the seal still attached, whereby one villein of Sutton sells land to another: D & C Charter no. 299; and for another, though the seal has been lost see D & C Charter no. 694.

[4] Though even at this date it would presumably be the law that only a 'free and lawful' man should have a seal. See P & M, II, pp. 223–4.

[5] These notes are taken from the Sutton court rolls, supported by D & C Charters nos. 204, 252, 299 and 314.

taining 8¼ acres) from the prior. In 1305 he bought two acres from the prior's former bailiff and in 1307 a parcel of meadow from a free tenant. In 1309 he made an exchange of land with the prior, and took up an additional 9½ acres and a parcel of meadow. In 1310 he bought 6 acres of arable for 20 silver marks. There is no reason to suggest that this record is exhaustive; yet there are here notices of seven transactions in no more than ten years. Five of them brought him an additional 26 acres of land; three of them involved him in the payment of rents totalling 36s. a year; and two of them alone in the expenditure of nearly £15 in entry fine or purchase money. Such a man was thriving into the yeomanry.

III

The tendencies evident in the villeinage at the beginning of the fourteenth century were precisely those which, at an earlier date and under more favourable circumstances of law and custom, were evident in the free tenancies. In fact, it would seem to be possible to speak of a single economic trend in peasant society from the twelfth century onwards which by the beginning of the fourteenth century, was just beginning to be a *general* trend embracing all groups of the peasants. That trend was one towards the transformation of the unit of peasant landholding: the destruction of the rough equality of holdings in each of the several grades of the peasantry; the appearance of larger holdings in the hands of some men, which often meant smaller holdings for other men. This, on the peasant side, was the counterpart of the high farming on the great estate.

Two sets of influences unite in laying down the direction of this trend. In the first place, there were those influences which came from above, and in particular the continuous drift away from cultivation of the medieval bishops of Ely. In the twelfth century, the result had been to reinforce the ranks of the older free tenants with new groups of free or semi-free holders settled on assarted land or land taken from the villeinage. This arrentation of villein land did not even cease in the first half of the thirteenth century, but its enfranchisement was checked: and henceforward villein land, even when it was rent-paying land, ceased to drift over into the freehold. Nevertheless, the dispersion of all sorts of land into rent-paying tenements continued, and in the reigns of the three Edwards was making extensive inroads into both villeinage and demesne. In consequence, the lord's need for labour from the villeinage and his desire to exact it were both reduced; and more tenants than ever before were paying rent for land. There was less need to insist that tenements must be kept together to maintain a labourer; the lord could accede to peasant demands for licence to buy and sell land; there was no necessary prejudice in that to his rents and there was a profit to be made by selling his permission.

Yet that was one side of the picture only. The medieval bishops of Ely were powerful men as landowners, with authority enough in many instances to set the stage upon which economic forces played; they might even have authority enough to hold the villeinage together as a source of labour when, as early as 1251, there were signs that it was disintegrating. But this last fact alone is sufficient to suggest the operation of other forces which were almost independent of landlord policy. The quickening of economic life in England which goes back deep into the twelfth century did not pass the peasant by. Already at the beginning of the thirteenth century a peasant market in free land had been created; and the stratification of freeholders into winners and wasters, men with much land and men with little, was already far advanced. Already, at this date, the same tendencies had affected the villeinage too; and as the thirteenth century goes on, villein ancestors of the yeomanry make their appearance.[1] As labour services declined, villein tenure became no more than a species of peasant tenure, a species which might give the lord more arbitrary rights in the land of the tenant, but which was for all that not distinct in kind from other sorts of peasant tenure. As villeins bought free land and free men villein

---

[1] There is much in all this to suggest that Prof. Campbell (*The English Yeoman under Elizabeth and the Early Stuarts*) is inclined, even while acknowledging the fact that some yeomen had villein ancestors (pp. 15, 51), to exaggerate the importance amongst those ancestors of the medieval freeman (e.g. p. 11); and also to post-date the real origins of the yeomanry. Robert Furse's progenitors may have been 'plain and simple men and women of small possession' (quoted, p. 7); but sometimes these small possessions had been growing for a long time, even before the fourteenth century. Plainness and simplicity of life might last longer; in fact, it may not have been given up for a more ostentatious way of life before the reign of Elizabeth: see Hoskins, *Leicestershire Arch. Soc. Transactions*, XXII, pp. 42–5.

land, and as both alike paid rent for land, lines of economic difference cease to correspond to lines of legal status.[1] Already before the Black Death manorial England was rapidly becoming peasant England—a peasant England in which manorial survivals might be something of antiquities or at best formalities profitable to the bishop. The demesne of the bishops of Ely, the incidents of villeinage, even labour services still had a long history: but the lines of development were clear. Out of freemen and sokemen, *libere tenentes* and *censuarii*, virgaters and half virgaters the peasant heirs of demesne and villeinage had then been born.

[1] It is sometimes very hard to decide, in a given case, whether a man is a free man or a villein—as it is for example in the case of Eustace Ballard on the prior's manor of Swaffham Prior. Amongst the villeins he held a half virgate for his own life and his wife's—a tenement perhaps acquired by marrying a villein woman; and also another half virgate for four years until the heir came of age. In addition, amongst the free tenants, he held a messuage by charter which had once been villeinage; a messuage and half an acre at will according to the custom of the manor; and yet another messuage and 15 acres of land on a life lease. In all he had a substantial small farm of some 50 acres for which he paid rents totalling 34s. a year: D & C Extenta Maneriorum, 12 Edw. II.

VI

THE HONOUR OF ST ETHELDREDA

IN the foregoing pages, attention has been focused from time to time upon the way in which the interest and convenience of medieval bishops of Ely influenced the distribution of land and of those obligations which were commonly attached to land. We have been concerned, however, in the main only with a part of the bishop's influence, with the operation of economic interest and routine in the workings of a great estate. But the bishops were more than mere economic men or, for that matter, religious men. Kings,[1] bishops,[2] even the humbler priors of Ely[3] spoke constantly in the twelfth century about the honour of St Etheldreda; and in the thirteenth century the bishop was said to hold his possessions *per baroniam*.[4] For the present purpose, we need make no too careful enquiry into the meaning of these terms. The important fact is that the bishop's estate was not only an economic, but also a feudal, unit held in chief of the king in return for the performance of certain duties. The character, and the changes in the character, of those duties must be our first concern. This will provide an introduction to the arrangements which the bishop made to carry them out, to some of the social consequences of those arrangements, and to some of the social classes which were thrown up by those arrangements.

---

[1] Henry II, for example: 'Henricus dei gracia Rex Anglie...omnibus militibus qui tenent de honore sancte Etheldrede' (Liber M, f. 84).

[2] 'Nigellus dei gracia Elyensis ecclesie episcopus universo clero suo, baronibus, ministris, hominibus et amicis suis Francis et Anglis tocius honoris sancte Aetheldrede': Trin. MS. O. 2. 1, f. 150; and compare Bodl. Laudian Misc. 647, ff. 114 (Bishop Longchamp), 116d, 118 (Bishop Eustace).

[3] Liber M, f. 241; Coucher Book, f. 213d; Cott. Claudius C xi, f. 343d for charters of Prior William (?1133–44).

[4] *FA*, ii, 148, 150, 428; iii, 395; *RH*, ii, 430; it was because he so held that the bishop complained against being tallaged in Cambridge for the mill he had there: *Memoranda de Parliamento*, 51.

I

The history of the barony, of course, begins only with the Normans, who settled in England under a leader desirous of preserving in England those usages to which he and his ancestors had been accustomed in Normandy.[1] The starting-point of that history was the imposition of a *servitium debitum* of forty knights upon Ely abbey in or about the year 1070.[2] This quota remained the primary basis for calculating feudal burdens incident upon the abbey and bishopric of Ely for the rest of the Middle Ages; and its history is too well known to call for more than brief discussion here.[3]

From time to time attempts were made to revise the original *servitium*. Rufus is said to have raised the abbey's obligation from forty to eighty knights, an increase which may have been abandoned by Henry I.[4] Henry II in 1168 tried to use, not the traditional *servitium*, but the $56\frac{1}{4}$ fees of old enfeoffment revealed by the returns of 1166, as a basis for the assessment of a feudal aid;[5] but he had abandoned the attempt before the end of his reign.[6] John might adopt the same policy during the interdict[7] and Henry III might try to do so in 1229–30;[8] but these were exceptional exactions and commonly unsuccessful.[9] The Conqueror's work endured long, despite the fact that by 1166 it had but little reference to the military resources of the barony, and by the later thirteenth century to its military obligations.

At least as early as 1277, in fact, the forty knights' fees at which the barony of Ely had been rated was a fiscal rating only; for in that year there is definite evidence of a new military

---

[1] 'Usus ergo atque leges, quas patres sui et ipse in Normannia habere solebant, in Anglia servari volens', etc.: *HE*, II, c. 101.
[2] See above, pp. 67–8.
[3] See especially Chew, *Ecclesiastical Tenants-in-Chief*.
[4] See below, p. 161.
[5] *Pipe R*, 14 Hen. II, 102; *RBE*, I, 48, 363–5; Chew, *op. cit.* p. 19.
[6] *Pipe R*, 33 Hen. II, 80.   [7] *RBE*, I, 151.
[8] *Pipe R*, 14 Hen. III, 62.
[9] There is in fact no sign that the bishop met the charges on the fees which he did not recognize even after 1168 or 1230. For the use of the traditional forty fees as the basis for assessing feudal aids in 1244 'de auxilio prelatorum domino Regi concesso...contra transfretacionem suam in Wasconiam' and in 1305 for the marriage of Edward I's daughter, see Cott. Tiberius B II, f. 250d and Exch. KR Lay Subsidy Roll, 81/3, m. 7.

rating of six knights only as the service due from the bishop.[1] When this new quota was established is not clear; but it is characteristic enough of the practice of cutting down military obligations in the thirteenth century—a practice often going back to John's reign and firmly established by the middle of the reign of Henry III.[2] Even this new quota, however, showed a tendency likewise to become merely a unit of fiscal calculation —a means of calculating the amount of the bishop's fine for his military service.[3] The actual military force which the bishop had to produce may have been reduced still further to five knights,[4] perhaps because, when Gilbert Pecche surrendered the barony of Bourn to the king in 1284, the bishop thereby lost the service of $5\frac{1}{4}$ fees.[5] But this has little importance. We have reached the end of the progressive reduction of feudal quotas; and within the next generation or so the feudal levy ceased to play any significant part in military organization.

Of course, it is true that the feudal obligations of the bishop of Ely were not limited by this military obligation and the various fines and scutages which derived from military obligations. Even the king's right to resume the temporalities during a vacancy, and the king's right to have a share, even the last word, in the appointment of bishops were rights which owed something to analogies drawn from feudal custom. Bishops of Ely, like other barons of the honour of England, no doubt owed suit to the king's court; and when the suitor was as old a statesman as Bishop Nigel, for example, the advice which he had to give

[1] Chancery Misc., Bdle. 9/2: 'H. Elyensis episcopus recognoscit servitium sex militum pro quo satisfecit in Garderoba regis pro ducentis et 40. marcis.'

[2] Mitchell, *Studies in Taxation*, pp. 300–9, 362–3; Painter, *Feudal Barony*, pp. 39 ff.; Chew, *op. cit.* pp. 28 ff.

[3] See LTR Misc., Bdle. 1/13 and Chew, *op. cit.* p. 73.

[4] In 1322 the bishop's contingent for the muster at Newcastle-on-Tyne against Robert Bruce consisted of two knights and six serjeants for five knight's fees: Chancery Misc., Bdle. 5/10. As early as 1295 the bishop fined in 500 marks for his service in Gascony; and this would imply a quota of five knights if the fine was fixed at the normal rate for that campaign: *Cal. Close R*, 1307–13, 469; Chew, *op. cit.* p. 70.

[5] The reduction of the resources of his barony by the loss of these fees was the subject of complaint by the bishop in 1305, already some time after Gilbert's death which took place in 1291: *RP*, I, 163; *Memoranda de Parliamento*, 75.

might well be advice worth listening to.[1] But on the whole the military obligations of the barony of Ely were those which had the more important consequences of a sort relevant to this study; and to some additional points about them we must turn now.

Military obligations were of two main sorts: duties of castle guard and the provision of a due contingent of knights in the king's army. So far as castle guard was concerned, the bishop at first had sent his knights to help to garrison Norwich castle; and in addition had made an annual payment to that castle and helped with labour in maintaining its fortifications. This duty was abolished by Henry I (for the enormous fine of £1000); instead, the bishop's knights were to do guard service in the Isle of Ely.[2] This was a privilege in which Henry II would support the bishop if the knights of St Etheldreda defaulted in their duty,[3] and was one of the many liberties of his see confirmed to Longchamp by Richard I.[4] But the privilege was also a duty, for the carrying out of which the king held bishops responsible—as Henry III did in 1260, Edward I in 1274, and Edward II in the time of the Ordainers.[5]

How far there were castles to guard in the Isle is another matter. The Conqueror seems to have taken over some sort of fortification at *Alrehede*;[6] but this castle had to be repaired by Bishop Nigel in about 1140, while the ruins on the Cherry Hill at Ely are probably the remains of that stone castle built by the same bishop at the same time.[7] But nothing much more is

---

[1] See the fine filial piety with which Richard FitzNeal extols his father's knowledge of exchequer matters and Henry II's respect for that knowledge: *Dialogus de Scaccario*, I, 8 (Stubbs, *Select Charters*, pp. 217–18). Nigel was certainly sitting as a baron of the exchequer as late as 1165, though stricken with the palsy the year before: Madox, *Exchequer*, p. 743.

[2] *Pipe R*, 31 Hen. I, 44; D & C Charter no. 3 (printed from chartulary sources by Bentham, Appx. XVIII and *Mon. Angl.* I, 482).

[3] See his writs in Liber M, ff. 83, 84 and Bodl. Laudian Misc. 647, f. 99d (and also below, Appx. II, p. 281).

[4] D & C Charter no. 13: 'Et sit quieta de warda militum in castello nostro de Norwico, ita quod milites de honore sancte Adeldrede qui solebant facere wardam in predicto castello faciant eam in Ely ad summonitionem Elyensis episcopi.'

[5] *Close R*, 1259–61, 37; *Cal. Pat. R*, 1272–81, 52; 1307–13, 489, 490; 1317–21, 46; 1321–4, 44, 63.

[6] *HE*, II, c. 111; for the problems connected with the identification of this place see *VCH Cambs.* II, 384, n.

[7] Trin. MS. O. 2. 1, ff. 142–42d. The account of Ely castle in *VCH Cambs.* II, p. 29 seems to avoid most of the difficulties connected with its history.

heard of the wooden fortress at *Alrehede*; while Ely castle was clearly a ruin in the thirteenth century and may have been one of the adulterine castles which Henry II put down.[1] Only Wisbech castle had a longer history: if there is no certainty when it was built, there was certainly a constable there in 1213,[2] and the site on which it stood was not finally cleared until 1794.[3] Yet castles may have been relatively unimportant in a place so well defended by nature as the Isle of Ely, defences which made it from time to time a camp of refuge for rebels. Aldreth causeway was probably defensible without a fortress, and the duty of defending it still had a formal existence at least in the fourteenth century.[4] In the thirteenth, there was also an elaborate arrangement for gathering up the knights of St Etheldreda for defence of the Isle. Five of the bishop's knights had messuages in Ely pertaining to their fees so that they could summon the other knights of the barony for their guard service. These men, moreover, may have been chosen as representative of the geographical extent of the honour. Simon Lisle's and Warin de Saham's fees were at Hinton Hall and Mepal in the Isle; but Henry Pelryn's was at Catmere Hall in Littlebury (Essex), Stephen de Marisco's at Walsoken in Norfolk, and Henry Muschet's at Fen Ditton and Triplow in Cambridgeshire.[5] This may have been a fairly recent arrangement in 1222; but lesser men had performed the same duty at earlier times. In 1169 there was a serjeant at Fen Ditton for summoning the knights of the bishopric, and he may have had the assistance of three other men described as summoners and living in Ely.[6]

[1] As Bentham thought (p. 137). It had disappeared by the time of John of Fountains, for he speaks of a messuage 'super ripam ad pontem ubi castrum quondam situm fuit': Bodl. Laudian Misc. 647, f. 124d.

[2] This was that Gervase, the fees and socage tenements of whose bailiwick were surveyed by the crown a few years earlier during the Interdict: *CRR*, VII, 5; *Book of Fees*, I, 628–31.

[3] *VCH Cambs.* II, p. 47.

[4] In 1361 the half fee at Mepal, which was mortified to the advantage of the Prior and Convent, had been held 'per servicium inveniendi unum hominem armatum ad custodiendum unum pontem de Alderhith per 40. dies contra hostes domini regis si forte insula Elyensis per inimicos regis obsideatur': D & C Charter no. 1122.

[5] Cott. Tiberius B II, f. 86d; Cott. Claudius C XI, f. 25d: 'Isti quinque debent wardam et debent summonire alios milites de baronia Episcopatus pro loco et tempore ad faciendum wardam in Ely.'

[6] *Pipe R*, 16 Hen. II, 95–6.

Practically nothing is known about the way in which the system of guard duty in the Isle worked in practice; but a little more can be said about the way in which the bishop fulfilled his other duty of providing knights for the king's army. A brief history of the bishop's knight service can only begin in the reign of Henry II, when a continuous series of Pipe Rolls commences. Bishop Nigel may have sent knights for the four campaigns on the continent between 1156 and 1162: certainly he paid no scutage for them,[1] but this may just possibly have been due to the fact that he was excused scutage as a baron of the exchequer.[2] After an interval of a quarter of a century, service was again performed, apparently, in every campaign between 1189 and the Interdict;[3] and after it, in the Biham campaign of 1221, the Welsh campaign of 1223, and the Bedford campaign of 1224.[4] After 1224 the knights of the barony of Ely fought only on rare and isolated occasions. Hugh of Northwold produced his service for the Gannoch campaign of 1246,[5] and John of Hotham for the Scottish campaign of 1322.[6] Finally, when the feudal levy was called out in 1327, the bishop again sent service; but it was a strange force which presented itself at York. It amounted to no less than 172 men-at-arms and included two bannerets and 35 knights.[7] This looks far more like an indentured retinue than any feudal service which might have been proffered for many a long year; and certainly the bishop required payment for them from the day 'the said men-at-arms were assembled at York'.

In short, military service seems only to have been normally performed from the barony of Ely during the relatively brief period between 1189 and 1224. Before and after that period we

---

[1] Baldwin, *Scutage and Knight Service in England*, p. 20; *Pipe R*, 7 Hen. II, 45, 48–9.

[2] *Dialogus de Scaccario*, I, c. 8 (p. 95) and compare *RBE*, II, p. clvi and Poôle, *Exchequer in the Twelfth Century*, p. 125.

[3] Normally this has to be inferred from the fact that the bishop does not appear in the Pipe Roll as paying scutage, or has quittance from scutage by the king's writ (presumably for service). Only occasionally is there a positive statement like Longchamp's protest against a charge for scutage for not having his knights in the Welsh campaign of 1189: 'sed eosdem et longe plures habuit in eodem exercitu....Et ideo cum Angelis et Archangelis quietus est': *Pipe R*, 2 Ric. I, 116.

[4] Chew, *op. cit.* pp. 52–3.   [5] *Ibid.* p. 52.

[6] Chancery Misc., Bdle. 5/10.

[7] Willard and Morris, *The English Government at Work 1327–1336*, I, pp. 344–6.

6

are more concerned with the history of scutage. The antiquity of this method of commuting feudal service into a mere money payment needs no reiteration; it was and must have been almost as old as knight service itself.[1] So far back we cannot go in the barony of Ely; but there has survived a well-known charter of Henry I, the two versions of which may be set out side by side:

<table>
<tr><td>A[2]</td><td>B[3]</td></tr>
<tr><td>Henricus Rex Anglorum archiepiscopis, episcopis, abbatibus, comitibus, baronibus, vicecomitibus et omnibus fidelibus Francis et Anglis tocius Anglie salutem. Sciatis me condonasse ecclesie S. Aetheldrede...quadraginta libras de illis centum libris quas predicta ecclesia solebat dare de scutagio quando scutagium

per terram evenerit....</td><td>Henricus Rex Anglorum archiepiscopis, episcopis, abbatibus, comitibus (baronibus, vicecomitibus et omnibus fidelibus Francis et Anglis tocius Anglie)[4] salutem. Sciatis me condonasse ecclesie S. Aetheldrede...quadraginta libras de illis centum libris quas predicta ecclesia solebat dare de scutagio quando scutagium currebat per terram meam Anglie ita quod ecclesia non dabit inde nisi sexaginta libras quando scutagium per terram evenerit....</td></tr>
</table>

This document dates from the year 1127;[5] its authenticity in the 'B' version has also been questioned.[6] In fact, however, there would seem to be no cause to suspect that the 'A' version is other than a rather natural copyist's mistake. Nothing essential is added to the document in the 'B' version; it has survived unabbreviated in a good twelfth-century text (Trinity MS. O.2.41); and it is unlikely to have been the product of a later age, particularly in and around 1166, since scutage at that time

[1] Stenton, *English Feudalism*, pp. 177 ff.
[2] Cott. Titus A i, f. 32; Trin. MS. O. 2. i, f. 113 d.
[3] Cott. Tib. A vi, f. 109; Trin. MS. O. 2. 41, f. 125; Liber M, f. 78. This charter has been printed by Bentham, Appx. XXI; Round, *Feudal England*, p. 268 and *EHR*, vi, p. 629; Hall, *RBE*, p. clii.
[4] The passage in brackets appears only in Trin. MS. O. 2. 41 and in Cott. Tib. A vi.
[5] Farrer, *Outline Itinerary of Henry I*, no. 555.
[6] By Hall, *RBE*, ii, pp. cliii–clvi. He considers that the repetition 'quando scutagium currebat per terram' (itself a suspicious phrase at this date) and 'quando scutagium per terram evenerit' is foreign to charters at this date; that the abbreviated style of salutation in the 'B' versions he knew showed that the copyist was not working from an original; and that Round had printed this instrument from late and very inferior texts (a perfectly valid criticism). He was inclined to suggest that the 'B' version dated from the reign of Henry II when the question of scutage was a burning one.

was not being levied at a figure as high as £60 from the barony of Ely. Finally, there can be no question of the general sense of Henry's concession being in any way cast into doubt; for that has two unequivocal sources of support. The first is a bull of Innocent II, dated 27 April 1139, confirming to Bishop Nigel the possessions and liberties of his see, including this remission of £40 of scutage.[1] The second is that entry on the Pipe Roll which shows that Bishop Hervey was paying very dearly for the king's acquittance 'de superplus militum Episcopatus', a reference which can only be to this charter.[2]

If the document itself, even in its longer form, is unquestionably a genuine document, it is another matter to interpret what is implied in it. The words of the charter do not, for instance, tell us how scutage was calculated in the reign of Henry I;[3] there is nothing in it to show at all clearly that what was at issue was the bishop's *servitium* (perhaps even the increase of the *servitium* by Rufus) and that it was hereby reduced.[4] In fact, a strict reading of the text would support quite strongly the argument that at this date scutage was levied at a fixed round figure for each barony, and that it was not yet a charge assessed according to the number of knights which made up a baron's *servitium debitum*.[5]

On the other hand, once the connection with the entry on the Pipe Roll is allowed, the matter assumes a different complexion. The 'superplus militum' must refer to knights over and above something; and one obvious assumption is that it refers to knights enfeoffed over and above the bishop's *servitium debitum*. In that case, Henry I may have anticipated (in this instance at least) Henry II's policy of 1166–8 of taxing such fees as the barons had created over and above their traditional quota.[6] In

---

[1] 'Remissionem quoque quadraginta librarum de scutagio prout ab eodem rege noscitur institutum et scripto firmatum': Holtzmann, *Papsturkunden*, II, no. 21 and cf. no. 35 (a bull of Lucius II of 1144).

[2] *Pipe R*, 31 Hen. I, 44; and compare Round, *Feudal England*, p. 269 and Stenton, *English Feudalism*, p. 179.

[3] They certainly do not provide clear proof that scutage was paid 'in accordance with the number of knights owed by the tenants [-in-chief]': Baldwin, *Scutage and Knight Service in England*, pp. 2–3.

[4] As suggested by Chew, *Ecclesiastical Tenants-in-Chief*, p. 9.

[5] As Hall argues: *RBE*, II, p. clvi.

[6] For this and what follows, see Stenton, *English Feudalism*, pp. 179–81 and Painter, *English Feudal Barony*, p. 34.

support of this assumption we may vouch the fact that the £60 of scutage which Bishop Hervey would still pay represented a charge of 30s. on each of the 40 fees of his *servitium*; and this seems to have been the charge which applied in the bishopric of Norwich about 1119, according to one interpretation of a grumbling letter from Herbert Losinga.[1] Such may have been the case; but unfortunately even the Pipe Roll, Henry I's charter and Bishop Herbert's letter all taken together are none of them definite enough to be conclusive. The kind of charge that scutage was in the time of the first bishop of Ely must still remain a matter of conjecture. The most that can be said is that it was already in 1127 a well-known charge; well enough known to have assumed a conventional figure which could be changed as a matter of privilege, at the high price Henry I demanded for a privilege.

The remaining chapters in the history of scutage can be passed over quickly, since they follow the familiar pattern. Under Henry II, in 1166 the bishop paid certain sums in commutation for service, but it was not a scutage; rather these payments were in lieu of providing a number of serjeants for the Welsh campaign of that year.[2] The so-called scutage of 1168 was again no scutage: it was a feudal aid for the marriage of the king's daughter. On this occasion Bishop Nigel paid at once the 40 marks charged against the traditional 40 fees at which his barony was assessed. He did not pay, however, an additional £10. 16s. 8d. assessed upon 16¼ additional fees of old enfeoffment which had been revealed by his *carta* in 1166;[3] there is in fact no sign that he ever did pay this sum. Before the end of the reign, moreover, agreement had been reached. If during the vacancy of 1169–73 scutage for the Irish campaign of 1172[4] was charged against all the 73½ fees created in the barony of Ely, in 1187 the scutage of Galway was assessed only upon the accepted 40 fees.[5] It was the same during the first half of the thirteenth century: only during vacancies or when the bishopric was in the king's hand for some other reason were all the fees of old enfeoffment brought under charge for scutage.[6] There

[1] Quoted Round, *Feudal England*, p. 270.
[2] *Pipe R*, 12 Hen. II, 85; Baldwin, *op. cit.* pp. 27–8.
[3] *Pipe R*, 14 Hen. II, 102.   [4] *Ibid.* 18 Hen. II, 117.
[5] *Ibid.* 33 Hen. II, 80.
[6] During the interdict, for example, or the vacancy of 1256–7: *RBE*, I, 151; Pipe R, no. 102, m. 7d.

were attempts at other times by Henry III's government to revive the policy of 1166; but they were met with stolid resistance.[1] By contrast, payment seems to have been made promptly on the accepted basis of 40 fees: for the Gascon campaign of 1242 and the Scottish campaign of 1244, for instance.[2] By that time, however, the history of scutage as such was almost over.

As early as 1265,[3] and regularly under Edward I and Edward II,[4] the bishop paid a fine instead of scutage. This fine was calculated on the basis of the revised *servitium* of six knights, at a rate which varied from 20 marks per knight in 1306 and 1314 up to 60 marks in 1300, 1310 and 1323. Even the lowest rate of fine was equal to a scutage on 40 fees at the highest rate (3 marks per fee) at which scutage seems to have been levied. On nine out of the eleven occasions when the bishop made fine under the first two Edwards, the crown gained by the new system; on three of those occasions it took three times the sum that Henry III or his progenitors had ever done.

It might be worth while, in conclusion, to set down a few figures which may indicate how much of a burden scutage was upon the barony of Ely. The position can be shown by tabulating the amounts paid in scutages and feudal aids for three roughly equal periods:

	Fines or scutages ($£$)	Feudal aids ($£$)	Total ($£$)
1165–89	114	153	267
1230–56	291	173	464
1300–23	1240	80	1320

Henry III's scutages produced two and a half times as much as Henry II's; scutages and aids combined about twice as much. That perhaps just about kept pace with the increase in the bishop's income. Under Edward I and Edward II, on the other

---

[1] In 1230 payment was still outstanding from 1217 on fees the bishop did not recognize; and no payment was made on a similar charge for the scutage of Brittany raised in 1230: *Pipe R,* 14 Hen. III, 57, 62. In 1250 and 1251, the bishop was owing £37 for two scutages in respect of the fees he did not recognize; and he showed likewise no sign of paying a similar charge for the aid for knighting the king's eldest son in 1252 and later: Pipe R, no. 95, m. 22; no. 96, m. 11; no. 98, m. 3 d; no. 99, m. 18 d; no. 100, m. 4 d. For payment of the aid on his 40 fees, see Exch. Receipt R (Auditors), nos. 23, 25.

[2] Cott. Tiberius B 11, f. 250 d; *Close R,* 1242–7, 203–4.

[3] *Cal. Pat. R,* 1258–66, 522.

[4] Chancery Misc., Bdles. 5/2, 5/3; LTR Misc., Bdle. 1/13; *Cal. Fine R,* 1, 85; *Cal. Scutage R,* 366, 379, 396.

hand, fines and aids produced five times as much as the scutages and aids of Henry II, while the bishop's net income had increased only threefold. True, these changes were passed on to the bishop's tenants; but even regarded as charges on his income they rose only from 1% a year under Henry II to 2% under Edward I. That might be a contributory factor to discontent in an age which had no love for taxes; but it cannot be said to be oppressive. All the money the bishops of Ely paid in scutages and fines looks small in bulk beside the debt Bishop Hervey owed to the Crown in 1130 for a variety of fines. It stood at £1450, and that year he had paid nearly £400.[1] Scutages can have had very little influence upon medieval society compared with the problem of providing maintenance for those forty knights which the Conqueror had made the *servitium debitum* of Ely abbey. It is to this problem in the history of the barony of Ely that we must now turn.

II

In the upper ranges of society, the main force which determined the distribution of property between the Conquest and the reign of Henry II was the military obligations imposed by the Crown upon the barons. Moreover, although in later generations this force became of less effect, the property relationships it had created did not disappear, however much they might be modified under other and newer influences. If only for that reason, the age of enfeoffment remains one of abiding interest, as one of the great formative periods in our history. In providing maintenance for a band of foreign fighting men, the barons of the conquest and of the next few generations parcelled out much of the soil of England into portions upon which the knight could grow into a knight of the shire, and the knight of the shire into a gentleman. It hardly matters at what point we enter upon the history of medieval England; sometime or another we must come back to the endowment of the knighthood.

At the same time, no too simple view can be taken of the process of enfeoffment. Fees were not created at one blow. There were not always the same number of fees in a barony, even apart from human fatality or default of heirs. Many influences determined the pattern at any given time, not all of

[1] *Pipe R*, 31 Henry I, 44.

them working in the same direction. There were the power and will of the crown to command service, and the severity of the obligations it was willing to impose. There was the calculation which a baron must have made about the amount of his land he could afford to subinfeudate; and the value of his knights to him with or without regard to the king's demand for service (and in a reign like Stephen's obligations imposed by the Crown might be a small matter by comparison with baronial self-interest or even the instinct of self-defence). There was the attitude of the knights themselves: their willingness or unwillingness to be mere fighting men, even to be fighting men at all. On an ecclesiastical barony, there was the influence of the international church, which had views in the matter, a growing law in which those views were embodied, and a developing machinery through which that law could be enforced. The history of the barony of Ely is not without interest from more than one of these points of view.

If they could be taken at their face value, Bishop Nigel's *carta* of 1166 and the returns to the inquest into knight's fees in 1210–12 would provide a convenient index to the stages in the progress of enfeoffment. At the latter date, the bishop had created some 82 fees. Of these $56\frac{1}{4}$ had been created before 1135, $16\frac{1}{2}$ between 1135 and 1166, and a further $9\frac{1}{2}$ between 1166 and 1212 (mostly in the district of extensive assarting in the Cambridge and Norfolk Marshland). That would make a nicely graduated curve: subinfeudation gradually decreased in intensity from the first wholesale distribution of lands in the critical years at the end of the eleventh century down to a few casual gifts of assarted land at the end of the twelfth century to favoured servants, even favoured relatives,[1] and on a more or less honorary basis. Unfortunately, the facts were a great deal more complicated.

The first phase in the history of enfeoffment was, as we have seen, probably more or less completed by the end of the Conqueror's reign. That phase was governed by its own specific conditions: by the necessity to provide the *servitium debitum* of

---

[1] A number of these fees were in all probability the reward of service or propinquity. We find Simon Lisle, who had been the bishop's seneschal, holding one-sixth of a fee at Elm in 1212; and one of the numerous Longchamp clan with one-twelfth of a fee at Wisbech.

forty knights which the Conqueror imposed on the abbey; and by the seizure of many of the abbey's lands in the early days of the conquest, lands whose holders provided a major part of these forty knights. During this phase, too, there was no sign of disagreement between the monarchy and the church about the propriety of imposing military burdens upon an ecclesiastical estate. At the same time, the king was prepared to make some return for this acquiescence characteristic of the age of Lanfranc. William I's efforts to secure restitution of the abbey's property, though generally only in the shape of lordship over knight's fees, was one such contribution. Henry I carried on the work: in 1127 he was commanding that holders of lands which had been sworn to St Etheldreda by the Domesday inquest should do their knight service to the bishop; and he reinforced the verdicts of forty years earlier by another verdict before his own justiciar.[1] Bishop Hervey's exertions against these intruders were noted by the chronicler; and the implication is that he had substantial success in completing the long process of recovery which goes back through the Domesday inquest to the famous plea at Kentford and that hardly less celebrated plea in the years 1071–75.[2]

Yet this was one phase only in the history of enfeoffment; and before Bishop Hervey's time another had already opened under different conditions and with different actors. The increase in the abbey's quota from forty to eighty knights in the reign of Rufus is ill-documented; but if the tradition is a good one, that increase must have stimulated further subinfeudation. At the same time, there were other currents running in an opposite direction. The intimate companionship of church and state

---

[1] See Henry's writ printed by Bentham, Appx. XVI from Liber M, f. 76, and particularly the phrase 'et unde verbum ostensum est coram iusticia mea'; and compare D & C Charter no. 6 (printed from chartulary copies by Bentham, Appx. XIX and *Cartae Antiquae Rolls* 1–10, no. 51): where holders of lands 'recognoscant eas et teneant de predicta ecclesia et episcopo de Ely... faciendo inde ecclesie servicium milicie secundum tenuras et secundum hoc quod servicia statuta sunt in eisdem terris. Et ita quod barones et vavassores easdem terras tenentes sint quieta erga me et alios dominos suos de tanto servicio quantum inde episcopo et ecclesie predicte facere debuerint in statuto servicio milicie.'

[2] Trin. MS. O. 2. 1, f. 112d: 'subiectis suo dominatui aut penitus expulsis qui terras ecclesie de eo recognoscere noluerunt'. On many of the points raised in this paragraph see above, pp. 67–70 and my remarks in *EHR*, LXII, pp. 438–56.

during the age of Lanfranc did not long outlast the Conqueror's reign; and from Anselm's time new notions of propriety in the relationship of king to church, and about the way the great ecclesiastical feudatory should act towards the properties in his charge, were creeping across Europe from Rome. The accession of Stephen opened the floodgates; and in the years before the anarchy there was much activity in the barony of St Etheldreda.[1]

This activity began at the very beginning of Stephen's reign, so far as we can see without specific papal stimulus. Bishop Nigel ordered a great survey to be made of the possessions of his church; and then, at a plea held before nine hundreds at the old Iron Age fortress of Wandlebury in the Gog-Magog hills, enforced recovery of a number of properties which had been alienated from his church.[2] By 1138, the Papacy had taken the matter up, and Innocent II commanded Nigel to recover lands which had been lost.[3] A few months later,[4] in confirming the rights of the convent of Ely, Innocent ventured upon an amplification of this instruction. He confirmed the conventual property 'so that from those lands which the monks have or which you have reserved for episcopal use, it should not be permissible for you or your successors or the said monks to alienate any of them or to put them out in knight's fees (*militari officio deputare*); but rather you ought to recover those which have been so alienated, and, when they have been recovered, you should have power freely to retain them in the right and dominion of your church'. In the meantime Nigel had already been active in this direction, following up, no doubt, the verdicts of Wandlebury; for the papal legate and the prelates of England were commanded to see that his sentence of excommunication upon intruders into his lands was firmly observed, and King Stephen was instructed to give counsel and aid in the same endeavour.[5]

---

[1] These sentences, of course, could not have been written without reference to Brooke, *The English Church and the Papacy*.

[2] Trin. MS. O. 2. 1, ff. 127d–128.

[3] Holtzmann, *Papsturkunden*, ii, no. 17 (5 Dec. 1138).

[4] *Ibid.* no. 21 (27 Apr. 1139).

[5] *Ibid.* nos. 22 and 23. Holtzmann's dating (29 Apr. 1139) is preferred here to that of Round (1142—*Geoffrey de Mandeville*, p. 412). These two letters were issued on the same day as another (Holtzmann, no. 24) excusing Nigel and Abbot Robert of Thorney from attendance at the Lateran council which Round himself assigned to 1139: *EHR*, viii, p. 516.

So far things had gone when the whole question was complicated by the round of confiscation and restoration during the years of the anarchy. The Papacy did not change its mind. In 1150, Eugenius III informed the bishop and convent that the canons forbade bishop or abbot to alienate the lands of their church; and he revoked as erroneous those grants which had been made from the property of the church of Ely, not only by Abbot Richard and Bishop Hervey, but also by Bishop Nigel.[1] Reading this in the light of the earlier letter of Innocent II, it would seem that there must have been much enfeoffment by all these three prelates.

On the other hand, and in the light of these papal letters, there must also have been a time when Bishop Nigel reversed the policies of his predecessors; when he was not creating, but resuming, knight's fees. There are one or two cases when we can be fairly sure that some of the property recovered by the plea of Wandlebury round about 1135 had previously been military tenures rather than lands absolutely withheld from the church. One such case is the manor of Pampisford in Cambridgeshire. It was recovered at Wandlebury; but earlier it had been granted by Bishop Hervey to his nephew, the Archdeacon William the Breton, for the service of one knight—a grant confirmed by Henry I at Ealing in 1127.[2] Its recovery in 1135 was presumably genuine enough; since, although it was granted away again as a knight's fee before 1166, Walter of Pampisford held it then of the new enfeoffment, suggesting a real break in continuity since the time it had been held by the warlike Archdeacon William.[3]

Nor is this the only instance in which Archdeacon William seems to have been ejected from a military tenement. In the years 1149–53, the prior and convent of Ely had a long and

<hr />

[1] Holtzmann, no. 63 (17 Mar. 1150).

[2] BM Add. 9822, f. 70d (below, Appx. I, p. 280).

[3] RBE, I, 364. There may be a certain amount of confusion about the early archdeacons of Cambridgeshire. Bentham supposed that there was a single Archdeacon William who assumed office c. 1116 and died about 1160; and Holtzmann, op. cit. II, p. 222n. hardly clears the matter up. It seems more likely in fact that there were two successive archdeacons called William: the first, William the Breton and Hervey's nephew (Trin. MS. O. 2. 1, f. 122); and a second, William de Laventona, who was one of Bishop Nigel's closest advisers from 1143 onwards (ibid. ff. 146, 150–50d, 163d). If this is granted, the reference to a William, who was former archdeacon in the litigation about Stetchworth discussed in the following paragraph, becomes comprehensible.

interesting struggle with his son Henry, who had usurped their rights in the manor of Stetchworth.[1] The details are unimportant for the present purpose; but it is significant that the monks complained that Henry put this land 'non aliter quam ad militare officium et ad seculares usus', and that he was supporting his claim with allegedly forged charters of Bishop Hervey and Prior Vincent.[2] We seem to have a reference here to another manor in which Bishop Hervey had enfeoffed his archdeacon; we also know that Stetchworth was one of the places which Nigel recovered at Wandlebury, and that it was Bishop Nigel who settled the manor upon the convent between 1135 and 1138.[3] All in all, it seems, the fees of Archdeacon William were treated with scant respect by Bishop Nigel when he tried to set his house in order; and Stetchworth at least remained part of the conventual endowment for the rest of the Middle Ages.

In the light of these instances, some of the other lands resumed at Wandlebury may well have been military tenures which make no appearance in the fees of the old enfeoffment in 1166. Lands recovered at Triplow, Little Gransden and Terrington were probably retained in the episcopal demesne;[4] West Wratting was conferred upon the monks;[5] and so for a time was Marham,[6] where William de Warenne and Hugh de Montfort had usurped the abbey's rights before 1086.[7] But in this latter case, the earl of Warenne retained his claim with marvellous pertinacity.

[1] Trin. MS. O. 2. 1, ff. 154 d–63; Holtzmann, *op. cit.* II, nos. 61–2, 64, 67–8, 71, 74, 79.

[2] Holtzmann, *op. cit.* II, no. 61.

[3] Stetchworth was not one of the manors given to the convent by Bishop Hervey (D & C Charter no. 51; it does, however, appear in the inflated version printed by Bentham, Appx. XXVI) but it did form part of Nigel's endowment of the cathedral priory: Trin. MS. O. 2. 1, f. 134 d; Cott. Vespasian A XIX, f. 43 d.

[4] Little Gransden can only be the bishop's demesne manor; the land at Triplow can hardly be the hide of land which Hardwin de Scalers usurped, since there is no sign that this was ever recovered, being held in 1166 by Theobald fitzFulk of the barony of Hugh de Scalers (*RBE*, I, 369).

[5] This again is likely to refer to the demesne manor; there seems to have been no break in the continuity of the military tenement made out of the three hides which Hardwin seized there: it was almost certainly part of the three fees of old enfeoffment held by Stephen de Scalers in 1166, since he was found granting land to St Radegund's nunnery in that village about this time: *Dd*, I, 190 d; *RBE*, I, 363; *Cal. Charter R*, III, 223. And West Wratting again was conferred on the monks by Nigel, not by Hervey.

[6] For Nigel's charter, see D & C Charter no. 53 (1).

[7] *Dd*, II, 159 d, 212 d, 238.

Perhaps he took the manor back during the anarchy, for he was one of those who were to be compelled in 1158 to restore property they had usurped from the church of Ely.[1] Eventually he had his way: in a settlement made in the year 1200, he was allowed to keep the manor for the service of one knight and a gift to the monks of land worth 100s.[2]

Other lands recovered in 1135 sooner or later found their way back into the hands of military tenants—but not without an interval. That we may assume to have been the case where lands, resumed by the bishop in 1135, appear as fees of the new enfeoffment (i.e. as creations of the period after 1135) in the bishop's *carta* of 1166. The fees in Streetley[3] and Mepal[4] are cases in point. In other instances—Impington and Cottenham, for example[5]—lands recovered in 1135 were not demised once more to military tenants until after 1166. Finally, the case of Coveney in the Isle is not without some interesting points. Sometime before 1163, it was granted to Ralf fitzOlaf, ancestor of the Lisles of Rougemont and steward of Bishop Nigel, for a rent of 5s. a year by Prior Alexander of Ely. In his charter confirming the grant, the prior had some suggestive remarks to make: 'we will not warrant anyone who says he has a grant or confirmation made by us in the time of Bishop Hervey, when we had no copy of our seal; or even in the time of Bishop Nigel when he had our lands and goods in his possession'.[6] Now Coveney was not one of the manors Hervey gave to the convent;[7] but we may infer from Prior Alexander's charter that he had

[1] Holtzmann, *op. cit.* II, no. 98.

[2] *Rotuli Curiae Regis*, II, 179, 274.

[3] The one fee of the new enfeoffment held by Jordan de Samford in 1166 lay in Streetley and Brightwell (Suff.).

[4] The fee held by Ralf fitzRichard in 1166 (*RBE*, I, 364) is probably Mepal. At the beginning of the thirteenth century it was held by Warin de Saham, who also held Henny of the prior and convent for 4s. a year; and this latter holding had been granted to one Richard fitzRalf (probably the father of Ralf fitzRichard) by Prior William (1133–44?): Trin. MS. O. 2. 41, f. 288; Liber M, f. 241.

[5] The bishop's lands in Impington were acquired by Simon Lisle in about 1201; they had previously been in the hand of Simon fitzEva, but it is not certain how far back the latter's title went: *Rotuli de Oblatis*, 157; *Rotuli Curiae Regis*, I, 25, 75. Nor is it certain when the senior branch of the Lisle family acquired Cottenham, but certainly after 1166.

[6] Cott. Claudius C xi, f. 346d; Coucher Book, 213d (printed below, Appx. XIII, p. 287).

[7] It does not appear in D & C Charter no. 51.

granted it away to someone. But so had Bishop Nigel (or so it had been granted in Bishop Nigel's time) when he had the priory's possessions in his hand: most probably then in the first two years of his episcopate, when he is said to have set a certain Ralf or Ranulf in charge of both his own and the conventual estate.[1] The actual deed in question may have survived—a charter in which Prior William (1133–44?) granted Eye and Coveney to Eustace the bishop's butler for the service of half a knight.[2] Both may have been resumed into demesne in 1135; and though Eye returned to the butler's fee,[3] Coveney must at some time or another have been given to the convent before Prior Alexander gave it to the Lisles.

Pampisford, Stetchworth, Coveney—here are three places where there were knight's fees in the reign of Henry I which did not find a place amongst the fees of the old enfeoffment in 1166; the same may well have been true of some of the other places which Bishop Nigel resumed in the first days of King Stephen. If we take the second phase in the history of the barony to cover the time from the accession of Rufus to the *carta* of Bishop Nigel in 1166, it is clear that this phase must be divided up into a number of sub-periods. The fact that Rufus raised the *servitium debitum* of the abbey, perhaps also the fact that Bishop Hervey had relatives and hangers-on[4] to provide for, stimulated Abbot Richard and Bishop Hervey to create military tenures: a dispersion of the lands of the church contrary to the canons for which Eugenius III was still to remember them in 1150.[5] But from 1135, perhaps under papal influence, this tendency was reversed. Bishop Nigel was busily engaged in resuming fees granted away by his predecessors when the outbreak of civil war again completely changed the whole situation.

Bishop Nigel's embroilment in the conflict between Stephen

---

[1] Trin. MS. O. 2. 1, ff. 126d–7, 132d.

[2] Coucher Book, f. 213d.

[3] It is the fee of new enfeoffment held by Peter *pincerna* in 1166: *RBE*, I, 364.

[4] Apart from the archdeacon, his nephew, Hervey may have brought to Ely some others who make a first appearance in the barony of Ely at this time: Ralf the Burgundian, who had a messuage in Ely near his master; Harolf, whom he enfeoffed in the manor of Hoo; William Pelryn and Osbert of Hinton, no doubt first holders of fees in Littlebury and Hinton Hall which were of old enfeoffment in 1166: Liber M, ff. 145, 146; Douglas, *Feudal Documents*, p. cl; D & C Charters nos. 51, 52B; Coucher Book, f. 217.

[5] Holtzmann, *op. cit.* no. 63 and above, p. 168.

and the Empress Matilda is too well known to need discussion here;[1] but the military commitments in which that conflict involved him are important for the present purpose. In 1140 he was making the castles of the Isle defensible; but in the same year Stephen laid siege to the Isle and drove the bishop's knights out of Aldreth castle. After Stephen's defeat at Lincoln in 1141 Nigel's private army reassembled, and Geoffrey de Mandeville was sent against them: an expedition which ended with the sorry sight of Geoffrey marching into Ely bringing with him the bishop's knights with their feet tied under their horses.[2] Emergencies of this sort must soon have called a halt to the policy of resuming knight's fees which Nigel had taken up in 1135; indeed, there is nothing surprising in the charge, brought at an ecclesiastical council in 1143, that 'bona ecclesie sue in milites dissipaverat'.[3] A number of lands, some of them lands resumed in 1135, had to be granted away to procure military followers or to buy political support. The fees of the new enfeoffment in 1166 still bear witness to this brief but important period in the history of the barony.

Probably the majority of the fees created after 1135 had as a prime objective the provision of a military force for the civil war; but perhaps we may instance in particular a few fees held by men who were clearly very close to the bishop in this period. Such a man was Ralf fitzOlaf, Nigel's chamberlain in 1144 and associated with the bishop at an even earlier date, who at some time or another was accommodated with military tenements at Northwold and at Nedging.[4] Such another was a man also with a significant name: that Albert *anglicus* who had a fee in Hertfordshire in 1166 and who was one of the men who acted as guarantor for the bishop's fine to have the king's peace in 1144.[5] But political expediency also left some mark. We may probably assign to this period an unfortunately incomplete charter wherein

[1] See particularly Round, *Geoffrey de Mandeville*.
[2] Trin. MS. O. 2. 1, ff. 142–4; Bodl. Laudian Misc. 647, ff. 86 d–87.
[3] *Ibid.* f. 88 d; Trin MS. O. 2. 1, f. 145 and compare Round, *op. cit.* p. 412.
[4] Trin. MS. O. 2. 1, ff. 146, 150.
[5] *Ibid.* f. 150 d; *RBE*, I, 365. The fact that both Ralf and Albert may have been of English or Anglo-Danish stock is not without interest as a pointer to circumstances which may have reopened the ranks of the aristocracy to men of native stock. Nor do these men stand alone in Nigel's entourage: there are also references to Godric *miles* of Walsoken and Godwin *miles* who had property in Ely—Thorney Red Book, I, f. 189; Bodl. Laudian Misc. 647, f. 114.

Nigel granted to Earl Aubrey II lordship over two fees in the Rodings (Essex) and over the fee Hugh de Bray held (at Landbeach in Cambridgeshire);[1] the grant of demesne manors at 'Brunesthorp' and Mundford to Hugh Bigod;[2] and, in the same way, the acquisition of a fee in Hertfordshire by a member of the Valoignes family, active like the earls on the side of the empress.[3] It need hardly be added that we must add to these deliberate grants of fees losses of property which were quite involuntary— lands that were seized by Geoffrey de Mandeville in the Isle, by the king without the Isle, and by their followers everywhere.[4]

The reign of Henry II was the time when many problems were settled in the barony of Ely, some which may go back to the Norman conquest, some of them product of Nigel's enfeoffments and Nigel's misfortunes. The crown stepped in decisively to establish order, following upon the tradition which the Conqueror had begun and Henry I had carried on. It was in the king's court at Northampton that controversies were settled between Ranulf Glanville and the Ardernes, and between both and the bishop, about the service of two knights due from the manor of Fimborough in Suffolk.[5] It was in the king's court at Windsor that Roger Bigod recognized that he owed the service of six knights for land held of the bishop in Suffolk;[6] and so closed a controversy which may go back to the Conqueror's time and which was still at issue in 1166.[7] It was of King Henry that the first Robert Lisle sought confirmation of the fees he and his father had accumulated by gift of Bishop Nigel and others.[8] After a century of disorderly growth, full of stops and starts and violent changes of front, the feudal structure of the barony of Ely was at last reduced to order and coherence.

[1] Morant, *History of Essex*, II, p. 447. The subject of the charter was, no doubt, the two fees of Simon de Roding which Earl Aubrey had in 1166. The early history of Landbeach, which the charter states had been granted to Aubrey I by Robert de Oilli and to Aubrey II by William de Cursun, is extremely obscure.

[2] Liber M, f. 89 (see below, Appx. III, p. 281).

[3] *RBE*, I, 365; Round, *op. cit.* p. 172.

[4] See the letter of Pope Lucius II in 1144: Holtzmann, *op. cit.* II, no. 40.

[5] Liber M, f. 89 (a charter of 1177–88).

[6] *Ibid.* f. 89 (a charter of 1177–86), printed below, Appx. III, p. 281.

[7] *RBE*, I, 364.

[8] Coucher Book, f. 214, confirming *inter alia* the grants made to Robert by Bishop Nigel in a charter to be found *ibid.* f. 213 and in Cott. Claudius C XI, f. 344.

Moreover, there was no going back to the policy of resuming knight's fees which had been pursued at Wandlebury and for which Innocent II had pressed in 1138 and 1139. To have done so would have been to repudiate the feudal obligations which the Conqueror and Lanfranc had imposed upon the church, and which there is no sign that Henry II ever thought to surrender. The papal attitude had not changed: Eugenius III made that perfectly clear in 1150,[1] and in 1156 Hadrian IV gave Nigel three months in which to resume the lands he and his predecessors had granted away on pain of suspension from episcopal office if he failed.[2] When it appeared that the threat would in fact be put into effect the king was compelled to step in to secure postponement of this sentence.[3] After that, there is no sign that the issue was pressed further; but this had been a preliminary trial of strength between the crown and the papacy in which the former seems to have had the support of the prelates of England.[4] Henry II, it must have been clear, was another man than Stephen.

Of the later history of subinfeudation in the barony, very little need be said. Less than ten fees altogether were created after 1166. One or two, like the recognition of the earl of Warenne's title to Marham, might result from a settlement of old disputes. A few were created to reward faithful servants, like the half fee Robert Lisle held in Cottenham in 1212 or the fee in Impington which Simon Lisle had acquired by about 1200.[5] But the greatest number of new 'knights' were established in the Marshland, though the service they represented was inconsiderable. An elaborate calculation might tell us that some four fees were created there; but almost without exception they were fractional fees, twelfths, sixths, quarters and so on.[6] Men such as these cannot have been enfeoffed primarily with a view

---

[1] Holtzmann, op. cit. II, no. 63.   [2] Ibid. no. 92.
[3] Ibid. nos. 93, 96, 98–100.
[4] Archbishop Theobald loyally urged Nigel to recover the property he had dispersed (Trin. MS. O. 2. 1, f. 169), but the Pope himself stated that postponement of sentence on the bishop had been granted at the request of the king, the archbishop and the bishops of England: Holtzmann, no. 100.
[5] Caius 485/489, f. 15; Rotuli de Oblatis, 157.
[6] See the list of 1208–13 in Book of Fees, I, pp. 628–9; and compare the entry regarding Nicholas the clerk at Doddington in 1222: 'idem tenet triginta acras de assarto per servicium militare, scilicet per octavam partem': Cott. Tiberius B II, f. 98.

to military service. Support they might be for the constable of Wisbech castle; but their real importance was probably that they were men of enterprise or men who had won reward from the bishop in an area where assarting provided a readily available fund of land for new settlers, great and small. These were men of a different sort from those 'milites episcopi' whom Geoffrey de Mandeville had fought and conquered.

In the early thirteenth century there are signs once more of a tendency to reverse the whole policy of subinfeudation, though on this occasion the motives would seem to be economic and have little to do with the canons or the papacy. Hugh of Northwold, that astute manager of his estate, from time to time bought out a military tenant. He bought the Lisles out of Northwold and turned the manor into a demesne manor;[1] he did the same with the Wintringhams in Totteridge,[2] and with the Westons in Tyd.[3] Yet such a policy was hardly likely to produce large scale results. The enfeoffment of military tenants which had been virtually completed in the twelfth century had created a powerful vested interest in the land which, at that late date, could neither be disregarded nor extinguished. That interest still leaves its imprint upon our English countryside; knights as well as barons have given Christian names to many a Saxon village.

III

In this connection, then, it is time to look a little more closely at the knights of St Etheldreda: to see what sort of men they were, what were their relations with the bishop, with other magnates and with the king. Such an undertaking is limited perforce by the nature of the evidence; it also demands an artificial limitation if it is to remain within the bounds of an essay such as this is. Before the thirteenth century, the materials for a history of the knights are painfully meagre; on the other hand, once the great series of government records has begun the evidence, if never complete, is sometimes embarrassing in quantity and variety. For that reason, in what follows, attention has been concentrated mainly upon the Cambridgeshire fees of the

---

[1] At a cost of 400 marks: Caius 485/489, ff. 4, 8 d, 9 d.
[2] For 200 marks: *ibid.* f. 164; Bodl. Laudian Misc. 647, ff. 129 d, 132 d, 133 d.
[3] For 40 marks: Coucher Book, f. 228.

barony and the men who held them between the accession of King John and the death of Edward II.

To take first questions first: what sort of men were they, these knights of St Etheldreda? or, to put it more exactly and as Henry I did, these barons and vavassors holding of the church of Ely? Here one thing is clear: they were different sorts of men at the same time and at different times. In 1086, 1166, 1212 and later some of the men holding knight's fees in the barony of Ely were barons, not of the honour, but of the kingdom. The descendants or successors of Roger Bigot, William of Warenne, Hardwin de Scalers, Picot, and Guy of Rembercurt—men ordered by the Conqueror to serve the abbot of Ely—continued to hold in the bishop's barony as well as of the king 'per baroniam'. From time to time, these barons of the conquest were joined by newer men, men who throve to a barony by the king's favour or even the bishop's favour. This whole group of 'baronial knights' calls for first consideration.

A goodly number of this group have titles which go back to the original settlement of the Normans. They include the Bigod earls of Norfolk, with six fees of the bishop in Norfolk and Suffolk;[1] the earls of Clare with fees in Broxted and Clenchwardon;[2] and the earls of Warenne who never relinquished that claim they had staked in Marham before *Domesday Book* was made.[3] They include also the Scalers of Whaddon and the Frevilles of Shelford, inheritors of Hardwin's barony which was divided between his two sons soon after 1086;[4] the Foliots and Ledets to whom the barony of Guy de Rembercurt descended;[5] and the Pecches, barons of Bourn, to whom descended a great part of the lands amassed by Picot and Hervey de Bourges.[6]

All of these men have a venerable title; all of them hold of the king in chief 'per baroniam';[7] but in terms of social status,

---

[1] *RBE*, I, 364.   [2] Caius 485/489, ff. 14d, 15d.
[3] See above, p. 169.   [4] *FFC*, 209.   [5] *FFC*, 245.

[6] The Pecche family was already established in 1086 as undertenants in Essex, Norfolk and Suffolk. Its rise to baronial status was probably due to William Pecche's marriage with the daughter and heiress of Hervey de Bourges, and to his son's with one of the coheiresses of Robert Peverel, to whom Henry I had granted most of Picot's lands: *GEC*, x, 331–6 and see the pedigree in *FFC*, p. 160.

[7] Some of the references are as follows: Scalers of Whaddon—*Cal. Inq. pm*, II, 309; Frevilles of Shelford—*ibid.* v, 228–9; *RH*, II, 540; Pecche of Bourne—*ibid.* II, 520–1, 526; *FA*, I, p. 171.

of wealth and of control over men we can hardly speak in the same breath of Clare and Scalers, of Warenne and Pecche. The earl of Warenne in the late thirteenth century had an income of £2000 a year or more; the earl of Clare in 1263 (even excluding his lands in Wales and Ireland) one of £1800, and he was paying scutage in the thirteenth century on some 450 knights' fees.[1] With some of the other families mentioned the situation was very different; and a few details may be worth consideration.

Of the minor baronial families holding in the honour of Ely, the barons of Bourn were probably the most substantial. Unfortunately there is no detailed survey of their estate, probably because Edward I used the chronic indebtedness of Gilbert Pecche[2] to secure the barony for himself and his Queen.[3] Even so, it is a far cry from the 450 fees of the earldom of Clare in the thirteenth century to the 17½ fees which Hamon Pecche returned in 1166, when he was also providing the service of two knights from his own demesne.[4] What the income of the family was there is nothing to tell us. Their lands were moderately extensive;[5] but few of their manors were demesne manors and not all their demesne manors had a demesne.[6] It seems clear that we must think in hundreds, not thousands, of pounds. Certainly the lands and fees surrendered to the Crown by Gilbert Pecche in 1284 were worth only £124 a year;[7] they may not have exhausted Gilbert's resources, but that gives us an indication of their order of magnitude.

If these resources seem small beside those of Clare or Warenne,

[1] Painter, *English Feudal Barony*, pp. 42–3, 174, 177.

[2] As early as 1270 he was indebted to Jews; in 1275 to the earl of Cornwall for £800; in 1280 to one Jewish creditor alone for 500 marks. The story of his deepening distress can be followed in *Exchequer of the Jews*, I, pp. 252–3; II, pp. 176, 266; III, p. 297; *Cal. Pat. R*, 1266–72, 441; *Cal. Close R*, 1272–9, 238; 1279–88, 80; LTR Mem. R. no. 51, m. 9.

[3] Westcliffe in Kent was secured in 1280 and most of the rest of Gilbert's lands in 1284: *RBE*, I, p. cxxviii; *Cal. Close R*, 1279–88, 25, 80; *Cal. Charter R*, II, 281; BM Add. 5837, f. 190.

[4] *RBE*, I, 366–7; a total of about 19 fees accords well enough with scutage records, etc., later: *Pipe R*, 8 Ric. I, 280; 3 John, 139; *Book of Fees*, II, 913, 918, 921.

[5] Extending to perhaps ten counties in the early thirteenth century: *Rot. Litt. Claus.* I, 120, 250–1, 326, 371, 571; II, 104; *Rolls of the King's Court in the Reign of Richard I*, p. 38.

[6] There was no sign of cultivation even in their capital manor of Bourn in 1279: *RH*, II, 520–1.

[7] *Cal. Charter R*, II, 281.

we must still remember that the death of Gilbert's father had been thought worthy of mention by Matthew Paris;[1] and that when we turn to the two families which inherited the barony of Hardwin de Scalers, we have still lesser men upon our hands. In the thirteenth century half the barony was still held by Hardwin's descendants; the other half had passed by marriage to the Hertfordshire family of Freville. Both families had highly localized interests, and their property was restricted to the four adjacent counties of Cambridge, Hertford, Norfolk and Suffolk. Both had three or four demesne manors, and an income of £50 or £60 a year.[2] Both owed the service of some 15 knights;[3] but they seem to have enfeoffed somewhat sparingly and often in fractional fees,[4] and by the fourteenth century these fees were looked upon as wasted land.[5] Both in the twelfth century, not without difficulty, paid the relief of a baron;[6] but in the thirteenth they were turning into the country gentlemen they really were. Thomas de Scalers, who succeeded in 1284 and died in 1341,[7] might even be taken as a typical member of that class. He was an M.P. for the county of Cambridge; he served on local commissions with other knights of similar substance; he was sheriff of Cambridge and Huntingdon.[8] In the fifteenth century the Frevilles too would represent Cambridgeshire in parliament, and they would still have an income of about £60 a year; but they were no longer barons or even knights, for in

---

[1] *Chron. Majora*, IV, 175.

[2] Geoffrey de Scalers of Whaddon in 1284 had an income of £54; Richard Freville in 1299 one of £58 and John his son one of £64 in 1312: Chancery Inq. pm, Edw. I, Files 38 (4), 87 (15); Edw. II, File 30 (10); AR no. 85, m. 9d. The unreliability of figures taken from the inquests *post mortem* is, of course, fully realized (see Kosminsky, *EcHR*, III, pp. 16ff.), but here and in what follows they are used rather as comparative indices, for which they will probably serve.

[3] *Rotuli de Oblatis*, 167, 168.

[4] In 1166 Hugh de Scalers returned only about 8 fees, and Stephen de Scalers (holding the later Freville moiety) 10 fees, of which only 7½ could be traced in 1312: *RBE*, I, 367–70; *Cal. Inq. pm*, V, 228–9.

[5] In 1312 the fees of the barony of Shelford 'non possunt extendere ad aliquem valorem quia non fecit aliquod servicium nisi scutagium quando currit': Chancery Inq. pm, Edw. II, File 30 (10).

[6] William de Scalers made fine in £100 for his father's lands in 1168 and had still not cleared the debt in 1188: *Pipe R*, 14 Hen. II, 105; 34 Hen. II, 40; Round, *Family Origins*, p. 232.

[7] Liber M, f. 515.

[8] *Returns of M.P.'s*, I, pp. 10, 13, 30; *PRO Lists and Indexes*, IX, p. 12; *Cal. Pat R*, 1292–1301, 515; *Cal. Close R*, 1288–96, 522.

1436 William Freville appeared under the rubric of esquires.[1] Behind these changes there lies an obscure revolution in society. Wide disparities of wealth were as characteristic of the twelfth as of the fourteenth and fifteenth centuries; but before these latter centuries the significance of tenurial relationship with the king had lost its force. By the end of the thirteenth century wealth and the power which wealth conferred had shifted the landmarks in medieval society; and the names of knight and baron were ceasing to imply tenures and becoming titles of honour.[2]

Under such circumstances it is not surprising to find that new barons as well as old were knights of St Etheldreda's honour. One of the most substantial was also one of the newest. This was Robert Tiptoft, whose devotion to Edward I went back to the time of baronial rebellion and the prince's crusade,[3] though his most consistent service was performed in Wales and the March of Wales.[4] Amongst his possessions he numbered Harston in Cambridgeshire and Strethall in Essex in the barony of Ely, though he had many other lands as we might expect of a man who counted the earl of Lincoln amongst the executors of his will.[5] He had in fact lands in six counties at least, and his income from them was set at £300 a year.[6] But Robert was merely founding the fortunes of his family: his more famous descendant, the fifteenth-century earl of Worcester, would have an income from land of £1000 a year.[7]

Other new families achieved an earlier distinction, like the Lestrange lords of Knockin, who acquired the Ely fee in Milton in 1276. *Novi homines* under Henry I, they acquired property in Norfolk by marriage into the family of Ralf fitzHerluin;[8] but like the Tiptofts, they owed their real importance to the Welsh march, and from the reign of Henry II they gradually grew in

[1] Wedgewood, *History of Parliament* 1439–1509, II, p. 384; Gray, *EHR*, XLIX, p. 632.

[2] On this whole question see Denholm-Young, *Collected Papers*, pp. 56–67; Treharne, *BIHR*, XXI, pp. 1–12; and Stenton, *History*, XIX.

[3] Powicke, *Henry III and the Lord Edward*, II, p. 699; *Cal. Pat. R*, 1266–72, 440, 441.

[4] R. J. Mitchell, *John Tiptoft 1427–1470*, p. 3.

[5] *Cal. Pat. R*, 1292–1301, 381.

[6] Chancery Inq. pm, Edw. I, File 85 (3).

[7] Gray, *EHR*, XLIX, p. 615.

[8] Round, *Peerage and Family History*, pp. 123–4.

stature as tenants in Shropshire both of the fitzAlans and of the crown.[1] John Lestrange V, who died in 1309, had property in at least five counties worth £125 a year;[2] property greatly increased when Roger Lestrange, his heir, inherited extensive lands from his kinsman, Ebulo de Montibus, and through his wife from Oliver de Ingham.[3] By the fifteenth century the Lestranges were a substantial, if not outstanding, baronial family with an income of some £400 a year.[4]

If the Lestranges and Tiptofts were primarily king's men, the Lisles, later barons of Rougemont, began in the bishop's service. Ralf fitzOlaf, founder of the family, was Bishop Nigel's steward; and from him acquired lands in Norfolk, Suffolk and Cambridgeshire which were the beginnings of the Lisle estate.[5] From this point, the property of the family grew fairly consistently for five generations. Robert Lisle I obtained Exning with his wife;[6] Robert II married one of the co-heiresses of the steward's fee in the honour of Richmond, and had interests at the beginning of the thirteenth century which extended into Northampton and Lincolnshire;[7] Robert III married one of the co-heiresses of John de Wahull in 1213 and came into her property when she died in 1221.[8] Robert IV, again, married a sister and heiress of Warin fitzGerold,[9] and Robert V a co-heiress of John de Mucegros.[10] Warin Lisle, who followed Robert V, was clearly a man of substance: in 1296 his six demesne manors in Cambridge, Suffolk and Bedford were valued at over £100 a year,[11] a sum which should probably be doubled in order to take account of his Cambridgeshire properties held of the honour of Richmond and the manors in

---

[1] H. le Strange, *Le Strange Records*, pp. 24, 31–3.

[2] Chancery Inq. pm, Edw. II, File 16 (6).

[3] *Cal. Inq. pm*, VII, 463–7; VIII, 374–81; IX, 133–4.

[4] Gray, *EHR*, XLIX, p. 617.

[5] For confirmation of these and other lands in Cambridgeshire acquired by purchase and with his wife, see the charter of Henry II in Coucher Book, f. 214d.

[6] Rymer, *Foedera*, I, I, 42.

[7] Farrer, *Honours and Knight's Fees*, III, p. 172; CRR, III, 345; VI, 168.

[8] *Rot. de Oblatis*, 487; *Exc. e Rot. Finium*, 3, 72–3; *Rot. Litt. Claus*, I, 329, 338–9, 470.

[9] *GEC*, VIII, pp. 69ff.

[10] Farrer, *op. cit.* III, p. 173; but her name seems to have been Mabel, not Alice: Close R, 55 Hen. III, m. 5d.

[11] Chancery Inq. pm, Edw. I, File 82 (9).

Hertfordshire and Oxfordshire he had inherited in 1293 from the Fortibus estates.[1] Over and above these demesne lands, we can trace about a dozen knight's fees held of the Lisles in the early fourteenth century scattered over nine or ten counties.[2] The Lisles were less notable than the vigorous and pushing Robert Tiptoft, but they were still very substantial men beside the Scalers and the Frevilles.

The barons of the honour and in the honour, then, were a various body of men. The same is true of the vavassors. Again there were men with wide interests, scattered estates and considerable substance; and there were also men with lesser substance and property less widely spread. Others again had interests which hardly transgressed the boundaries of the county in which they lived; while by the end of the thirteenth century there were also men holding fees, minutely subdivided, who can have been little more than substantial peasants.

In the category of substantial men, holders of ancient serjeanties and recipients of royal favour in the thirteenth century provide more than one example. Such were the Argentems of Wymondeley in Hertfordshire, held by serjeanty of the butlery from Henry I's time.[3] They were holding land of the bishop in Meldreth at least as early as 1212. In 1318 John de Argentem had property in six of the eastern shires, an income of £100 from his demesnes, and seven fees were held of him which were worth about £65 to their holders.[4] Such, again, were the fitzAuchers, foresters of Waltham from Henry II's time,[5] who acquired a fee of the bishop in Pampisford by marrying its heiress.[6] At the end of the thirteenth century, they had lands in Hampshire, Wiltshire, Cambridgeshire and Essex worth perhaps £40 a year.[7] Such, finally, were the Peverels of Sampford Peverel, whose main estate lay in the west country and was

---

[1] Cal. Inq. pm, III, 98–9 with values taken from Chancery Inq. pm, Edw. III, File 66 (37).

[2] Cal. Inq. pm, v-vii, passim; Cal. Close R, 1302–7, 273.

[3] Farrer, op. cit. II, p. 238.

[4] Chancery Inq. pm, Edw. II, File 68 (2).

[5] Farrer, op. cit. II, p. 289.

[6] Cal. Inq. pm, IV, 112–13.

[7] Chancery Inq. pm, Edw. I, File 110 (9). The successor to the estate married one of the co-heiresses of John de Bellewe and added to it a good deal of property in Yorkshire: Cal. Close R, 1307–13, 440–1; Cal. Inq. pm, VIII, 160.

worth in 1300 about £50 a year.[1] Their connection with the barony of Ely was a venerable one, for Jordan of Sampford held a fee in Streetley and Brightwell before 1166.[2] Other men were rising to a similar substance in the later thirteenth century through the favour of the king. Peter de Chauvent was one: king's knight in Henry III's time, steward and chamberlain of the household under Edward I,[3] he secured the manor of Impington in the barony of Ely.[4] His income was probably greatly understated by the £40 of land he held at his death.[5] Another was Roger Loveday, Edward I's justice, who at his death held a manor in Elm of the bishop of Ely and other lands worth £75 a year.[6]

Men of this sort, however, were not of the common run of country gentlemen; and to discover the latter we must descend still lower in the social scale. Not untypical was the Burdeleys family, holders of a fee of the bishop in Madingley; of the manor of Stagsden in Bedfordshire from a number of lords; and of Scoulton in Norfolk by serjeanty of the king's larder.[7] In 1283 these lands brought in an income of only about £24 a year;[8] yet on such an income Geoffrey de Burdeleys, who succeeded to the estate in that year, contrived to be one of those men who were running the counties of a much governed England for the king. His interests lay chiefly in Cambridgeshire: in that shire he collected taxes, acted as a conservator of the peace, sat on many judicial commissions, conducted an inquest into the payment of scutage and into the collection of pavage in the county town, and sat twice as one of the knights of the shire in the king's

[1] Chancery Inq. pm, Edw. I, File 94 (5).

[2] RBE, I, 364.

[3] Close R, 1259–61, 246; Tout, Chapter in Medieval Admin. History, II, pp. 25–6, 43–4. In 1295 Edw. I described him as 'dilectus et secretarius miles': Cal. Chancery Warrants, I, p. 50.

[4] Apparently by taking advantage of the insolvency of Simon Lisle: Cal. Pat. R, 1266–72, 398.

[5] Chancery Inq. pm, Edw. I, File 107 (24); but before his death he had transferred to his son the manor of Wapham which Henry III had given him: Cal. Pat. R, 1266–72, 211; 1301–7, 55.

[6] Chancery Inq. pm, Edw. I, File 49 (5).

[7] Cal. Inq. pm, II, 277.

[8] Chancery Inq. pm, Edw. I, File 34 (2); this accords exactly with his payment of 180 marks to redeem his property under the Dictum of Kenilworth: KR Mem. R, no. 42, mm. 26, 26 d. His manor of Madingley included dependent military tenures in Rampton, Cottenham and Comberton.

parliament.[1] There were his like about everywhere in thirteenth-century England: Wattishams and Cockfields in Norfolk and Suffolk; Colvilles, Muschets and Maners in Cambridgeshire; Hayes and Berners in Essex. Their incomes sound slight to our ears, but they were doing a wonderful part of the work of government.

Yet below them there was another rung in the ladder of feudal tenants—the one or two manor men of strictly localized importance. It is much harder to obtain information about them, since the king was seldom concerned with them or their property; but a private inquest *post mortem* held by the bishop in 1316 lifts the curtain for a moment. It was concerned with the quarter fee of which Thomas of Elsworth had died seised in Hardwick, consisting in all of some 80 acres of demesne land and 2s. 5d. in rent.[2] We cannot be sure, of course, that this was all the land which Thomas had. He may also have held a quarter fee of the honour of Richmond in Whaddon,[3] together with Picot's fee in Conington—five virgates of land and some £2 in rents in 1279.[4] If these were all properties of the same man, we seem to be dealing with a pushing new man rising on the tide of thirteenth-century prosperity. At Conington, he had displaced the Blancgernuns, at Whaddon the Sahams and at Hardwick Sir Hugh de Estcote. What his total resources were it is hard to say, £15 to £20 perhaps: he was a rising man, but still of a substance less than the Burdeleys.

Lower still amongst this group we should probably place Robert de Aula, holding a quarter fee in Over of the bishop in which he had no demesne land at all.[5] In addition, he seems to have held 40 acres as a hundredor at Linden End and a quarter fee in Graveley as a tenant of the abbot of Ramsey.[6] We may reasonably doubt if his income was much over £5 a year. Not dissimilar in social status may have been William Jake of Eversden with about 80 acres for quarter of a fee;[7] or Richard

---

[1] *Cal. Pat. R*, 1292–1301, 104, 515; 1313–17, 49, 108, 124, 506, 580–1, 584; 1317–21, 460, 542; *Cal. Fine R*, II, 218–19; III, 59; *Returns of M.P.'s*, I, pp. 15, 30.
[2] Cott. Claudius C XI, f. 322.   [3] *FA*, I, p. 150.
[4] *Ibid*. p. 148; *RH*, II, 467–8.   [5] Coucher Book, f. 240.
[6] Caius 485/489, f. 53; *RH*, II, 472.
[7] *RH*, II, 511–14. Of this he had only about 20 acres in demesne, and the remaining 60 acres brought in only about 3s. in rents. On the other hand he was a great dealer in small parcels: he had taken up ten plots from nine different men and containing a further 20 acres, of which he sub-let about

Belebuche with a hide of land in Westwick for the same service;[1] or Thomas Aliquid with the like amount of land for like service in Willingham. There were thriving peasants in the thirteenth century with as much substance; and like many a one of them Thomas Aliquid found his men for the lord's boon days and rode with them to see they did their work well.[2]

It is, moreover, not without interest that we discover that in 1303 this last tenement was held by Walter Aliquid and *partners*; that in 1327 Walter paid a mere 6*d.* to the fifteenth of that year; and that by 1428 this hide which had been a quarter fee in Willingham was broken up into four parcels which cannot have represented more than peasant holdings.[3] This tendency towards disintegration is not without parallel elsewhere. The fee of one knight which the Clement family held in Harston throughout the thirteenth century was in 1346 divided between John Gauge, Millicent Saleman and their partners. In Suffolk, the fee of the Wattisham family in Wattisham, Hitcham and Brettenham had by 1346 been divided into a half fee and two quarters; whilst the two fees of the Ulvistons in Debenham, Wetheringsett and Kenton were even more minutely subdivided into some ten fragments.[4] This disintegration of fees might have more than one consequence. The land might pass directly into the hands of men of peasant status, as the Aliquid fee must have done and as the bishop's own demesne was beginning to do during the same period. Equally, the fragments might go to augment larger units of property, as in the case of the half fee which the Saham family held in Whaddon. It broke up into two portions: a quarter fee which went to swell the property which Thomas of Elsworth was building up, the other quarter (possibly by marriage) to augment the property of the Scalers family, already the main landholders in the village.[5]

---

10 acres. But clearly he cannot have cultivated more than a virgate, and his military service was no more than an obligation for scutage, which he sub-divided amongst his tenants.

[1] *RH*, II, 407–8: he had kept about 75 acres in demesne.

[2] Caius 485/489, f. 116d. The family in the early thirteenth century had also held land in Willingham of the honour of Brittany: St John's College Muniments, Drawer XXXIV, no. 107.

[3] *FA*, I, pp. 148, 185; KR Lay Subsidy, 81/6, m. 9.

[4] *FA*, I, p. 165; V, pp. 71, 93.

[5] *PQW*, 103; *FA*, I, p. 150. Landowning as well as peasant families at this time sometimes add much to their holdings in the shape of small plots of land.

These fragments of biography in the foregoing pages may also call for a word or two on some of the factors which influenced the rise and fall in the social scale of the men who held military tenements in the barony of Ely. Some reduction of status might be implied by the fact that, by the thirteenth century, the holder of a fee was no longer a knight by definition, that knighthood was becoming a title of honour but sparingly applied. There was also, however, a reshuffle of landed property going on; and in the process, some families were falling—families of the lesser baronage like the Pecches; families of a typical knightly sort like the Lisles of Hinton Hall;[1] even new rich families like the Chauvents[2] and Lovedays.[3] In each case, the symptoms were the same: a chronic and pressing weight of debt, which had to be got rid of eventually by the sale of land. But if we search for the causes of this embarrassment, we are reduced to speculation. It may be that the barons of Bourn had, at an early date, enfeoffed knights too generously and left themselves too slender resources in demesne to provide an adequate cash income in the conditions of the thirteenth century. It may be that a small estate, like Simon Lisle's of Hinton Hall, divided between Somerset and Cambridgeshire was an unmanageable property

The Abingtons of Abington-in-the-Clay are not untypical. In 1247 their manor had been worth £11. 18s. od.; in 1274 three additional holdings had been added to the manorial nucleus and it was valued at £11. 19s. 4d.; in 1294 there were nine additional parcels and the value was £18. 9s. 9d.: Chancery Inq. pm, Hen. III, 5 (15); Edw. I, 5 (6), 68 (6).

[1] This family, as consistent in the bishop's service as the Lisles of Rougemont, suffered a rapid eclipse in the later thirteenth century. About 1272 Simon Lisle owed about £360 to Jews, a debt granted by the king to Peter de Chauvent who secured Simon's manor in Impington in settlement: *Exchequer of the Jews*, II, pp. 43–6, 54, 66–8; AR no. 84, m. 8. In 1281 he was raising money from Robert Burnell on his manors in the Isle, and in 1287 and 1291 Robert was in possession of Simon's Somerset manors: *Cal. Close R*, 1279–88, 130, 478; 1288–96, 137. Finally in 1289 he granted all his Cambridgeshire lands, for what consideration we do not know, to the bishop of Ely: Cott. Claudius C xi, f. 22d.

[2] Peter de Chauvent's son began to disperse his father's property almost immediately. He was clearly hopelessly in debt to Geoffrey Seman, member of a prominent family in the borough of Cambridge who in the end secured the manor of Impington in settlement: *Cal. Close R*, 1313–18, 465, 498; 1318–23, 335; 1324–7, 322. Rye, *Cambridge Fines*, pp. 91, 92.

[3] Richard Loveday was in trouble for arrears of rent at Elm in 1299; and by the end of the second decade of the fourteenth century these lands had passed to Walter Langton in discharge of Richard's debts: AR no. 95, m. 27; Chancery Inq. pm, Edw. II, File 70 (7).

at a time when circumstances were calling for greater personal supervision over it. It may well be that, in the last resort, the accidents of personal capacity were the deciding factors. In an age of high farming, in an age of violent inflation and very rapid social change, the complex bureaucracy of a large estate might make the ability of its owner a matter of less concern; on smaller estates, the owner must have counted for more.

The circumstances which might help a family to rise in the social scale are sometimes a little clearer to us. The rewards of service to the king or to some other great man might lay the foundations of a family's fortunes: as it did for the Lisles of Rougemont, for the Tiptofts and Lestranges, for Peter de Chauvent and Roger Loveday. Such service not only gave opportunities for acquiring land, but also for securing other concessions of the sort which makes the landed income of a man like Robert Tiptoft no very adequate indication of his real substance. The grant of offices of profit under the crown, of properties forfeited by the Disinherited, of fines under the Dictum of Kenilworth, of wardships and marriages, of the custody of vacant bishoprics and other lands in the king's hand, of debts owed to Jews—such pickings were a concomitant of royal favour and must have contributed in no small measure to the rapid rise of the Tiptofts.[1] A stake in the Welsh march might offer substantial chances of increasing property as the English hold on Wales was consolidated; some endowment with economic virtues no doubt helped a man in thirteenth-century England. But for families great and small the surest of all the ways to augment the family property was to marry an heiress. That had founded the fortunes of the Pecche family soon after the Conqueror's time; it brought the fitzAucher foresters of Waltham to Pampisford; it was almost an article of faith that a Lisle must marry a woman of property. A business-like knight in thirteenth-century England might prosper if he managed his resources well; but his business acumen had perhaps been most strikingly displayed upon his wedding-day.

---

[1] This summary is based upon entries in the close, patent and fine rolls for the later years of Henry III and the reign of Edward I—entries which can easily be followed in the indices to the printed calendars. Robert's offices included, not only the justiceship of West Wales for most of Edward I's reign, but also at one time or another those of constable of Portchester and Nottingham castles, keeper of Bestwood Forest and the Shepherdry of the Peak, etc.

The knights of St Etheldreda, then, as the thirteenth century drew on, were a motley company. There were the great men of England. There were old barons becoming new gentry, meeting and mingling with other families starting from a humbler place in the ladder of tenure, and both alike busy about the affairs of their counties. There were a few families passing out of this solid core of local substance and climbing towards the newer peerage which was to dominate the closing period of medieval England. Below all of them holders of fees were falling out of the knighthood; and, from a deeper stratum of society, thriving peasants were encroaching upon the lands which once had supported fighting men. All this was a far cry from the society described in Bishop Nigel's *carta*, which lists the men who had garrisoned the castles at Aldreth and Ely and whom King Stephen and Geoffrey de Mandeville had fought and defeated. It is time to return to that time of troubles and look finally at the changes which took place in the relationship between the bishop and his knights.

IV

These changes must take account of a continuous process whereby feudal property was slowly dispersed at various stages of a lengthening tenurial ladder; and, in consequence, the bishop was separated by one or more intermediaries from the actual holders of the land. Owing to the immediate post-conquest circumstances, this had often been true from the beginning; for as early as 1086 Picot and Hardwin and Guy de Rembercurt had enfeoffed military tenants in lands which they had recognized they held of the abbot of Ely. In the twelfth century, instances were multiplied—when political expediency persuaded Bishop Nigel, for example, to grant fees in Landbeach and Aythorpe Roding to the earl of Oxford. The progress of this trend may be illustrated by tabulating the facts about twenty-one Cambridgeshire fees (one of which was divided into two moieties in the course of the thirteenth century).

Date	Demesne	Fees held directly of the bishop	One Mesne Lord	Two Mesne Lords
1086	10	5	6	—
1212	—	13	7	1
1250–79	—	10	10	2

The tendency evident in these figures may have been partly due at some periods to political needs—needs to procure fighting men or the support of influential magnates; and to the operation of the laws of inheritance and the details of family settlements. It was, however, probably also influenced in the thirteenth century by the large amount of buying and selling land which arose out of economic causes. In turn, all those things combined to complicate the feudal relationships into which any given man might enter. The fitzAuchers were no very eminent family; but in 1304 Henry fitzAucher held in the west country of the earl of Salisbury, in Cambridgeshire of the bishop of Ely, and in Essex of the king, the honour of Boulogne and the abbot of Waltham. To these lands his son was to add others in Yorkshire held again of the king, of John Mowbray and of Sir William de Ros.[1] There is no need to multiply such illustrations; they belong to the commonplaces of late feudal history. Equally clearly, however, loyalty was not infinitely divisible. The complexity of tenurial relationships at the end of the thirteenth century can only mean that, in fact, they had been divorced very largely from that personal loyalty which once they had implied; that most of the obligations they had once imposed had evaporated; and that the feudal barony as a community in society and government had to all intents ceased to exist.

Of course, the formal incidents of feudal tenure went on being exacted. The earl of Norfolk and marshal of England did homage for the lands he held of the bishop in the thirteenth and four-teenth centuries,[2] as doubtless his ancestors had done since they had recognized the bishop's lordship in the court of Henry II.[3] Probably he did so in words which were not dissimilar to those which have come down to us from an even later time: 'I become your man and homager from this day forward and faith shall have to you before all men living for the land I hold of you of your lordship, except the faith I owe to my sovereign lord; so help me God and the Holy Dame'.[4] In like manner, reliefs

---

[1] *Cal. Inq. pm*, IV, 112–13; VII, 53; VIII, 160.

[2] So Roger Bigod did homage to Bishop John of Kirkby at the Exchequer in 15 Edw. I and Earl Thomas to Bishop John of Hotham in the chamber-lain's room next the painted chamber in 4 Edw. III: Cott. Claudius C xi, ff. 22 d, 328 d; Coucher Book, f. 224 d.   [3] See above, p. 173.

[4] Cott. Claudius C xi, ff. 22 d, 23 in what appears to be a fifteenth-century hand. For homage rendered for land in Madingley in 10 Hen. IV and for

were no doubt paid at succession to a military tenement at the beginning of the fourteenth century[1] just as they had been paid in the twelfth century.[2] It is possible that knights as well as free tenants may have made a gracious aid to the bishop from time to time;[3] occasionally, where prerogative rights did not interfere, the bishop may have enjoyed the wardship of an heir or the marriage of a daughter or a son.[4] But if these rights persisted, it is unlikely that they were of much profit to the bishop; they were also mere incidents, incidental to the main purpose of military tenure in its origins.

There is, unfortunately, practically no evidence about the performance of military service by the knights of St Etheldreda. They were clearly not performing that service at the beginning of the fourteenth century: the bishop's contingent in 1327, as we have seen,[5] looks like an indentured retinue; and not one of the knights or serjeants sent on the 1322 campaign by the bishop can be identified as one of his military tenants.[6] This service was done, however, after a lapse of three-quarters of a century since last the bishop had sent his quota to the Gannoch campaign of 1246; and it may not be unreasonable to assume that, in that long period, arrangements for the exaction of military service had become obsolete. We can only suppose that between 1189 and 1246, when the bishop commonly sent his contingent to the king's army, he had in fact called upon the military tenants of his barony to perform the obligations of their tenure. Perhaps the service which William Muschet performed in Ireland in 1210[7] (though the bishopric was then in the king's hand during the interdict) is an instance of such service actually being done.

So we are left with scutage, and the different things that might happen when that charge was levied. In the twelfth

a homage ceremony in the bishop's chapel at Downham in the reign of Edward IV see *ibid.* f. 23 and Coucher Book, f. 210.

[1] In 1299 John de Freville paid £7. 10s. for 1½ fees in Shelford, etc.; and in 1310 the keepers of the see specifically reported that there were no reliefs during the period: PRO Min. Accts, 1132/10, 12.

[2] For some examples see *Pipe R,* 17 Hen. II, 115–17.

[3] The prior at least seems to have procured a royal writ to take an aid from his knights: *Pat. R,* 1225–32, 334.

[4] For such claims in respect of the heirs of Robert de Aula and Thomas of Elsworth, see Coucher Book, f. 240 and Caius 485/489, f. 369d.

[5] Above, p. 159.

[6] Chancery Misc., Bdle 5/10 (Marshal's Roll, 16 Edw. II).

[7] *FFC,* p. 206.

century, so far as we can see, either the bishop produced his quota of knights and no question of scutage arose; or the bishop paid scutage to the king on forty fees, and collected from the eighty fees or thereabouts in his barony an amount double that which he had paid. All attempts by Henry II and Henry III to divert all or part of this 'unearned increment' to the exchequer were unsuccessful. In the thirteenth century, the alternatives were more numerous. Again, the bishop might serve—either with forty knights or more commonly with a much reduced quota (not necessarily composed of military tenants of his barony); or he might pay scutage on forty fees; or he might pay a fine which, in the later part of the century, was calculated in terms of the reduced quota due from his barony which had been recognized by the time of Edward I. Whichever course the bishop followed, the Crown's action was the same: a writ was issued to the bishop to take a scutage from his military tenants when he sent knights to the Biham campaign in 1221,[1] when he paid scutage in 1217,[2] and when he fined for service in 1282 or 1303 or 1310.[3]

In the first of these three cases, where the bishop had sent his knights, scutage would doubtless be levied only from those fees which had provided no knight for the bishop's quota (an arrangement which would in the long run make it possible to send a purely hired force as was done in 1322). In the second instance, the bishop would make his profit as in the twelfth century. But when the bishop fined for his service, as he did from the beginning of Edward I's reign onwards, it was another matter. In 1300, for example, he paid a fine of £240;[4] but scutage was levied only at a rate of £2 on the fee.[5] The bishop must, therefore, have paid at least £80 from his own pocket, even assuming (and it is a doubtful assumption) that he was still able to tax all his eighty fees. Of course, he might make a profit still; as he should have done in 1303 when he was able to fine in £120.[6] On the balance, however, if scutage was normally levied at £2 a fee in the reign of the first two Edwards, the bishop's income from this source cannot quite have covered

---

[1] Chew, *Ecclesiastical Tenants-in-Chief*, p. 52n.; *Rot. Litt. Claus.* 1, 475.
[2] *Ibid.* 372; *Pipe R*, 14 Hen. III, 57; Madox, *Baronia Anglica*, p. 95 (quoting Pipe Roll of 2 Hen. III).
[3] *Cal. Scutage R*, 366, 379, 396.
[4] LTR Misc., Bdle. 1/13, m. ·1.   [5] KR Lay Subsidy 242/65.
[6] LTR Misc., Bdle. 1/13, m. 2.

his outgoings in fines.[1] Edward I and Edward II had succeeded where Henry II and Henry III had failed: they had diverted the profitability even of commuting military service from the bishop to the Crown.

This change was worked out concurrently with that other change which made military tenure merely scutage-paying tenure. Time and time again we read of military tenements, of tenements held by military service, namely that they pay so much for scutage when scutage runs.[2] This purely fiscal conception of military tenure had by the thirteenth century become so normal that, like other normal obligations resting upon the land, the payment of scutage had become a charge annexed to holdings and had been pushed down the ranges of society to the peasantry. At Quy in 1279 we read that the whole vill owed scutage;[3] at Rampton that Gilbert Pecche owed scutage to the bishop, John de Burdeleys to Gilbert Pecche, and Robert Lisle to John de Burdeleys—and that even Robert's villeins, even his cottars, paid their share of this burden.[4] Such arrangements might go back for some time. Sometime early in the thirteenth century the bishop increased the service due from the Wintringham fee in Totteridge from one-quarter to half a knight; a little later he bought out the tenant and took the manor back into demesne. But the men of the manor continued to answer for the scutage due from a quarter fee, each according to the size of his tenement.[5]

[1] Income and outgoings would have balanced more or less if the bishop had been able to tax all the fees he once had had; but it seems clear that he was not able to do so, for example, in the case of the fees Gilbert Pecche surrendered to the crown: see above, p. 177.

[2] In 1273 Simon Daubeny 'debuit servicium dimidii militis quando scutagium currit'; in 1279 Edmund Pecche held half a fee in Eye for homage and scutage: Chancery Inq. pm, Edw. I, File 2 (1); *RH*, 11, 442.

[3] *RH*, 11, 496.

[4] *RH*, 11, 451. With this instance may be compared the devolution of scutage in the Coleville fee in Impington. There were no villeins, but the free tenants of the manor paid scutage to Henry de Coleville, Henry to Alexander le Lord, Alexander to Gilbert Pecche and Gilbert to the bishop (pp. 464–5). In Henry fitzAucher's manor at Pampisford, scutage was paid not only by the customary tenants, but also by sub-tenants of his free tenants, and even sub-tenants of sub-tenants of his free tenants (p. 415). At the same time there was nothing novel in villeins paying scutage at this date; some of them had done so before the end of the twelfth century: *CRR*, I, 16 (a Northants case of 1196), and see A. L. Poole, *Obligations of Society in the XII and XIII centuries*, p. 47.

[5] Caius 485/489, ff. 164d–5: 'Juratores dicunt quod quando scutagium evenerit tunc omnes prescripti (tenentes) respondebunt domino de uno

7

This was an old enough arrangement in this case to have made scutage no more than another customary rent before the middle of the thirteenth century: customary and already immutable despite Hugh of Northwold's bargain with his military tenant which had doubled the amount of scutage which the bishop demanded of him.

In these ways, then, between the time of Bishop Nigel and the time of John of Hotham military service degenerated into scutage, scutage into a customary rent, and something from which the bishop of Ely could no longer even profit in face of Edward I's manipulation of the fiscal side of his feudal rights. The obsolescence of these military aspects of feudalism determined the fate of yet another obligation of the military tenant. It was the right of the lord of a great honour to hold a court to which his military tenants owed suit, a court which could enforce the performance of feudal obligations. That point was put clearly enough in the writ in which Henry II called upon the knights of St Etheldreda's honour to perform their castle guard in the Isle of Ely.[1] If they did not do so, he said, the bishop would proceed against them through their chattels and the fees they held of him until they were willing to obey. If the bishop was going to act in accordance with that good old law which was later written into the thirty-ninth clause of the Great Charter, he could only have distrained upon their goods and disseised them of their fees by lawful judgement in the court of the honour.

There are indeed signs of this honour court in our records; that is not the difficulty. The difficulty is to isolate it from all the other courts with which it shares the appellation of 'curia Eliensis'. That title was anything but an exclusive title. It might refer to a court of freemen living in the southern part of the Isle; a court that would later be called the court of the hall or the court of the palace. It might refer to a court held in virtue of the bishop's liberty in the Isle. Still, there are cases where the 'curia Eliensis' must have been a court of the honour, a court of knights. We have, for instance, a copy of a fine made in the

quarterio militis'; and Alan the son of Thomas held 41 acres and 'dabit scutagium quando evenerit secundum porcionem tenementi sui cum aliis'.

[1] Liber M, f. 85; Bodl. Laudian Misc. 647, f. 99d (printed below, Appx. II, p. 281).

court of William Longchamp, elect of Ely, on 2 December 1189, before Osbert the seneschal, Walter fitzHugh and William Muschet, as well as other knights present on that day.[1] The court in question can hardly have been a court for the Isle or some part of the Isle: for the land with which that fine was concerned lay at Fincham in Norfolk and William Muschet, who was one of those present, held not in the Isle but in the shire proper. The case, like another five years later of which we have also a record, was set on foot by the king's writ of right; and once again in this later case the land was not in the Isle, but at Impington in the geldable part of the shire.[2] Doubtless, too, it was the jurisdiction of his honour court that the bishop was defending when he claimed cognizance of cases arising in the king's courts and concerned with property elsewhere than in the Isle of Ely: in the case, for example, between Ranulf Despencer and John de Camera in 1199, which probably had to do with land in Westwick.[3]

Such a court of knights, moreover, could even be assembled as late as 1229. In that year both bishop and prior died, and the question arose whether or not the king's keepers of the bishop's temporalities ought to seize also the conventual possessions. The issue was decided by an inquest; and in the end the king relinquished his claim to the conventual property in such a circumstance. The letters notifying this decision were a precious document; and for that reason they were read in the court of Ely, so that the knights there assembled could be witnesses to their tenour should such a situation recur.[4] But the most valuable part of the record of these events is that it includes a list of eighteen of the knights present on that occasion, of whom sixteen can be positively identified. Five had their main holdings in the Isle of Ely. Six others had fees which lay in Cambridgeshire

[1] Cott. Tiberius B II, f. 254.

[2] *Rot. Curiae Regis*, I, 34, 64. The record is very corrupt and reads 'Prumptune'. The identification with Impington is based on the fact that the claimant in the case was Simon the son of Eva, who in 1201 gave land in Impington to Simon Lisle by charter, land which Simon held in 1212 of John the son of Simon: *Rot. de Oblatis*, 157; Caius 485/489, f. 14d. The issue here, incidentally, was settled by judicial duel in the bishop's court.

[3] *CRR*, I, p. 89; for the Despencer lands in Westwick in the twelfth century see *FFC*, pp. 35–7; but John de Camera held there of the bishop in 1212: Caius 485/489, f. 14d.

[4] Bodl. Laudian Misc. 647, ff. 132d–3.

outside the Isle (and these included Richard de Scalers, Baron of Shelford). Of the rest, there was Giles of Wattisham and Hervey Thurmod, tenants at Wattisham and Rattlesden in Suffolk; Robert de Ulmo, tenant of an unidentified fee in Hertfordshire in 1212; Geoffrey of Wintringham and Richard Chewelle, tenants of Totteridge and Hatfield in the same county; and Walter Pelryn, holder of a fee at Catmere Hall in Littlebury, Essex.[1] The list ends with the usual 'et multis aliis', but even the names it cites would constitute a representative enough gathering of the knights of the barony of Ely.

That, however, is the last time the honour court appears in the records, so far as can be seen. This may have been due in the main to the general influences which were undermining feudal jurisdiction everywhere by the beginning of the thirteenth century. At the same time, two special reasons may have made the bishop of Ely the more acquiescent in this withering away of his honour court. Firstly, throughout his estate and over all his hundreds the bishop enjoyed (or was making good his claim to enjoy) amercements imposed by the king's justices.[2] He had little reason, therefore, to feel concern about the superior attractiveness of the wares offered by the royal courts. Long before 1229, instead of claiming his own court where such antique processes as the duel[3] still flourished, he would claim instead his liberty,[4] or more exactly the amercement in virtue of his liberty.[5] The new Angevin justice may have eaten away much of the jurisdiction of the bishop's honour court, but it abated in no way the profit he derived from the administration of justice.

If the bishop's general liberty contributed in this way to the decline of the honour court, so also did the particular and special liberty he enjoyed in the Isle. The 'curia Eliensis' of which most is heard in the thirteenth century is a court of the bishop's 'itinerant justices'. Already before 1229, in 1220, such a court

---

[1] Caius 485/489, ff. 157d, 173d, 314d, 322d; Cott. Tiberius B II, f. 247d; Bodl. Laudian Misc. 647, 132d.

[2] The bishop was allowed the amercements from the eyre of 1223 in his Norfolk and Suffolk hundreds, and from all his lands and fees: *Rot. Litt. Claus.* I, 539–40, 583, 628.

[3] See above, p. 193, n. 2.

[4] *CRR*, II, 224 (Cambridgeshire, 1203); v, 128 (Norfolk, 1207).

[5] *CRR*, IV, 120 (1206, Suffolk): 'Episcopus Eliensis petit misericordiam per libertatem suam.'

seems to be hearing a plea between Alan de Fitton and William
Longchamp about land in Leverington, a plea which was heard
'in curia Elyensi et per breve domini Regis de morte anteces-
soris'.[1] There were, of course, knights in the court; but with
them two or three freehold tenants, the reeve of the hundred,
Solomon the goldsmith of Ely and the janitor of the priory—and
all of them were tenants in the Isle. In short, with the king's
courts doing what the honour court had done outside the Isle;
with this court of the bishop's itinerant justices doing all that
the king's courts could do within the Isle—there was no real
function left for the honour court to perform. In fact, to all
seeming, it quietly disappeared about this time. It was at this
time, too, that the other functions of the barony were disappearing. It was the last age of military service, for never again
after 1246 did the bishop exact service from his fees. Knight's
fees became merely pieces of property which occasionally paid
scutage, valueless to the bishop just as the fees of the barony of
Shelford were to their lord because they did no service save
scutage when it ran.[2] More and more of them had disappeared
from the bishop's view behind a screen of mesne tenancies.
Some of them were already tending to disintegrate. The feudal
community had become at best a fiscal community.

One consequence of this group of changes must have been the
disappearance of that close personal association between knights
and bishop, of which one of the main foci must have been the
honour court, and to which the witnesses of the twelfth century
charters are some sort of testimony. The knights, of course,
were part only of the entourage of a feudal bishop: he was also
accompanied in the charters by members of his ecclesiastical
familia, by his household servants, even by visiting strangers.[3]
Still, a bishop like Nigel was often in the company of his
knights: not only his steward, chamberlain, butler and despencer
(men who were also military tenants of the barony); but also
plain knights like Jordan of Hinton, the Beche family, the
Picots, Ralf fitzRichard, Humphrey fitzGeoffrey, and William

[1] D & C Charter no. 833; and cf. Egerton MS. 3047, f. 211d.
[2] See above, p. 178, n. 5.
[3] D & C Charter no. 52 B (printed Douglas, *Feudal Documents*, p. cl from
Liber M, f. 145). It is a charter of Bishop Hervey's witnessed by the abbot
of Thorney; the archdeacon of Cambridgeshire and three other clerks; the
bishop's steward and five other knights; and half a dozen 'ministri episcopi'.

Muschet (from Cambridgeshire); Hugh de Berners from Essex; Albert Anglicus and the Pelryns from Hertfordshire; Stephen de Marisco from Norfolk.[1] This composite picture has some similarities with the record of 1229; it implies a degree of personal association which must have made the community of the honour comprehensible in human terms, as well as in administrative and judicial terms.

More than that, this personal association of bishop and knights provided much of the administration of the barony. The honour court itself, here as elsewhere, must have done work which was as much administrative as judicial; and as late as 1229 the facts about the king's rights during vacancies could be committed to its collective memory as the safest repository for such facts. But the knights were also a reservoir of administrative personnel. The early stewards of Ely—Ralf fitzOlaf under Nigel, Osbert Longchamp under his uncle, Simon Lisle under Eustace[2]—were either holders of military tenements or they were almost automatically provided with such holdings. Here again the situation was changing in the early thirteenth century, and Matthew Christien, who was John of Fountains' steward, was already another sort of man than his predecessors had been. He may have started his career as the bishop's steward,[3] but from this office he passed easily into the royal service—as a keeper of the vacant see in 1229, a collector of taxes in the liberty of Ely in 1232, a justice to enquire into the doings of Peter de Rievaulx in 1234.[4] From this wider experience, he could then return to the bishop's service: he was Hugh of Northwold's attorney in 1236,[5] one of his justices in 1243,[6] and he may even have become steward once again.[7] He may have thriven to knighthood,[8] but there is no sign that he

---

[1] These remarks are based upon an examination of over thirty of Nigel's charters, scattered over a number of sources. His acts would amply repay systematic collection.

[2] For Ralf, see Gray, *Priory of St Radegund*, pp. 74–7; D & C Charters nos. 53 (1), 53 (2); Liber M, ff. 154, 155, 158; for Osbert, Cott. Tiberius B II, f. 254; and for Simon, D & C Charter no. 822 and *CRR*, II, 136; VII, 5.

[3] D & C Charter no. 833; Liber M, ff. 169–74.

[4] *Close R*, 1227–31, 177; 1231–4, 160, 573; *Cal. Liberate R*, I, 137–8.

[5] *Close R*, 1234–7, 380.

[6] D & C Charter no. 140.

[7] Cott. Vespasian A XIX, ff. 100, 101 d.

[8] He is given the title 'dominus' in Bodl. Laudian Misc. 647, f. 139 d.

was ever enfeoffed in a military tenement in the barony of Ely.[1] He was not so much a successor of the old feudal stewards as the first of those professional administrators who carried on so much both of royal and private administration alike in thirteenth-century England. But this is parcel of wider changes in methods of administration to which we must return in a later chapter. All that concerns us here is the fact that in the administration of the bishop's barony, as in other things, feudal ties were weakening. The king himself at this time was shifting the burden of political and military responsibility from the barony to the shire. In the shire, the king's government brooked no inter-mediary, such as the feudal tenant-in-chief had been, in the work of government—save where privilege could be successfully asserted and the franchise which supported that privilege could stand the test of frequent 'quo warrantoing'. As part of this shift of responsibility, the knight was being called into the king's service; his field of operations was that community of the shire which waxed as the community of the honour waned. No doubt feudal loyalties continued to cast long shadows over this changing world. The Lisles of Rougemont had founded their family fortune in the service of Bishop Nigel, but they were beginning to take up the king's service as sheriffs of Cambridge-shire before the twelfth century was out.[2] Yet throughout the thirteenth century they remained wonderfully faithful to an ancient loyalty: acting as the bishop's justices[3] and still to be found about his person,[4] even though they were a much more substantial family than once they had been. But such consistency might already seem old-fashioned in that century. Bishop Nigel's castles were already in ruins; his successors were ceasing to send the knights of the honour to the host; and the honour

[1] He was, however, granted assarted land for a money rent in the Marsh-land: Liber M, f. 175 and a roll entitled 'De terris in Wisbech' amongst the D & C muniments. I am indebted to G. J. A. Becket for letting me have a transcript of this latter document.

[2] *Memoranda Roll*, 1 *John*, 4.

[3] In 1243, 1272 and even as late as 1348: D & C Charter no. 140; Liber M, ff. 374, 626.

[4] Robert Lisle (? IV) was one of the jurors who heard the king's letters about the convent's rights in 1229 (Bodl. Laudian Misc. 647, f. 133); and one or another member of the family was constantly attesting the bishop's charters: Liber M, ff. 162–6 (Eustace), 172, 173, 175 (John of Fountains), 175, 177 (Geoffrey de Burgh), 184, 188 (Hugh of Northwold).

court was disappearing—all things which had given a binding character to the feudal relationship. All that remained was a spasmodic and impersonal cash nexus, to which no oath of homage could give real or continuous life.

Nevertheless, more remained of the honour of St Etheldreda than a few old-fashioned loyalties. The abbots and bishops had done more than demand service from their knights in their castles, their military contingents and their honour court. They had also conceded to them no small part of the rights over land and men which had been gathered up before 1066. The endowment of the knighthood with land had a greater permanence than the fleeting device of government represented by the feudal army and the community of the honour. This endowment persisted after the obligations it had entailed had ceased to be significant obligations; it became in the end the endowment of an unpaid local ruling class ready for the king's service. With all the shifts of circumstance and fortune which governed the descent of manors, there is that much continuity between the work of the last abbots and the first bishops in providing for the knights of St Etheldreda, and the busy scene of the county courts of eastern England in Hugh of Northwold's time, when Scalers and Burdeleys and Muschets were already about the work of 'self-government at the king's command'.

VII

THE LIBERTY OF ST ETHELDREDA

WHEN, in the final chapter of this essay, we come to study the administration of the lands of the bishop of Ely, a considerable number of officials of a variety of sorts will have to be passed under review. But in that chapter we shall also be very much concerned with courts; for very often in the affairs of estate or barony there was no more propriety in administrative action without due process of law than there was in the affairs of the Nation. In this chapter, therefore, it will be necessary to complete the study of those rights the medieval bishops had which, so to speak, created the courts which played so great a part in administration. We might say that the bishop's feudal rights created that honorial court of Ely which still had some sort of existence in 1229; a court which could apportion and exact feudal duties from the knights of the honour and, at the same time, define and maintain the rights which the knights enjoyed by virtue of shouldering such duties. In a like manner we may say that the bishop's territorial rights created those manorial courts in which was exercised that jurisdiction over villeins which was 'the very life blood of the agrarian and economic system'.[1] We shall have much more to say of them.

These courts, however, did not exhaust the jurisdictional powers exercised by the medieval bishops of Ely. There were other courts, too, forming part of that complex of powers and privileges which went to make up the franchise or liberty of the church of Ely. This liberty must be considered at this point, for it conferred a further body of rights upon the bishops which, like their feudal and territorial rights, created administrative institutions. It will be convenient, in considering this liberty and its consequences, to follow the pattern of privilege rather than that of geography. We have to deal, so to speak, with successive layers of privilege superimposed one upon the other. There was a common substratum uniform throughout the bishop's lands and hundreds. At certain points this common

[1] Maitland, *Select Pleas in Manorial Courts*, p. lx.

basis was built upon by the addition of those powers which the king would exercise in royal hundreds. Finally, at one point only, in the Isle of Ely, there was yet another storey: a complex of privileges which may almost justify Coke's description of the Isle as a county palatine,[1] a description which would imply that the bishop's power and authority within the Isle was kinglike.[2]

In describing the liberty, we can afford to cast our net widely. In general terms, the medieval bishops took their stand upon the words of instruments drawn up before there were bishops: upon Edgar's charter, upon the Confessor's charter (forgery though it might be), upon the Conqueror's confirmation of the Old English liberty after the famous plea at Kentford. Very early the cathedral priory was claiming that it should enjoy the same liberty as the bishops had. Bishop Hervey may have conceded to them nothing of the sort, but the monks at sometime or another may have fabricated proof that he had done so;[3] and Bishop Nigel certainly did make this concession in his settlement with them round about 1135.[4] This concession in turn, fully established during the thirteenth century (chiefly during the disputes which arose between the monks and the king's keepers during vacancies),[5] was given a definitive form in a charter of Robert of Orford in 1303 in which the *verba generalia* of Bishop Nigel were interpreted in adequate detail and in the light of the controversies raised during nearly two centuries.[6] All this is

[1] *Institutes of the Laws of England*, IV, c. 39: 'In divers statutes it is called the County Palatine of Ely.' There are, certainly, a few references to the county palatine of Ely after the end of the Middle Ages: in a legal record concerned with a customary tenant in the Isle in Edward VI's reign preserved by Bentham, and in the King's Lynn Assembly Book, *s.a.* 1610: CUL Add. 2962, f. 7; *Hist. MSS. Commission*, 11th Report, Appx. III, pp. 151, 177.

[2] Coke, *Institutes of the Laws of England*, IV, c. 36.

[3] There is no mention of any such general privilege in the original of Hervey's charter (D & C Charter no. 51), but in the inflated version printed by Bentham, Appx. XXVI, he is made to grant the monks their court 'cum universis libertatibus et consuetudinibus que in terris meis que mei iuris sunt servantur'.

[4] In words almost identical with those of the forgery quoted above: 'et curiam suam ipsis concedo cum universis libertatibus suis et consuetudinibus que in terris que mei iuris sunt servantur': Cott. Vespasian A xix, ff. 43 d–5; Trin. MS. O. 2. 1, ff. 134d–5.

[5] Liber M, ff. 138, 612. In 1272 'jurati dicunt quod Prior et conventus habent omnes libertates sicut Episcopus infra insulam et extra in omnibus terris et tenementis suis per cartas suas'—liberties which the jurors go on to enumerate in great detail.

[6] D & C Charter no. 74A.

a matter of good fortune: we can look to the prior's liberty as well as the bishop's for a description of the medieval liberty of the church of Ely.

I

We may properly begin with the ground floor of the liberty, with the franchise co-extensive with the lands and hundreds of St Etheldreda. In 1272 this was described as giving the prior and convent the right to hold their courts and leets in all their manors; to attach and arrest felons in all their lands; to have a prison for all men arrested in their lands and for their tenants arrested everywhere; to execute judgement upon their men and to receive judicial profits from them in the shape of amercements, fines and forfeited chattels.[1] A better classification of these rights may be drawn, however, from the bishop's defence of his liberties in Huntingdonshire in 1286.[2] Of judicial privileges, he claimed the right to hold the view of frank-pledge in all his manors and to plead all pleas the sheriff could plead in virtue of his office or of the king's writ. Closely related to these judicial privileges were the administrative rights claimed by the bishop: to execute and make return upon all royal writs, to arrest and imprison all criminals taken in his manors and bring them before the king's justices, and to execute the sentence imposed upon them. The profit lay, finally, in the fiscal liberties the bishop claimed: the right to the forfeited chattels of felons and the year and a day in their lands; the right to all amercements and fines imposed by the king's justices upon the bishop's men and lands—a right which, in this very eyre, diverted £11 from these Huntingdon manors to the bishop's pocket.[3] We may pass over more hurriedly the bishop's claim to have warren in all his manors as granted by charter of Henry III,[4] and the grant of exemption from toll which went back to a concession of Richard I;[5] but the three main aspects of the liberty demand closer consideration.

Taking first his fiscal liberty, outside the Isle the bishop in the main simply profited from the activity of the king's

[1] Liber M, f. 612. [2] Coucher Book, ff. 232–3.
[3] Cott. Claudius C XI, f. 328. [4] Mon. Angl. I, p. 486.
[5] D & C Charter nos. 13 and 14. In virtue of this privilege in 1251 the mayor and bailiffs of York were told to cease vexing the bishop and his men in that city by reason of any toll: Close R, 1247–51, 426.

justices. As his liberty was defined in Hertfordshire in 1279, in Huntingdonshire in 1286, in Cambridgeshire in 1299,[1] he enjoyed in the first place the right granted by Henry III in 1233 of receiving all the amercements imposed upon all his men, lands and fees and all the fines issuing from those amercements.[2] From the late twelfth century onwards the main occasions from which such profits accrued were the sessions of itinerant commissions—of the justices of the forest,[3] above all of the justices of eyre.[4] In the ampler liberty enjoyed by bishop and prior in their Norfolk and Suffolk hundreds this privilege extended, not only over all their lands and men, but over all the lands and men within the hundreds.[5] The issues might not be inconsiderable: we hear about £143 from the eyre of Robert de Lexinton in Norfolk and Suffolk in 1237;[6] allowances totalling £80 are to be found on a single Pipe Roll from about the same period.[7]

This profitable right of receiving the amercements and fines from his men and lands included, of course, a share equivalent to his property in common fines made by tithings and vills, hundreds and counties.[8] In fact, such communal payments leave a very early mark on the records. In the earliest pipe rolls, the bishop was already receiving a proper share of murdrum fines.[9] When the eyres began, however, dereliction of communal responsibility became expensive in other matters than mysterious homicide: and the bishop received his due

[1] Coucher Book, ff. 232–3; Liber M, ff. 121–2; AR no. 95, m. 52d.

[2] D & C Charter no. 24.

[3] Notices become very numerous towards the end of the twelfth century: e.g. *Pipe R*, 27 Hen. II, 101, 104, 106; 1 Ric. I, 24, 27, 193. For later instances see *Memoranda R*, 1 *John*, 36 and Coucher Book, f. 200d (52 Hen. III).

[4] Time and time again the barons of the exchequer have to be instructed by the king to honour this liberty: see *Rot. Litt. Claus.* I, 583; II, 143; LTR Mem. R, no. 14, m. 7; *Close R*, 1234–7, 242.

[5] *Rot. Litt. Claus.* II, 143, 202; *Close R*, 1234–7, 229.

[6] BM Add. 41612, f. 19.

[7] *Pipe R*, 14 Hen. III, 96, 343, 344.

[8] Note, e.g., the terms of an extract from a pipe roll copied into Cott. Tiberius B II, f. 249d: 'Vicecomes Cantebr' reddit compotum...de misericordiis hominum, villarum et decenarum quorum nominibus proponitur hoc signum ELY in rotulo de itinere W. de Eboraco. In thesauro nihil etc.'

[9] *Pipe R*, 31 Hen. I, 45, 97; 3 Hen. II, 97; 4 Hen. II, 127–9, 166. This privilege, together with exemption from Danegeld, the bishop was unable or unwilling to confer on his tenants; it was carefully reserved when Nigel granted land in Triplow to Chatteris abbey: Cott. Julius A 1, f. 136d.

profit from the failings, the falsehoods and the neglect of tithings and vills, hundred juries and hundred courts, counties and county courts—from that whole crop of 'common fines' which did so much to make England a much governed England.[1] His share of such fines represented the majority of the profit the bishop reaped from the Huntingdonshire eyre of 1286: only three of his men were amerced, and the sum they paid amounted only to about one-sixth of the total which went to the exchequer at Ely.[2]

A second category of profits from the king's justice which was being claimed before the middle of the thirteenth century,[3] and certainly as a matter of common form by the time of the *quo warranto* enquiries of Edward I, was the bishop's right to have the chattels of all his men condemned as felons and the year and a day's waste of their lands. The latter privilege was being enjoyed at the latest by the years 1253–5, somewhat to the embarrassment of the sheriff of the day from whom the exchequer went on trying to extract the income he ought to have received from the waste of the lands of one of the bishop's felonious tenants.[4] Even Edward I's purge of the judicial bench in 1289 redounded to the prior's profit, though not without some doubt and questioning on the part of the king's advisers: for Thomas de Weyland had been the prior's tenant at Brandeston and elsewhere in Suffolk.[5] It was in part the tendency of the exchequer to question this very liberty which led the bishop to petition the king for redress in 1318, a petition which led to the comprehensive confirmation of the rights of the church of Ely in the parliament of York in that year.[6]

It remains to speak of certain fiscal liberties which progressively became of lesser importance and even completely obsolete. The charters of Henry I were much concerned with the quittance of Bishop Hervey's lands from payments such as

---

[1] E.g. *Pipe R*, 32 Hen. II, 14, 66, 67; 1 Ric. I, 49, 189, etc.
[2] Cott. Claudius C xi, f. 328.
[3] Cott. Tiberius B ii, f. 249d.
[4] Pipe R, no. 106, m. 17d. 'Johannes le Moyne debet 8l. li. 17. sol. 4. den. ob. de duobus debitis...sed non debet summoneri de 19. li. 8. sol. 8. den. de anno et vasto terre Willelmi de Shelford...quia Episcopus Eliensis habuit annum et vastum terre predicti Willelmi eo quod tenuit terram predictam de feodo eiusdem Episcopi.'
[5] BM Add. 41612, ff. 19d–20; *Cal. Fine R*, i, 271.
[6] *Rotuli Parliamentorum Anglie hactenus Inediti*, 68.

wardpence;[1] those of Richard I with gelds and danegelds;[2] while Abbot Samson's kalendar would note that the Ely manors in the St Edmund's hundreds of Suffolk did not scot for gelds and sheriff's aid.[3] Some of these acquittances might still leave a mark upon some of the minor customary rents paid by the bishop's tenants in the thirteenth century, but that was all. The right of the bishop to collect for his own use the danegeld,[4] the *dona* of counties,[5] and the *dona* of boroughs paid by his tenants,[6] evaporated with the passage of these taxes into the limbo of obsolete fiscal devices. Neither bishop nor prior ever obtained a similar exemption from paying the taxes on movables which, from the thirteenth century onwards, became the main method of raising extraordinary revenue. At best, they were able to assert an administrative liberty: the privilege of collecting taxes in their own lands, but for the use of the king.

Here we may leave the records of the exchequer and turn to those of chancery and the king's justices, and to the administrative side of the liberty of Ely. In the administration of justice, both bishop and prior claimed to exclude completely the king's bailiffs in everything which preceded and succeeded trial;[7] and many of the implications of this claim are well brought out in a case which came before the itinerant justices in Cambridge in 1286.[8] A man had been appealed of murder in the prior's manor of West Wratting, and he was arrested and imprisoned there by the prior's bailiffs. He was taken by them to the county court for a preliminary enquiry on a writ *de odio et atia* but, having failed to substantiate his allegation of malice, he was returned to the prior's prison to await the coming of the itinerant justices. Preliminary work of this sort is always before us, as when the bishop's bailiffs seize a tenement to which the succession is disputed and hold an inquest to determine the rightful heir, or carry out arrests in various places in the bishop's fees.[9]

[1] D & C Charters nos. 3, 4; Bentham, Appx. XVIII, XX.
[2] D & C Charters nos. 13, 14.
[3] CUL Add. 6006, f. 103.
[4] *Pipe R*, 31 Hen. I, 46, 49, 59, 62, 94, 99; 2 Hen. II, 14, 16, 17, 20; 8 Hen. II, 47–8, 65–6 (the bishop received about £60 in all).
[5] *Ibid.* 2 Hen. II, 14, 16, 18, 20; 4 Hen. II, 133, 135.
[6] *Ibid.* 5 Hen. II, 53 (a *donum* from the borough of Cambridge).
[7] E.g. *RH*, I, 197, 461 (Hunts. and Norfolk).
[8] AR no. 86, m. 44.
[9] E.g. AR no. 82, mm. 10, 31.

Indeed, the prisons of bishop and prior can seldom have been empty, although they were so numerous that they must often have been no more than improvised gaols.[1]

Perhaps that was the reason for the importance of the gaols both bishop and prior had in Ely and the bishop in East Dereham. It was a matter of complaint by the Huntingdonshire jurors in 1276 that the bishop had taken men from that county to his gaol at Ely;[2] and by the Norfolk jurors that he had taken men wherever he found them in the shire (and particularly from the Marshland manors) and sent them to East Dereham gaol, or even out of the shire altogether into Cambridgeshire (presumably to Ely).[3] This last complaint may explain how it was that in 1251 a man could be outlawed for non-appearance in Norfolk when in fact he was in prison at Ely,[4] but East Dereham gaol was the normal prison for the bishop's men in his Norfolk liberty.[5] The two prisons at Ely served a similar purpose for the liberty in the Isle and even in the shire outside the Isle.[6]

Having transacted this preliminary business for the king's justices, the bishop's bailiffs then carried out the work which followed the coming of the judges. Not only did they collect fines and amercements, and take over the lands and chattels of felons and outlaws; they also did such hanging as there was to be done. Gallows were part of the normal paraphernalia of the bishop's liberty,[7] and there were numerous instances when they were put to use.[8] At Pulham in Norfolk it was even an incident of the tenure of William Akerman and five of his

[1] We hear of the prior's gaol at Stetchworth as well as West Wratting, and of prisoners being kept in the prior's house at Melbourn and in his *curia* at Stapleford. Prisoners were also held in the bishop's *curia* at Colne in Hunts. under guard of the cottars and tofters: AR no. 82, mm. 24d, 27; no. 85, m. 4; Caius 485/489, ff. 104–5 d.

[2] *RH*, I, 197.

[3] *RH*, I, 461, 472; and for a man taken from the Marshland to prison at East Dereham, see AR no. 568, m. 1 d.

[4] *Cal. Inq. Misc.* I, 561.

[5] As it had been for a long time: see *Rot. Litt. Claus.* II, 54, 56; *Pat. R,* 1225–32, 151.

[6] For a man accused of murder at West Wratting and imprisoned at Ely to await trial, see Cott. Vespasian A xix, f. 100.

[7] *RH*, I, 438, 461, 472; II, 143, 152, 607 for a number of manors in Huntingdonshire, Norfolk and Suffolk.

[8] AR no. 82, m. 24d for hangings in both the bishop's and the prior's lands in Cambridgeshire.

peers that they would hang men condemned for theft in the manor.[1]

Sometimes, royal officers were excluded as effectively from the liberty when taxes had to be collected. In 1224 both bishop and prior were collecting by their own bailiffs the carucage granted by the clergy and the crusading taxes;[2] and again in 1225 the fifteenth of movables levied generally in that year.[3] In 1232 and 1237, special collectors were appointed for the liberty,[4] and in the latter case all that appears on the final account of the taxors is a note of the lump sum received from the bishop's lands, without any of the customary detail.[5] Again in 1253, when an aid was levied for knighting the king's eldest son, the bishop accounted directly at the exchequer;[6] and in 1270, when the king's taxors assessed the twentieth even in the Isle, the king conceded that this should not be taken as a precedent.[7] It is none the less possible that it did in fact become a precedent; at least in 1327 the bishop's and prior's lands in both the Isle and the shire were assessed with the same searching detail as all the other lands of Cambridgeshire.[8]

In fact, however, these exclusive rights in fiscal and legal administration were no more than particular aspects of the bishop's right to have the return of all royal writs in all his lands[9]—to execute, in short, all the duties of local administration at the king's command which, outside of liberties, would be the responsibility of the sheriff and his minions. What happened is illustrated by a writ of 1299.[10] The collectors of the tenth and the sixth in Cambridgeshire had not paid over their takings in full, and the sheriff was ordered to distrain for the residue. The sheriff endorsed the writ with the note that he had taken appropriate action against Thomas de Scalers; but the other

[1] Caius 485/489, f. 227; for similar obligations in the Isle, see below, p. 225, n. 6.

[2] *Pat. R*, 1216–25, 494, 508 for payments made by the bishop into the wardrobe; *Rot. Litt. Claus.* I, 593.

[3] *Ibid.* II, 40, 82.   [4] *Close R*, 1231–4, 160–1; 1234–7, 558.

[5] Exch. KR Lay Subsidy 81/1.

[6] Exch. Receipt Rolls (Auditors), no. 23, m. 3; no. 25, m. 3.

[7] *Cal. Pat. R*, 1266–72, 418.

[8] Exch. KR Lay Subsidy 81/6.

[9] For Herts see *RH*, I, 188, 192–4; Hunts, p. 197; Norfolk, p. 461; Cambridgeshire, pp. 51–3 and Cott. Domitian A xv, ff. 147–7 d; and the Isle, AR no. 95, m. 65.

[10] KR Returns of Writs, Bdle. 1, File 10 (15).

collector, Simon de Bradenham, was living in the bishop's liberty, so he had passed the king's writ to the bishop's bailiff who had taken from Simon goods to the value of £1.

The work done by the bishop's bailiffs in virtue of this liberty is no more capable of neat classification than is the work of the sheriff in the geldable; it covered all the administrative functions of government. Like the sheriffs, the bailiffs must have received their stacks of writs: about the collection of the king's debts;[1] about the production of parties before the barons of the exchequer or others of the king's courts;[2] about the levying of distresses as part of such proceedings;[3] about distraints to secure payment of fines and amercements;[4] and about the action needed to alleviate the flood danger in the Norfolk Marshland.[5] Such a list could be extended indefinitely; but there is hardly need to do so. We need only note that when the king sent messengers to the sheriff of Cambridgeshire, they might often go on to the bishop;[6] and part of the normal expenditure of the keepers of the see in 1302 was the cost of carrying the king's writs to Cambridge from time to time.[7] The exclusion of all royal agents which this liberty implied was a right which the bishop was willing to defend by methods which were sometimes questionable, if always vigorous. The men of Huntingdon may have had cause to say that the bishop's liberty in the soke of Somersham in 1276 was a liberty which impeded the king's justice; for when Elias the hundredor entered it to levy distresses, the bishop's men seized his horse and kept it until he had given up what he had taken.[8] At Glemsford in Suffolk, they acted with more formal legality: they raised the hue and cry against a royal bailiff and sub-bailiff coming on a similar errand.[9] But there were more lawful ways of proceeding: when the king had granted to another return of writs within the bishop's

---

[1] LTR Mem. R, no. 26, m. 16 (these and the references which follow are merely a selection).

[2] CRR, II, 284; III, 46, 241; KR Mem. R, no. 31, mm. 6d, 8d, 10d.

[3] AR no. 90, m. 4.   [4] RH, I, 197, 467.

[5] Cal. Pat. R, 1281–92, 203.

[6] Cal. Liberate R, I, 38, 131, 433; though normally, of course, the responsibility would be left with the sheriff. It would be his task to decide which writs the bishop must execute, and forward them to him, no doubt through one of his bailiffs errant (see Cam, Hundred and the Hundred Rolls, pp. 135–6).

[7] PRO Min. Accts, 1132/11.

[8] RH, I, 197.   [9] RH, II, 144.

liberty, a fourteenth-century bishop might proceed by bill in parliament and have the matter determined before the chancellor.[1]

Turning to the bishop's judicial liberty, its character is well enough summed up in the description of the manor of Rattlesden in 1251.[2] Although that manor lay within the liberty of St Edmund's, the bishop still had toll and team, infangentheof and utfangenetheof; he had his gallows and tumbril, the views of frank-pledge and of measures, and the right to plead pleas of *vee de naam* and all other pleas the sheriff could plead with or without royal writ. This was not perhaps an altogether unusual liberty; but it did include all of the jurisdiction the sheriff would exercise in the geldable in his tourn, in his hundred and his county courts.

This liberty the bishop exercised in his courts leet, which seem usually to have been held in each of his manors[3] once a year.[4] Here frank-pledges were viewed and the assizes of bread and ale administered, and all those things done which the hundred bailiff would do in the geldable at the view of frank-pledge which preceded the twice yearly sheriff's tourn.[5] At least from Huntingdonshire there is explicit testimony that all this was done 'secundum constitucionem comitatus', following, that is to say, the articles which the sheriff administered elsewhere;[6] and commonly the bishop's vills owed no suit to the sheriff's tourn, nor did the king's bailiff attend at the bishop's leet.

A number of records of these courts leet have survived, and we can say something about them.[7] In most of them the pro-

---

[1] *Year Books, 12 & 13 Edw. III*, 243.   [2] Caius 485/489, f. 313 d.

[3] Though manors might be grouped for the purposes of the leet, particularly where there were sub-manors in or near one of the bishop's manors. More of this will be said later. But a single court was also held for the four vills of the 'leta integra' of the bishop in the Norfolk Marshland, on which see Douglas, *East Anglia*, pp. 195 ff.

[4] At Great Shelford and Littleport, for example: PRO Min. Accts, 1132/14, 1133/1; Maitland, *Court Baron*, p. 110.

[5] Cam, *Hundred and the Hundred Rolls*, pp. 185–6.

[6] *RH*, I, 197; Coucher Book, ff. 232–3.

[7] The following account is to some extent a composite one based upon the following rolls: (i) Those printed by Ault, *Court Rolls of Ramsey and the Honour of Clare*, pp. 173 ff., for the joint leet held by the bishop, the abbot of Ramsey and the prior of Lewes at Walsoken. (ii) The Littleport rolls of 1316–25 in Maitland, *Court Baron*, pp. 122–46. (iii) A number of scattered rolls from Elm, Wisbech, Tyd and Leverington between 28 Edw. I and 14 Edw. III in the Ely Diocesan Registry. (iv) The rolls of the prior's leet at Sutton between 21 and 31 Edw. I in the Dean and Chapter's muniments.

cedure seems to have been the same. Offences were presented by a jury, often of twelve men and sometimes identified with the capital pledges of the vill;[1] though these presentments were sometimes submitted to the verdict of a special inquest jury constituted *ad hoc*,[2] or even of a jury of freemen to declare upon a matter so fundamental to the bakers of the village as the current price of corn.[3] At the same time, such methods of proof existed side by side with more archaic methods like wager of law; indeed, where an inquest jury was used, it was often set apart from the normal process of the court in that it was a privilege which had to be bought. All this was probably like enough to the process in the views where the hundred bailiff presided; and the same is true of the business transacted according to these rules. The tithings were corrected and disciplined. Errant bakers and ale-wives were regularly fined for breach of the assizes.[4] Justice was done in matters of petty crime—hamsoke, larceny, assault and blood-drawing, and upon a lady who was a common slanderer of her neighbours. A civil jurisdiction was also exercised: in the guise of a criminal plea by means of an action of trespass, and in matters of convention and debt where the king's courts might not always have offered so efficient a remedy.[5]

But there were also other matters that came before the court leet. A great deal of time was taken up in dealing with common nuisances: obstructing sewers and roads and footpaths; making purprestures from the common 'ad nocumentum ville'; grazing pigs on the fen dykes to the danger of all; keeping a leprous wife

---

[1] Normally at Sutton and see also *Court Baron*, pp. 110, 145 (though at Littleport there are also traces of double presentment by the capital pledges and a jury of freemen).

[2] *Ibid.* pp. 131, 144; Sutton Court Leet, 21 Edw. I (Martinmas).

[3] *Court Baron*, p. 139. Where the word of free men was necessary, the capital pledges may not have been able to provide it because they were always villeins. This seems certainly to have been the case at Sutton; and it may have been that a freeman did not need to be in a tithing, despite the fact that Bracton speaks with two voices on the point (P & M, 1, p. 568); for there was a man at Leverington who 'non fuit in decena quia liber': AR no. 95, m. 69.

[4] So regularly that it may explain the complaint in 1276 in Norfolk that the bishop, like the abbot of Ramsey, 'uses this liberty other than he ought, in that he takes redemption when he ought to administer judgement and justice', in other words when he ought to use his tumbrils and other *iudicialia*: *RH*, 1, 458, 461.

[5] For a number of cases see *Court Baron*, pp. 113–16, 124–5, 126, 131.

in the village or failing to repair a common road. The village community seems very prominent in some of these entries; and offences against its common interest were sometimes decided in the light of 'ordinances', of 'statutes', of 'the bilawe' which regulated common affairs.[1] Closely analogous was the appointment of communal officials in the court: ale-tasters, affeerers of amercements, constables of the peace, dykereeves, even common swineherds.[2] At the same time, the community of the vill or manor was only one of the parties to the law day. The court was usually called 'curia et leta'; manorial business, the lord's business, often preceded (and was even mingled with) the business of the view;[3] and no very sharp distinction was drawn between franchisal jurisdiction and domanial.[4] So the capital pledges, along with all their other duties, might have to present a man who set up a handmill in prejudice to the lord's mill; ladies in the villeinage who had made themselves liable to leyrwite; villeins who had fled or married without licence; a hayward who carried on the lord's farming inefficiently.[5] The leets, like others of the bishop's courts, were part of the machinery for the management of his estate. To that part of their work we must in due course return.

At the same time, all this normal business of the view and the domanial business sometimes added to it did not exhaust the justice the bishop might do in any of his manors. In 1317, when he admitted his military tenant, Geoffrey de Coleville, into the already tripartite partnership of the leet at Walsoken, and granted that he might send his steward and a clerk and take the amercements of his men, he reserved 'regal jurisdiction' to himself.[6] For the bishop had more than the right to hold the view of frank-pledge. He could hear all those pleas the sheriff

---

[1] For offences 'contra ordinacionem ville' and 'contra statutum ville' see Sutton Court Leet, 31 Edw. I (St Luke); and for the 'bilawe' of Littleport see *Court Baron*, p. 112. Seignorial interest may have counted for much in the formation of these manorial codes (see Lennard, *Economic Journal*, LIII, pp. 85–6); yet at Wilburton in 1251 the lord only received half the proceeds from offences against the 'belawe': Caius 485/489, f. 49.

[2] Elm, 28 Edw. I, 13 Edw. II, 14 Edw. III; Tyd, 28 Edw. I (all at Pentecost).

[3] Cf. Maitland, *Court Baron*, p. 110.

[4] Ault, *Private Jurisdiction in England*, p. 105.

[5] *Court Baron*, p. 123; Sutton Court Leet, 21 Edw. I (Martinmas).

[6] *Cal. Pat. R*, 1317–21, 36–7.

could hear without writ: pleas of *vee de naam* which normally would fall to the sheriff;[1] and major criminal actions initiated, not by presentment, but by appeal[2] together with a summary jurisdiction over hand-having thieves.[3] He could also plead those pleas which the sheriff could hear when he had the king's writ: doubtless pleas of debt and contract under the writ *justicies* and pleas upon the writ *de nativo habendo*,[4] and certainly pleas under the writ of right where the grand assize was not invoked.[5] The record of a case initiated by such a writ in the bishop's hundred court at Wisbech is well known;[6] it immediately provoked a command that all the free tenants were to attend the next court for its hearing. The many free tenants in all the bishop's lands who owed suit for afforcement,[7] for afforcement as for the king's writ[8] or for the king's writ,[9] suggest that pleas entertained in virtue of this franchise were no very extraordinary events.

There remains only the relationship of the bishop's liberty to other administrative authorities (franchisal, communal and royal) in the shires in which it lay. This, however, raises a preliminary question about the extent of the liberty of Ely as it has been described above. There can be no question that it included all the demesne manors of the bishop and prior. Sometimes it

---

[1] Cam, *Hundred and the Hundred Rolls*, p. 210.

[2] Morris, *Early English County Court*, p. 123. The bishop was claiming his court in such cases in the Norfolk Marshland in 1204 and 1213, and in 1206 a similar claim was allowed with the customary admonition to do right to the parties: *CRR*, III, 224; IV, 243; VII, 2.

[3] The local courts seem still to have possessed this jurisdiction in the thirteenth century (P & M, II, pp. 494 ff.). When exercised by the bishop his court would have to be specially afforced, as had the prior's court at Newton where one free tenant owed a suit to the leet 'et si latrones capti fuerint et debent adiudicari, tunc venit ad curiam': D & C Extenta Maneriorum, 12 Edw. II. In this connection we may note the case of a man in 1257 'qui captus fuit cum quodam bove furato apud Walpol et in curia episcopi Elyensis convictus et suspensus': AR no. 568, m. 1 d.

[4] Morris, *op. cit.* pp. 117–21.

[5] The manor of Bramford in 1251 'habet in se libertatem...ad placitandum breve recti magnum et parvum': Caius 485/489, ff. 358 d.

[6] See Cam, *Liberties and Communities*, p. 200.

[7] At Wiggenhall, many of the tenants owed suit both to West Walton and Wisbech 'pro afforciamento': Caius 485/489, f. 215 d.

[8] E.g. *ibid.* f. 307 d (Hartest): 'pro afforciamento curie ut pro breve domini regis'.

[9] E.g. a military tenant owed suit to the court of Wetheringsett 'pro breve domini regis': *ibid.* f. 341 d.

extended further, as when the manors held by the bishop's tenants owed suit to courts leet in the bishop's demesne manors,[1] or when the bishop's steward held the view in the tenant's manor.[2] But on the whole these were exceptional cases. Generally the more substantial military tenants of the bishop had acquired the right to hold their own courts leet by grant or usurpation.[3] This might be true even in the highly privileged area of the Isle, where Bishop Hervey had granted to the abbey of Thorney hundredal jurisdiction in its manor at Whittlesey: a grant which was interpreted by Hugh of Balsham in 1278 as including the view of frank-pledge, the amends of bread and ale and measures, pleas of bloodshed and hue and cry, pillory and tumbril and the execution of sentences requiring corporal as well as pecuniary punishment, and all the other things which pertained to the view.[4]

These sub-franchises, if so we may call them, were limited generally to the right to hold the view of frank-pledge. Unlike the demesne manors of the bishop, however, they did not always have exemption from suit to the sheriff's tourn. The fee held by the Bray family in Landbeach, for example, had owed such suit until the 1260's, when it had been withdrawn doubtless during the time of troubles.[5] In the same way, though the king's bailiffs were rigorously excluded from the bishop's lands, more than one tenant in his barony had to admit these royal officers at the holding of his view.[6] Everything suggests, in fact, that these smaller franchises had grown up in no very tidy way. No doubt the early bishops had granted away many lands with privileges of sake and soke and infangentheof and so on, and by the thir-

---

[1] The manors of Henry de Sandewico and Geoffrey de Burnaville in Caston and Darmsden owed suit to the bishop's leet at Barking; the abbess of Chatteris owed suit at Willingham for her holding in Quy: Caius 485/489, f. 333; Coucher Book, f. 240d.

[2] He held the view in all the bishop's fees in Cottenham in 1279; and also in the Peverel fee in Streetley in the thirteenth and fourteenth centuries: RH, II, 411; Cott. Claudius C XI, f. 121d; Coucher Book, f. 235d.

[3] Even some quite small men might have the view, like Robert de Aula for his quarter fee in Over: Cott. Claudius C XI, f. 366d.

[4] CUL Add. 3020, ff. 167, 176d–7.

[5] RH, II, 453; and for suits similarly withdrawn 'to the liberty of Ely' at Milton, Impington and Rampton, see RH, I, 51.

[6] This was true of the manors of the abbess of Marham and William Belet in Marham, and of the Coleville manor in Lolworth (which also owed a suit to the tourn): RH, I, 458; II, 457.

teenth century this was being interpreted as conferring a right to hold the view of frank-pledge. In this way a formidable body of customary claims may have been built up, but claims which were also various and very seldom grounded on valid royal concession.

However they were acquired, these rights became part of the bundle of property rights comprised in a manor. They would pass with an heiress when she married, and so long as they had been exercised without interruption from a time beyond which no man's memory ran, the king's justices soon began to allow them. It was in this way that William de Baldak justified his view in Landbeach in 1299, for he had married Agnes, heiress of the Brays, and she had the requisite customary right.[1] It was in this way, too, that Henry fitzAucher could defend his view in Pampisford, for he too had married an heiress with a customary title to the liberty.[2] In this latter case, however, there was something more: his wife's claim went back in some way to those privileges which Bishop Hervey had conferred upon Archdeacon William. He had the charter, moreover, by which Henry I had confirmed the grant of Pampisford to the archdeacon with sake and soke, toll and team and infangentheof.[3] He was able to buttress his customary right by having this charter enrolled upon the rolls of the justices of eyre.[4]

It was a different matter where a manor passed by enfeoffment. Peter de Chauvent acquired the Lisle fee in Impington as a return for paying Simon Lisle's debts to the Jews;[5] and in 1279 he had the view of frank-pledge there without either the bishop's bailiff or the king's.[6] In 1299 the day of reckoning came. He claimed his view because Simon Lisle had granted him the manor with all its liberties, and Simon and his ancestors had had the view time out of mind. The king's pleader was quite categorical. This liberty Peter claimed to have was a royal liberty; only the king could grant it; and if Peter could produce no better title to it, then he demanded judgement for the king.[7]

---

[1] *PQW*, 105.

[2] *PQW*, 99–100; he still had the liberty at his death in 1303, for its profits were included in the valuation of the manor: Chancery Inq. pm, Edw. I, File 110 (9).

[3] BM Add. 9822, f. 70d (for this see above, p. 168 and below, Appx. I, p. 280).

[4] AR no. 90, mm. 10, 16. [5] *Cal. Pat. R*, 1266–72, 398.

[6] *RH*, 11, 464. [7] *PQW*, 105.

In all this talking, there was no intervention from the bishop of Ely. Long ago the Lisles may well have owed the liberty to the bishop's grant; but like land and service, franchises too had passed down the scale of subinfeudation. In consequence, and as a general rule, the bishop had little control over the franchises of his tenants in the thirteenth century and little obvious interest in them. They had become a matter for the king's justices to discuss, commonly in terms which had little real relevance to the disorderly process of growth which, while it explained many of the common features they had inherited from the liberty of Ely, had led also to much variety in the detailed privileges, involved.

This rather long digression has at least some point in illustrating the fact that, outside his hundreds and the Isle of Ely, the bishop's liberty was confined in the main to his demesne manors. But so far as those manors were concerned, it was a universal liberty. The bishop's franchise was not impaired by the fact that Feltwell and Northwold lay in Ralf de Tony's hundred of Grimshoe; Bridgeham in Robert de Tateshall's hundred of Shropmanford; and Pulham in the earl of Norfolk's half hundred of Earsham[1]—though the liberty did not exempt the bailiff of Pulham from doing suit to Earsham hundred court.[2] It was the same in Suffolk. The bishop had the same privileges as elsewhere in the St Edmundsbury hundreds, privileges which had given rise to protracted litigation at the beginning of the thirteenth century.[3] But here again, the bishop's manors owed suit to the abbot's hundreds,[4] and when the bishop attempted to extend his liberty to the detriment of the abbot's and in a manner not warranted by his charters (in setting up a market at Lakenheath, for instance), the king was on the abbot's side.[5]

---

[1] Caius 485/489, ff. 222, 267d, 275, 283.

[2] *Ibid.* f. 222: 'Ballivus istius manerii debet sectam de hundredo in hundredum per annum vel dabit per annum 2. solidos ad festum sancti Michaelis, et hec ad voluntatem dicti comitis.' At an earlier date this suit had been an incident of the tenure of one of the bishop's free tenants: Cott. Tiberius B II, f. 184d.

[3] *Rot. Curiae Regis*, II, 6–7, 66; *CRR*, II, 136, 140; III, 84, 277; IV, 98; V, 58, 132–3, 157; *Placitorum Abbreviatio*, 70.

[4] Caius 485/489, ff. 300, 307d–8, 313d, 352–2d; Cott. Tiberius B II, f. 194; CUL Add. 6006, f. 104d.

[5] *CRR*, II, 135–6, 140–1, 211, 266; *Pipe R*, 4 John, 114.

These instances illustrative of the relationship between the bishop's liberty and the liberties of others indicate clearly enough that, despite the fact that the bishop could plead all pleas which the sheriff could plead, his franchise did not exempt his lands from customary suits to shire and hundred courts (even when some of the latter were also in private hands). In Cambridge-shire, suit to shire and hundred was an incident of tenure at Triplow, Great Shelford and Willingham.[1] In Norfolk, there were tenants who performed such suits, 'scilicet pro manerio'.[2] It goes almost without saying that similar suits were owed to the courts held by the king's justices of eyre,[3] for in that case there was no question of exemption from their jurisdiction; the bishop had only a right to the amercements they imposed upon his men. It may seem somewhat less logical that his manors owed suit to the shire and hundred courts when in fact he could do all the justice himself which those courts could do so far as his own men were concerned. One explanation would seem to be that in fact these suits were older than the sort of court-holding franchise the bishop had in the thirteenth century. They were suits 'de veteri conquestu' like Robert de Aula's suit at Over;[4] they were suits 'pro manerio', representing the demesne and perhaps incident upon tenements created out of the demesne, which may date from Henry I's reorganization of the local courts.[5] Whatever the explanation, these suits remained cus-tomary obligations upon the bishop's manors, and commonly tenurial obligations upon certain tenements in those manors. The bishop's men (unlike the pleas in which they were in-volved) could not be withdrawn from the courts of the sheriff

---

[1] Caius 485/489, ff. 117, 136, 141 d; Cott. Tiberius B II, 215, 218 d. Such suits were equally widespread in the bishop's fees: RH, II, 407, 434, 451, 452-3, 464-5, 477-8, 485, 495-7 (Westwick, Teversham, Rampton, Milton, Impington, Over, Swaffham Prior, Quy).

[2] Caius 485/489, ff. 201 d, 202; Cott. Tiberius B II, f. 167 d.

[3] E.g. at Pulham (Cott. Tiberius B II, f. 184 d); Barking (Caius 485/489, f. 333 d); Hitcham (ibid. f. 324); Wetheringsett (ibid. f. 342), etc. Again there are many examples from the bishop's fees, as in the fitzAucher manor at Pampisford, where three of the customary tenants 'adiuvabit ad quattuor homines et prepositum coram Iusticiariis itinerantibus': RH, II, 415. Simil-arly, the bishop's hundred and a half of Mitford in Norfolk appeared before the justices by a jury of eighteen men: AR no. 562, m. 2 d; no. 564, m. 3 (1250); no. 577, m. 75 (1286).

[4] Cott. Claudius C XI, ff. 366-6 d.

[5] Maitland, EHR, III, p. 420.

or the courts of private hundreds; or if they.were withdrawn 'because of the liberty of Ely', that was usurpation, a matter to be presented before the king's justices.[1] Only in the Isle of Ely was the bishop's liberty completely insulated from the normal workings of local administration.

II

Before dealing with the liberty of the Isle as a whole, however, we must first look at the next storey in the bishop's liberty, the jurisdiction the bishop exercised in his hundreds. For this purpose we may exclude the Suffolk hundreds which the abbots possessed: they were granted to the prior and convent by Bishop Hervey in his charter to the monks. The bishop's franchise was limited to the hundred and a half of Mitford in Norfolk and the 'two hundreds' of the Isle of Ely.

The franchise in Mitford hundred presents few difficulties. It was, we are told in 1251, free in the bishop's hand. In it his bailiffs made all attachments and returned all writs and pleaded all pleas the sheriff could plead—and this by grant of the king's ancestors from a time beyond memory.[2] To these rights may be added others which the bishop had generally: the rights of appropriating and collecting amercements imposed by the king's justices.[3] These are more or less the rights the bishop had every-where; there is only one addition to the general formula used for the bishop's rights in any of his manors—in Mitford hundred the bishop collected amercements and the rest 'tam de alienis feodis quam de suis propriis'.[4] The bishop not only had the hundred court; the liberty of Ely already described was co-extensive with the hundred.

It was a liberty which gave rise to a good deal of quo warran-toing. As early as 1222 the bishop and sheriff were at odds over it, and the former was commanded to show his title which, it would seem, he was able to do.[5] In 1225 the sheriff was once

---

[1] E.g. *RH*, I, 50, 51; II, 451, 452: suits withdrawn at Coton and Teversham in 1276, and at Rampton and Milton in 1279.

[2] For 1251 see Cott. Claudius C XI, f. 233 d and Cott. Domitian A xv, f. 120; and cf. *RH*, I, 443 for 1276.

[3] E.g. LTR Mem. R, no. 7, m. 12 d.

[4] Cott. Domitian A xv, f. 120.

[5] LTR Mem. R, no. 7, m. 12 d; *Rot. Litt. Claus.* I, 539–40, 628.

more told to hold an inquest into the bishop's rights in open county court; in the same year he was to have twelve knights at Westminster to give their verdict on what the bishop's liberty had been at the outbreak of the war between John and his barons; and finally he was ordered to see that the bishop had his customary franchise.[1] Despite all this enquiry John of Fountains was able to have neither liberty nor court in the hundred;[2] and in 1230 there was again trouble over the bishop's right to collect amercements in the fees of other lords.[3] In the end it took all Hugh of Northwold's vigour to obtain a settlement. In 1232 the justices of eyre were again commanded to make enquiry; and the sheriff at last produced a jury of knights at Cambridge on St James's day which pronounced in favour of the bishop's right to return writs, make attachments, impanel juries, plead all pleas in his own court which the sheriff could plead, and collect amercements in his own and other fees.[4] This long wrangle, in July 1233, moved Henry III to confirm the liberties granted to Ely by Richard I and to issue a charter which at last defined the bishop's rights in his Norfolk hundred and the prior's in his five and a half hundreds of Suffolk[5]—a charter which the sheriff was ordered to read in his county court and observe for the future.[6]

If general principles were settled, it was another matter in regard to detail. There was much trouble about the exercise of the coroner's office in the hundred. In 1250 the bishop's bailiffs claimed that no coroner should enter the hundred and that they themselves exercised the office: about this the justices felt they must speak with a higher authority, since no warrant was shown. In 1257 the same claim was reiterated; and this time the liberty was taken into the king's hand because felonies were concealed and no one was convicted for them. In 1286, however, the hundred bailiff, even the hundred bailiff's clerk, were still exercising the office of coroner,[7] and it is clear that they were keeping

---

[1] *Rot. Litt. Claus.* II, 18, 46, 65; and for an account of the inquest Bodl. Laudian Misc. 647, f. 130d.

[2] CUL Add. 2950, f. 127.   [3] *KR Mem. R, 14 Henry III*, 43, 60–1.

[4] *Close R, 1231–4*, 138; CUL Add. 2950, f. 127.

[5] D & C Charter no. 23; *Cartae Antiquae Rolls* 1–10, no. 14.

[6] *Close R, 1231–4*, 237; and cf. mandates to the barons of the exchequer, *ibid.* 1234–7, 229, 242.

[7] On all this see AR no. 562, m. 3; no. 564, m. 3; no. 568, m. 4; no. 577, mm. 32, 32d.

proper rolls of their work in this capacity.[1] It may have been to prevent these recurring difficulties that a writ was issued early in the fourteenth century which allowed the bishop to have his own coroner for the hundred, to be elected on receipt of the king's writ.[2] This licence may have permitted the bishop's bailiff to continue to exercise the coroner's office, as he was certainly doing in the fifteenth century.[3]

No doubt such troubles were characteristic enough of the history of private hundreds in the age of reform at the exchequer. The organization of the hundred, in the same way, has many parallels elsewhere. The hundredal manor had shifted between 1086 and 1251 from East Dereham to Shipdham. At the latter place the suitors from all the vills of the hundred had to present themselves, suitors who were generally free tenants or semi-free, their suit a tenurial duty. Sometimes the obligations of the vill were acquitted by sending six men of whom one might be a priest—an arrangement which recalls the ancient representation of a vill in the local courts by the priest, the reeve and four men.[4] Apart from the income derived by the bishop from the hundred court itself, some of the villages paid sheriff's aid and 'forwache' (perhaps analogous to the wardpence paid elsewhere),[5] and most of them cert money which was payable at the view of frank-pledge.[6] At the same time the bishop, it would seem, did not always manage to retain the view. In 1379 his bailiff accounted for the perquisites of leets in only fourteen of the eighteen villages of the hundred; in 1276 the bailiffs of Costessey had withdrawn suits from the hundred[7] and were questioning the bishop's right to hold a leet at Westfield, while the lords of Hockering had withdrawn Geoffrey le Parmenter who ought to have been geldable for the amends of bread and

[1] Extracts from these rolls have been preserved in Cott. Domitian A xv, ff. 130 ff., some of which date from c. 1281.
[2] Cal. Pat. R, 1317–21, 330.
[3] Cott. Domitian A xv, f. 138.
[4] All this has been worked out by Douglas, East Anglia, pp. 146, 148–55.
[5] Neilson, Customary Rents, pp. 128, 158. She takes 'forwache' to be a payment for 'castle-guard or some other watching service'.
[6] For all this see the list of the assized rents of the hundred in Caius 485/489, ff. 251 d ff. (1251) and the account of the bailiff of the hundred in 1379 summarized by H. M. Cam, Liberties and Communities, p. 197.
[7] They had also withdrawn suits in 1257 from East Tuddenham, Thurston, Yaxham and Westfield: AR no. 568, m. 5.

ale.[1] But these once again were the troubles of any holder of a private hundred, just as much as they were the troubles of the king in hundreds which were geldable.

When we turn from Mitford hundred to the hundreds of the Isle, much that is commonplace in the former immediately disappears. No doubt there are many reasons for the complicated history of the hundreds of the Isle. It was an old and compact immunity; almost every acre in it was held by bishop or prior who had, therefore, a greater freedom in shaping its institutions; its very geography was radically altered by extensive assarting in the twelfth and thirteenth centuries. The hundreds of the Isle have less stability and less uniformity of organization than the hundreds of the geldable or an isolated private hundred like that of Mitford. Indeed, there is a problem of geography which demands discussion before turning to problems of jurisdiction.

The emergence of three separate hundreds—the hundreds of Ely, Wisbech, and Witchford—seems to have been a development which took place after 1066,[2] although it was fully worked out by the thirteenth century. Wisbech hundred included Wisbech itself, together with its dependent hamlets of Leverington, Newton, Tyd, Elm and Upwell:[3] hamlets linked closely to the administrative offices in Wisbech castle upon the walls of which the customary tenants laboured; to Wisbech market, the economic centre of the northern fenland; and to the great demesne manor of Wisbech Barton on which the customary tenants owed harvest boons. Witchford hundred was less compact, and lacked the economic unity of its northern neighbour. It included the eleven villages in the south-western corner of the Isle, together with the outlying soke of Doddington and, almost at the gates of Peterborough, the village of Whittlesey.[4] It has much of the character of a merely administrative unit, like most of the medieval hundreds.

[1] *RH*, I, 443. [2] See above, pp. 31–3.

[3] See Wisbech Hundred, 31 Edw. I (Circumcision) where the marginal entries of fines and amercements are each distinguished by a note about where the offender lived; and 31 Edw. I (St Nicholas) where the total issues at the foot of the roll are similarly divided between the constituent villages of the hundred.

[4] Wren's Note Book, f. 277; PRO Min. Accts, 1132/11; and the fourteenth-century rolls of the hundred court (EDR Court Rolls, C 7).

Ely hundred, on the other hand, is a great deal more elusive. We hear of it in Bishop Eustace's time;[1] it included Ely, Downham and Littleport in 1251;[2] there were profits to be accounted for from the hundred in 1286;[3] and in 1285 and 1299 the presentments made by the hundred of Ely before the king's justices included offences committed, not only in Ely, but also in Brame, Stuntney, Quaveney, Northney and Littleport.[4] In short, the hundred in the thirteenth century must contain Ely and its hamlets together with the villages of Littleport and Downham, even though the hundred seems sometimes to go under the name of the 'vill of Ely'.[5]

Yet even if we can identify the hundred, it is another matter to discover its court. No Ely court rolls have survived from any period earlier than the fifteenth century; and amongst these rolls those which bear most resemblance to the records of a hundred court are the rolls of the 'curia de Berton', the court at the Barton gate. They are meagre in their contents, which consist mainly of pleas of debt and convention, familiar residual business of the hundred courts at a late date. In addition there are a few registrations of land transfers like those which appear regularly enough upon the rolls of Wisbech hundred.[6] Apart from these rolls, extracts from others which have since been lost have been preserved by Bishop Wren and show that in the fourteenth century the jurisdiction of the Barton court extended over Little Thetford, Stuntney, Chettisham, Downham and Littleport.[7] All this looks sufficiently like a court for the hundred of Ely.

At the same time, and if this is true, the Barton court had some strange peculiarities. It was a weekly court: more like the court of a borough[8] than the court of a hundred, and that despite

---

[1] A grant of land 'de wara hundredi de Ely': Bodl. Laudian Misc. 647, f. 116d.

[2] Caius 485/489, ff. 19, 29d, 34d.   [3] PRO Min. Accts, 1132/9, 1307/2.

[4] AR no. 90, mm. 9–10; no. 95, mm. 65d–7. If we add Downham this would agree well enough with the bounds of Ely hundred shown on Speed's map in 1610.

[5] In 1285, 1310 and 1316, for example: AR no. 90, m. 9; PRO Min. Accts, 1132/12, 13.

[6] EDR Gaol Delivery Rolls E 1 (16–20 Hen. VI).

[7] For this and much of what follows see Wren's Note Book, ff. 256, 301, 317–20.

[8] P & M, I, p. 658.

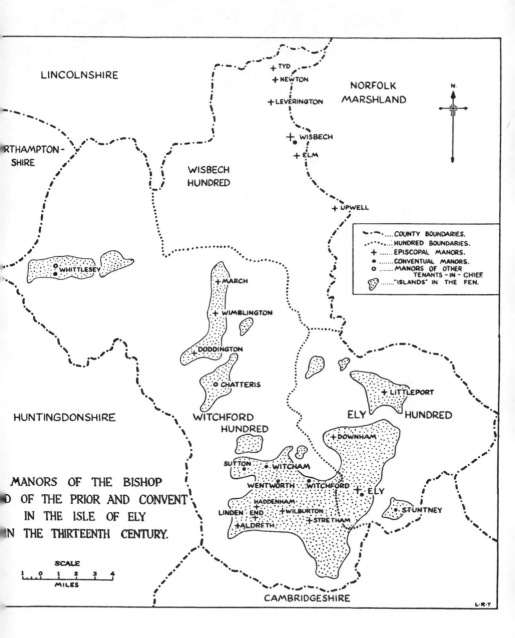

LINCOLNSHIRE

+ TYD
+ NEWTON

NORFOLK
MARSHLAND

+ LEVERINGTON

N.

RTHAMPTON-
SHIRE

WISBECH
HUNDRED

+ WISBECH

+ ELM

+ UPWELL

COUNTY BOUNDARIES.
HUNDRED BOUNDARIES.
+ ....EPISCOPAL MANORS.
● ....CONVENTUAL MANORS.
○ ....MANORS OF OTHER
        TENANTS - IN - CHIEF
....."ISLANDS" IN THE FEN.

WHITTLESEY

+ MARCH

+ WIMBLINGTON

+ DODDINGTON

○ CHATTERIS

HUNTINGDONSHIRE

WITCHFORD
HUNDRED

+ LITTLEPORT

ELY HUNDRED

+ DOWNHAM

SUTTON   ● WITCHAM

WENTWORTH   ● WITCHFORD

+ ELY

● STUNTNEY

MANORS OF THE BISHOP
D OF THE PRIOR AND CONVENT
IN THE ISLE OF ELY
N THE THIRTEENTH CENTURY.

HADDENHAM
LINDEN END   + WILBURTON
+ ALDRETH   + STRETHAM

SCALE

1 0 1 2 3 4
MILES

CAMBRIDGESHIRE

L·R·T

the fact that the 'city' of Ely hardly became a borough in any real sense in medieval times. Secondly, much seignorial business was done in it: lands were demised at farm, tallages exacted, labour services enforced, licences to marry given and payments of relief made. Thirdly, two of the entries preserved by Wren make the Barton court look as though it was purely a court of villeins, for in them defendants there seek the 'Curia Palacii' because they were free tenants.[1] These entries raise a number of problems which it is best to discuss separately.

One of the possible explanations might be that the Barton court was a court similar to the 'Curia Bondorum', 'Curia de Bondis' or 'Curia Nativorum' which made its appearance in Wisbech hundred in the reign of Edward II. Its records were enrolled with the proceedings of the hundred court, even on the same membrane; its jurisdiction extended over the whole hundred of Wisbech;[2] and like the hundred court it seems to have met at three-weekly intervals.[3] The business it transacted was also much like that of the hundred court: on the one hand, the usual trespasses, assaults, and pleas of debt and convention; on the other hand, much seignorial business in connection with the alienation and inheritance of customary land, the enforcement of labour services, and so on.[4] If from this point of view it is difficult to distinguish between the hundred court and the 'curia bondorum', there does seem to be some sort of theory that the latter was the proper court where a villein or villein land was concerned. So when John Markaund was attached to answer in the hundred for unjust detention of beasts belonging to John Page, he could answer that, since the distress had been taken in the lord's customary land, the case ought to be heard in the 'Curia Bondorum'.[5] The court, in fact, was a kind of halimote for the whole hundred, and it had a great future. As time went on, in terms at least of its profitability, it completely overshadowed the hundred court and the halimotes in the

[1] Wren's Note Book, ff. 319, 320. 'In placito transgressionis...venit defendens et petiit liberam curiam ad palatium quod libere tenens' (33 Edw. III); 'Defendens in curia de Berton petit Curiam Palatii ut liber tenens' (40 Edw. III).

[2] As shown by cases in Curia Bondorum, 5 Edw. II (Ascension).

[3] Curia Bondorum, 12 Edw. II (St George): 'Dies datus est in tribus septimanis.'

[4] Curia Bondorum, 7 Edw. II (Holy Cross).

[5] Wisbech Hundred, 7 Edw. II (Trinity).

8

individual manors,[1] perhaps because the control of the customary land-market was gradually concentrated in it.

Unfortunately, from a point of view of explaining Wren's extracts about the Barton court, there does not appear to have been a similar development at Ely. In the first place, it is clear that free tenants did appear in the Barton court.[2] Secondly, it does not seem to be possible to draw a direct comparison between the hundred court of Wisbech and the 'Curia Palacii' of Ely, a court which long ago proved such a sore puzzle to Bentham.[3] Before returning to the Barton court, something must be said of this court to which a defendant at the Barton might appeal if he were a free tenant. Again, the earliest surviving rolls date from the end of the fifteenth century.[4] They are the records of a court held annually on the Monday after Michaelmas, and consist merely of a list of essoins or suits not performed. All they tell us is that suitors should have come from Chatteris, Witchford, Witcham, Wentworth, Wilburton, Stretham, Little Thetford and Sutton—that and a total of 53s. 6d. in fines at the foot of the roll. But even this information is of some value. Almost all of these vills lie in Witchford hundred, and many of them were held, not by the bishop, but by the prior. Therefore, the 'Curia Palatii' can hardly be a 'free' hundred court for the hundred of Ely; nor can it be a feudal court, a free court of feudal tenants.

So let us look again at the suitors of the court. Wren has preserved an entry from a roll of Witchford hundred court of 14 Richard II, in which the heirs of John of Quy did homage for the lands their father had held in Haddenham and for which he had done suit to the hundred and to the 'Curia Palatii'.[5] Now there was a John of Quy who held a military tenement in Haddenham in 1346 and 1302, a tenement which had been held in the first half of the thirteenth century by Richard and Nigel

[1] Wisbech Castle Accts, 12–13 Hen. VIII: by this date the perquisites of the 'Curia Bondorum' amounted to £125 out of a total revenue of £135 from courts of all sorts in the hundred.

[2] E.g. the payment of relief in 43 Edw. III for free tenements in Ely and Chettisham: Wren's Note Book, f. 320.

[3] CUL Add. 2962, f. 5 d: 'Queerie, he wrote, whether it be not the same with the principall Court', the court which sat in the Aula Episcopi, and tried cases involving life and limb. In this he was pretty clearly wrong.

[4] EDR Court Rolls, C 6: Curia Palatii, 11, 13 and 15 Edw. IV.

[5] Wren's Note Book, f. 279.

de Chewelle.[1] The last-named in 1251 had owed suit to the bishop's court in Linden End and 'ad curiam de Ely'.[2] The 'court of Ely', therefore, in the thirteenth-century records is the same court as the 'Curia Palatii' in the records of the fourteenth and fifteenth centuries. At this earlier period, it is clear that suit was owed from Linden and Haddenham, Stretham,[3] Sutton,[4] Witcham,[5] Wilburton,[6] and Doddington;[7] also by the abbot of Ramsey in Chatteris[8] and the five knights of the barony who held messuages as summoners in Ely.[9]

If this much can be said of the suitors, we can say nothing about the business of the court. Wren notes that, in the courts of 15 and 16 Richard II, nothing was done except the exacting of fines for default of suit.[10] True, in 1285, a plea of convention or debt in the halimote at Littleport was postponed to the 'curia de Ely',[11] much as difficult cases from the halimotes might be transferred to Wisbech hundred court. But before the end of our period, such cases might go from Littleport to the bishop's council rather than the court in his palace;[12] and the very development of the council, so characteristic of the later Middle Ages,[13] may have helped to hasten the decline of the 'Curia Palatii'. In the end, however, we still know very little about this court. Its name tells us that it met in the bishop's palace. It was not a court of tenure, for its suitors were drawn from all the villages of the southern part of the Isle; some of them, significantly, were *hundredarii*. In the thirteenth century, it met every

[1] *FA*, I, pp. 151, 173; Cott. Tiberius B II, f. 107 d; Caius 485/489, f. 52 d.
[2] Caius 485/489, f. 52 d: Nigel only owed suit at the manor court on the coming of the seneschal.
[3] *Ibid.* ff. 41 d–2 d.
[4] D & C Charter no. 197.
[5] *Ibid.* nos. 76–8; Coucher Book, ff. 218 d–19.
[6] Caius 485/489, ff. 47–7 d (most of the *hundredarii*).
[7] Only at the Easter and Michaelmas courts both in 1251 and the fourteenth century: *ibid.* f. 63; Wren's Note Book, f. 303. On the other hand the bishop granted a wood in March (in the soke of Doddington) in 1227 for a rent and *four* suits a year to the court of Ely: *Cal. Charter R*, I, 55.
[8] In 1294 it was allowed that the abbot might do this suit by two of his tenants: Coucher Book, f. 213; *Cart. Rames.* I, 215–16.
[9] Caius 485/489, f. 20 d.
[10] Wren's Note Book, f. 304.
[11] *Court Baron*, pp. 119–20.
[12] *Ibid.* p. 127.
[13] Levett, *Studies in Manorial History*, pp. 21 ff.

three weeks like the typical hundred court.[1] May this not be, then, the shadow of what had once been the court of the two hundreds of Ely, before those hundreds had become geographical entities, and before the 'ferthyng' of Wisbech had been added to the Isle? This court may have met alternately at Witchford and Ely; the double suit which the hundredors owed to Witchford hundred and the court of Ely may have been originally but one suit. At the heart of the franchise, this court of Ely or court of the palace might have developed along the same lines as the abbot of Ramsey's *banlieu* court at Broughton.[2]

Yet events seem to have conspired against the 'Curia Palatii'. The development of the bishop's council may have robbed it of a supervisory jurisdiction over the halimotes. It never managed to absorb the 'palatine' liberties of the bishop in the Isle, which were exercised by special commissioners—the bishop's justices itinerant, justices of gaol delivery, justices of oyer and terminer, etc. It never exercised any control over the hundred court which arose in the 'ferthyng' of Wisbech. Witchford hundred acquired its own independent hundred court. In fact, the 'curia de Ely' was dead, it seems, before ever it acquired the grander name of 'Curia Palatii'—because it had no function left to fulfil. And here we return to the problem which provoked this long digression: the problem of the court of Ely hundred. Whatever the 'curia de Ely' may have done in the thirteenth century—and sometime or another it must have exercised the functions of a hundred court, however wide its field of operation —the court of Ely hundred in the fourteenth and fifteenth centuries can only have been the court of the Barton. There is much that is unorthodox about it. It may have been in origin merely the domanial court of the vill of Ely, though exercising a jurisdiction over all the hamlets clustered about the town itself. The extent of its jurisdiction may have made that domanial court a suitable court upon which the hundredal jurisdiction might be devolved; its original character may have made it a court in which a freeman could be arraigned only with doubtful pro-

---

[1] Three-weekly suit was required from the abbot of Ramsey (Chatteris) and the Pelryn tenement in Witcham; as it was from the holding of which Peter de Chauvent was seised at his death in Stretham, Haddenham and Thetford: Coucher Book, f. 213; D & C Charters nos. 76–8; *Cal. Inq. pm*, IV, 94.

[2] Ault, *Court Rolls of the Abbey of Ramsey*, pp. xxxvii ff.

priety; its weekly sessions may be testimony to the tendency for Ely to grow from a village to a city. At least, it completes the tale of that variety which characterizes the hundred courts of the Isle of Ely in the Middle Ages.

Having said so much of the hundreds, we can turn now to the composition and powers of their courts—a discussion which, for lack of evidence, must ignore the hundred of Ely. Wisbech and Witchford hundreds, on the other hand, do not seem to have been large assemblies; and in both of them suit was a tenurial obligation. Wisbech court was the smaller of the two. In 1251 some eighteen military and free tenants in Wisbech and its hamlets owed suit;[1] and a certain number of others could be called upon when the king's writ had to be pleaded.[2] In Witchford hundred, on the other hand, the obligation to suit was far less selective, and was still characteristically an incident of free tenure. At Linden End and Wilburton all the *hundredarii* seem to have owed suit to the hundred,[3] at Stretham most of the free tenants,[4] at Whittlesey (in the abbot of Thorney's manor) all the free tenants.[5] But if it was a free man's duty, it adhered so closely to the land that only the bishop's express dispensation could remove it;[6] otherwise it passed with the land to a man's heirs, or to any grantee to whom he might transfer the holding.[7] Witchford hundred court, then, had this difference from Wisbech hundred court. Its suitors were more numerous because Saxon sokemen had survived in the hundred and their descendants continued to attend its court—indeed, became burdened with the duty of doing so. In Wisbech hundred, on the other

---

[1] Caius 485/489, ff. 74–4d, 84, 88d–9, 96d, 98.

[2] Not only in Outwell and Leverington, but also in Tilney and Wiggenhall in the Norfolk Marshland: Caius 485/489, ff. 84, 98, 214d, 215d; Cott. Tiberius B II, f. 172d.

[3] Caius 485/489, ff. 47–7d, 53.   [4] *Ibid.* ff. 41–2d.

[5] Thorney Red Book, I, ff. 176d–7.

[6] This is illustrated by a charter of Hugh of Balsham acquitting Thomas Balsham of the suits 'in quibus tenetur ratione terrarum et tenementorum suorum quas idem tenet in insula Elyensi'. Suit to the hundred was not the only duty which fell upon the hundredors: 'et quia predictus Thoma et alii terras consimiles tenentes in predicto hundredo sectam ad furcas de Aldrehee cum contingat aliquem ibidem suspendi facere tenetur, et ibidem moram facere debent quousque suspensus fuerit mortuus', this suit too is remitted: Bodl. Laudian Misc. 647, ff. 169d–70.

[7] For sales of land subject to suit to the hundred see D & C Charters nos. 197 (Sutton), 726 (Witcham).

hand, the suitors were either survivors of a far smaller original population or a few tenants deliberately enfeoffed in a district of rapidly growing population to satisfy the need of the hundred court for suitors.

Unlike the court of the Barton, both Wisbech and Witchford hundred courts met at three-weekly intervals.[1] Both seem to have met on fixed days: Witchford on Tuesdays and Wisbech on Thursdays, though for two years during Edward II's reign the Wisbech court also changed over to Tuesday. Wisbech hundred was always held at Wisbech itself; but Witchford hundred court was more mobile, meeting at Witchforstone, Witchamlowe, Haddenham and Sutton.[2] Both courts, like the court of Mitford hundred, were centres for the collection of customary payments. At Wisbech the most important was the 'ferthyngsilver' payable by many of the free and some of the customary tenants[3] (the name of this payment again recalls the original status of this hundred). The dues rendered at Witchford hundred were a more miscellaneous collection: the rents of the *hundredarii*,[4] payments for the right to hold the view of frankpledge[5] and for the maintenance of Aldreth causeway,[6] 'hedburghsilver' paid by the prior so that his villeins did not go to the bishop's tourn,[7] and 'wanersylver' payable 'de quolibet habente bestiam'.[8]

---

[1] For what follows in general material has been drawn from the rolls of Wisbech hundred for the years 30 Edw. I–12 Edw. II and for Witchford hundred for the years 12–14 Ric. II—both in the Ely Diocesan Registry. The three-weekly sessions were broken by a Christmas vacation, so there were seventeen courts held yearly: see Cam, *Liberties and Communities*, pp. 198 ff.; Wisbech Castle Accts, 17–18 Edw. III, etc. In 1222, on the other hand, Witchford hundred court met fortnightly: 'sciendum quod quilibet hundredarius debet semel sequi hundredum infra quindecim dies' (Cott. Tiberius B II, ff. 107d, 105—Linden End and Wilburton). This would have been the normal practice of the reign of Henry II; it was changed to an interval of three weeks between courts by an ordinance of 1234: P & M, I, pp. 538, 557.

[2] Wren's Note Book, f. 276.

[3] Caius 485/489, ff. 74 d–99.

[4] On these hundredal rents see above, p. 117.

[5] The abbot of Thorney for his leet in Whittlesey, for instance: Thorney Red Book, I, ff. 176 d–7; Liber M, ff. 378–9.

[6] From the Ramsey manor in Chatteris: Hearne, *Sprot's Chronicle*, pp. 209–12.

[7] This may be the same as the payment to 'frendleshundret', the meeting of the court at the seneschal's coming after Michaelmas, which was annexed to many holdings in the prior's manors: e.g. D & C Charter no. 275 (Sutton).

[8] On these payments in general see Wren's Note Book, ff. 277–80, 286.

Rent collecting was, however, a minor function of the hundred court, which must mainly be of interest to us as a judicial and administrative tribunal. From the former point of view, the rolls of Witchford hundred are not of major interest. They are late, they are concerned mainly with petty debts: for by the reign of Richard II the competence of the court had been eaten away by the growth of the jurisdiction of the bishop's justices of the peace.[1] Wisbech hundred court at the beginning of the fourteenth century was clearly a much more active tribunal, and it is possible to say something about both its procedure and the business which came before it. Cases were initiated there for the most part in the traditional way, by verbal process. A offers himself against B, C appeals D, E makes a plaint, a plaint which is called a *querela*. Only occasionally does a case begin otherwise: but in 1260 the prior of Norwich was party to a plea in this court 'per breve regis',[2] and in 1305 Hamon of Walton brought the king's writ of right into the court.[3] In whatever way the case began, the next step was always the same: the securing of all the parties in the court, and perhaps of an expanded body of suitors if the king's writ came into the plea. This object was attained in a number of ways: by attachment, by the nomination of pledges bound to produce their principals, by taking a variety of distresses which would in the long run extend to pledges who failed to produce their principal or a master who must be compelled to produce his servant when the latter has nothing whereby he might be distrained.[4]

When all the parties and suitors were present, the case could proceed. In this connection 'clearly the suitors were still the judges, even if the hundred bailiff presided and kept the rolls'.[5] But judgement might still be a long way off when the parties appeared in court. Sometimes an *ad hoc* inquest jury was empanelled in the court to testify to some point, and the suitors

[1] See Cam, *Liberties and Communities*, p. 198.
[2] *Close R*, 1259–61, 162.
[3] Wisbech Hundred, 33 Edw. I (Pentecost); Cam, *op. cit.* p. 200.
[4] Wisbech Hundred, 34 Edw. I (day illegible): William Pepir was summoned to answer Eleanor le Webestere, but the bailiff reported that he had nothing whereby he might be distrained. On the other hand he was in the mainpast of Richard Baxtere: 'ideo preceptum est distringere predictum Ricardum ad habendum manupastum suum'. For a similar case in the halimote at Littleport, see *Court Baron*, p. 127.
[5] Cam, *op. cit.* p. 201.

would pronounce judgement in the light of its verdict.[1] In other cases the halimotes were instructed to make enquiries in order to supplement the information before the hundred court: about a dispute over succession to land in Tyd, a claim for damages where corn was stolen from a man's field, whether or not a man was a villein, whether a man had been disseised of villein land.[2] In 1307, the halimotes were even commanded to carry out a survey, and certify the results to the next hundred court, of all the fees and tenements the bishop had in the hundred.[3]

These are examples of the way in which the hundred court acted as the apex of the hierarchy of courts which the bishop had in Wisbech hundred. It clearly acted in a supervisory capacity over the halimotes, presumably where cases were specially difficult or beyond the normal capacity of the manor courts. In some senses, too, the halimotes acted as the agents of the higher court. On one roll we read how two pledges were in mercy for failing to produce Richard Priour to answer charges against him 'prout patet in ultima halimota'; in another that Nicholas de Aula and John Adger were to be distrained to have Bartholomew de Leanveys to do fealty in the hundred court as it appeared from the last halimote.[4] Cases might also be sent down to the halimote for determination, as well as come up from the halimote to the hundred court.[5] Finally the hundred court was continually issuing commands that judgements should be properly executed, judgements made not only in the halimotes but also in the courts leet.[6]

The hundred court itself was, in turn, subject to supervision. Many cases were postponed when unforeseen difficulties arose: when the prior claimed his court in a plea of trespass, when Thomas Morel claimed his court over a defendant he alleged to be one of his men, or when both the prior and Thomas Doreward claimed their courts in a plea of debt 'et magna est altercacio inter partes'.[7] In such cases, no doubt, it was necessary to

---

[1] Wisbech Hundred, 30 Edw. I (Assumption), 31 Edw. I (St Nicholas).

[2] *Ibid.* 30 Edw. I (Assumption); 31 Edw. I (Conversion of St Paul); 34 Edw. I (St Catherine); 35 Edw. I (Lent, St Barnabas).

[3] *Ibid.* 35 Edw. I (Lent).

[4] *Ibid.* 31 Edw. I (Conversion of St Paul); 35 Edw. I (Lent).

[5] For a case sent down to the halimote, *ibid.* 30 Edw. I (St Luke); for one sent up to the hundred, 31 Edw. I (Conversion of St Paul).

[6] E.g. *ibid.* 35 Edw. I (Lent, St Barnabas).

[7] *Ibid.* 30 Edw. I (Michaelmas, St James); 33 Edw. I (Pentecost).

consult the records or higher authority, as it was when problems arose about the incidents to which a free woman holding in the villeinage was liable: judgement was adjourned 'et interim consulendum est'.[1] Such consultation might be with the bishop and his council, for it was they who pronounced upon the need for appointing a temporary beadle in Leverington.[2] In more routine matters, the authority of the seneschal might be enough: he might pardon an amercement imposed for a false appeal, or authorize the alienation of a villein tenement.[3] Higher still was the supervision exercised by the king, whose writ of right could initiate proceedings, whose statutes (like the statute of *Quia Emptores*) prescribed the law that the court would administer,[4] and who would authorize the sheriff to omit nothing because of the bishop's liberty when no justice was to be had from the bishop's court. The hundred court of Wisbech was not only part of the hierarchy of courts in the Isle of Ely; it was also part of the machinery through which justice was done at the king's command by bishop and sheriff alike.

There is, however, still a final point to be made about the business which was transacted in the hundred court of Wisbech. A great deal of it, of course, consisted of the normal petty civil and criminal jurisdiction of a hundred court. But also, as we shall see in much greater detail in another place,[5] there was much seignorial business done in the hundred: business connected with the incidents of free tenure and with villein men and villein land. Much of this last business in the long run may have been segregated in sessions of the 'Curia Bondorum', acting as a kind of super-manorial court for the whole hundred. If so the loss of business to the hundred court probably made for its decline from that state of intense activity evident in its rolls at the beginning of the fourteenth century.

If seignorial business does not appear on the rolls of Witchford hundred, there are (as we have seen) signs of it also in the records of the Barton court at Ely. The reason for this contrast between Witchford hundred court on the one hand and those of Ely and Wisbech on the other would seem to lie once again in

---

[1] Wisbech Hundred, 2 Edw. II (St Barnabas).
[2] *Ibid.* 35 Edw. I (St Barnabas).
[3] *Ibid.* 33 Edw. I (Lent), 35 Edw. I (Lent).
[4] See Cam, *op. cit.* p. 200.   [5] See below, ch. VIII.

some of the differences in the history of these courts to which attention has been drawn. Witchford hundred court stands in the direct succession to that court which had once exercised the hundredal jurisdiction over the two hundreds of the Isle; moreover, the bishop had demesne only in some four of its dozen villages. In the court of such a hundred the bishop's seignorial affairs would have been an intrusion. At Wisbech, on the other hand, the hundredal jurisdiction may well have been tacked on to the court of an economic complex, the old 'ferthyng' of Wisbech; and the fact that most of the land in the hundred was the bishop's land meant that there was no very real necessity to distinguish between tribunals in which the bishop exercised franchisal and domanial rights. The court of the Barton may, likewise, have originated in a court for a similar economic district with a unity imposed upon it by intercommoning rights and by common labour services on the Barton farm commuted only in the twelfth century. Some of the characteristics it had possessed in those early days the Barton court may have carried over into the time when it inherited from the 'curia de Ely' its hundredal functions.

This picture of diversity may be concluded by calling attention to yet another distinction between the hundreds of the Isle. No sheriff held his tourn in the Isle of Ely; but there is nothing uniform about the arrangements the bishop made to fill this gap. What happened in Ely hundred is very obscure: probably the business of the tourn was devolved upon the courts leet in the various manors, like that which the bishop held in his own great manor at Ely.[1] At Wisbech, on the contrary, the business of leet and tourn were fused in a single court leet for all the vills of the hundred held annually on the Wednesday after Pentecost;[2] in that court, each vill came forward in turn by a presenting jury of twelve (there is no sign of the capital pledges), and the busi-

---

[1] There are rolls of the Ely Court Leet in the Diocesan Registry for 14 and 49 Hen. VI and 11–17 Edw. IV. Ely hundred may well have resembled Clackclose hundred in Norfolk from this point of view: it was, perhaps, no more than a complex of leets: Cam, *Hundred and the Hundred Rolls*, p. 187; Ault, *Court Rolls of the Abbey of Ramsey*, pp. xliii–xliv.

[2] This seems to be quite clear from a comparison of the dates of the courts leet held in this hundred as shown by the rolls which have survived amongst EDR Court Rolls, C 7 and C 8. In 28 Edw. I proceedings in the leet for Wisbech, Elm, Tyd, and Upwell are all entered on two membranes tied together at the head.

ness of that vill was completed before passing on to the next. Only Witchford hundred conforms to something of the normal pattern. The right to hold the view of frank-pledge was often in other hands than the bishop's,[1] and the usual business preliminary to the tourn was clearly done in the manorial courts leet. The bishop then held his tourn, as the sheriff would do in the geldable, on St Michael's day at Witchfordstone and on St Peter's day at Witchamlowe.[2] At this tourn, presentments were made by juries of freemen, which seem to have passed on presentments made to them by the reeve and four men from each vill.[3] The number of free jurors was never the customary twelve,[4] but they presented all the usual offences and omissions with which any sheriff's tourn would be concerned[5] before the competence of that court was absorbed by the growing powers of the justices of the peace.

In these notes on the hundreds of the Isle, stress has been placed inevitably upon their differences, differences which can be explained in the light of the diversity of character shown by different parts of the Isle. But when we find that the hundred courts of Wisbech and Ely were dealing with seignorial business, or that the leet and tourn were fused in Wisbech hundred, these facts correspond to no rule of law or principle of jurisdiction. It was merely that this was the convenient way for the bishop to order his affairs, given the character of the district concerned; and that in fact circumstances were such that the bishop could consult convenience in determining what character and what

[1] The prior had the view in all his manors; the abbot of Thorney in Whittlesey; while Henry fitzAucher claimed the view in Little Thetford and William of Tuddenham in his manor in Sutton, Chatteris and Hinton Hall: Thorney Red Book, I, 176 d–7; AR no. 86, m. 16; no. 90, m. 10; no. 95, m. 65.

[2] For what follows, Turnus Vicecomitis Rolls, 53 Edw. III, 18 Ric. II, and 7 Hen. VI.

[3] In the margin of the rolls, opposite the list of jurors, appears the rubric 'libera inquisicio'; and the name of John Drenge was erased from the list of Chatteris jurors 'quia nativus'. On the other hand, each group of entries in the body of the roll was prefaced with the phrase: 'Juratores supradicti similiter cum quattuor hominibus et preposito presentant quod etc.'

[4] There was a separate free jury for each vill, and in 1376 it consisted most commonly of six or eight men. But Doddington mustered only four in 1376 and three in 1394.

[5] The presentment of the Haddenham jurors in 18 Ric. II are typical enough: default of suit, bloodshed, hamsoke, false raising of the hue and cry, slander, hindering the constable, a habitual disturber of the peace, breach of the assizes of bread and ale, defaults of the ale-tasters and the *vigilator*, etc.

powers his courts should have. Those circumstances arose out of the fact that the bishop enjoyed a veritable immunity in the Isle of Ely, which gave him a free hand to order his courts as he would, provided such justice was done as would satisfy a king's demands. The nature of this immunity in its higher ranges is the next point calling for attention.

III

In the year 1305, the bishop of Ely was petitioning in parliament. He and his predecessors, he declared, had enjoyed cognition of all pleas within the Isle of Ely, so that no minister of the king might meddle therein to execute any duty of his office. But now, owing to the negligence of the king's keepers during the last vacancy, in that they had neglected to claim this liberty, the king's justices were unwilling to recognize it. Here the matter passed from parliament to the King's Bench;[1] but the bishop had done no more than echo that monk of Ely priory in the twelfth century who stated that the Isle was exempt from every sort of judgement and authority, so that no servant of exaction might meddle therein or disturb the possessions of the Saint.[2] This was the liberty which would later be called the palatine liberty of the Isle.

The extent of the liberty the bishop enjoyed in the Isle was succinctly described by the knights and free tenants of Cambridgeshire in 1261.[3] No sheriff or bailiff might enter the Isle for any purpose; instead, they should send all original writs concerning the Isle to the bishop's bailiffs for execution. When the king's justices came into the shire, once again, the sheriff should hand over all original writs; and the bishop himself was able to determine all pleas, including pleas of the crown, by his own justices. There is more precision still in the claims made by the bishop's attorney before the justices of oyer and terminer appointed to enquire into the oppressions of local officials in 1341.[4]

---

[1] Maitland, *Memoranda de Parliamento*, p. 41; *RP*, I, 162.

[2] *HE*, p. 6; the phrasing is suggestive of an exclusive banlieu liberty: compare for example Henry I's confirmation of St Edmund's liberty printed in Douglas, *Feudal Documents*, p. 62 and the description of the liberty of Glastonbury in *Mon. Angl.* I, 62 referred to by Lobel in *Oxford Essays presented to H. E. Salter*, p. 130.   [3] AR no. 82, m. 3.

[4] On this commission see Lapsley, *EHR*, xxx, p. 10.

Whenever anyone holding land or resident within the Isle was involved in any plea, that plea should be determined before the bishop's justices, who ought to have cognizance of all pleas arising in the Isle. So when justices came to Cambridgeshire, they should hand to the bishop's attorney a transcript of their commission and the articles of their enquiry, and the bishop would then assign justices to carry out the commission according to its tenour and according to the law and custom of the realm.[1]

In the thirteenth century the bishop's immunity appears most prominently in connection with the descent of the justices of eyre upon the shire of Cambridge. Only when the bishopric was in the king's hand would royal justices sit in the Isle;[2] normally the writs were handed over to the bishop's seneschal and the bishop was commanded to do full and speedy justice.[3] Naturally the bishop also received the profits of the justice he did, and the administration of deodands and other profitable windfalls. In this last connection, however, he would not be allowed to claim as a deodand a shirt into which a Norman merchant had sewed £50, which he had sent on the way to Caen on the back of a servant and in which the servant had been drowned in the river at Littleport.[4]

The bishop's liberty, however, was equally effective against other sorts of judicial visitation. The king was almost certainly acting in defiance of the bishop's rights when, in 1231, he constituted a commission of assize to hear an assize utrum regarding a tenement in Wisbech; and it was probably sharp practice when the session of the commission later moved to Cambridge because of the liberty of Ely.[5] More characteristic, to all seeming, was the conduct of similar justices in 1250. They sat at Tyd within the Isle; but they exercised no jurisdiction there, and an assize

---

[1] BM Add. 9822, ff. 33d–4d.

[2] This is the explanation for the fact that King John himself did justice in the Isle round Martinmas 1210 (CRR, VI, 52–3, 63, 72); that William de Saham and his colleagues sat there in 1286 (AR no. 90, m. 6; Sayles, Select Cases in the Court of King's Bench, I, p. clxi); and John of Berwick and his colleagues in 1299 (PRO Min. Accts, 1132/10).

[3] In 1272, for example: 'Memorandum quod omnia brevia impetrata versus Episcopum Eliensem et homines suos quoscunque et alios ius suum infra insulam de Ely prosequentes tradita sunt Waltero de Wylburgham, senescallo predicti Episcopi, et dictum est ei quod plenam et celerem iusticiam exhibeat etc.': Coucher Book, f. 235.

[4] Cal. Pat. R, 1313–17, 52, 80–1.   [5] Pat. R, 1225–32, 508.

of novel disseisin concerning land in that village was successfully claimed by the bishop's bailiffs.[1] In the same manner, the king's justices of the market were told to supersede their office in the Isle;[2] exemption was obtained in 1305 from the visitation of the new-fangled justices of trailbaston;[3] and later still against justices of oyer and terminer.[4]

The Isle, however, not only excluded the jurisdiction of these visiting courts; it also excluded the jurisdiction of the central courts. There was, of course, discussion about this liberty. In 1260, there was a plea between the bishop and the abbot of Thorney about unjust distraint by the former in Whittlesey. At first the bishop successfully claimed the case from the court of common pleas, but it was later revoked for decision before the king and council on the ground that the abbot held, not of the bishop, but of the king in chief.[5] This, however, was a delicate matter involving two great men; and it should be noted that it was to the king and council that the case was reserved. In 1272 there was a very similar case with the abbot of Ramsey as the other party, the distraint having taken place in Chatteris. The bishop's claim that he ought to have the case in his own court was quickly set aside because some of the king's council and the barons of the exchequer wished the matter to be closed by agreement if possible. An agreement was finally reached which obviated the necessity of deciding upon this delicate matter of jurisdiction.[6]

It was another matter where lesser men were concerned. In 1297, for instance, Michael of Littleport pleaded in the King's Bench that he had been assaulted and robbed by various men from Sutton; but before the case could proceed the bishop's bailiff came and craved his lord's liberty, and the case was transferred to the bishop's court.[7] There are transcripts of many similar cases amongst the Ely records. The bishop claimed

---

[1] AR no. 1177, m. 6.   [2] *Cal. Close R*, 1272–9, 167.
[3] BM Add. 9822, ff. 31 d–32 d; for the commissions of trailbaston set up as a result of an ordinance of 1304, see Holdsworth, *Hist. of English Law*, 1, pp. 273–4 and Cam, *Studies in the Hundred Rolls*, pp. 73 ff.
[4] E.g. in 8 Edw. II: CUL Add. 2950, ff. 156–7.
[5] *Close R*, 1259–61, 174.   [6] *Select Cases in the Exchequer of Pleas*, p. 65.
[7] Coucher Book, f. 200 d: 'Et super hoc venit Robertus Hereward, ballivus Episcopi Eliensis, et petit libertatem domini sui de Ely, et dictum est dicto Michaeli quod sequatur in curia ipsius Episcopi de Ely ita quod iusticia sibi fiet, alioquin quod redeat hic in statu quo nunc est etc. Et dies datus est in curia predicti Episcopi etc.'

successfully from the King's Bench the jurisdiction over men
who entered his park at Haddenham in 1308; over men who broke
into the prior's house at Sutton, assaulted his servant and cut
down his timber; over John the son of William of Wisbech who
robbed Robert Beauveis and abducted his wife; over a case of
violent assault at Tyd in 1363.[1] From the Common Pleas in the
same way he claimed a case about property in Elm in 1312, pleas
of convention involving property in Wisbech and Ely, and a plea
dower relating to property in Wisbech.[2] In brief, the liberty the
bishop had in the Isle constituted an immunity against every
sort of royal justice. It was a liberty greater than the abbot of
Reading had in his franchise or than the archbishop of York had
at Beverley and Ripon[3]—for in these the king's judges sat side
by side in judgement with the stewards of the lords of the
franchise. It was a liberty equivalent to such banlieu liberties
as those of Glastonbury, Ramsey and Bury St Edmunds.[4]

There is a good deal of evidence for the agencies through
which the bishop exercised this superior jurisdiction. In the
thirteenth century, so far as can be seen, he held only one sort
of court for the purpose: a court called in 1220 and 1243 merely
'curia Elyensis';[5] a court which at the beginning of the fourteenth century was held 'coram X, Y and Z iusticiariis et aliis
eiusdem Episcopi fidelibus ibidem presentibus';[6] and a court
which on a number of occasions was held before the bishop's
itinerant justices.[7] This is the court which has left a rich collection of fines settling cases which began commonly with a royal
writ and often in the royal courts.[8] No rolls have survived from

---

[1] Coucher Book, f. 218d; Cott. Claudius C xi, f. 358d; CUL Add. 2950,
ff. 132, 134–6.
[2] Cott. Claudius C xi, ff. 136d; CUL Add. 2950, ff. 136–9.
[3] LTR Mem. R, no. 14, m. 4; Lobel, Essays presented to H. E. Salter,
pp. 126–8.
[4] Lobel, op. cit. pp. 128–30 and The Borough of Bury St Edmund's, pp.
113–16; Ault, Private Jurisdiction in England, pp. 112–25.
[5] D & C Charter no. 833 and BM Egerton MS. 3047, f. 211d (a plea of
mort d'ancestor about land in Leverington); D & C Charter no. 140 (a plea
about land in Witchford).
[6] Thorney Red Book, i, f. 201; ii, f. 384; Liber M, f. 626.
[7] Thorney Red Book, i, f. 175d; ii, f. 382; D & C Charters nos. 184, 846;
Liber M, ff. 347, 374 (these instances date from the years 1246, 1247, 1248,
1260, 1272).
[8] In one case, all the stages can be traced. In 1314 Master Geoffrey de
Fresyngfeld brought a plea of convention in the Bench about property in Ely

the court of the bishop's itinerant justices; but the character of the bishop's liberty would be enough to suggest that, in addition to this jurisdiction he was exercising in civil cases, he would exercise all the criminal justice that the king's judges would administer outside the Isle. This impression is confirmed by notes in later account rolls about seven condemned felons taken from Ely to the gallows at Aldreth and the purchase of two empty wine barrels for two women condemned to death by burning,[1] as well as by notes from the rolls of the bishop's itinerant justices from about the years 1260–75 preserved in a conventual register. They were doing all the king's justices would do, not only in executing criminal justice, but also in hearing presentments about escaped felons, claims to liberties and the verdict of a coroner's quest upon the chattels of felons.[2]

In the later Middle Ages the omnicompetence of the court of the bishop's itinerant justices seems to have been dispersed amongst a number of commissions. True, even at the beginning of the sixteenth century we hear still of the bishop's judges 'ad omnia placita',[3] but this may refer to a commission of gaol delivery or oyer and terminer. The first of these commissions is heard of as early as 1286, when the bishop's justices of gaol delivery adjudged to death a tenant of the convent;[4] and again in 1299 when a commission to deliver Ely gaol had been given to the bishop's steward together with Fulk Baynard and Richard de Belhous.[5] It would seem, however, from the proceedings of the eyre of 1286 that the king issued the commission to deliver, and that the bishop merely took executive action upon it.[6] At

against Alexander de Rypton and his wife, but the bailiff of the liberty intervened and claimed his master's court (Cott. Claudius C XI, f. 326 d); the fine levied in the bishop's court which settled the matter is preserved in D & C Charters nos. 485 and 918. For other fines see the references in the previous notes, and also D & C Charters nos. 151 (printed below, Appx. XVII, p. 290; here the extract from the roll of the bishop's court is annexed to the charter), 161 (a grant of land to the convent 'prout in quadem fine levata in curia domini... episcopi Eliensis per breve domini Regis... plenius continetur'), 918, 1161.

[1] CUL Add. 2953, f. 2.

[2] Cott. Vespasian A XIX, ff. 99 d ff. (extracts are printed below, Appx. XVI, p. 290).

[3] Reg. N. West quoted CUL Add. 2945, f. 167.

[4] AR no. 90, m. 9.   [5] AR no. 95, m. 66 d.

[6] AR no. 90, m. 7 d: Hugh de Cressingham, the bishop's seneschal, claimed that the gaols of the Isle should be delivered by the seneschal and that no one

any rate, such justices continued to be appointed: in 1326 justices of gaol delivery held no less than three sessions at Ely, and commissions directed to them are to be found in bishop's registers in 1414 and 1515.[1]

In the later Middle Ages, however, the bishop's justices of assize were probably more important still. Towards the end of the fourteenth century they were holding three sessions a year, just as the king's assize justices were;[2] and the bishop clearly had his justices of assize early in the reign of Edward II.[3] Over and above these rights, the bishop seems also to have claimed to issue commissions of oyer and terminer as they were necessary;[4] and in the fourteenth century to have his own justices of the peace, who sat in Richard II's reign at Ely, Wisbech, Whittlesey, Sutton and Haddenham, and in the reign of Henry VII at Ely and Wisbech.[5] This last liberty was one which was carefully reserved to the bishop in the statutes regulating the appointment of justices of the peace and *custodes rotulorum* in the sixteenth century.[6]

One final power the bishop had in virtue of his liberty in the

else ought to have the record of the delivery or of the process of pleading. 'Et milites de patria assidentes Justiciarii hic quesiti fuerunt si ipsi unquam vidissent quod dominus Rex constituisset per breve suum milites de patria Justiciarios suos ad deliberandam gaolam in ista libertate; ad quod surrexit Willelmus Muschet et dixit quod sic, et quod ipse simul cum aliis militibus de patria fecerunt deliberacionem gaole in ista libertate de quibusdam prisonibus ad impetracionem hominum prioris de Ely; et super hoc protulit warantum suum et rotulos suos de sua deliberacione, et dixit quod ipse examinavit prisones et totum officium... exequebatur. Ideo consideratum est quod dominus Rex remaneat in statu pristino concedendi hoc warantum et constituendi Justiciarios suos etc.'

[1] CUL Add. 2953, f. 13; Reg. T. Bourchier and Reg. N. West quoted in CUL Add. 2945, ff. 140, 167.

[2] CUL Add. 2953, f. 3; Holdsworth, *Hist. of English Law*, i, p. 276.

[3] When a quitclaim regarding 20 acres of land in Elm was enrolled 'coram Iusticiariis eiusdem Episcopi apud Ely ad assisas capiendas assignatis': Cott. Claudius C xi, f. 318.

[4] In the early fourteenth century the question arose whether Hugh of Northwold's privilege to the men of Littleport to cut sedge in Rakfen was prejudicial to the other commoners in that fen. The prior addressed a *querela* to the bishop about it; and the bishop appointed his seneschal and the prior to hear and determine the rights of the case according to the oath of good and faithful men of the Isle: Cott. Claudius C xi, f. 361 d.

[5] CUL Add. 2953, ff. 3, 9; and for the Wisbech hundred bailiff collecting amercements imposed by the J.P.'s in 1489-90 see Cam, *Liberties and Communities*, p. 197.

[6] 27 Hen. VIII, c. 18; 3 & 4 Edw. VI, c. 1.

Isle: the right of issuing commissions to his own coroners to exercise their office according to the law and custom which governed it.[1] Coroners, indeed, were very thick upon the ground in the Isle, for it is clear that there was at least one for each of the hundreds.[2] As usual, moreover, the arrangements made to fill the office in the different hundreds were not the same. In 1299 the coroners of Wisbech and Witchford hundred were both said to be elected by the men of the hundred;[3] but none the less the coronership of Wisbech hundred seems to have shown strong tendencies to become hereditary.[4] In Ely hundred there is no question that the coronership was an hereditary serjeanty in the hands of the Baret family.[5] Still, despite this variety in the form of their appointment, these coroners performed the common duties which royal coroners performed in the geldable, and had their quarrels with the latter over the right to hold inquest upon a corpse discovered in Marmere on the disputed borderland between the shire and the Isle.[6] They took the depositions of approvers, and held inquest in cases of murder and upon the bodies of men found drowned in mysterious circumstances.[7] They were, in short, fulfilling the terms of their commission to

[1] A fifteenth-century commission is preserved by Bentham in CUL Add. 2951, f. 83: 'Philippus...Eliensis Episcopus omnibus ad quos presentes littere pervenerint salutem. Sciatis quod constituimus et ordinamus Johannem Dunholt coronatorem nostrum hundredi nostri de Wicheford infra insulam nostram Eliensem, dantes et concedentes eidem Johanni plenam potestatem et mandatum nostrum generale ad debito modo faciendum et exercendum officium predictum et omnia et singula que ad officium predictum secundum legem et consuetudinem regni Anglie pertinent etc.'
[2] E.g. AR no. 95, mm. 64, 66d, 69.
[3] *Ibid.* m. 65: John Pelryn was coroner of Witchford and John le Marchaund of Wisbech hundred 'per eleccionem tocius communitatis'.
[4] In 1279 and 1286 the coroner was Martin le Marchaunt, who also seems to be referred to in 1299 as Martin de Leverington; he was succeeded by his son John who is referred to indifferently as John de Leverington, John the son of Martin and John le Marchaund: AR no. 90, m. 6; no. 95, mm. 64, 69; D & C Charters nos. 720, 724–5, 852, 999, 1026.
[5] The serjeanty of being coroner of Ely hundred was clearly laid down in 1251, when Lodovic Baret and Ralf Barbur held 36 acres of land 'et debent esse coronatores et replegiare homines episcopi'; while the coronership was included in the list of serjeanties in 1286: Cott. Claudius C xi, f. 26d; AR no. 90, m. 9. The office seems to have descended from Lodovic to his son Nicholas and then to William Baret at the beginning of the fourteenth century: AR no. 90, m. 6; no. 95, m. 64; D & C Charters nos. 148, 149A, 151, 446, 481, 750, 805, 947, 963, 1160.
[6] AR no. 86, m. 48d; no. 90, m. 8.
[7] AR no. 90, mm. 6, 9d *et passim*.

exercise their office and all that pertained to it according to the law and custom, not of the Isle, but of the realm of England.

If this discussion of the liberty began with immunity uppermost in our minds—an immunity which encouraged institutional diversity and great flexibility in the powers which courts might exercise—we come back none the less to the law and custom of England in the end. That law and custom in Bracton's time may have taken up à great deal from the customs of folk and the customs of districts; but still its essential quality remained its commonness. Particularity and diversity had in fact been fused into a single corpus of law and custom in the unifying practice of the king's administration and the day to day work of his judges. It is the relationship between the king's government and franchise, the impact upon an immunity of the common law and custom of the realm, which constitutes the last problem to be discussed in connection with the liberty of St Etheldreda.

IV

The description of the liberty which has been given in the foregoing pages has rested in the main upon materials of the thirteenth and fourteenth centuries, since no evidence of an earlier date exists for a study of the liberty as a working system. But there is a modification needed. The franchises of medieval England were not formed at a blow: they have their own processes of growth, their own history. The medieval bishops were not unaware of the fact, for when they claimed their liberties, a good deal of historical record was vouched in their support.[1] They would claim view of frank-pledge by King Edgar's charter; chattels of felons and the right of their bailiffs to arrest, imprison and to execute the judgements of the king's courts in virtue of a charter (to all seeming a forged one) of King Edward the Confessor; and other liberties again by grant of Richard I and Henry III. In all this there are signs of growth and change: change at least in the emphasis placed at different times upon the different constituents of the liberty.

In the thirteenth century, the liberty of Ely was everywhere a court-holding liberty. Everywhere its men were withdrawn

[1] See the bishop's claim of his liberties in Hertfordshire in 1279 and Huntingdonshire in 1286: Coucher Book, ff. 232–3; Liber M, ff. 121–2.

from the jurisdiction of tourn, of hundred and of shire; in some hundreds the church exercised the hundredal jurisdiction over the whole of those hundreds; in the Isle there was no jurisdiction save that exercised by the bishop's own justices. Yet, as we have seen, this may not always have been so; there is no absolutely conclusive proof that the Anglo-Saxon abbots had enjoyed from the beginning a court-keeping franchise, not even in the Isle of Ely.[1] Whatever the truth may be about the state of affairs before 1066, it is certain that the church of Ely was holding courts in its hundreds shortly after the conquest. Henry I's writ can mean nothing else, where he commands all barons holding in the bishop's hundreds to come to the pleas in the bishop's hundreds at the summons of the bishop's bailiffs as—we should note—they had done in his brother's and his father's time.[2] In the Isle, the fact that the hundred courts were clearly the bishop's courts is evident from a charter of Bishop Hervey's to Thorney abbey in 1128, which is clarified by another from Bishop John of Rochester and confirmed by Henry I.[3] Bishop John says that Hervey has given up the suit to Witchford hundred which he had been accustomed to exact from the abbot's manor in Whittlesey: Hervey's charter (which is echoed by Henry I) that he has granted to the church of Thorney 'all those customs and secular causes which the church of Ely has in its hundreds of Witchford...excepting properly royal customs which pertain neither to him nor to his church'. Whatever other significance these documents have, they make it quite clear that it was from his own hundred court that Bishop Hervey granted this exemption.

It is also not without interest to note that, at a later time, the liberty the abbot of Thorney had in Whittlesey was a right to hold his own view of frank-pledge with all that pertained to the view 'saving to the bishop and his successors causes and things which demand judgement of life and limb according to the law and custom of the realm'.[4] May we not presume that the bishop's right to the view arose partly out of a similar exemption from the

[1] See above, pp. 25 ff.
[2] Bentham, Appx. XXIII.
[3] Thorney Red Book, I, ff. 24d, 166, 167 (see Appx. VI, p. 284, XIV, p. 288).
[4] *Ibid.* I, 176d–7 (an agreement between the bishop and the abbot in 1278).

jurisdiction of the local courts throughout his lands? The right to the forfeiture of all its men which the church of Ely had possessed since King Edgar's day must certainly have helped to create this exemption. Once exemption had been asserted, however, cases in which the bishop's men were involved, and which would have gone in the normal course to the shire and hundred courts, may have been added to the work already done in the manors by domanial courts. It must have been some such injection of public business into the manorial courts which accounts for the 'curie et lete'[1] in which the bishop's franchisal powers were most prominently and most generally exercised in the thirteenth century.

In the first century or so after the conquest, the liberty of Ely may have amounted to little more than these rights just discussed together with administrative powers to exercise the jurisdiction involved. The bishop had his courts in his hundreds and the hundredal jurisdiction over all his men: that may have been enough for a twelfth-century immunity, supplemented as it was by judicial powers over villeins in the courts of manors and over knights in the court of the honour of St Etheldreda. In the thirteenth century, probably from Henry II's time, the liberty had to move with changing times if it was to remain an immunity. The old shrieval jurisdictions from which exemption had been gained were on the wane; they were being replaced by new and more powerful royal courts; the sheriffs were busier than ever, but they were 'ministerial sheriffs', no longer viceroys in the shire.[2] The bishop of Ely might still have to answer from time to time about the warrant he had for his views, his hundreds and the rest; but the defence of his liberty at bottom was now concerned with other things. It was concerned with his rights as against the king's travelling justices and the king's central courts; it was concerned with the profit they extracted from his men; it was concerned, not with the judicial, but with the administrative activities of sheriffs, as the 'king's maids of all work' in the shire.[3]

These were the problems which were settled (more or less) after much discussion before the itinerant justices and in the

---

[1] See above, p. 210.
[2] Cf. Templeman, *Sheriffs of Warwickshire*, p. 4.
[3] Cam, *Liberties and Communities*, pp. 27–8.

charters of Henry III,[1] Edward II[2] and Edward III.[3] The
bishop was permitted to enjoy the profits of justice done by the
king's judges throughout his lands and in all his hundreds. But
if the liberty was no longer everywhere a judicial immunity,
it remained an administrative immunity from which, provided
there had been no default of justice on the bishop's part, the
sheriff and his subordinates were rigorously excluded and in
which the bishop's bailiffs transacted all the multifarious business of government. Only in the Isle of Ely was a complete
judicial immunity maintained; elsewhere all that was added was
the right to plead all pleas the sheriff could plead under the
authority of new-fangled writs. Naturally enough the evolution of administrative immunity and a lucrative fiscal privilege
created problems in an England which was being straitened
into 'a united *regnum*, not a loose federation of jurisdictions'.[4]
Problems were bound to arise until it became clear that an
immunity was only a franchise, and that the duty of a franchise
holder was to administer the king's government, for his own
profit maybe, but also (in the words of a judgement of the early
fourteenth century) as 'the king's minister for upholding and
carrying out in the king's name and in due manner what belongs
to the royal authority'.[5]

Even to put it so, however, perhaps lays too much stress upon
a notion that in the thirteenth century there was a taming of
liberties, a harnessing of their machinery to the machinery of
the state. Even the England which had been no more than
a 'federation of jurisdictions' had been born in 'the friendly co-
operation of William the Conqueror with his companions'; and
that first feudal age bequeathed to the thirteenth century, in the
mind of king and baron alike, a keen sense of their mutual

[1] For the background and references to this charter, see above, pp.
216–17.

[2] The occasion for Edward II's charter is made clear in *Rotuli Parliamentorum hactenus Inediti*, 68–70 and see my remarks in *EHR*, LXII, pp. 454–5.
For Edward's charter see *Cart. Rames.* I, 118–19 and *Cal. Charter R*, III,
397–8. It was followed immediately by a mandate to the barons of the
exchequer to allow the bishop and prior the issues of the green wax in all
their hundreds and lands: BM Add. 41612, f. 58.

[3] *Cal. Charter R*, IV, 79.

[4] Powicke, *Henry III and the Lord Edward*, I, p. 116.

[5] *Placitorum Abbreviatio*, 257 quoted Cam, *Liberties and Communities*,
p. 184; and see the whole argument of ch. XIV of the last-named work.

interdependence.[1] There is much to illustrate this fact in the history of St Etheldreda's liberty, despite an increasingly severe scrutiny of its privileges from the early part of the thirteenth century onwards.

Of course the bishop's liberty entailed, not only profit and privilege, but also responsibility—just as the sheriff's office did. If the bishop or his officers failed to obey the royal mandate, then the liberty would be classified as one of those which impeded common justice.[2] If the bailiffs of the liberty failed to produce parties to a plea or to notify the sheriff of the names of pledges, they would be summoned before the king's court to show reason for their neglect;[3] and as early as 1204 the sheriff would be instructed to omit nothing because of the bishop's liberty when the bailiffs of St Etheldreda had in fact failed in their duty.[4] Once again the sheriff would be told to enter the bishop's liberty when the latter ignored the king's command to free beasts taken as distress from the abbot of Thorney[5] or failed to account at the exchequer for royal debts levied within the liberty.[6] More than that, the sheriff would get a writ of aid directed to the inhabitants of his shire if it appeared that the liberty was sheltering malefactors, and the support of a special commission of oyer and terminer when it appeared that the men of the liberty had acted in a high-handed, even a disorderly way; or if the bishop had failed to maintain Earith causeway as he ought to have done.[7] Once again the sheriff would be ordered to enter the liberty, with four lawful knights from his shire, to make a record of a plea in the bishop's court when a false judgement had been given there;[8] or in order to make an inquest into the bishop's lands and chattels in the less usual eventuality of the bishop having been convicted before the king of certain felonies.[9] The ultimate sanction behind all these interventions was the threat that a liberty misused should be forfeit. This would seem to be the sanction Henry III was invoking as early

[1] Powicke, op. cit.; Rolls of the Justices in Eyre for Gloucestershire, etc. (ed. D. M. Stenton), p. liii.

[2] RH, I, 49.   [3] CRR, II, 284; III, 46.

[4] CRR, III, 241.   [5] Cal. Close R, 1272-9, 73.

[6] KR Mem. R, no. 43, m. 11.

[7] Cal. Pat. R, 1272-81, 100; 1292-1301, 379; RP, I, 314.

[8] AR no. 95, m. 30.

[9] KR Ext. and Inq., Bdle. 9, File 2: this of course was Bishop Thomas Lisle, found guilty of harbouring and concealing a murderer in 1356.

as 1225, when he wondered much that the bishop had released certain men delivered to him to keep in his prison; and told the bishop to restore them to prison without delay, as he wished to have his liberty maintained.[1]

These instances, however, indicate no settled hostility to the bishop's liberty; merely a determination to insist upon the view that a franchise (as much as the geldable) was part of the *regnum*, and subject to the king's overriding authority. In themselves they have no more and no less significance than similar disciplinary action against sheriffs or other royal officers. Where there had been no carelessness or inefficiency or abuse in the exercise of privilege, the story was a different one. The king's government stood behind the administration of the liberty, not only as mentor and even schoolmaster, but also as its support. It would step in to aid the bishop when his houses were demolished while he was beyond the seas on the king's business; or when corn was stolen from his fields while he was in Rome; or when disorders too great for his own resources to cope with broke out in his manors and his courts.[2] The sheriff would be told to help the bishop in distraining his tenants to mend the sea-dykes in the Marshland, or to compel the men of Dunwich to render the 24,000 herrings they owed annually to the monks of Ely.[3] There seems to have been little limit to the king's willingness to accommodate the bishop: in 1226, before the bishop had a proper gaol in his Norfolk liberty, a special commission was hurriedly appointed to try two murderers arrested there, because the bishop had nowhere he could properly keep them.[4] The bishop's judicial rights also commanded respect: sheriffs were told not to hold pleas in their county courts which should properly be held in the liberty of Ely,[5] and royal justices to respect the bishop's liberties as he had enjoyed them in the past.[6] Edward I was even willing to promise amends should his courts of the steward and the marshal, when they were in those parts, in any way infringe

---

[1] *Rot. Litt. Claus.* II, 67.

[2] *Cal. Pat. R,* 1247–58, 526; 1272–81, 178–9; 1301–7, 93.

[3] *Close R,* 1256–9, 475–6; KR Mem. R, no. 28, m. 5.

[4] *Rot. Litt. Claus.* II, 159.

[5] Mandates to the sheriffs of Essex and Cambridgeshire in *Close R,* 1242–7, 84; 1247–51, 103.

[6] See the mandates to the itinerant justices in Norfolk in 1228: *ibid.* 1227–31, 80; and to justices of assize in Suffolk in 1224: *Pat. R,* 1216–25, 486.

the exclusive liberty of the Isle—a promise only made, however, after the matter had received parliamentary discussion.[1]

In all this, the 'friendly co-operation' of the king and his companions does not seem so far distant after all, despite writs of *quo warranto* and all the discipline which was necessary to turn federation into *regnum*. There was much discussion about the liberty of St Etheldreda during all this period; much questioning of its powers, its privileges and its exemptions. But that did not mean the end of its capacity to change and develop with changing times. The liberty may have lost the judicial immunity it acquired in the twelfth century when it had shut out the sheriff—or lost it, at least, everywhere except in the Isle. But in return, it gained an extended fiscal privilege and an enhanced administrative immunity everywhere; and in the Isle a judicial immunity equipped with all the institutions designed to administer the new common law. By the end of the fourteenth century this had come to include the right of the bishop to nominate his own justices of the peace.

Still, that was in the Isle; and in the Isle, it was sometimes claimed at a later time, the bishop had a palatine liberty.[2] In fact this does not seem to have been so. Generally, at least, when the bishop appointed judicial commissions, they seem to have acted on royal writs and a royal commission rather than on the bishop's writ and the bishop's commission.[3] There were many things which were peculiar about the courts of the Isle; but, in acting upon the king's writs or in acting so that no king's writ would be evoked by anything doubtful in their action, those courts still administered the law of England and their officials were subject to all the scrutiny which fell upon others administering that law. The Isle was an exclusive banlieu liberty, a very privileged liberty, even if it was not a palatinate in medieval times; it was none the less an integral part of the government of England, censured as such and sustained as such.

---

[1] Maitland, *Memoranda de Parliamento*, pp. 146–7; *Select Cases in the Court of King's Bench*, III, p. cxxiv.

[2] On palatine liberties, see Coke, *Institutes of the Laws of England*, IV, c. 36 and Holdsworth, *Hist. of English Law*, I, pp. 109–32. For the distinction between palatine liberties and banlieu liberties like that of the Isle of Ely, see Lobel, *Essays presented to H. E. Salter*, p. 134.

[3] See the terms in which the bishop claimed his liberty, discussed above, pp. 232–3.

For that reason, moreover, the liberty in general and the liberty of the Isle in particular are a striking illustration of the permanent contribution made to medieval English government by feudal notions about the essential co-operation between king and aristocracy in the work of administering the realm. It was the persistence of this notion which made it thinkable that a franchise could take up and embody into its working in the thirteenth century the new law, the royal law, and the institutions that law engendered. This fact, in turn, reacted upon the domestic matter of how the bishop ordered his affairs. The casual and amateur character of the methods used in administering his lands and rights in early times may have been suitable enough in an estate managed along customary lines, in a barony with its own self-regulating machinery, in a liberty concerned with customary courts and the 'good old law'. These methods were obsolete in the circumstances of the thirteenth century. One of those circumstances was the fact that St Etheldreda's liberty had become part of a kingdom, the affairs of which were increasingly conducted by the professional administrator and the professional judge; and 'civil servants' were no unusual occupants even of its bishop's stool. The history of that liberty, therefore, is significant from the point of view of the changes which took place in the device of government in medieval times; it has also a significance for the methods of administration which were employed in the lands, the barony and the liberty of Ely, whether they were administered in the interest of bishop or king or in that common interest where no dividing line can be drawn.

VIII

ADMINISTRATION

TOWARDS the end of the tenth century, Abbot Brihtnoth took thought for the administration of the abbey's property which he had helped Bishop Ethelwold to accumulate. He chose from amongst the brethren a trustworthy man, Leo by name, 'cui rei familiaris commisit preposituram'. No doubt Leo had the assistance of reeves of manors (about whom we hear a century later) in his task of cultivating lands and looking to the sowing of divers fruits; but the administration of the lands of St Etheldreda was carried on with very meagre resources in these early days.[1] Moving forward three centuries, a very different picture is presented to us in the vacancy accounts of the later thirteenth century. Bailiffs stand by the side of the reeves of the manors; travelling bailiffs and stewards and auditors link the manors with the bishop's household and supervise the judgements which the homages still give in the bishop's courts; the bishop's household has acquired many separate departments, each staffed by many officials. Some of these administrators were more than trustworthy: they were men of technical training. One of them had legal training enough to have acted as the bishop's attorney before he became his seneschal; another knowledge enough of the canon law to proceed from the office of seneschal to the office of official of the diocese. Many of them could pass from the bishop's service into the administrative service of the king; one of them could even become one of the king's judges.[2]

Clearly, these domestic matters of administration are symptomatic of larger changes. Behind the development of administrative resources in the bishopric of Ely lie great constitutional changes: the astonishing inventiveness of the Angevin line in the art of government, and the ways in which that inventiveness diversified and deepened the responsibilities of the holders of franchises. Economic changes told in the same way: the management of a great estate in the high-farming age called for more

[1] *HE*, II, c. 54.
[2] Further detail on these points will be found below, pp. 265-9.

detailed supervision, more technical capacity in the bishop's officers and a greater readiness to take decisions which were properly economic decisions than had the management of an estate 'farmed' in the customary manner. Social changes also had a part to play. As feudal relationships lost their meaning, feudal institutions likewise withered away; and an administrative void was left over which the professional in administration could extend his province. Above all, the professional himself had appeared: a fact which calls for a knowledge of more than English intellectual history if some day we are going to understand it. There are problems here which would take us too far if an attempt were made to tackle them in this study; in this chapter, therefore, the nature of the changes which took place in estate administration will be described so far as the materials allow. The background of those changes can only be rough-sketched; it is the background, not only to the history of the church of Ely, but also to the history of the realm of England in the high Middle Ages.

I

A detailed reconstruction of the administrative history of the episcopal estate of Ely is precluded at once by the fact that no central financial records have survived. At best we can hope to establish, in the first instance, a broad impression of how the bishop's administrative institutions developed. Such a chronological framework, in turn, will provide a standard of reference in estimating the real importance of different institutions at the time when we can discern them most clearly, in the later thirteenth and early fourteenth centuries.

So far as the twelfth century is concerned, no single document reveals the administrative arrangements the bishops had made to manage their affairs; but attestations to episcopal charters indicate the main groups of men upon whom they relied to transact the business of bishopric, barony, estate and liberty. These groups included more than one sort of man—a fact illustrated by a charter of the first of the bishops.[1] There were at least three groups of men in the 'court' of Bishop Hervey when it was considering the disposition of Stretham church. There were the officials: the seneschal and the 'ministri episcopi'.

---

[1] Douglas, *Feudal Documents*, p. cl, and see above, p. 195 and n. 3.

There was the episcopal household: the archdeacon and a number of clerks. Finally, there were the knights, tenants of the honour of St Etheldreda; the testing clauses of most of the early charters show that their duty to give aid and counsel and court service to their lord was not one that rusted for lack of use. Doubtless, the distinctions made here are rough and ready ones: Hervey's archdeacon was enfeoffed in a military tenement and at this stage the greater officers of the bishop were commonly military tenants of the barony of Ely. But the dividing lines grew sharper with the passing of the years.

No attempt will be made here to deal further with the ecclesiastical *familia* as an element in administration. It remains, of course, a constant element; in many of Bishop Eustace's charters, for instance, clerks are almost the only witnesses,[1] and in the days of Bishop John de Ketene his chaplain and the rectors of Haddenham and Westley Waterless would be at his side in dealing with the matter of the bishop's bakery.[2] To discuss the bishop's *familia* adequately, however, would involve a digression into diocesan administration foreign to the purposes of this study. Its members must be taken for granted, except to the extent that they engage our attention on other grounds.

The official group keeps closely enough to the pattern which is well known in other feudal households. The seneschal is always before us. There was also a constable in Hervey's time and Nigel's;[3] and a marshal who, in Hervey's time, was responsible for the regulation of the bishop's household[4] and who still was to be found amongst the bishop's officers (if somewhat obscurely) in the early fourteenth century. Nigel and Eustace also had their butler;[5] while the chamberlain was prominent under Nigel and Longchamp[6] and could still, in Bishop

---

[1] E.g. D & C Charters nos. 62 (no laymen), 63 (four laymen with seven clerks), 64 (five laymen with eight clerks), 65 (two laymen with thirteen clerks).

[2] Coucher Book, f. 217.

[3] D & C Charter no. 51; Liber M, f. 155.

[4] The rights and duties of Bishop Hervey's baker were to be defined 'secundum disposicionem marescalli nostri', who seems to have enforced the 'assisa hospicii nostri' which regulated the arrangements for providing bread for the bishop's table: Coucher Book, f. 217 (printed below, Appx. V, p. 283). All this would be in line with the marshal's duties in the king's household; see Madox, *Exchequer*, p. 33.

[5] Liber M. ff. 154, 155, 158, 162 (2).

[6] *Ibid.* ff. 151–6, 162–5.

Eustace's day, lay stress upon his ministerial relationship with his lord.[1] Most of these men were typically feudal officers: holders of fees and the sort of men who could share the views and attitudes of the varying body of knights and others who made up the bishop's 'curia'. Even at this date, however, there were signs of an incipient professionalism. Bishop Nigel's seneschal had already acquired his own clerk;[2] and it may be no coincidence that it is in the lifetime of that bishop, born and trained as a member of the greatest official dynasty of the twelfth century, that we find notices for the first time of what were later to be the four terms of the exchequer of Ely [3]

There is nothing to suggest that any of these officers received any salary as their counterparts did in the thirteenth century. Many of them clearly received grants of land either as a fee for the performance of their office or to sustain them whilst they served the bishop. The steward and butler in the twelfth century were always military tenants of the barony; and Nigel granted land in Ely and Hartest to William de Camera, his *serviens*,[4] and to Geoffrey his *famulus* a 40-acre tenement in Snailwell for a rent of 6s. 8d. and 'pro servicio suo nobis impenso et impendendo'.[5] Even Bishop Hervey's baker had a tenement in Ely attached to his office.[6] Many of the smaller offices—coronerships, the office of boatman, the office of forester and so on— became in this way hereditary serjeanties; but this hereditary principle did not succeed in capturing the chief offices of administration, and in particular the office of seneschal. That may have helped to make easier the transformation of the bishop's administrative system in the thirteenth century.

Meantime, the local side of twelfth-century administration leaves few marks on the records. In 1169–73, when the see was vacant after Nigel's death,[7] there are few signs of the complex

[1] St John's College Muniments, Drawer III, no. 36: 'Universis sancte matris ecclesie filiis ad quos presens scriptum pervenerit Simon camerarius E. Elyensis episcopi salutem', etc.
[2] D & C Charter no. 54.
[3] Liber M, f. 157 and see below, pp. 256–7.
[4] D & C Charters nos. 53 (2), 54; the former was confirmed by Henry II: *ibid.* no. 11 printed by Delisle-Berger, *Recueil des Actes de Henri II*, no. 337.
[5] Caius 485/489, f. 35.
[6] Coucher Book, f. 217 (below, Appx. V, p. 283).
[7] See *Pipe R*, 16 Hen. II, 95–6; 17 Hen. II, 115–17; 18 Hen. II, 115–17; 19 Hen. II, 161–2.

hierarchy of officials which later gave cohesion to the scattered lands of the bishop. Of travelling officials we hear only of summoners to gather the bishop's knights for their service in the Isle. Of manorial officers, two serjeants are mentioned as looking after two manors which were not at farm; otherwise the keeper during the vacancy (and, we may suppose, the bishop at other times) dealt with farmers of manors—men who might indeed be bailiffs or reeves,[1] but who might also be (as we know from other places)[2] men of substance and local standing. No doubt this minimized the amount of administrative staff necessary; although there are references to *servientes*—bailiffs, no doubt, in charge of manors or courts whose duties can only be surmised for lack of documentation.[3] The impression which remains, none the less, is that the bishop managed with an ecclesiastical *familia* and a primitive feudal household at the centre and the slightest of hierarchies scattered over the estate. By comparison, the advance of professionalism in the thirteenth century amounted to a veritable revolution.

The progress of administrative organization is visible enough in the vacancy accounts.[4] Of course, these records do not tell us everything. When no bishop existed, his household (and above all his wardrobe) falls out of the picture. But it is quite clear that by the second half of the thirteenth century there was a kind of permanent civil service in the lands of the bishop of Ely; that it persisted, bishop or no bishop; and that it commanded salaries commensurate with the professional skill requisite for the duties it performed. The seneschal was acquiring local deputies—three of them in 1256 and five in 1299—and there

[1] For instance, the term 'firma prepositorum' in Ranulf Flambard's division of the abbey's income between abbot and convent; while Bishop Hervey certainly had a reeve at Fen Ditton: *HE*, II, c. 136; Liber M, f. 145 (below, Appx. VII, p. 284).

[2] One illustration is the connection of the Cockfield family with the St Edmund's manors of Semer and Groton, for which see Galbraith, *Studies in Medieval History presented to F. M. Powicke*, pp. 283 ff. There is an interesting instrument wherein Abbot Samson demised these manors to Adam son of Robert of Cockfield in CUL Mm. IV. 19, f. 223. For similar instances on the estate of St Benet of Holme, see West, *Register of St Benet of Holme*, nos. 124, 132.

[3] For example, in Nigel's charter confirming the rights of the convent: 'Concedo eis eciam omnes servientes suos de omnibus ministris suis ut eos cum suis mansuris libere possideant': Trin. MS. O. 2. 1, ff. 134d–5.

[4] For what follows, see Pipe R, no. 101, m. 4 (1256) and PRO Min. Accts, 1132/10, 11, 12, 13 (1299, 1302, 1310, 1316).

was a constable of Wisbech castle who acted in a similar capacity in the Marshland bailiwick. There were two receivers at the bishop's exchequer; one or two permanent attorneys in the king's courts; and, highest paid of all the bishop's officers, two auditors who in their perambulations about the estate impressed upon it a uniform standard and a uniform efficiency of administration. These officials in turn controlled a complex local hierarchy: hundred bailiffs with their sub-bailiffs, beadles and clerks; manorial bailiffs with their subordinate reeves, haywards and a variety of other agents. It is the operation of this complex hierarchy which can be studied in some detail in the records of the thirteenth and early fourteenth centuries.

II

It is a matter of convenience to examine the administrative arrangements of the thirteenth-century bishops under two main heads: to consider first economic administration and domestic housekeeping, and secondly judicial administration and the offices concerned with the bishop's public or quasi-public functions. Such a division, however, is purely a matter of convenience which approximates no more than very roughly to the facts of the thirteenth century. In private, as in public, administration 'divisions were not made along functional lines'.[1] Many of the bishop's officers—the seneschal at one end of the scale, haywards and beadles at the other—played a part that was both economic and judicial. To this overlapping attention will be drawn from time to time; for the moment let us look at the administrative aspects of the episcopal economy, and make what we can of it despite the lack of receiver's accounts.

It is best, perhaps, to begin at the bottom with manorial administration. In it, the central position occupied by the reeve is some testimony to the painful process of adjustment required in turning a customary and amateur system of administration into the highly centralized system of the thirteenth century. Traditionally, the reeveship was an office to which each and all of the lord's customary tenants were liable;[2] it might therefore

---

[1] Plucknett, *Concise History of the Common Law*, 134.
[2] E.g. at Wetheringsett 'dominus potest facere prepositum suum de quocunque voluerit viginti acras tenente'; or at Kelshall 'Iuratores dicunt quod

be expected to 'go the rounds' and to be allotted by annual election in the manor court.[1] From all these points of view the reeve's office was typical of an administration essentially amateur. For the same reason, the reeve received no salary: his payment consisted in acquittance from his customary works, commonly the right to eat at the lord's table in harvest time,[2] and a few traditional perquisites of minor importance.[3] None the less, it was upon the reeve that primary responsibility rested for the whole conduct of the manorial economy, a responsibility attested by the *compotus* which he had to present yearly at the bishop's exchequer for audit. He was responsible for the rents due from the manor, and for transmitting cash from time to time to the bishop's exchequer.[4] He paid the salaries of officials attached to the manor,[5] and dispensed the customary liveries of food to the manorial *famuli* and to boon workers in harvest time;[6] he paid any wages there were to be paid. He was responsible for the condition of plough-beasts and for the state of the hedges about the fields and the *curia*;[7] he answered for the issues of grain and sold what was surplus both of grain and livestock. For all these tasks a very great deal was asked in terms of skill and devotion from men whose duty was discharged by necessity rather than by choice.

Doubtless, reeves were in a large measure forced to be efficient; they were closely watched by the auditors, by bailiffs, by their neighbours who would be asked to speak about the conduct of the lord's husbandry in the manor court. Yet there are also signs that, in the fourteenth century, the bishops appreciated

dominus potest facere prepositum de quocunque tenente dimidiam virgatam': Caius 485/489, ff. 155d, 350.

[1] As the reeve was elected at Wisbech: e.g. Wisbech Halimote, 5 Edw. II (St Dionysius).

[2] Caius 485/489, ff. 124, 155d, 350, etc.

[3] At Fen Ditton he received half an acre each of wheat and barley and the right to put four plough-beasts into the lord's pasture; at Wetheringsett, he got forage and straw for his horse when he rode on the lord's duty, and the branches from the bottoms of the hay and cornstacks in the lord's *curia* and the old fences about the stacks—doubtless as firewood: *ibid.* ff. 124, 350.

[4] 'Et portabit redditum usque in Ely ad quodlibet scaccarium'; while in the Marshland, where there was no demesne, the reeve's duty was specifically stated to be the collection of rents: *ibid.* ff. 84d, 92d, etc, 350.

[5] Wisbech Barton Acct, 13–14 Edw. II.

[6] Sutton Halimote, 35 Edw. I (St Peter).

[7] Sutton Court Leet, 32 Edw. I (St Etheldreda).

9

the value of experience as much as the efficacy of coercion. Once a good man had been found for the office of reeve, he might continue to hold it for a considerable number of years. Robert Almar, for instance, was reeve at Great Shelford from 1321 to 1328; William Charite from 1328 to 1340; and Adam atte More at least for the five years which followed 1340. It was the same at Wisbech: John Mariot served eight years at least, Adam Sweyn seven years, Robert Blak and John Tyd five years each.[1] Even the traditional reeveship of the manor was beginning to be an office for a quasi-professional rather than an out-and-out amateur.

The reeve's main colleague in the manor was a man called in some places a hayward, in others a beadle: both seem to have done much the same sort of work and they can probably be fairly regarded as the same official. They were, like the reeve, elected from the body of customary tenants; again like the reeve, they were rewarded by being excused their customary works and had a few other perquisites of a minor sort.[2] Their duties on the economic side included the collection of rents in money and kind;[3] looking after the lord's fields and meadows;[4] and seeing to the sowing of the lord's demesne.[5] In addition to rent collecting, however, the beadles of Wisbech hundred made summonses, attached parties to be before the court, carried out orders given by the hundred court, and collected amercements according to extract rolls handed over to them by the constable of the castle.[6] If the beadle here was the executive of the hundred

---

[1] This information is taken from the account rolls of these two manors.

[2] For election, see *Court Baron*, p. 128: for the perquisites of the office e.g. Caius 485/489, f. 350: ¼ acre each of wheat and barley and ½ acre of oats; gleanings from the hayfields; grazing rights on the banks, balks and footpaths. All this is very similar to the 'serjeanty of the beadlery' on the St Edmund's manor of Westley—an acre each of barley and rye, another rood of barley, a saddlebag full of the lord's seed was the beadle's reward there, though he also received a livery of corn every two months: CUL Ff. II. 33, f. 92d. At Elm and Leverington a special tenement was attached to the beadle's office, perhaps comparable with the Budell-land at St Albans: Caius 485/489, ff. 84d, 92d; Levett, *Studies in Manorial History*, p. 116.

[3] D & C Treasurer's Roll, 18–19 Edw. II.

[4] *Court Baron*, p. 140.

[5] The reeve of Great Shelford usually answered for corn sown by tally drawn against the hayward: PRO Min. Accts, 1132/14.

[6] Caius 485/489, f. 84d; Wisbech Hundred, 35 Edw. I (Lent and St Barnabas); AR no. 95, m. 70d (where a beadle produced the extract rolls in his own defence).

court, at Littleport the hayward seems to have been equally the executive of the manor court. He it was who had to retain the body of a man until the bishop had been satisfied about certain damages; who had failed to take gage and pledge to prosecute from plaintiffs; who had kept for himself forfeitures and amercements arising from the lord's court.[1] In short, the lord asked more of his villeins than labour, rent and servile incidents; he also asked them to fulfil most of the managerial tasks in his manors. His paid administrators acted only as supervisors, even though some of them (in the persons of the manorial bailiffs) had taken up their residence within the manor before the end of the thirteenth century.

Bailiffs or 'servientes' in charge of manors appear at least as early as 1256; and doubtless these were the men described as 'servientes ultra waynagium' in 1310.[2] Some, at least, of them looked after two manors.[3] Unlike the reeve and the hayward, however, the bailiff was a salaried official, paid normally at the rate of 2d. a day. That is one of the few things that can be said about the bailiff; indeed, almost the only function he performed of which there is specific evidence was on some occasions to superintend the threshing.[4] Doubtless, however, he exercised a far more general supervision over agricultural operations; and he must have presided sometimes in the halimotes, though there are times when the seneschal or sub-seneschal sat there[5] (as they did more usually in the courts leet).

If the activities of the bailiffs are hard to discern, it is harder still to obtain more than the most fragmentary information about the central financial offices upon which the bishops relied. Of their household offices, the wardrobe leaves more traces than any other. Clearly it was a highly organized department by the middle of Edward II's reign; clearly also it fulfilled a dual

---

[1] Maitland, *Court Baron*, pp. 120, 140–1.

[2] Pipe R, no. 101, m. 4; PRO Min. Accts, 1132/12.

[3] The reeve of Great Shelford paid only half the stipend of the bailiff of that manor; the other half no doubt was paid in the other manor under his control: *ibid.* 1132/15. In the fifteenth century Wilburton and Stretham had a common bailiff: Liber B, no. 183.

[4] The reeve often warranted his account for the issues of the grange by tallies drawn against the bailiff: PRO Min. Accts, 1132/14; Wisbech Barton Accts, 8–9 and 14–15 Edw. II. But the bailiff might be replaced in this duty by a granger appointed temporarily for the purpose.

[5] As at Littleport in 1324: *Court Baron*, p. 137.

function. In the first place, it was a travelling office of receipt accompanying the bishop and to which the bishop or his ward-rober might order payments to be made from the manors.[1] Secondly, it took the necessary executive measures to provide for the material needs of the bishop and his entourage. Wardrobe bills commanded the despatch of malt and eggs from Shelford 'ad expensa hospicii', of malt from the same manor to the bishop's house in London, of grain from Wisbech to the bishop at York when he was there on the king's business.[2] They were also used to warrant expenditure on fuel for the kitchen which the reeve incurred when the bishop came to the manor;[3] and, in general, to control the flow of grain and livestock from the manors for the bishop's consumption, whether he was at Ely or Hatfield or Somersham.[4] Obviously, the wardrobe had both a financial and a secretarial staff.

The remaining officials of the household are little more than names. There was a larderer who received the cattle, sheep, pigs, fowls and eggs which wardrobe bills had brought to the household.[5] There was, at least at one moment, a 'receptor bladi'.[6] There was a chamberlain,[7] a steward of the household,[8] a marshal,[9] and a butler as late as the fifteenth century.[10] In the absence of central financial records, however, there is very little that can be said about these officers.

There remain two groups of officers—the officers of the bishop's exchequer and his auditors—about whom we are in very little better case. So far as the exchequer is concerned, it is to all seeming first mentioned in a charter of Bishop Geoffrey

[1] E.g. Wisbech Barton Accts, 8–9 Edw. II (£5 paid into the wardrobe at Somersham); 15–16 Edw. II (£28 paid into the wardrobe in response to the lord's letters, and receipt warranted by sealed letters of Nicholas de Stoketun and William de Outhorpe). The latter was an experienced member of the wardrobe staff; he was wardrober at least from 1321 to 1333.

[2] *Ibid.* 13–14 Edw. II; PRO Min. Accts, 1132/14.

[3] PRO Min. Accts, 1132/15.

[4] *Ibid.* 1132/15, 1135/8; Wisbech Barton Accts, 8–9 Edw. II.

[5] PRO Min. Accts, 1132/15, 1307/2.

[6] *Ibid.* 1132/14 (Great Shelford, 15–16 Edw. III).

[7] D & C Charter no. 131 (1273–88).

[8] BM Add. 41612, f. 6 (1276): there is nothing to identify him with either receiver or wardrober, positions he seems to have filled in some households: Denholm-Young, *Seignorial Administration*, pp. 15–16.

[9] Coucher Book, f. 217; and for a fifteenth-century marshal, Liber B, no. 57.

[10] *Ibid.* no. 40 (*temp.* Henry VI).

Ridel's in the late twelfth century;[1] while the four accounting terms mentioned in that charter can be traced back from charters of Eustace and Longchamp[2] to one of Bishop Nigel.[3] The latter may well have been the creator of the exchequer of Ely. Apart from that there is not a lot we can say about it. In 1262 it was presided over by an officer the bishop called his treasurer,[4] in 1299 and later by two receivers—both of them clerks and both of them in receipt of 6d. a day for wages and 4 marks a year for robes.[5] It was to these officers at Ely that the majority of cash payments from the manors were made, commonly no doubt at the quarterly account days;[6] and these payments were acknowledged by tallies which the reeve could produce to satisfy the auditors.[7] But there is nothing to tell us about the procedure of the bishop's exchequer, although we know that the receivers were not always content merely to receive revenue. Sometimes they also surveyed its sources, as William de Migele did when he visited Shelford in 1333 or John de Ely when he went to Somersham in 1382, possibly to clear up the aftermath of the peasant rebellion.[8]

In these journeys, however, the receivers may have trespassed upon the province of the auditors. There can be no question about the imprint left by these officers even upon our very scanty records. Their place in the official hierarchy was well established in 1299. Two of them were paid at the rate of 1s. a day, with the usual 4 marks for robes: a rate considerably higher than that paid to receivers or sub-seneschals or even to the constable of Wisbech castle.[9] This may well be a crude expression in terms of hard cash of the comparative importance of the auditor's office in the administration of the bishop's

[1] Granting 'centum solidos annuos de scaccario nostro in assuetis quattuor anni terminis' to the sacristy: Bodl. Laudian Misc. 647, f. 110.

[2] Egerton 3047, f. 10; Liber M, ff. 162 (2), 163.

[3] Liber M, f. 157.   [4] D & C Charter no. 105.

[5] PRO Min. Accts, 1132/10.   [6] E.g. Caius 485/489, f. 355.

[7] E.g. Wisbech Barton Accts, 14–15 Edw. III: 'Liberate Magistro Willelmo de Migele receptori apud Ely 6. libre per 2. tallias.'

[8] PRO Min. Accts, 1133/1, 1307/3.

[9] PRO Min. Accts, 1132/10: 'In vadiis duorum clericorum audientium compota prepositorum et ministrorum episcopi', etc. By the fifteenth century the number of auditors had increased to four: Wren's Note Book, f. 210. Taking it that the auditors were paid at a rate equivalent to about £18 a year, comparative rates for other officers were: the constable of Wisbech £13. 6s. 8d.; sub-seneschals £10; receivers £9.

estate.[1] The accounts of Wisbech Barton show that the auditors, before the final audit of the reeve's accounts, visited the manors once or twice a year to hold a preliminary view of the accounts.[2] To satisfy them, every payment in cash the reeve had made, every livery made in kind, had to have its warrant—the lord's letters had to be produced for payments made at his command; sealed wardrobe bills for payments to the wardrobe or the delivery of foodstuffs to the household; tallies against the bailiff or hayward to verify the issues of the grange or the liveries of seed corn, or against the receivers to verify liveries to the exchequer at Ely. Payments or liveries without some such warrant as these would be simply disallowed;[3] and the reeve's opportunities for making an illicit profit must have been, if not precluded, at least circumscribed.[4] In all this work, the auditors impressed some sort of standard of honesty and efficiency upon the amateur administrators of the manor. But they did more than that. Their work, added to the constant stream of wardrobe missives and the peripatetic oversight of things in general exercised by the seneschals, did a good deal to give coherence and a working unity to the bishop's scattered lands. The auditors came to a place, not only to view the accounts, but also to view the manor; and sometimes also to transact a business deal that might seem too large for a mere reeve, like the sale of the wool clip at Wisbech Barton.[5]

In all this, of course, the administrative system on the bishop

---

[1] On the importance of officials 'sent out from the household' in the administration of great estates, see Denholm-Young, *Collected Papers*, pp. 160–1.

[2] This and the remarks which follow are based on the Wisbech Barton Accts; and compare Denholm-Young, *Seignorial Administration*, pp. 131 ff.

[3] At Wisbech, a claim for expenditure on looking after one of the bishop's wards was disallowed as 'sine warranto' (8–9 Edw. II); and so was a payment of 20s. to the reeve of Terrington 'quia non habet talliam' (11–12 Edw. III).

[4] At Wisbech the wages the reeve claimed to have paid the *famuli* were scaled down (14–15 Edw. II); the cost of washing and shearing 30 sheep was reduced from 9d. to 3½d. (15–16 Edw. II) and the cost of transporting wool to Ely was similarly scaled down (5–6 Edw. III). At Somersham in 21–2 Edw. III the price at which corn had been sold was revised by the auditors in an upward direction, because the reeves of Doddington and Willingham had sold at these higher prices at the same time (PRO Min. Accts, 1307/2). The penalties imposed upon reeves for falsification (or possibly even inefficiency) may also be regarded as an encouragement to honesty and efficiency: the enormous fine of £20 charged against the reeve of Wisbech Barton in 20–1 Edw. III, for instance.

[5] Wisbech Barton Accts, 8–9 Edw. II; 5–6 Edw. III.

of Ely's estate was like enough to that on other great estates around this time.[1] It was the sort of system called for by the conditions of the day—by a great estate economy directed both to competitive marketing and to the fluctuating demands of a peripatetic lord for sustenance. The harmonizing of these objectives alone called for much flexibility, much control, much centralization. At the same time, the long upward curve in prices and the cost of living called for efficiency: an efficiency transmitted outwards from the bishop's household to the reeves and haywards and the other amateur managers of manors. In these ways there had been a radical change in estate administration since the day when Bishop Nigel was alive and dead, when the feudal household would seem to have played a much more passive role in its relations with the farmers of manors. But then the economy of England had changed. It may never have been a natural or a subsistence economy; but it had been a customary economy—an economy which had much inflexibility, which changed slowly. What happened in the thirteenth century, above all else, was a great speeding up in the rate of change in economic affairs and the infusion of a greater flexibility into economic relationships and the utilization of economic assets. No small part in making this change possible was played by a new professional group—men like the bishop's wardrobe clerks and itinerant auditors who forced the customary routine of manorial farming to conform to the higher requirements of the economic unity of the estate. Such men deserve a place with their counterparts in the royal household in the direction they gave to the changing England of the high Middle Ages.

III

When we turn from the bishop's domestic offices to legal administration, we are at once on firmer ground. The activities of the judicial institutions in the estate and liberty of the bishops of Ely, if only because they were often concerned with problems which were public rather than private in character, leave their mark in the public records and leave it the more clearly as the liberty was subjected to the intense scrutiny which it received from

---

[1] See, of course, Denholm-Young, *Seignorial Administration*; and also Knowles, *TRHS*, 4th ser. XXVI, p. 46.

the Angevin state. A study of these institutions may begin with the office of seneschal. Even though he was more than a judicial officer, his pre-eminence amongst the bishop's ministers owed much to the fact that he was the bishop's natural representative in the exercise of the franchises which the see of Ely possessed.

It was perhaps some measure of this pre-eminence that, when the bishop was going beyond the seas, he appointed his seneschal and his official as his attorneys and committed to them the whole custody of the bishopric.[1] For the seneschal was the natural representative of the bishop and of his liberty in all secular matters. He acted as the bishop's attorney in cases pending before the royal justices[2] and in claiming the bishop's liberty before them.[3] It was to the seneschal that an order was sent to give respite to a man who was party to a case in the bishop's court, but had gone on the king's business to the exchequer;[4] it was the seneschal who mainperned to do right to a royal clerk indicted of a trespass in the bishop's court.[5] He also received the king's command during the troubled time of baronial rebellion to muster the bishop's knights in the Isle and to have its defences put in order,[6] just as he was sometimes sent by the bishop to fine at the exchequer for the military service due from the barony of Ely.[7]

It is, however, as a holder of courts that the seneschal figures most prominently in the records. He sometimes presided over the halimotes;[8] more frequently over courts leet;[9] and sometimes over the hundred courts at Wisbech and Witchford.[10] More important, he was clearly the central figure in the major

---

[1] KR Mem. R, no. 33, m. 9d; this arrangement was confirmed by the king and acknowledged by the king's itinerant justices; while the seneschal himself appointed attorneys to answer for him before the barons of the exchequer: *ibid.* no. 44, m. 5; *Cal. Pat. R*, 1258–66, 221; AR no. 82, m. 10.

[2] For instance, Simon Lisle in John's reign and Matthew Christien in the early part of Henry III's reign: *CRR*, II, 136, 154, 158; III, 175; LTR Mem. R, no. 4; KR Mem. R, no. 5, m. 13d.

[3] CUL Add. 2950, ff. 142, 144.

[4] KR Mem. R, no. 27, m. 23d; LTR Mem. R, no. 29, m. 14d.

[5] *Close R*, 1259–61, 453.   [6] *Ibid.* 37; *Cal. Pat. R*, 1266–72, 504.

[7] LTR Misc., Bdle. 1/13 (in 1300).

[8] At Ely in the fifteenth century (EDR Court Rolls, C 6) and at Littleport in the fourteenth (*Court Baron*, p. 137).

[9] E.g. Wisbech Court Leet, 28 Edw. I (Pentecost).

[10] For Wisbech hundred court, see Wisbech Hundred, 33 Edw. I (Lent); 35 Edw. I (Lent). In 1390–1 the seneschal presided at about half a dozen out of the seventeen meetings of the Witchford hundred court.

courts of the liberty which sat at Ely. When the king's justices came round to Cambridge in 1272, they handed over the writs against the bishop and his men in the Isle to the bishop's seneschal.[1] One result of this transfer was that, fourteen years later, a decision could be given about presentment of Englishry in the Isle in the light of the rolls of Walter of Wilbraham (seneschal in 1272) and his companions.[2] It was in the same eyre of 1286 (held in the Isle because the see was vacant) that the jurors said that 'all the seneschals of the bishop since the last eyre have held all the pleas of the crown, in delivering gaols, in pleas *de juratis et assisis*, and in pleading all writs which can be pleaded in the county court; and all this they have been able to do from time beyond memory'.[3] It was because they had exercised these powers in criminal matters that during vacancies the seneschals were often commanded to answer for the chattels of men whose hanging they had ordered;[4] and, because they also exercised this civil jurisdiction of the bishop's, the final concords levied in his court remain the best source for a list of seneschals.[5] Apart from presiding over these courts at Ely, the seneschals seem also to have had the custody of the mass of fines and writs and rolls which were the record of all their activities.[6] In view of the burden of this work it is hardly surprising that, in the reign of Richard II, Sir Thomas Skelton the seneschal should also be called the bishop's 'justiciar'.[7]

[1] Coucher Book, f. 235 (and see above, p. 233, n. 3).

[2] AR no. 90, m. 6: 'Compertum est per rotulos itineris Walteri de Wilburgham et sociorum suorum quod in hundredo de Wycheford fuit per juratores eiusdem hundredi quoddam murdrum presentatum', etc.

[3] AR no. 90, m. 9.   [4] AR no. 90, m. 9; no. 95, mm. 66d, 69, 70.

[5] For one such fine, with the extract attached from the roll of a court held before Hugh de Cressingham, then seneschal, see D & C Charter no. 151 (below, Appx. XVII, p. 290).

[6] See above, p. 236, n. 6 and D & C Charter no. 154, an indenture dated February 1300 recording how Guy of Tilbrook and Robert Hereward (two former seneschals) handed over to the prior for custody the feet of seven fines 'et viginti duo brevia patencia de placitis terre cum rotulis placitorum; et quattuor brevia patencia de deliberacione gaole cum rotulis eiusdem deliberacionis de tempore Johannis de Kyrkeby'; and, from the time of his successor, Bishop William of Louth, another seven fines 'et sex brevia patencia de placitis terre cum rotulis placitorum; et duo brevia patencia de deliberacione gaole cum rotulo eiusdem deliberacionis... et unum breve de Raap cum recordo quod Johannes filius Johannis de Debeham tulit versus Robertum de Schaddeworthe.'

[7] CUL Add. 2953, f. 9; we also hear of the bishop's 'justitiarius' in the fifteenth century: Cott. Claudius C XI, f. 340d.

On the other hand, judicial duties did not exhaust the duties or the competence of these medieval seneschals. Like their masters, and like their contemporaries in the bishop's exchequer, they were ever on the move; and in more than one of the bishop's manors in 1357 there was 'parva camera pro senescallo'.[1] These wanderings allowed them to carry out many miscellaneous duties. In the Marshland, they were concerned with the imposition of tolls upon merchandise passing down the fenland rivers to the sea,[2] or the levying of rates for the maintenance of fen banks and ditches.[3] They sometimes received money from subordinate officials and gave letters of quittance thereof, though they might forget to pay over the sum to the bishop's exchequer.[4] It was also the seneschal who held the inquests upon which the terrier of 1251 was based;[5] or those in 1333 to discover whether or not John the son of Robert Hubert was a villein and in 1346 to establish whether or not some of the bishop's land in Doddington had been illegitimately alienated.[6] It was also the seneschal who was ordered to lease certain demesne lands at Great Shelford and who, by his letters, appointed a repreeve there during harvest; who pardoned an entry fine for a villein holding at Littleport; and who was allowed expenses at Somersham 'per suos adventus pro statu manerii supervidendo'.[7] Unlike the stewards of St Albans, the seneschals of Ely (for all their absorption in the affairs of a great liberty) needed still in the fourteenth century that 'domestic and agricultural knowledge...indicated by Walter of Henley and the *Seneschaucie*'.[8]

The seneschal, of course, did not stand alone in the transaction of these multifarious duties. In the first place, his was not the last word and he was subject to supervision. His conduct in the manor courts might be guided by the bishop's writ of right;[9] and where a problem of peculiar difficulty arose the matter

---

[1] In the Isle, for example, at Doddington, Stretham (here it was 'aula cum camera pro senescallo'), Littleport and Haddenham: BM Add. 6165, ff. 141–2.
[2] AR no. 95, m. 70 d.
[3] *Ibid.* mm. 70, 70 d.
[4] *Year Books, 21–22 Edw. I*, 39.
[5] Coucher Book, f. 1, and above, p. 5, n. 7.
[6] CUL Mm. 1. 49, f. 156; Coucher Book, f. 237 d.
[7] PRO Min. Accts, 1132/14, 15; 1135/8; *Court Baron*, p. 137.
[8] See Levett, *Studies in Manorial History*, p. 103.
[9] *Court Baron*, pp. 121–2.

might be referred to the bishop's council,[1] of which the seneschal was only one of the members.[2] His instructions, again, might be countermanded by the bishop's letters; and when he did act, he might have very explicit instructions. He was told what rent he was to charge for the demesne land he was to lease at Shelford; he was told what the arrangements were about the disposition of amercements imposed on the prior's tenants in the bishop's courts.[3]

Secondly, the seneschal had a host of subordinates. By 1298 there were five sub-seneschals in five of the six bailiwicks into which the estate was divided (the sixth, the Marshland bailiwick, being governed in a similar way by the constable of Wisbech castle).[4] It is not easy to distinguish at times between these subordinate seneschals and the 'capital seneschal', as he was later called: and there is unlikely to have been a great deal of difference between the duties performed by him and those performed by these subordinates. The constable of Wisbech was in a slightly different position. It would appear from the commission given to Thomas de Lovetot in the mid-fourteenth century that he had three main duties. Firstly, he had the custody of the castle of Wisbech. Secondly, he had the oversight of all the manors of the Marshland bailiwick (not only Wisbech and its hamlets, but also the bishop's manors in the Norfolk Marshland). Finally, he had the duty of holding the hundreds, leets and halimotes in the said castle and manors.[5] A little later, on the appointment of Sir Nicholas Loveyn as constable in 1360, a concession was made in respect of this last duty: he could appoint a deputy for holding courts if he was not himself sufficiently 'instructed'.[6]

[1] *Court Baron*, p. 127; and for similar reservation at Wisbech hundred court see above, p. 229.

[2] In the later Middle Ages, membership of the bishop's council was usually specified in the seneschal's commission (e.g. CUL Add. 2953, f. 9). During the period covered by this study, however, the council has left few traces; though somewhere about 1236 Hugh of Northwold provided for his forester in Somersham 'deliberacione habita cum concilio suo': Coucher Book, f. 223 d.

[3] See the bishop's writ in Cott. Claudius C XI, f. 347 d: 'H. dei gracia Elyensis Episcopus Hugoni de Cressyngham senescallo suo salutem.... Mandamus quod liberari faceris Priori Elyensi extractas amerciamentorum tenencium suorum', etc.

[4] PRO Min. Accts, 1132/10.   [5] CUL Mm. I. 49, ff. 177–9.

[6] Coucher Book, ff. 237–7 d. There is, however, a good deal of evidence for the constable presiding over courts: e.g. Wisbech Hundred, 30 Edw. I

These powers vested in the constable helped to create a somewhat unusual state of affairs in the Marshland bailiwick. The
degree of responsibility he assumed for overseeing the manors
in his bailiwick is nowhere quite clear; but at least for the
manors of Wisbech hundred the castle was an important centre
for the collection of revenue as well as of administration. The
reeve of the castle accounted to the bishop for all the assized
rents of the hundred; for the farms of most of the fisheries, reed
beds, etc.; and for the issues of all the hundred courts, leets and
halimotes in the hundred.[1] The reeve of the Barton manor,
again, seems to have delivered to the reeve of the castle from
time to time substantial sums of money. Finally, the bailiff of
the hundred collected at Wisbech castle all the profits arising
in the hundred from the bishop's courts of higher jurisdiction.[2]
The fiscal role played by Wisbech castle was not, so far as we
know, paralleled by that of any other centre in any other bailiwick; but then Wisbech hundred was a peculiar hundred and
very much a hundred of the bishop's demesne lands. It must
have helped to make the accounting duties of the constable
more onerous than those which were undertaken by any of the
sub-seneschals elsewhere; and it is hardly surprising that he had
acquired a clerk to aid him as early as the second quarter of the
thirteenth century.[3]

Of other officers who fall within the seneschal's range of interests, so to speak, little need be said. Like most other holders
of great liberties, the bishop had his attorneys watching his
interests in the royal courts.[4] There was a multiplicity of bailiffs:

(Assumption): John son of Peter charged with a trespass 'venit in plena curia
et ex parte domini Regis super hoc per constabularium allocutus'. For the
constable holding courts leet, see AR no. 95, m. 71 d and Wisbech Court
Leet, 35 Edw. I (Pentecost).

    [1] Wisbech Castle Accts, 6–7, 17–18, 20–1, 21–2, 23–4, 24–5, 28–9 Edw. III.
    [2] Compotus of Wisbech Hundred Bailiff, 20–2 Edw. III. He accounts
for the perquisites of the 'magna curia de Ely' (possibly a court of gaol
delivery) and of the court of the bishop's justices of assize; also for certain
amercements imposed in the court of King's Bench which must presumably
have represented an infringement of the bishop's right to try crown pleas
in his own courts and for which the king had made amends by granting the
issues to the bishop by his charter.
    [3] The constable's clerk witnesses a charter of Hugh of Northwold in Liber
M, f. 189. A robe for his clerk as well as for himself were included in the perquisites of the constable's office when it was granted to Thomas de Lovetot.
    [4] PRO Min. Accts, 1132/10, 12: two of them paid at a rate of £3. 13s. 4d.
a year and receiving their robes.

a bailiff of the liberty of the Isle;[1] hundred bailiffs like those of Wisbech or Mitford hundreds; and bailiffs errant, either on horse or on foot.[2] The duties they fulfilled are close enough to the common run of a bailiff's duties to call for no extended comment; and they were accused of most of the misdeeds of which medieval bailiffs were capable.[3] Below them, of course, were the beadles and the haywards upon whom ultimate responsibility for producing parties and executing judgements seems to have fallen; at the lowest level there was the same lack of a clear cut functional division of labour as there was at the top—in the heterogeneous combination of judicial, administrative and agricultural duties performed by the seneschals.

Before leaving the bishop's administrative offices, a few words about the sort of men who were seneschals in the thirteenth century may not be out of place. They are the only officials about whom much can be known; but the knowledge which can be accumulated has some significance in view of the pre-eminence they enjoyed amongst the bishop's ministers. It has a further significance in view of the change from seneschals like Ralf fitzOlaf in Nigel's time, a baron of the honour of Ely, to the professional administrators of the thirteenth century who had little that was feudal or military about them. A turning point may almost be said to have been reached during the stewardship of Simon Lisle (?1202–13).[4] He may have been descended from

[1] This office was held jointly with the stewardship of the bailiwick of the Isle in the fifteenth century, and may have been so held even at this time: CUL Add. 2950, ff. 110, 112.

[2] In 1256 there were two 'capital riding serjeants' and twelve 'foot serjeants'; in 1299 there was an itinerant bailiff paid 10 marks a year for receiving and returning the king's writs: Pipe R, no. 101, m. 4; PRO Min. Accts, 1132/10.

[3] One accusation somewhat out of the common run is recorded in AR no. 95, m. 65: 'De Christianis usurariis mortuis. Dicunt quod magister Willelmus de Luda, Episcopus Eliensis, qui obiit, per Willelmum Boreward et Radulfum de Littlebir', ballivos suos istius hundredi [i.e. Witchford hundred], mutuavit diversis hominibus istius hundredi, videlicet apud Lyndon 40 quarteria frumenti, 60 quarteria ordei [etc.; similar loans of grain at Wilburton and Stretham]...capiendo pro quolibet quarterio predicti bladi octo denarios ultra summam quam vendi potuit in insula predicta a tempore quo predictum bladum mutuatum fuit...ita quod totum proficuum pervenit ad manus ipsius episcopi ipso sciente et precipiente.' Similar charges were levelled against the bishop and his bailiff in Wisbech hundred, though here they had charged a shilling above the market price of the grain.

[4] CRR, II, 136; VII, 5; and see Rot. Litt. Claus. I, 108.

a cadet branch of Ralf fitzOlaf's family; he was certainly a military tenant of the barony. But for him service with the bishop was a prelude and perhaps a training for more extended service with the king.[1] Many of the seneschals who followed him took the same path to promotion in the administrative service of the time; others came to the bishop's service from the king's service. In either case, however, it is clear that what counted by this time was some degree of professional competence for the office. In consequence, men of promise from outside the bishop's estate or men whose experience had been gained elsewhere found a ready entry to the bishop's service: the feudal *familia* of the bishops of Ely had, by 1215, more or less ceased to be a recruiting ground for administrative personnel.

There were, of course, some seneschals in the thirteenth century who were also tenants of the bishop's barony. Andrew of Ely (1278–9)[2] was representative of a family which had held a military tenement in Pampisford at least as early as 1212; while John de Estwode (1276)[3] and John of Quy (1282)[4] both held fees of the bishop—although in their case these fees may have been granted to them as a reward for the services they had rendered the bishop. Yet seneschals holding of other baronies are commoner still. Thomas de Ingaldesthorp (1225–8)[5] held fees of the earl of Warenne and the honour of Haughley in Norfolk, and of Margery Rivers and the earl marshal in Essex and Hertfordshire;[6] Richard Batayl (1237)[7] was a military tenant of Richard Munfichet in Essex;[8] Jordan of Daventry may have belonged to a family of minor tenants-in-chief in Northamptonshire.[9] But the bishop cast his net wide, and often outside the

[1] In 1215 he was *custos* of the honour of Richmond; an itinerant justice in 1218 and responsible for sending the Great and Forest Charters to the sheriff of Cambridge to be read in the county court; and twice he received payments from the exchequer to sustain himself in the king's service: *Rot. Litt. Claus.* I, 190, 350, 365, 377–8, 390; *Pat. R*, 1216–25, 146, 150, 158, 208, 257.

[2] AR no. 90, m. 6; D & C Charter no. 704. The dates given in brackets do not necessarily indicate the full period for which a man acted as the bishop's seneschal, merely a date at which they can positively be identified as acting in that capacity.

[3] Bodl. Laudian Misc. 647, f. 164.

[4] BM Add. 41612, f. 12 d.

[5] D & C Charter no. 69; *Cal. Charter R*, I, 84.

[6] *Book of Fees*, I, 477, 480; II, 906, 909, 1465; *Cal. Inq. pm*, I, 59.

[7] Bodl. Laudian Misc. 647, f. 137 d.

[8] *Book of Fees*, I, 480; II, 1162.   [9] *FA*, IV, 441, 445.

ranks of men we can recognize as military tenants. Geoffrey of Sandiacre was a tenant in Northamptonshire of St Andrew's Priory, Northampton, though he may have been connected with the Derbyshire family holding in the latter county and in Nottinghamshire.[1] Hugh of Cressingham was a Norfolk man; Sir Robert de Schadeworth may have come from the Lincolnshire family of that name;[2] and John de Bukelond seems to have come from Kent.[3] Robert of Madingley, finally, was probably a member of a family, holding extensively in the borough of Cambridge and in neighbouring Madingley, which provided the town with more than one of its early bailiffs and one of its early members of parliament.[4]

The diverse origins of these men is but one fact about them; it is also possible to recognize signs of professional competence which were the fruits of training and experience. Both Robert Hereward[5] and Nicholas of Cambridge[6] were bailiffs of the Isle of Ely before they were promoted to the office of seneschal. Hugh of Cressingham (1282–6) was acting as the bishop's attorney in the king's courts at Westminster in 1278,[7] a fact which suggests that he may have been a man with some legal training. Training of another kind—in the canon rather than the common law—had probably been acquired by Guy of Tilbrook. He was Bishop John of Kirby's seneschal, in which capacity he acted as one of the bishop's justices in 1289;[8] he was also a clerk and he became afterwards official of the diocese.[9]

Men of this sort were typical of the new professional class which staffed the private civil services of thirteenth-century great estates. Such men, however, were equally in demand for royal administration; and they passed easily back and forward

---

[1] *FA*, IV, 7; *Book of Fees*, I, 8, 151, 231, 374, 398; II, 1001, 1150.

[2] *FA*, III, 169, 196, 224.   [3] AR no. 95, m. 70.

[4] Maitland, *Township and Borough*, pp. 134–6, 140, 144, 155; Cam, *Liberties and Communities*, p. 26.

[5] He was bailiff of the Isle in about 1296–7 and became seneschal immediately afterwards: AR 95, mm. 64, 70; Cott. Claudius C XI, f. 321 d; D & C Charter no. 154; Phillimore, *Pleas of the Court of King's Bench, 1297*, 216.

[6] Bailiff in 1316, he was active as seneschal in 1321–3: Maitland, *Court Baron*, p. 121; PRO Min. Accts, 1132/14.

[7] Cott. Claudius C XI, f. 19; Bodl. Laudian Misc. 647, f. 170. The seneschal at this date was Andrew of Ely.

[8] D & C Charters nos. 154, 1161.

[9] AR no. 95, m. 66 d.

from one to the other.[1] We have seen this happen as early as John's reign to Simon Lisle, and a few years later to Matthew Christien.[2] Matthew's successor, Thomas de Ingaldesthorp, was equally versatile: he joined Matthew in the custody of the vacant see of Ely in 1229; before he became seneschal he had been under-sheriff of Norfolk, and afterwards he was keeper of Castle Rising and sheriff of Norfolk and Suffolk.[3] Another contemporary, Sir William Rusteng, after service as the bishop's seneschal was more than once a collector of taxes in Norfolk and he became escheator of that county in 1246.[4] And if this was true at the beginning of the century, it was at least as true at the end. Robert Hereward has been described as 'the king's clerk *par excellence*'. He was sheriff of Cambridgeshire from 1300 to 1301 and of Norfolk from 1301 to 1306; he was keeper of the vacant see of Ely in 1302, a commissioner *de wallis et fossatis*, an inspector of wines, a purveyor of grain for the king.[5] Yet he started his career, as we have seen, in the bishop's service; he was bailiff of the Isle before even he became the bishop's seneschal. Similarly, Robert of Madingley had a career which presents a striking parallel to that of Matthew Christien. He was the bishop's seneschal from about 1304 to 1310.[6] In the next decade, however, he was one of the king's justices of assize and of oyer and terminer, and he was an assessor of tallages for the king;[7] by 1317 this service seems to have brought him a knighthood.[8] Amidst all this work of national importance, however, he still sat as a judge in the bishop's court in 1314[9] and in 1317 he was a member of the bishop's council.[10]

In the last resort, these fragments of biography do no more than express in personal terms the conclusions already drawn from a study of the relationship between the liberty of Ely and the king's government in the thirteenth century. Because the Angevin kings enforced common standards, common responsi-

---

[1] Denholm-Young, *Seignorial Administration*, pp. 162–4.
[2] See above, pp. 196–7, 265–6.
[3] *Close R*, 1227–31, 149, etc.; 1231–4, 352; *PRO Lists and Indexes*, IX, 86.
[4] *Close R*, 1234–7, 189, 547; *Cal. Pat. R*, 1232–47, 483; *Book of Fees*, I, 491, 572; II, 1259.
[5] Cam, *Liberties and Communities*, p. 47; *Cal. Inq. Misc.* I, 511.
[6] D & C Charters nos. 156, 1078; BM Add. 9822, ff. 32, 33.
[7] Foss, *Judges*, III, p. 277; CUL Add. 2950, ff. 152 ff.
[8] Bodl. Ashmolean 801, f. 126.
[9] D & C Charter no. 918.   [10] Maitland, *Court Baron*, p. 127.

bilities and a 'common law' within liberties and without, the lords of estates and the lords of franchises were compelled to create an administrative system adequate to the responsibilities imposed upon them. Because the same tasks had to be performed in a liberty and in the geldable, because the same qualifications were requisite for their performance, a common pool of administrative officials came into existence—men who gained the same sort of experience and grappled with the same sort of problems whether they served the king or the bishop. The very existence of this official class, which pushed into the background the feudal household and the feudal court in seignorial administration, was a potent force in knitting together the *regnum* of Edwardian England. If there was a *common* law these men were, after all, the exponents of its commonness. It was a steward of the bishop of Ely who could, quite naturally, enter into an obligation before the king to exhibit justice 'secundum legem et consuetudinem regni nostri'.[1]

IV

Having enumerated a number of officials and discussed the functions of a few of them and the kind of men they were, we have not quite finished with administration. An administrative act in the Middle Ages often took the form of a judicial act— a judgement, a verdict, a declaration of law and custom. It often took place in a court; administrative offices often took on the appearance of judicial tribunals. Perhaps it was that medieval men did not distinguish clearly between different sorts of action; or perhaps it was an outcome of one of the very few basic constitutional notions of medieval times, a notion operative at all levels of society, that administrative action only acquired real validity when it was invested with due process of law. Before we can leave this question of administration, we must return to the courts that were held in the bishop's lands and the bishop's liberty, and the wonderful amount of administration which was done in them.

---

[1] 'Rex vicecomiti Cant' salutem. Quia Jordanus de Davintr', senescallus libertatis Episcopi Eliensis, manucepit coram nobis exhibendi dilecto clerico nostro Johanni Walerand plenam justiticiam secundum legem et consuetudinem regni nostri', etc.: *Close R*, 1259–61, 453.

The clearest exemplification of the administrative functions of courts, naturally enough, is to be found in the halimotes. It may be true that in the manor courts, as in the hundred court of Wisbech, the suitors were still the judges: but they judged often upon questions propounded by the lord's representative and for the purpose of facilitating the conduct of the lord's husbandry or protecting the lord's rights. Some of the things done in one halimote held at Wisbech may serve as illustration enough.[1] The performance of labour services was enforced, and men who did their service inadequately or inefficiently were punished.[2] Servile payments like heriot, leyrwite, etc. were exacted. The labour supply of the manor was ensured by recalling villeins who had fled or withdrawn,[3] preventing the alienation of villein land, and providing successors in villein holdings which had fallen vacant. In all these ways the basic requirements of the seignorial husbandry were safeguarded; if the homage judged, its judgement was about its own responsibilities. This method of enforcing common responsibility might go very far; on one of the conventual manors, when the hayward had been guilty of a variety of misdeeds, the whole vill was compelled to make amends because they had elected him to the office.[4]

These were the traditional functions of the manor courts; but, in the same way, their machinery was adapted to the changing administrative requirements of changing times. There may be no sign on this estate that the manor courts were the places in which the auditors conducted their scrutiny of the reeve's accounts;[5] but they had none the less a part to play in the detailed supervision exercised over manorial administration in the high Middle Ages. There are abundant signs that verdicts of the manor court were used to investigate the conduct of reeve

---

[1] What follows is based upon Wisbech Halimote, 34 Edw. I (Michaelmas).

[2] Like the man at Sutton who sent a 'wee lassie' instead of a man: 'Martinus le Chapman misit unam mulierculam ad opera domini ubi misisse debuit unum hominem': Sutton Court Leet, 8 Edw. II (St Luke).

[3] The attitude on this question is neatly summed up by an entry on the roll of the Sutton Halimote, 13 Edw. II (Pentecost), when an order was given to attach one of the prior's villeins 'quia nativus et fugitivus et rebellus [sic] erga dominum et ballivos suos'.

[4] Sutton Halimote, 23 Edw. I (St Thomas) and compare the fine of 20s. made by the whole vill for having elected an 'insufficient' reeve: Sutton Court Leet, 7 Edw. II (St Luke).

[5] As did happen on some estates: see Denholm-Young, *Seignorial Administration*, pp. 150–1.

or hayward towards the lord and towards their neighbours.[1] More important was the growing use of the manor court to register transfers of property, particularly as the demesne and the villeinage broke up and the market in land came to embrace all the varieties of peasant property. Mills and fisheries were put to farm in the manor court;[2] leases were made from the demesne in the manor court;[3] villein land was transferred in the manor court, from complete holdings down to the smallest of plots.[4] The jurisdiction over villeins exercised in the manor court may have been 'the very life-blood of the agrarian and economic system'; the very form of the court roll may have made it 'an economic document', a roll of 'the occasional profits of the manor'.[5] By the end of our period that roll was also being adapted to serve the purpose of a register of the dispersed rights of the lord in his demesne and his villeinage alike.

The bishop's lordship, however, was more than a lordship over villeins. He had free and military tenants as well as villein tenants; he had franchisal rights everywhere in his estate. One result of this was that the theoretical lines which ought to have separated different sorts of jurisdiction became blurred in administrative practice. The manor courts were very often concerned with tenures freer than villein tenures. Reliefs were exacted in the halimotes;[6] free tenants were called upon to perform homage in the halimotes, freemen who might even be sons of knights.[7] Some of this jurisdiction might have been more properly exercised in the bishop's feudal court, had that

---

[1] For example, the inquest made in the halimote at Littleport into the conduct of the hayward 'versus dominum et vicinos suos': Maitland, *Court Baron*, pp. 140–1.

[2] Sutton Halimote, 26 Edw. I (Purification), 7 Edw. II (Pentecost).

[3] E.g. Sutton Halimote, 32 Edw. I (Nativity).

[4] E.g. the sale of 20 perches of villein land registered in Wisbech Halimote, 30 Edw. I (Martinmas) and of 10 perches registered in Elm Halimote, 14 Edw. III (Holy Cross).

[5] Maitland, *Select Pleas in Manorial Courts*, pp. xiv, lx.

[6] At Wisbech Halimote, 34 Edw. I (Michaelmas) an order was given to take into the lord's hand a stall in the market and a free holding of 12 acres until the heir made satisfaction for his relief.

[7] Wisbech Halimote, 34 Edw. I (Michaelmas): both John son of Ralf Brid and Bartholomew son of Sir James de Belvaco were expected to appear to do homage, and when they failed to do so their lands were to be taken into the lord's hand.

court still been in working operation. Franchisal jurisdiction, too, was sometimes exercised in the manor courts: the assizes of bread and ale were enforced, the tithings controlled;[1] and even the procedure of the halimotes, with their juries of presentment, seems modelled on the procedure of the leet.[2] The conjunction of 'curia' and 'leta' characteristic of the estate, the blending of patrimonial and franchisal jurisdictions characteristic of the bishop's courts leet,[3] point in the same direction. We may classify jurisdictions, but these classifications have little relevance to practice. The rule followed was no theoretical rule; it was a rule of convenience.

Convenience, however, had to take account of a variety of circumstances; and the result is that there is much variety in the sort of business which might come before the same sort of court in different places. The court leet which the bishop shared with other lords at Walsoken[4] was purely a franchisal court, by contrast with the same court at Littleport where the business is adequately described by its title of 'curia et leta'.[5] A similar contrast may be drawn between two of the hundred courts of the Isle. Witchford hundred court was an orthodox hundred court enough; but it is a very different matter when we look at the records of the court held in the predominantly demesne hundred of Wisbech. Wisbech hundred court contributed to the administrative work of the bishop's estate almost as much as the leets and the halimotes did. It did very many things which can only be described as feudal or domanial business. Free tenants paid relief in the hundred court as well as in the halimote;[6] it heard the result of an inquest *post mortem* upon the lands of

---

[1] At Elm Halimote, 30 Edw. I (SS. Philip and James) there were 6 presentments for offences against the assize of bread and 33 for offences against the assize of ale; at Emneth Halimote, 20 Edw. II (St Luke) and Newton, 14 Edw. III (Holy Cross) this was almost the only sort of business recorded. For control of tithings, see Sutton Halimote, 20 Edw. I (St Barnabas).

[2] Juries of presentment were universal in the halimotes of Wisbech hundred: e.g. in 14 Edw. III (Holy Cross) at Leverington (a jury of 22), Elm (14), Newton (6), Wisbech (20) and Tyd (16). At Wisbech, 30 Edw. I (Martinmas) we find the more regular jury of twelve.

[3] Cf. Maitland, *Select Pleas in Manorial Courts*, p. xix.

[4] Ault, *Court Rolls of the Abbey of Ramsey*, pp. 175 ff.

[5] Maitland, *Court Baron*, pp. 107 ff.

[6] E.g. Wisbech Hundred, 31 Edw. I (Conversion of St Paul) where William the son of Hugh Riggisilver paid relief for his father's messuage, shop and lands in Wisbech.

Sir John de Vaux, and commanded that his heir (amongst other heirs) was to be brought into the court to satisfy the lord for his relief and to do homage.[1] But the hundred court was equally concerned with a great deal of purely domanial business, with many matters affecting the villeinage and the villeins. It was much concerned with the buying and selling of villein land: for it ordered such land alienated without licence to be taken into the lord's hand.[2] On the other hand it allowed alienation to take place by means of surrender in the hundred court, whereupon the grantee could have his seisin when he paid his entry fine.[3] There seem to be occasions when men sought the confirmation of the hundred court for transactions carried out in the halimotes: Adam Sewale, for example, paid a fine there to hold a villein tenement 'prout patet in ultima halimota'. They also sought confirmation for less regular transactions, as William of Cambridge and Alice Brom did when they were allowed to hold villein land at will which John Sything had given them by charter—a charter they gave up to the lord in the court.[4] And there were many other matters in which villeins figured: the halimote of Tyd presented its findings in the hundred court about a villein who had died without heirs;[5] heriot was exacted;[6] men were amerced for withdrawing from the halimote jury and paid marriage fine, while women paid leyrwite.[7]

The extent to which the hundred court of Wisbech meddled in such matters explains another fact already noticed.[8] Because it was so deeply involved in domanial business, it was natural that the hundred court should make use of the halimotes of the hundred for its own purposes; supervise them and draw cases to itself and out of their purview; and, in the end, throw off a kind of special session for villeins' affairs in the 'curia bondorum' which must have substantially curtailed the importance and the business of the halimotes in the hundred. Yet the important thing is not that the hundred court of Wisbech defied legal proprieties and the sphere of activity which legal purists

---

[1] Wisbech Hundred, 33 Edw. I (Lent) and cf. 35 Edw. I (Lent).
[2] E.g. ibid. 31 Edw. I (Circumcision), 33 Edw. I (Lent).
[3] Ibid. 32 Edw. I (Holy Cross); 7 Edw. II (St Laurence).
[4] Ibid. 35 Edw. I (Lent).   [5] Ibid. 33 Edw. I (Lent).
[6] Ibid. 35 Edw. I (Pentecost).
[7] E.g. Wisbech Hundred, 35 Edw. I (Lent, Pentecost and St Barnabas).
[8] See above, p. 228.

might assign to it. The important thing is that, where he could, the bishop would use even a franchise court for feudal and domanial business, much of it administrative business. It indicates how little distinction there was in men's minds between the various attributes of lordship and how much of administration was transacted under the guise of a judgement. The heterogeneous business of Wisbech hundred court is merely the counterpart of the miscellaneous duties of the bishop's seneschals—seneschals of courts, perhaps, but also responsible for assembling the knights of the barony for the defence of the Isle or coming 'pro manerio supervidendo'. It is likewise the counterpart of the dual personality of the haywards—in charge of the demesne corn fields and the collection of rents, but also the executives of the halimotes; and of the imposition upon the reeve, not only of the duty of conducting the manorial husbandry, but also of keeping the rolls of the tithings.[1]

In the last analysis, however, there may be another inference which can be drawn from these facts. Territorial lordship was still the most powerful element amongst the combination of powers exercised by the bishops of Ely on the day that King Edward I was alive and dead, just as it was the oldest element and had been the most constant and enduring. Many of the bishop's franchisal powers had merely been tacked on to institutions created in origin to serve domanial ends; and preoccupations about estate administration were compelling enough, where circumstances were favourable, to deflect the administration of franchisal powers to domanial purposes. The purely feudal lordship which the bishop had also exercised in the twelfth century and which had its own administrative requirements and institutions, had in the meantime lost most of its substantial character. Such regulative functions deriving from this stem as persisted into the thirteenth and fourteenth centuries had been dispersed between the courts and administrative offices managing the estate and the liberty (when they had not been lost entirely to the king's courts or the king's administrators). In this sense, as in others, territorial lordship and franchise,

[1] Sutton Halimote, 13 Edw. II (Pentecost): 'Dies datus est capitalibus plegiis usque ad proximam curiam ad habendum rotulum de eorum et decenarum suorum [sic] sub pena 20. s.'; 13 Edw. II (St Margaret): 'Capitales plegii...venerunt et fecerunt predictum rotulum et liberatus est in custodia Martini prepositi.'

which had existed before the establishment of the feudal community of the barony of Ely, continued also to live after it. This is true with all allowance made for the fact that the shape and form of territorial lordship in John of Hotham's time was something that Bishop Hervey (to say nothing of Abbot Brihtnoth) would have found changed out of all recognition; and that the liberty which Edward II confirmed in 1318 was a far different and a far more powerful thing than that soke King Edgar had given (whatever it may have meant) in the hundreds of the church of Ely and in all its lands.

V

There would be little propriety in giving to the last words of this essay the title of a conclusion. Certainly, in the previous pages, there have been a number of attempts to draw out of the records of the church of Ely some deductions about the progress of the lordship exercised by the abbots and the bishops of Ely, and about the influence they exercised upon those fragments of medieval society they had some power to shape. But how far such deductions, even where they are valid deductions from the evidence available, have been influenced by the chance survival of records is a matter for criticism from other and comparable estates. They have been put forward as hypotheses; and these last words can merely sum up some of the hypotheses.

From this point of view, it is convenient to have ended with a study of the administration of the bishop's estate. The force and character of his lordship can be measured to a large extent by the administrative resources at his disposal at different points of time. In that respect, the history of the administration of the estate serves to reinforce impressions derived from other parts of this essay: not only the impression that medieval lordship changed rapidly and profoundly, but also that the bishop's capacity to influence at least some sections of society acquired added strength in the generations which separate Bishop Hervey and Bishop John of Hotham.

Bishop Hervey, of course, had taken over a good deal from the abbots who were his predecessors: many knights enfeoffed in the barony of Ely, and much of the property which the abbots had garnered. But it seems to have been Hervey and his immediate successors who drew this heritage together into a recognizable feudal community and endowed it with institutions characteristic enough of an episcopal barony. The administrative system so created was not without its force, but it had a limited range by comparison with the systems of later times. Economically it was based upon the static and relatively inflexible device of 'farming' manors. Its central institutions were a household with functions still in the main domestic and undifferentiated, and a court which existed to declare the pre-existing custom of the honour. These central offices in turn seem to have had a restricted range of contacts with the local cells of the estate, the scattered manors between the Wash and the banks of the Thames. The officials of the barony, finally, are hardly unjustly described as amateurs: knights who were stewards or chamberlains or butlers; serjeants who were coroners or bakers or steersmen; reeves who were villeins, even any of the villeins. It was a system designed, not for change, but for stability.

Yet the system was faced with anything but stable circumstances, and in the end circumstances changed the system. It had to face the profoundly disturbing reallocation of political responsibility carried through by the Angevin kings. It was subjected to an economic revolution—of which the price revolution of the late twelfth and the thirteenth centuries was merely a part, perhaps merely a symptom. In consequence, the liberty of Ely was forced to assume responsibilities which demanded the most advanced administrative capacities of the age for their fulfilment. The bishop's estate had to adapt itself to an expanding and competitive economy, and at the same time find means of controlling the redistribution of wealth amongst the peasantry which was another consequence of economic change. The need was both for higher quality and greater detail in administration— for professional rather than amateur officers, for a positive and centralizing effort in place of the more negative principle of maintaining and exacting customary rights and customary duties. In the course of these changes, the barony of Ely and its institutions fell into the background. This could happen because the king asked less often for service, and knights looked less like fighting men; but as these functions of the barony declined, so also did the court of the honour give place to the courts of the liberty as the central judicial institutions in the bishop's lands, and the knights of the honour cease to be obvious recruits for the bishop's administration. Almost as much as in 1066 lordship had shifted its ground; but once again it had gained something from the change.

Before 1066, the lordship exercised by the abbots of Ely had been a very revolutionary lordship, even if it was also inchoate and based upon no single principle. Its major achievements had been the rapid accumulation of territorial possessions, personal dependants and some quasi-judicial privileges. The Norman Conquest entailed some losses of land and more of men; but over what remained the abbot's hold was consolidated by the reduction of the maze of pre-conquestual relationships into a single and easily comprehensible tenurial dependence. The addition of this feudal element to the lordship exercised by the abbots and bishops strengthened their hold upon the land and upon the service of the dependant; probably also it added to their equipment of courts through which territorial rights were maintained and services exacted.

Feudal lordship in this sense, however, was a passing phase. Like the older lordship of the abbots, feudal landlordship rested upon a customary economy. A new phase began when the passive exploitation of land by means of the 'farming' system was replaced by the progressive high-farming economy of the thirteenth-century great estate. More than that, the thirteenth century was also pre-eminently an age in which franchisal lordship was reaching maturity. The lords of honours were losing their old feudal powers of local administration; but some of them (and the bishop of Ely amongst them) were taking upon themselves the task of exercising a more modern and extensive authority which had its origin in the inventive capacities of the Angevin monarchy. Despite the disintegration of his barony and the loss of control over property which had been disposed in military tenements, the bishop of Ely still managed to strengthen the sinews of his lordship. Hugh of Northwold and his successors succeeded in augmenting the wealth which their estates brought in. They acquired new and growing franchisal powers which, though they were exercised on the king's behalf and 'secundum legem et consuetudinem regni Anglie', could also be used for more private and even more profitable ends.

They had their lawyer stewards, wardrobe clerks, itinerant auditors, even reeves serving year after year to further the augmentation of income and the due conduct of a liberty. These were the men in possession of the skills which the changing needs of medieval government and medieval lordship had called into existence.

It need hardly be said, of course, that this was far from the end of the lands and liberties of the bishopric of Ely. The liberty had still a very long history. Some of its powers survived the great centralizing of local authority under Henry VII and Henry VIII, and even the spoliation of the diocese of Ely by Elizabeth. The liberty of the Isle was still a functioning liberty when Bentham wrote: a matter of small profit and often by-passed, but also 'a matter of great convenience' to the inhabitants of the Isle 'since they have justice administered as it were at their very doors'. Perhaps it was the cold reason of philosophical radicalism which finally destroyed so patent an anachronism. Long before that, however, the thirteenth-century great estate had vanished, with the changing economic circumstances of the later Middle Ages. In that age of contracting economy, it was possible for men from the peasantry, grown to sufficient stature in the thirteenth century for this end, to enter into the heritage of the high-farming bishops. The signs of the times were there in our period, and some of the preparatory steps had been taken both by lord and peasant; but the history of the rentier landlordship of the later medieval bishops has still to be studied.

There is still a further problem which a study of a single estate can do nothing to resolve: the problem of the relationship between the various factors which contributed to the changing character of medieval lordship. There is no means of weighing the respective influence, at the same time or at different points of time, of economic and constitutional change, of the growth of legal doctrine or the advance of what we might call technical education. Moreover, even within the boundaries of one estate in these dark ages, it is never easy to see the part which men, individual men, have played; though some of them, we feel, must have played a much greater part than surviving records ever explicitly tell us. Some of the stewards may have done so—men like Matthew Christien or Robert of Madingley, who had capacity enough to make a career for themselves in the

king's service as well as the bishop's. And the same must be true
of some of the bishops. It has been hard to write of the estate
of the bishops of Ely without mentioning Hugh of Northwold.
He was the good monk-bishop; but perhaps he was also the
high-farming bishop *par excellence* in the history of the
bishopric of Ely simply because he was a monk in days when the
monastic order was the 'nurse of intelligent and broad-minded
landowners'. John of Kirkby and William of Louth, likewise,
may have contributed something to the institutions of estate and
liberty: Kirkby, trained at the chancery by Burnell and a man
who, as treasurer, left his mark upon the exchequer of England;
and Louth, for ten years keeper of Edward I's wardrobe when
the wardrobe was much of the government of a much-governed
England. Earlier still there is Nigel. The fragments of records
which have survived show what a mixed man he was. He often
lived like a baron and left the barony of Ely in something like
its final shape. He was often a great administrator in the national
field, and he may have spared some of his skill in giving an
exchequer to his estate. Yet this same man, this royal clerk and
feudal bishop, seems sometimes to have tried to carry out papal
views about the proper uses of ecclesiastical property. About
Nigel and Hugh of Northwold and the rest we shall never know
enough and generally we shall know only very little. For that
reason there will always be a vital chapter which can never be
written in a history of the lands and liberties of the bishopric
of Ely.

APPENDIX OF DOCUMENTS

No attempt has been made to present collated texts of the documents which follow. A satisfactory edition of the Ely charters is badly needed, but that is a large task and outside the intention of this appendix. All that is here intended is to present some sort of text of documents which will illustrate some of the points in the foregoing pages. For that reason, both punctuation and the use of capitals have been modernized throughout.

I

Writ of Henry I confirming to William, Archdeacon of Ely, the Manors of Pampisford and Little Thetford which had been granted to him by his uncle, Bishop Hervey

BM Add. 9822, f. 70d.
Date: August 1127 (?).

Henricus rex Anglie episcopo de Ely et priori et toto conventui et omnibus baronibus Francis et Anglis de honore de Ely salutem. Sciatis me concessisse Willelmo archidiacono de Ely, capellano meo, manerium meum de Pampesworda et manerium de Litleteotfort que Herveus episcopus de Ely, avunculus suus, ei dedit coram Rogero episcopo Sarisberiensi consensu prioris et conventus Eliensis ecclesie. Et volo et firmiter precipio ut bene et pacifice et honorifice teneat hereditario iure, scilicet manerium de Pampesword' pro servicio unius militis et manerium de Litleteotfort per servicium .v. solidorum quos reddet quoquo anno monachis predicte ecclesie sicut predictus episcopus et prior et conventus ei ea dederunt et concesserunt et cartis suis confirmaverunt, et teneat ea cum saka et soka et tholl et them et infangentheof et cum omnibus aliis consuetudinibus suis cum quibus episcopus predictus ea melius et honorabilius tenuit dum ea habuit in manu sua. Testibus Rogero episcopo Sarisberie et A. episcopo Lincoln' et T. cancellario et Roberto de Sigillo. Apud Eylingas in transitu meo.

II

Writ of Henry II commanding the Knights of the Honour of St Etheldreda to fulfil their guard duties in the Isle of Ely

Liber M, f. 85.
Date: 1155–89,[1] presumably 1172–89.

Henricus Dei gratia rex Anglorum et dux Normannorum et Aquitannorum et comes Andegavorum omnibus militibus qui tenent de honore Sancte Etheldrede et de episcopo Eliense salutem. Precipio vobis quod ad summonicionem episcopi Eliensis veniatis in insulam de Ely ad faciendum ibi wardas vestras sicut debetis et sicut vos vel antecessores vestri unquam melius facere solebatis. Et nisi feceritis ipse iusticiet vos per catalla vestra et per feoda que de ipso tenetis quod faciatis. Teste meipso. Apud Winton'.

III

Notification by Henry II that Roger Bigod has recognized in the King's court that he owes the Bishop of Ely the service of six Knights for lands his ancestors held of the Church of Ely in Suffolk; and that Bishop Geoffrey has claimed 'Brunesthorp' and Mundford on the ground of their alienation by Bishop Nigel 'in gwerra'

Liber M, f. 89 (another copy in Bodl. Laudian Misc. 647, f. 110d).
Date: probably 1177–86.

Henricus Dei gratia rex Anglorum et dux Normannorum et Aquitannorum et comes Andegavorum archiepiscopis, episcopis, abbatibus, comitibus, baronibus, iusticiariis, vicecomitibus et omnibus fidelibus suis Francis et Anglis tocius Anglie salutem. Sciatis quod Rogerus Bigod coram me in curia mea apud Windesor recognovit quod ipse et heredes sui debent ecclesie Elyensi et G. episcopo Elyensi et successoribus suis servicium sex militum de antiquis tenementis suis que antecessores eius tenuerunt in Sudfolc de ecclesia Elyensi. Et preterea predictus G. episcopus clamavit ibidem tunc adversus prenominatum Rogerum Bigod duo maneria, scilicet Brunesthorp et Mundeford, que conquerebatur esse alienata de dominica mensa episcopi Elyensis et donata a Nigello episcopo Elyensi antecessore suo comiti Hugoni patri predicti Rogeri Bigod tempore regis Stephani in gwerra. Quare volo et firmiter precipio

---

[1] There is a similar (though not identical) writ in Liber M, f. 84 witnessed by Bishop Richard of Winchester which must, therefore, belong to the years 1174–88. Another copy of the writ printed above is to be found in Bodl. Laudian Misc. 647, f. 99d.

ut predictus Rogerus Bigod et heredes eius faciant predictum servicium ecclesie Elyensi et prefato G. episcopo et successoribus eius de prescriptis tenementis que sunt in Sudfolc. Testibus. Gaufrido filio meo. Hunfrido de Buhun constabulario. Hugone de Creissi. Roberto filio Bern'. Gerardo de Canvill. Rogero filio Reinfr'. Apud Windesor.

IV

Charter of Bishop Hervey laying down the lands, etc. he had conferred upon the Cathedral Priory of Ely

D & C Charter no. 51.
Date: 1109–31 (presumably early in that period).

Herveus Dei gratia primus episcopus Elyensis ecclesie omnibus fidem Catholicam confitentibus salutem. Manifestum sit vobis omnibus me pro amore omnipotentis Dei et Sancte Marie perpetue virginis necnon et Sancti Petri apostolorum principis et Sancte Atheldrythe virginis et omnium sanctorum Dei et pro remedio et salute anime mee monachis eiusdem loci victum et vestitum separatim a rebus episcopalibus ordinasse et sic ordinatum inperpetuum concessisse, scilicet ad vestitum hec maneria subscripta: Stoke, Meltune, Cingestune, Baldereseie, Suthburne, Ryscemere, Ho cum saca et soca et omnibus consuetudinibus ad ecclesiam de Ely pertinentibus in quinque hundredis et dimidio de Wiclawe. Ad victum Winestune, Lachingehyde, Undeleie, Scepeie, Fotestorp, Stunteneie. Et in Lyteltedford tres virgas de terra, Suttune, Witleseie, et ecclesiam Sancte Marie de Ely cum terra et decimis ad ecclesiam pertinentibus, Wivelingham, Hardwic, Havocestune, Newetune, Meldeburne, Melrede, et duodecim sceppas segetum de filiis Hardwini. Et unam vaccariam de Bele et quattuor pensas casei de Dereford et triginta milia allecium in Dunewic et viginti millia anguillarum in Stunteneie et octo pensas salis et vineam unam et que pertinent ad illam. Et sex piscatores ad piscandum in aquis ubi solebant, cum mansionibus eorum, et octo (?) servientes cum mansionibus eorum. Et lig... solebant habere, et super ripam de Bluntesham unum hominem cum mansione una et quinque agris terre ubi ligna possint adunare et octo agros de prato. Ad luminare ecclesie Winteworda et Tydbrihtseie et apportatus altaris. Ad operationem ecclesie Hedfelde et Hadham et viginti solidos de ecclesia de Lytelbyri...de Ratendune unoquoque anno et dedicationes totius episcopatus excepta rectitudine archidiaconi et capellanorum episcopi. Et ad opus ecclesie offerenda que veniunt ad manus episcopi in Ely et omnis apportatus processionum de toto episcopatu in ebdomada Pentecosten. His testibus. Willelmo archidiacono. Gozelino clerico. Rodberto capellano. Turoldo clerico.

Salamone clerico. Gosfrido stabulario. Willelmo Peregrino. Osberno de Durclero. Wihtgaro. Alberto. Siquis vero malignitatis spiritu commotus hanc nostram concessionem et donationem infringere, contempnere vel abicere voluerit, a Deo et ab omnibus sanctis sit condempnatus et a nobis in quantum licet excommunicatus et a consortio omnium fidelium separatus nisi resipiscat. Fiat. Fiat. AMEN.

V

Charter of Bishop Hervey granting to Haldeyn the office of baker together with a messuage and eighteen acres of land in Ely

Coucher Book, f. 217 (another copy in Cott. Claudius C XI, f. 352). Date: 1109–31.

Notum sit omnibus fidelibus me Herveum Eliensem episcopum dedisse et concessisse Haldeyno, qui est serviens in meo pistrino, unam mansuram et octodecim acras terre arabilis in Ely et officium pistrini nostri, ita quod idem Haldeynus et sequaces sui habeant et percipiant totum brennum de pistrino nostro et quod sint de familia nostra cum duobus equis et duobus garcionibus ad liberationes et robas nostras, et quod inveniant in pistrino nostro quattuor fideles pistores qui sciant officium, vel plures si necesse fuerit, et inveniemus eis cibum et potum vel vadia sua sicut alii de hospicio nostro percipiunt; et cum palefridi nostri minucti[1] fuerint vel infirmi predictus Haldeynus vel sequaces sui invenient eis brennum si fuerit in pistrino in prima nocte minuctionis secundum disposicionem marescalli nostri, et si alias necesse habemus emere brennum ad palefridos nostros habebimus illud brennum pro racionabili precio; et si voluerimus facere grossum panem et integrum totum frumentum vel aliud bladum quodcumque simul fundatur, ita quod predictus Haldeynus et sequaces sui nichil inde percipiant et respondebunt de summa et pondere panum de qualibet summa secundum assisam hospicii nostri. Et quando pistores nostri rengient ad panem rengii faciendum inveniemus eis saccos de coreo ad nostrum rengium portandum. Habendum et tenendum dictam mansuram, octodecim acras terre arabilis et officium pistrini nostri cum omnibus commoditatibus et libertatibus supradictis per servicium quattuor exenniorum panum nobis et successoribus nostris annuatim faciendi bene et in pace et hereditarie imperpetuum. Hiis testibus. Iocelino. Henrico. Hasculpho. Radulpho presbytero. Nicholao. Radulpho Burgo. Radulpho Chaueware. et teste tota villata.

---

[1] The reference is to the practice of bleeding horses discussed, in Roman times, by Vegetius. The Rev. M. P. Charlesworth helped me to track this down, and see also Ducange, *Glossarium mediae et infimae Latinitatis s.v.* 'minuere'.

VI

*Charter of Bishop Hervey defining the liberty of
Thorney Abbey in its manor of Whittlesey*

Thorney Red Book, 1, f. 166.
Date: 1128.

Notum sit omnibus tam presentibus quam futuris me Herveum
Dei gratia Elyensem episcopum primum concessisse et in elemosinam
dedisse Thornensi ecclesie omnes illas consuetudines et causas seculares quas habebat Elyensis ecclesia in hundredis suis de Wichefort
de terra et de hominibus Thornensis ecclesie de Wytleseye, exceptis
propriis regalibus consuetudinibus que super terram illam evenerint
que nec ad me nec ad ecclesiam nostram pertinent. Hanc autem
donacionem feci in die qua egomet Thornensem ecclesiam dedicavi.[1]
Hiis testibus. Gilberto London' episcopo. Johanne Rofensi episcopo.
Walthefo abbate Croiland'. Henrico Huntend' archidiacono. Hugone
de Scalariis. Luca filio Walteri.

VII

*Charter of Bishop Hervey granting to Alfric his reeve
and his heirs a tenement in Fen Ditton*

Liber M, f. 145.
Date: 1109-31.

Herveus Dei gratia episcopus cum toto conventu fratrum Elyensis
ecclesie omnibus fidelibus eiusdem ecclesie salutem. Notum sit
cunctis presentibus et futuris me concessisse et dedisse per consilium
et consensum tocius conventus Alurico preposito meo de Dittun' et
Roberto heredi suo et cunctis heredibus suis post eum tres virgas
terre in eadem villa quas ante eum habuerunt tres rustici, scilicet
Hunningus, Wlnothus, Aedwinus Cacabred, et novem acras terre
desolatas ad supplementum terre sue et illas tres mansiones que ad
predictas virgas pertinent. Et pro illis tribus virgis dabit unoquoque
anno in meam firmam unam marcam argenti pro omni servicio et pro
omni consuetudine. Monachis vero dabit ipse Aluricus et heredes
sui post eum eandem terram habentes unoquoque anno tres summas
de farina, unam in festivitate sancte Etheldrede que est in vigilia
sancti Johannis Baptiste et duas in alia festivitate eiusdem virginis
que est post festivitatem sancti Michaelis. Hiis testibus. Gocelino.
Waltero. Nicholao. Turoldo. Willelmo clericis. Ricardo. Beraldo.

---

[1] The date of the dedication of the restored church at Thorney is given as
1128 in Thorney Red Book, 1, f. 167d.

Harsculfo. Willelmo. Waltero. Jordano. Alano militibus. Henrico. Roberto. Sihtrico. Ordmero. Willelmo. Ricardo. Gosfrido. Symone. et aliis quampluribus.

VIII

Charter of Bishop Nigel permitting Storic of Witcham
to divide his holding between his two sons

Egerton MS. 3047, f. 62d.
Date: 1132–*c.* 1160 (i.e. before the death of Archdeacon William).

Nigellus Dei gratia Eliensis episcopus omnibus hominibus de honore sancte Etheldrede Francis et Anglis salutem. Sciatis me concessisse Storico de Wycham ut dividat terram suam duobus filiis suis, videlicet Radulfo clerico et Colsweino, hereditario iure. Et volo ut idem filii sui post mortem ipsius teneant bene et honorifice et hereditarie faciendo servicium quod eidem tenemento pertinet. Testibus. Willelmo archdiacono. Ricardo de Sancto Paulo. Gilberto capellano. Johanne Peregrino. Huberto clerico. et multis aliis.

IX

Charter of Bishop Nigel confirming to the monks of Ely a gift
of land made to them by Wigar the priest in Stretham

Liber M, f. 158.
Date: 1133–69.

Nigellus Dei gratia Elyensis episcopus omnibus hominibus de honore sancte Etheldrede salutem. Universitati vestre notum facimus nos concessisse et presenti carta nostra confirmasse ecclesie sancte Etheldrede et monachis nostris Elyensibus in liberam et perpetuuam elemosinam duas acras et unam rodam terre et tres rodas prati in Straham quas Wigarus priest dedit et concessit eidem ecclesie et monachis in exitu vite sue, sicut liberam terram suam quam dare et vendere potuit. Volumus igitur et precipimus quod prefata ecclesia et monachi predictam terram et pratum libere et quiete et honorifice tenendo possideant, salvo servicio quod ad hundredum pertinet. Testibus. Huberto clerico. Gaufrido capellano. Magistro Ern' et Johanne medicis. Magistro Rogero. Magistro Henrico. Magistro Willelmo. Henrico clerico.

10

X

Charter of Bishop Nigel confirming Bishop Hervey's relaxation of the ploughing service which had been owed at the Barton Farm by all the ploughs of the Island of Ely

D & C Charter no. 56.
Date: 1163–9 (Prior Solomon succeeded about 1163).

Nigellus Dei gratia Elyensis episcopus omnibus hominibus de honore sancte Adeldrede salutem. Condono imperpetuum araturam carrucarum totius insule de Ely quam faciebant Bertune de Ely, quam eciam predecessor noster bone memorie, Herveus episcopus, antea condonaverat. Hoc autem condonavi pro salute anime mee et predecessorum meorum et prohibeo auctoritate divina ne amodo ab aliquo successorum meorum exigatur. Testibus. Ricardo Eliensi archidiacono. Salamone priori. Johanne de Sancto Albano. Roberto Crestien. Waltero Pilato clericis. Waltero de camera et Willelmo. Alberto Anglico. Roberto filio dapiferi. Radulfo filio Ricardi. Willelmo molendinario. Willelmo filio Turchilli. Paiano clerico.

XI

Charter of Bishop Longchamp confirming to the monks of Ely a gift of land made to them by Ralf the clerk in Witcham

D & C Charter no. 58.
Date: 1190–7.

Willelmus Dei gratia Elyensis episcopus, Apostolice Sedis legatus, et domini regis cancellarius omnibus Christi fidelibus ad quos littere iste pervenerint salutem. Noverit universitas vestra nos dedisse et concessisse ecclesie sancte Adeldrede de Ely et monachis ibidem Deo servientibus totam terram que fuit Radulfi clerici de Wicham quam tenuit de nostro soccagio in eadem villa; quam idem Radulfus dedit eisdem monachis cum corpore suo pro anima sua; ita plenarie et integre sicut eam melius tenuit et integrius die qua fuit vivus et mortuus pro eodem servicio pro quo idem Radulfus inde facere solebat hundredis. Et ideo volumus ut prefati monachi teneant predictam terram bene et in pace, libere, quiete et honorifice in terris, masagiis, croftis, pratis et pasturis et in omnibus rebus ad prefatum feodum pertinentibus. Et ut hec donatio rata sit et inconcussa eam sigilli nostri munime corroboravimus. Hiis testibus. Reginaldo Bathon' episcopo. Warino Ebroic' precentore. Johanne de Manestun'. Ricardo de Sancto Eadmundo clericis. Magistro Eustachio. Roberto de Insula. Waltero de Tifford. Turoldo de Hegeneton. Michaelo

Pelerin. Petro de Lindona et Ricardo de Nortun qui hanc cartam scripsit et multis aliis.

XII

Charter of Bishop Eustace confirming to the monks of Ely a gift of land made to them by Osbert of Witcham in Witcham

Liber M, f. 163 (2).
Date: 1197–1215.

Eustachius Dei gratia Elyensis episcopus omnibus ad quos presens carta pervenerit salutem in vero salutari. Noverit universitas vestra nos dedisse et concessisse ecclesie beate Etheldrede de Ely et monachis ibidem Deo servientibus totam terram que fuit Osberti de Wicheham quam tenuit de nostro soccagio in eadem villa, quam idem Osbertus dedit et quam de assensu nostro dare potuit eisdem monachis cum corpore suo pro anima sua, ita plenarie et integre sicut eam melius tenuit et integrius pro eodem servicio quod idem Osbertus inde facere solebat hundredis. Quare volumus et firmiter precipimus ut prefati monachi habeant et teneant predictam terram bene et in pace, libere, quiete et honorifice in terris, massagiis, croftis, pratis, pasturis et in omnibus rebus ad predictum feodum pertinentibus. Et preterea concessimus eisdem monachis pro quadraginta solidis quos ipsi nobis dederunt, et quietum clamavimus in curia nostra de Ely, Everardum le Paumer de Litleport cum omnibus catallis suis. Hiis testibus. Radulfo capellano. Magistro Thoma de Driffeld. Magistro Nicholao de Derlege. Magistro Johanne Blundo. Magistro Galfrido Grim. Ricardo de Ronhale. Simone de Insula. Roberto de Insula. Roberto de Welles. Michaelo Pelerin. Eudone de Tefford'. Radulfo de Pinu. et multis aliis.

XIII

Charter of Prior Alexander granting the Isle of Coveney to Ralf Dapifer for an annual rent of five shillings

Cott. Claudius C xi, f. 346d (another copy in Coucher Book, f. 213d). Date: c. 1151–63.

Alexander prior et totus conventus Eliensis ecclesie omnibus filiis et fidelibus ecclesie sancte presentibus et futuris salutem et oracionem. Noverit vestra fraternitas nos donasse et presenti carta concessisse Radulpho dapifero nostro et amico insulam de Coveneya cum omnibus pertinenciis sive in terra sive in aqua et marisco in feudo et hereditate de nobis tenendam per servicium quinque solidorum annuatim inde reddendorum pro omni consuetudine et servicio sibi et heredibus suis post ipsum. Et sciatis quod nos non warrantizamus aliquem qui dicat se habuisse donacionem vel confirmacionem factam a nobis de predicta insula tempore domini Hervei episcopi quando nos non habuimus copiam sigilli nostri vel eciam tempore domini Nigelli episcopi quando ipse habuit terras et res nostras in saisina sua, quia nullam donacionem vel confirmacionem warrantizamus ante hanc nostram donacionem que facta est communi voluntate nostri conventus et ad utilitatem et honorem nostre ecclesie. Volumus igitur et precipimus firmiter quod tam prefatus Radulphus quam heredes sui post ipsum libere et quiete et honorifice ipsam insulam cum appendiciis suis per predictum teneant servicium.

XIV

Charter of John, Bishop of Rochester, recording on behalf of Thorney Abbey the liberties in its manor of Whittlesey conceded by Bishop Hervey[1]

Thorney Red Book, i, f. 167.
Date: 1128.

Notum sit omnibus tam presentibus quam futuris quod ego Iohannes Dei gratia Roffensis episcopus vocacione domini Hervei Elyensis episcopi dedicacionem Thornensis cenobii interfui, presente eodem episcopo domino Herveo et domino Gilberto venerabili London' episcopo. Ubi autem ad dotem ecclesie conferendam proventum est, venerabilis pater Herveus divino tactus spiritu Thornensi ecclesie in presencia nostra et cleri et populi dotem huiusmodi dedit. In villa siquidem que Witleseya dicitur, cuius due partes ad Thornense Monasterium pertinent, tercia vero ad Elyense, episcopus Elyensis super terram abbatis que in Wytleseya erat huiuscemodi consuetudinem habuerat, quod ad hundredum suum apud Wicheford homines abbatis qui in predicta manebant villa venire consueverant, unde multas et frequentes inquietaciones abbas Thornensis et homines sui patiebantur. Hanc autem consuetudinem et quicquid iuris aut consuetudinis Elyensis episcopus aut antecessores sui in memorata terra habuerant idem episcopus Thornensi monasterio, in presencia nostra et venerabilis abbatis Roberti et congregationis sue et monachorum Elyensium qui presentes fuerunt et hanc dotem concesserunt, imperpetuum condonavit, Radulfo secretario Elyensi cultellum suum episcopo Elyensi offerente eodemque episcopo dotem per eundem cultellum super altare positum confirmante hoc videlicet tenore, ut homines abbatis Thornensis in Wytleseya manentes ad hundredum apud Wicheford' nullatenus veniant, nec episcopus Elyensis aut successores sui hanc vel aliam consuetudinem ab eis exigant, sed quieti et liberi ab omni subieccione episcopi Elyensis suorumque successorum permaneant.

[1] For Hervey's charter see above, Appx. VI.

XV

Agreement between the Abbot and Convent of Thorney and the free men of Leverington about newly assarted land[1]

Thorney Red Book, 1, ff. 186d–7.
Date: 1216–36.

Notum sit omnibus Christi fidelibus presens scriptum visuris vel audituris ita convenisse inter abbatem et conventum Thorn' ex una parte et Walterum filium Walteri et Alanum de Fitton' et Johannem filium Gaufridi et Willelmum filium Roberti et Adam filium Lewini et Johannem clericum et Gaufridum de Cruce et Petrum filium Willelmi et Robertum de Fittun' et Radulfum Rote et Elyam filium Gaufridi et Rogerum filium Maud et Thomam filium Walteri et Thomam filium Gothe et Adam filium Johannis et Alexandrum filium Aluredi et Walterum Rote et Adam de Cruce et Petrum Franceys et Alanum filium Radulfi et Adam Catting et omnes eorum participes ex altera in Leverington': videlicet quod prefati homines et eorum participes in Leverington' concesserunt predicto abbati Thorn'.xxx. acras terre propinquiores Trokenholt in nova purprestura inter dravam que venit de terra Gervasii de Runmere et veterem ripam de Fulhilt nomine vicesime quinte partis abbati et conventui in eadem purprestura pertinentis. Et si dicti homines aut eorum heredes aliam fecerint purpresturam in marisco de Leverington' inter veterem ripam et divisam inter eos et Wisebech', dictus abbas et conventus Thorn' et eorum successores vicesimam quintam partem suam habebunt. Concesserunt etiam dicti homines quod totum dominicum dicti abbatis et conventus circa Trokenholt erit sewiciatum eodem sewicio quo terras suas sewiciant. Ad huius autem convencionis confirmacionem fideliter et sine fraude observandam, Robertus Dei gratia Thorn' abbas sigillum suum una cum predictis sigillis Walteri et Alani huic scripto in modum cirographi confecto apposuit. Predicti autem homines ad istam convencionem fideliter observandam pro se et heredibus suis et eorum participibus tactis sacrosanctis evangeliis corporale sacramentum prestiterunt. Hiis testibus. Domino Rogero de Causton', tunc constabulario de Wysebech. Domino Roberto de Marisco. Domino Ada de Tyd. Ricardo filio presbyteri de Neuton'. Bartholomeo filio eius. Johanne Soupeseure. Johanne de Gravele. Nicholao clerico. Alano de Nevile. Bartholomeo de Sancto Edmundo. Radulfo coco. Rogero filio domini Ade de Tyd.

---

[1] The rubric refers to this as 'scriptum cirographatum inter liberos homines de Leverington' et abbatem', etc.

XVI

Extracts from the rolls of the Bishop's Itinerant
Justices in the Isle of Ely

Cott. Vespasian A xix, ff. 101–101 d.
Date: 1260–72.

Placita apud Ely coram Roberto de Leveryngton priore Elyense,
Philippo de Insula et Jordano de Aventr'[1] tempore Hugonis episcopi
etc.

Stephanus filius Ailbod' de Ely incarceratus in prisona Prioris
de Ely in Witles'; evasit etc.

Matilda filia Rogeri fabri inventa fuit mortua in prisona prioris
de Ely apud Wycham etc.

Willelmus vicarius de Wycham interfecit Margeriam de la Sale
et fuit in prisona prioris de Ely etc.

Rogerus capellanus incarceratus fuit in prisona prioris de Ely et
evasit ad ecclesiam beate Marie etc.

Placita apud Ely coram priore et Waltero de Wilburham,[2] Roberto
de Insula, Andrea de Ely et aliis Justiciariis Itinerantibus ibidem anno
regni regis Henrici lvi. incipiente tempore Hugonis episcopi etc.

Presentatum est quod prior Eliensis clamat habere warennam
infra insulam et currit cum leporariis et capit lepores etc. Et
juratores dicunt quod dictus prior semper et predecessores sui usi
sunt huiusmodi warenna. Ideo concessum est quod habeat etc.

Rogerus de Fakenham et Galfridus de Kirkfledam suspensi;
catalla eorum .xij. solidos; Prior de Ely recepit etc.

XVII

Quitclaim by Reginald Pecche and Agnes his wife to the Prior and
convent of Ely of a rent in Ely made in the Bishop's court at Ely

D & C Charter no. 151.
Date: 1282.

Universis Christi fidelibus presentes litteras visuris vel audituris
Reginaldus Pecche et Agnes uxor eius ac relicta domini Thome de
Hicworthe militis, defuncti, salutem in domino sempiternam. Noverit universitas vestra quod nos concessimus, remisimus et omnino
quietum clamavimus in curia domini episcopi prout continetur in
rotulis eiusdem curie domino Johanni priori Elyensi et eiusdem loci
capitulo totum jus et clameum quod habuimus vel aliquo modo
habere potuimus nomine dotis per mortem dicti domini Thome de

---

[1] Seneschal *c.* 1260–7.   [2] Seneschal *c.* 1267–72.

Hicworthe in triginta et duobus solidis annui redditus quos dictus dominus Thomas de Hicworthe in villa de Ely quondam percipere consuevit, super qua dote nos dictum priorem Elyensem in curia domini regis per brevem dicti domini regis implacitavimus. Et si contingat quod ego Reginaldus uxore mea superstite viam universe carnis fuero ingressus, volo et concedo quod heredes mei et assignati mei quicumque ad dictam dotem dicti annui redditus warantizandam teneantur. Et ad maiorem huius rei securitatem faciendam, uterque nostrum corporale prestitit sacramentum. Pro hac autem concessione et omnino quieta clamacione dedit nobis prior Elyensis quattuor marcas argenti. In cuius rei testimonium presentibus litteris sigilla nostra apposuimus. Hiis testibus. Q....de Ely. Hugone de Cressingham, tunc tempore domini episcopi Elyensis senescallo. Philippo de Sepeye. Thoma clerico de Berton. Hugone ad portam. Nicholao Barath. Johanne pistore. Hugone Lespicer. Roberto coco. et aliis.

(The following extract from the rolls of the
bishop's court is attached to the charter)

Ely: Placita tenta ibidem coram Hugone de Cressingham die lune post clausum Pasche anno regni regis Edwardi x°.

Johannes prior de Ely per attornatum suum optulit se .iiij°. die versus Reginaldum Pecche et Agnetem uxorem eius de placito medietatis .xl. solidorum redditus cum pertinenciis in Ely unde eum implacitant etc. Et predicti Reginaldus et Agnes veniunt et remittunt et quietum clamant eidem priori totum jus et clameum quod habuerunt vel habere potuerunt in predicta medietate .xl. solidorum redditus cum pertinenciis nomine dotis ipsius Agnetis et predictus Prior eisdem satisfecit etc.

LIST OF FULL TITLES OF THE AUTHORITIES REFERRED TO IN THE TEXT AND THE NOTES

I. MANUSCRIPT SOURCES

(1) *Ely Chronicles, Registers and Chartularies*

Trinity College Library, Cambridge:
    MS. O. 2. 1.
    MS. O. 2. 41.

British Museum:
    Add. MS. 9822.
    Add. MS. 41612.
    Cott. MS. Claudius C xi.
    Cott. MS. Domitian A xv.
    Cott. MS. Tiberius A vi.
    Cott. MS. Tiberius B ii.
    Cott. MS. Titus A i.
    Cott. MS. Vespasian A xix.
    Egerton MS. 3047.

Ely Diocesan Registry:
    Liber B.
    Liber M.
    The Old Coucher Book (Liber R).

Gonville and Caius College, Cambridge:
    MS. 485/489.

Bodleian Library:
    Laudian Misc. 647.

Cambridge University Library:
    Add. MS. 3468 (The Black Book of Ely).

(2) *Other records of the church of Ely*

Ely Diocesan Registry (for the classification of these records see Gibbons, *Ely Episcopal Records*):
Bailiffs' Rolls (D5(1)—Downham; D5(2)—Stretham, etc; D7—Wisbech Castle; D8—Wisbech Barton).
Bishop Wren's Note Book, G2.
Court Rolls (C6—Ely halimotes, leets and *curie palacii*; C7—Elm, Emneth, etc., halimotes and leets; Witchford hundreds and *turnus vicecomitis*; C8—Wisbech hundreds, leets, halimotes and *curie bondorum*).
Plea and Gaol Delivery Rolls, E1 (Ely).

Muniments of the Dean and Chapter of Ely:
Charters.
Extenta Maneriorum, 12 Edw. II.
Obedientiary Rolls of the Treasurers, Cellarer, Granetar, Hostiller and Steward of the Prior's Hospice.
Sutton Court Rolls.
Cambridge University Library:
James Bentham's Collectanea: Add. MSS. 2945, 2950, 2951, 2953, 2962.
Wilburton Acct. Roll 6–7 Hen. IV: Doc. 817.

(3) *Public Records*

Assize Rolls nos. 82–6, 90, 95, 562, 564, 568, 577, 1177.
Chancery Inquisitions post mortem, Henry III–Edward III.
Chancery Miscellanea, Bdles. 5/2, 5/3, 5/10, 9/2.
Curia Regis Roll no. 104.

Exchequer records:
KR Extents and Inquisitions, Bdle. 9, File 2.
KR Lay Subsidy Rolls, 81/1, 3, 6; 242/65.
KR Memoranda Rolls, nos. 5, 27–8, 31, 33, 42–4.
KR Returns of Writs, Bdle. 1, File 10.
LTR Memoranda Rolls, nos. 4, 7, 14, 26, 29, 30, 51.
LTR Miscellanea, Bdle. 1/13.
Pipe Rolls nos. 95–6, 98–102, 106.
Receipt Rolls (Auditors), nos. 23, 25.
Ministers' Accounts (General Series), Bdles. 766/10, 1132/9–15, 1133/1, 1135/8, 1307/2–4; (Duchy of Lancaster Series), Bdles. 288/4716–7.

(4) *Various Manuscript Sources*

Bodleian Library:
Ashmolean MS. 801.

British Museum:
Add. MSS. 5837, 6165.
Cott. Julius A 1 (Register of Chatteris Abbey).

Cambridge University Library:
Baker MS. Mm. 1. 49.
Cottenham enclosure award: Doc. 630(87).
Red Book of Thorney Abbey (Add. MSS. 3020, 3021).
Registers of the abbey of Bury St Edmunds:
Add. 6006 (Abbot Samson's Kalendar).
Ff. 11. 33.
Mm. iv. 19.
Muniments of St John's College, Cambridge.
Charters of the Hospital of St John the Evangelist, Cambridge.

II. PRINTED SOURCES

These sources have been indexed throughout under the title of the book, not under the name of the editor; the only exceptions are in the case of medieval chronicles, etc., of which the author is known, where references are given under his name. In this and the following section, the place of publication is London unless it is stated to be elsewhere.

Acta Sanctorum Iunii...quae collegit Johannes Bollandus etc., t. IV (Antwerp, 1707).

Acta Sanctorum Ordinis Sancti Benedicti, t. II, ed. J. Mabillon (Paris, 1669).

Anglia Sacra sive collectio historiarum de archiepiscopis et episcopis Angliae ad annum 1540, ed. H. Wharton (2 vols., 1691).

Anglo-Saxon Charters, ed. A. J. Robertson (Cambridge Studies in English Legal History, Cambridge, 1939).

Anglo-Saxon Chronicle, ed. B. Thorpe (RS, 2 vols., 1861).

Anglo-Saxon Wills, ed. D. Whitelock (Cambridge Studies in English Legal History, Cambridge, 1930).

Bede, *Historia Ecclesiastica Gentis Anglorum*, ed. C. Plummer, in *Bedae Opera Historica*, vol. I (Oxford, 1896).

Book of Fees (3 vols., 1921–31).

Bracton's Note Book, ed. F. W. Maitland (3 vols., 1887).

Calendar of Chancery Warrants, I (1927).

Calendar of Charter Rolls, I–IV (1903–12).

Calendar of Close Rolls, 1272–1327 (9 vols., 1892–1908).

Calendar of Fine Rolls, I–III (1911–13).

Calendar of Inquisitions post mortem, I–IX (1906–17).

Calendar of Liberate Rolls, I–III (1917–37).

Calendar of Miscellaneous Inquisitions, I (1916).

Calendar of Patent Rolls, 1232–1327 (13 vols., 1894–1913).

Calendar of Scutage Rolls, in *Calendar of Various Chancery Rolls* (1912).

Cartae Antiquae Rolls 1–10, ed. L. Landon (Pipe Roll Society, n.s., vol. XVII, 1939).

Cartularium Monasterii de Rameseia, ed. W. H. Hart and P. A. Lyons (RS, 3 vols., 1884–94).

Cartularium Saxonicum, ed. W. de G. Birch (3 vols., 1885–93).

Chronicle of Hugh Candidus, translated C. and W. T. Mellows (Peterborough Museum pubns., n.s., I (part I), Peterborough, 1941).

Chronicon Abbatiae Ramesiensis, ed. W. D. Macray (RS, 1886).

Chronicon Monasterii de Abingdon, ed. J. Stevenson (RS, 2 vols., 1858).

Close Rolls, 1227–72 (14 vols., 1902–38).

Codex Diplomaticus aevi Saxonici, ed. J. M. Kemble (English Historical Society, 6 vols., 1839–48).

Court Baron, ed. F. W. Maitland and W. P. Baildon (Selden Society, IV, 1891).

Court Rolls of the Abbey of Ramsey and the Honour of Clare (Yale Historical Pubns. (Texts), IX, New Haven, 1928).

Crawford Collection of Early Charters and Documents, ed. A. S. Napier and W. H. Stevenson (Oxford, 1895).
Curia Regis Rolls, I–VIII (1923–38).
Dialogus de Scaccario, ed. A. Hughes, G. C. Crump and C. Johnson (Oxford, 1902).
Domesday Book, I–II (ed. A. Farley, 1783); IV (ed. H. Ellis, Rec. Comm., 1816).
Earliest Northamptonshire Assize Rolls, ed. D. M. Stenton (Northamptonshire Record Society, V, Lincoln, 1930).
Ecclesie de Bernewelle Liber Memorandorum, ed. J. W. Clark (Cambridge, 1907).
'Ely Chapter Ordinances and Visitation Records', ed. S. J. A. Evans, in *Camden Miscellany*, XVII (1940).
'English Weights and Measures, Select Tracts and Table Books relating to', ed. H. Hall and F. J. Nicholas, in *Camden Miscellany* XV (1929).
Excerpta e Rotulis Finium in Turri Londinensi asservatis, 1216–72, ed. C. Roberts (Rec. Comm., 2 vols., 1835–6).
Exchequer of the Jews: Calendar of Plea Rolls of, ed. J. M. Rigg (Jewish Historical Society of England, 3 vols., 1905–29).
Feudal Aids (6 vols., 1899–1921).
Feudal Documents from the Abbey of Bury St Edmunds, ed. D. C. Douglas (British Academy Records of the Social and Economic History of England and Wales, VIII, 1931).
Foedera, Conventiones, Litterae etc., ed. T. Rymer (edition A. Clarke, etc., Rec. Comm., 1816–30).
Grosseteste, Robert—*Epistolae*, ed. H. R. Luard (RS, 1861).
Historical Manuscripts Commission Reports, 11th Report, Appx. III (1887); 12th Report, Appx. IX (1891).
Inquisitio Comitatus Cantabrigiensis, subjicitur Inquisitio Eliensis, ed. N. E. S. A. Hamilton (Royal Society of Literature, 1876).
KR Memoranda Roll, 14 Henry III, ed. C. Robinson (Pipe Roll Society, n.s., XI: Princeton, 1933).
Liber Eliensis ad fidem codicum variorum, ed. D. J. Stewart (Anglia Christiana Society, 1848).
Memoranda de Parliamento: Records of the Parliament holden at Westminster, 28 February 33 Edward I, ed. F. W. Maitland (RS 1893).
Memoranda Roll, 1 John, ed. H. G. Richardson (Pipe Roll Society, n.s., XXI, 1943).
Memorials of St Edmund's Abbey, ed. T. Arnold (RS, 3 vols., 1890–6).
Monasticon Anglicanum, by W. Dugdale (ed. of J. Caley, H. Ellis and B. Bandinel, 1846).
Monasticon Cluniacense Anglicanum, or Charters and Records among the Archives of the Abbey of Cluni, ed. G. F. Duckett (2 vols., Lewes, 1888).
Norfolk Portion of the Chartulary of the Priory of St Pancras of Lewes, ed. J. H. Bullock (Norfolk Record Society, XII, 1939).

Papsturkunden in England, I–II, ed. W. Holtzmann (Berlin, 1930–5).
Paris, Matthew—*Chronica Majora*, ed. H. R. Luard (RS, 7 vols., 1872–84).
Patent Rolls, 1216–32 (2 vols., 1901–3).
Pedes Finium or Fines relating to the County of Cambridge, ed. W. Rye (Cambridge Antiquarian Society, Octavo pubns., XXVI, 1891).
Pipe Rolls:
　Magnus Rotulus Scaccarii de anno 31° *Henrici I*, ed. J. Hunter (Rec. Comm., 1833).
　Pipe Rolls, 5 Henry II—10 John and 14 Henry III (Pipe Roll Society pubns., 1884–1945).
　The Great Roll of the Pipe, 2–4 *Henry II*, ed. J. Hunter (Rec. Comm., 1844).
　The Great Roll of the Pipe, 1 *Richard I*, ed. J. Hunter (Rec. Comm., 1844).
　The Great Roll of the Pipe, 26 *Henry III*, ed. H. L. Cannon (Yale Historical Pubns. (Texts), V: New Haven, 1918).
Placita de Quo Warranto, ed. W. Illingworth and J. Caley (Rec. Comm., 1818).
Placitorum Abbreviatio, ed. G. Rose and W. Illingworth (Rec. Comm., 1811).
Pleas of the Court of King's Bench, Trinity Term, 25 *Edward I*, 1297, ed. W. P. W. Phillimore (British Record Society, Index Library, XIX, 1898).
Recueil des actes de Henri II . . . concernant l s provinces françaises et les affaires de France, ed. L. Delisle (revú E. Berger, 3 vols., Paris, 1916–27).
Red Book of the Exchequer, ed. H. Hall (RS, 3 vols., 1897).
Register of the Abbey of St Benet of Holme, ed. J. R. West (Norfolk Record Society, II n.p., 1932).
Rolls of the Justices in Eyre for Gloucestershire, Warwickshire and Staffordshire, 1221–2, ed. D. M. Stenton (Selden Society, LIX, 1940).
Rolls of the King's Court in the Reign of Richard I, ed. F. W. Maitland (Pipe Roll Society, 1891).
Rotuli Curiae Regis, ed. F. Palgrave (Rec. Comm., 2 vols., 1835).
Rotuli de Oblatis et Finibus in Turri Londinensi asservati, ed. T. D. Hardy (Rec. Comm., 1835).
Rotuli Hundredorum, ed. W. Illingworth et J. Caley (Rec. Comm., 2 vols., 1812–18).
Rotuli Litterarum Clausarum, ed. T. D. Hardy (Rec. Comm., 2 vols., 1833–44).
Rotuli Parliamentorum, I–II (n.p., n.d.).
Rotuli Parliamentorum Anglie hactenus Inediti, ed. H. G. Richardson and G. O. Sayles (Camden Society, 3rd Ser., LI, 1935).
Royal and other Historical Letters illustrative of the Reign of Henry III, ed. W. W. Shirley (RS, 2 vols., 1862–6).
Sacrist Rolls of Ely, ed. F. R. Chapman (2 vols., Cambridge, 1907).

Select Cases in Chancery, 1364–1471, ed. W. P. Baildon (Selden Society, X, 1896).
Select Cases in Manorial and other Seignorial Courts, ed. F. W. Maitland (Selden Society, II, 1888).
Select Cases in the Court of King's Bench in the Reign of Edward I, ed. G. O. Sayles (Selden Society, LVI, LVII and LVIII, 1936–9).
Select Cases in the Exchequer of Pleas, ed. H. Jenkinson and B. E. R. Formoy (Selden Society, XLVIII, 1931).
Sprot, Thomas, *Chronica*, ed. T. Hearne (Oxford, 1719).
Walter of Henley's Husbandry, ed. E. Lamond (Royal Historical Society, 1890).
Year Books:
21–2 Edward I, ed. A. J. Horwood (RS, 1873).
33–5 Edward I, ed. A. J. Horwood (RS, 1879).
2–3 Edward II, ed. F. W. Maitland (Selden Society, XIX, 1904).
12–13 Edward III, ed. L. O. Pike (RS, 1885).

III. SECONDARY AUTHORITIES

AULT, W. O., *Private Jurisdiction in England* (Yale Historical Pubns. (Misc.), X, New Haven, 1923).
BALDWIN, J. F., *Scutage and Knight-Service in England* (Chicago, 1897).
BELOE, E. M., 'Freebridge Marshland Hundred and the Making of Lynn', *Norfolk Archaeology*, XII (1895).
BENTHAM, J., *The History and Antiquities of the Conventual and Cathedral Church of Ely* (2nd. ed., Norwich, 1812).
BEVERIDGE, W., 'The Yield and Price of Corn in the Middle Ages', *Economic History*, I (1926–9).
BLOCH, M., *La Société féodale: formation des liens de dépendance* (Paris, 1939).
— 'The Rise of Dependent Cultivation and Seigniorial Institutions', *Cambridge Economic History*, vol. I (Cambridge, 1941).
BLOMEFIELD, F., *An Essay towards a topographical History of the County of Norfolk* (11 vols., 1805–10).
— *Collectanea Cantabrigiensia* (Norwich, 1750).
BÖHMER, H., 'Das Eigenkirchentum in England', in *Texte und Forschungen zur englischen Kulturgeschichte: Festgabe für Felix Liebermann* (Halle, 1921).
BROOKE, Z. N., *The English Church and the Papacy* (Cambridge, 1931).
CAM, H. M., *Liberties and Communities in Medieval England* (Cambridge, 1944).
— *Studies in the Hundred Rolls* (Oxford Studies in Social and Legal History, ed. P. Vinogradoff, vol. VI, no. xi: Oxford, 1921).
— *The Hundred and the Hundred Rolls* (1930).
CAMPBELL, M., *The English Yeoman under Elizabeth and the Early Stuarts* (Yale Historical Pubns. (Studies), XIV: New Haven, 1942).

CHADWICK, H. M., *Anglo-Saxon Institutions* (Cambridge, 1905).
— *Origin of the English Nation* (Cambridge, 1924).
CHEW, H. M., *English Ecclesiastical Tenants-in-chief and Knight Service* (Oxford, 1932).
COKE, Sir EDWARD, *Institutes of the Laws of England, the Fourth Part* (edn. of 1817).
Complete Peerage of England, etc. by G.E.C. (new edition in process of publication, 1910 ff.).
DARBY, H. C., *The Medieval Fenland* (Cambridge, 1940).
— 'The Domesday Geography of Cambridgeshire', *PCAS*, XXXVI (1936).
— 'The Fenland Frontier in Anglo-Saxon England', *Antiquity*, VIII (1934).
DENHOLM-YOUNG, N., *Collected Papers on Medieval Subjects* (Oxford, 1946).
— *Seignorial Administration in England*, (Oxford Historical Series, Oxford, 1937).
DODWELL, B., 'East Anglian Commendation', *EHR*, LXIII (1948).
— 'The Free Tenantry of the Hundred Rolls', *EcHR*, XIV (1944-5).
DOPSCH, A., *Economic and Social Foundations of European Civilisation*, trans. M. G. Beard and N. Marshall (1937).
DOUGLAS, D. C., *Social Structure of Medieval East Anglia* (Oxford Studies in Social and Legal History, ed. P. Vinogradoff, vol. IX: Oxford, 1927).
— 'Fragments of an Anglo-Saxon Survey from Bury St Edmunds', *EHR*, XLIII (1928).
— 'The Norman Conquest and English Feudalism', *EcHR*, IX (1939).
DUCANGE, C., *Glossarium medie et infime Latinitatis* (6 vols., Paris, 1840-6).
DUGDALE, W., *The History of Imbanking and Drayning of divers Fens and Marshes* (2nd. ed., 1772).
FARRER, W., *An Outline Itinerary of King Henry I* (Oxford, 1919; repr. from *EHR*, XXXIV, 1919).
— *Feudal Cambridgeshire* (Cambridge, 1920).
— *Honours and Knight's Fees* (3 vols., London and Manchester, 1923-5).
FOSS, E., *Judges of England* (9 vols., 1848-64).
FOWLER, G., 'Fenland Waterways Past and Present: South Level District'; Part I, *PCAS*, XXXIII (1933); Part II, *PCAS*, XXXIV (1934).
FOWLER, G. H., 'The Devastation of Bedfordshire and the surrounding Counties in 1065 and 1066', *Archaeologia*, LXXII (1922).
FOX, C., *Archaeology of the Cambridge Region* (Cambridge, 1923).
GALBRAITH, V. H., 'The Death of a Champion (1287)', *Studies in Medieval History presented to F. M. Powicke*, ed. R. W. Hunt, W. A. Pantin and R. W. Southern (Oxford, 1948).
'The Making of Domesday Book', *EHR*, LVII (1942).

GANSHOF, F. L., *Qu'est-ce que la féodalité?* (Bruxelles, 1944).

GIBBONS, A., *Ely Episcopal Records* (Lincoln, 1891).

GIBBS, M. and LANG, J., *Bishops and Reform*, 1215–72 (Oxford Historical Series, Oxford, 1934).

GOEBEL, J., *Felony and Misdemeanour*, 1 (Foundation for Research in Legal History, Columbia University: New York, 1937).

GRAHAM, R., *English Ecclesiastical Studies* (Society for Promoting Christian Knowledge, 1929).

GRAY, A., *The Priory of St Radegund, Cambridge* (Cambridge Antiquarian Society Octavo Pubns., XXXI, Cambridge, 1898).

GRAY, H. L. 'Incomes from Land in England, 1436', *EHR*, XLIX (1934).

HARDY, T. D., *Descriptive Catalogue of the Materials relating to the History of Great Britain and Ireland*, 1 (RS, 1862).

HILTON, R. H., *Economic Development of some Leicestershire Estates in the Fourteenth and Fifteenth Centuries* (Oxford Historical Series, Oxford, 1947).

HOLDSWORTH, W. S., *History of English Law*, 1 (4th ed., 1931).

HOLLINGS, M., 'The Survival of the Five Hide Unit in the Western Midlands', *EHR*, LXIII (1948).

HOMANS, G. C., *English Villagers of the Thirteenth Century* (Cambridge, Mass., 1942).

HOSKINS, W. G., 'The Leicestershire Farmer of the Sixteenth Century', *Leicestershire Archaeological Society Transactions*, XXI (1941–2).

HOWARD, H. F., *The Finances of St John's College, Cambridge* (Cambridge, 1935).

HURNARD, N. D., 'Anglo-Norman Franchises', *EHR*, LXIV (1949).

JAMES, M. R., *The Western Manuscripts in the Library of Trinity College, Cambridge* (Cambridge, 4 vols., 1900–4).

JOLLIFFE, J. E. A., 'English Book Right', *EHR*, L (1935).

— 'The Age of the Folk in English History' in *Oxford Essays in Medieval History presented to H. E. Salter* (Oxford, 1934).

KNOWLES, D., *The Monastic Order in England* (Cambridge, 1940).

— *The Religious Orders in England* (Cambridge, 1948).

— 'Some Developments in English Monastic Life, 1216–1336', *TRHS*, 4th Ser., XXVI (1944).

KOSMINSKY, E. A., 'Services and Money Rents in the Thirteenth Century', *EcHR*, V (1935).

— 'The Hundred Rolls of 1278–9 as a Source for English Agrarian History', *EcHR*, III (1931).

LAPSLEY, G. T., 'Archbishop Stratford and the Parliamentary Crisis of 1341', *EHR*, XXX (1915).

LENNARD, R. V., Review of Homans, *English Villagers of the Thirteenth Century*, *Economic Journal*, LIII (1943).

— 'The Destruction of Woodland in the Eastern Counties under William the Conqueror', *EcHR*, XV (1945).

— 'The Economic Position of the Domesday Villani', *Economic Journal*, LVI (1946).

LENNARD, R. V., 'The Economic Position of the Domesday Sokemen', *Economic Journal*, LVII (1947).

LE STRANGE, H., *Le Strange Records: a Chronicle of the early Le Stranges of Norfolk and the March of Wales*, A.D. 1100–1310 (1916).

LETHBRIDGE, T., 'The Car Dyke, the Cambridgeshire Ditches and the Anglo-Saxons', *PCAS*, XXXV (1935).

LEVETT, A. E., *Studies in Manorial History*, ed. Cam, H. M., Coate, M. and Sutherland, L. S. (Oxford, 1938).

LEVISON, W., *England and the Continent in the Eighth Century* (Oxford, 1946).

LOBEL, M. D., *The Borough of Bury St Edmunds* (Oxford, 1935).

— 'The Ecclesiastical Banleuca in England' in *Oxford Essays in Medieval England presented to H. E. Salter* (Oxford, 1934).

LUNT, W. E., *The Valuation of Norwich* (Oxford, 1926).

MADOX, T., *Baronia Anglica: a History of Land Honours and Baronies and of Tenures in Capite* (1741).

— *History and Antiquities of the Exchequer* (1711).

MAITLAND, F. W., *Domesday Book and Beyond* (Cambridge, 1897).

— *Township and Borough* (Cambridge, 1898).

— 'History of a Cambridgeshire Manor', *Collected Papers*, ed. H. A. L. Fisher, II (Cambridge, 1911).

— 'The Suitors of the County Court', *EHR*, III (1888).

MILLER, E., 'The Ely Land Pleas in the Reign of William I', *EHR*, LXII (1947).

— 'The Estates of the Abbey of St Alban', *Hertfordshire Architectural and Archaeological Society Transactions* (1938).

MITCHELL, R. J., *John Tiptoft*, 1427–1470 (1938).

MITCHELL, S. K., *Studies in Taxation under John and Henry III* (Yale Historical Pubns. (Studies), II: New Haven, 1914).

MOORMAN, J. R. H., *Church Life in England in the Thirteenth Century* (Cambridge, 1945).

MORANT, P., *History and Antiquities of the County of Essex*, 2 vols. (1768).

MORRIS, W. A., *The Early English County Court* (University of California pubns. in History, XIV, no. 2: Berkeley, 1925).

NEILSON, N., *Customary Rents* (Oxford Studies in Social and Legal History, ed. P. Vinogradoff, II, no. 4: Oxford, 1910).

PAINTER, S., *Studies in the History of the English Feudal Barony* (Johns Hopkins University Studies in History and the Social Sciences, LXI, no. 3, Baltimore, 1943).

PELL, O. C., 'Upon Libere Tenentes, Virgatae, and Carucae in Domesday Book', *PCAS*, VI (1891).

PLUCKNETT, T. F. T., *Concise History of the Common Law* (3rd ed., 1940).

— 'Bookland and Folkland', *EcHR*, VI (1935).

POLLOCK, F. and MAITLAND, F. W., *History of English Law before the Time of Edward I* (2nd ed., Cambridge, 1923).

POOLE, A. L., *Obligations of Society in the XII and XIII Centuries* (Oxford, 1946).

POOLE, R. L., *The Exchequer in the Twelfth Century* (Oxford, 1912).

POSTAN, M. M., 'The Chronology of Labour Services', *TRHS*, 4th Ser., xx (1937).

— 'The Rise of a Money Economy', *EcHR*, xiv (1944).

POWER, E., *The Wool Trade in English Medieval History* (Oxford, 1941).

POWICKE, F. M., *King Henry III and the Lord Edward*, (2 vols., Oxford, 1947).

— 'Observations on the English Freeholder in the Thirteenth Century', *Wirtschaft und Kultur: Festschrift zum 70. Geburtstag von Alfons Dopsch* (Baden bei Wien, 1938).

Public Record Office Lists and Indexes, ix: 'Sheriffs of England and Wales to A.D. 1831' (1898).

REANEY, P. H., *Place-Names of Cambridgeshire and the Isle of Ely* (English Place-Name Society pubns., xix: Cambridge, 1943).

Returns of Members of Parliament, i (1878).

ROBINSON, J. A., *The Times of St Dunstan* (Oxford, 1923).

ROUND, J. H., *Family Origins and other Studies* (ed. W. Page, 1930).

— *Feudal England* (repr. of 1909).

— *Geoffrey de Mandeville* (1892).

— *Studies in Peerage and Family History* (1901).

— *The Commune of London and Other Studies* (1899).

— 'Nigel, bishop of Ely', *EHR*, viii (1893).

SAVINE, A., 'English Customary Tenure in the Tudor Period', *Quarterly Journal of Economics*, xix (1905).

SEEBOHM, F., *Tribal Custom in Anglo-Saxon Law* (1911).

SMITH, R. A. L., *Canterbury Cathedral Priory: a Study in Monastic Administration* (Cambridge, 1943).

— *Collected Papers* (1947).

STENTON, F. M., *Anglo-Saxon England* (Oxford History of England, ii: Oxford, 1943).

— *The First Century of English Feudalism* (Oxford, 1932).

— Introduction to *The Lincolnshire Domesday and the Lindsey Survey*, ed. C. W. Foster and T. Longley (Lincoln Record Society, xix: Horncastle, 1924).

— 'St Benet of Holme and the Norman Conquest', *EHR*, xxxvii (1922).

— 'The Changing Feudalism of the Middle Ages', *History*, xix (1935).

STEPHENSON, C., 'Commendation and related problems in Domesday', *EHR*, lix (1944).

STEPNIAK, *The Russian Peasantry* (1905).

TAWNEY, R. H., *The Agrarian Problem in the Sixteenth Century* (1912).

TEMPLEMAN, G., *Sheriffs of Warwickshire in the Thirteenth Century* (Dugdale Society Occasional Papers, no. 7, Oxford, 1948).

TOUT, T. F., *Chapters in the Administrative History of Medieval England* (6 vols., Manchester, 1920–33).

TREHARNE, R. F., 'Knights in the period of Reform and Rebellion, 1258–67', *BIHR*, XXI (1946).

Victoria County Histories:
  Cambridgeshire and the Isle of Ely, I–II (1938–48).
  Essex, I (1903).
  Huntingdon, I (1926).
  Kent, III (1932).
  Northamptonshire, I (1902).
  Suffolk, I (1911).

VINOGRADOFF, P., *English Society in the Eleventh Century* (Oxford, 1908).
— *The Growth of the Manor* (2nd ed., 1911).
— *Villainage in England* (1892).

WEDGEWOOD, J. C., *History of Parliament*, 1439–1509 (2 vols., 1936–8).

WELLS, S., 'The Laws of the Bedford Level Corporation': in *The History of the Draining of the Great Level of the Fens called the Bedford Level* (2 vols., 1830–2).

WILLARD, J. F. and MORRIS, W. A. (ed.), *The English Government at Work*, 1327–36, I (Pubns. of the Medieval Academy of America, XXXVII: Cambridge, Mass., 1940).

INDEX